Forms of Justice

Forms of Justice

Critical Perspectives on David Miller's Political Philosophy

Edited by Daniel A. Bell
and Avner de-Shalit

ROWMAN & LITTLEFIELD PUBLISHERS, INC.
Lanham • *Boulder* • *New York* • *Oxford*

ROWMAN & LITTLEFIELD PUBLISHERS, INC.

Published in the United States of America
by Rowman & Littlefield Publishers, Inc.
A Member of the Rowman & Littlefield Publishing Group
4720 Boston Way, Lanham, Maryland 20706
www.rowmanlittlefield.com

P.O. Box 317, Oxford OX2 9RU, United Kingdom

British Library Cataloguing in Publication Information Available

Library of Congress Cataloging-in-Publication Data

Forms of justice : critical perspectives on David Miller's political
philosophy / edited by Daniel A. Bell and Avner de-Shalit.
        p. cm.
Includes bibliographical references and index.
  ISBN 0-7425-2178-8 (cloth : alk. paper) — ISBN 0-7425-2179-6 (pbk. :
alk. paper)
  1. Social justice. 2. Miller, David (David Leslie) Principles of
social justice. I. Bell, Daniel (Daniel A.) II. De-Shalit, Avner.
  HM671 .F67 2002
  303.3'72—dc21   2002006365

Printed in the United States of America

∞™ The paper used in this publication meets the minimum requirements of
American National Standard for Information Sciences—Permanence of Paper
for Printed Library Materials, ANSI/NISO Z39.48-1992.

To David and Sue Miller

Contents

Acknowledgments

The first drafts of most of this volume's chapters were presented at Nuffield College, Oxford, in June 2000. We would like to thank the president and members of Nuffield College for their warm hospitality and kindness. Special thanks are due to Sue Miller for her enthusiasm, support, and help with this project. We want to thank our editor, Mary Carpenter, for her encouragement and help. Finally, as always, Yifat, Daniel, Hillel, Shiri, Julien, and Bing were most understanding and patient.

Adam Swift's contribution draws on his earlier article, "Public Opinion and Political Philosophy: The Relation between Social-Scientific and Philosophical Analyses of Distributive Justice," in *Ethical Theory and Moral Practice* 2, no. 4 (1999): 337–363. Used with kind permission from Kluwer Academic Publishers.

Introduction

Daniel A. Bell and Avner de-Shalit

Who should rule a political community? What obligations do we owe to the poor? What is a fair wage? More generally, how should we distribute the good and bad things in life? Is there a single principled answer to these questions?

"Yes," reply most great political philosophers. The answer to these questions can be framed in terms of one fundamental principle of justice. Plato argued that "justice in the city" consists of putting the most talented members of the community in charge of political decision making and dividing the rest between a class of soldiers and a class of producers. Mill argued that justice consists in the set of enforceable rules that have the effect of promoting the greatest possible amount of happiness. Rawls argued that justice consists in the equal distribution of "social primary goods" such as liberty, opportunity, and wealth, unless an unequal distribution is to the advantage of the least favored. These general principles can be further divided into a number of subprinciples that provide guidance in cases of conflicting political values, but the rest is simply a matter of implementation.

In his book *Spheres of Justice*, Michael Walzer famously questioned this approach. Justice, he argued, is pluralistic in nature. Members of a political community value different kinds of social goods, and they relate to them as forming different "spheres of justice." Justice, then, consists in respecting the relevant criteria of distribution within each "sphere." In contemporary liberal democracies, for example, health care should be distributed according to the principle of need, and political rights should be distributed according to the principle of equality. Walzer defends his conclusions by appealing to the reflective beliefs people hold about the institutions and practices of their own society.

The proper *site* for justice, Walzer argues, is the state. Questions of justice always arise within a bounded political community, and obligations—beyond

1

a bare minimum of prohibitions against murder, torture, and slavery—do not extend beyond the boundaries of one's state. Moreover, Walzer seems to take it for granted that the state is the main institution for implementing justice. Justice is realized once the state enacts policies that allow for the implementation of the various shared understandings informing the distribution of social goods within the politically organized community.

But is it really just to adopt a "hands-off" approach when people living in neighboring states are victimized by natural or human-made disasters? What obligations do we owe to refugees from faraway lands? Can the West (or the North, as many experts see it) justifiably make use of most of the world's resources, leaving "the rest" to pay the environmental costs? Should multinational companies operating in the Third World be constrained by codes of conduct? Can the IMF continue to impose "structural adjustment programs" on poor countries without any accountability whatsoever? These questions cannot be answered without principles of justice that are transnational in scope, and Walzer's theory seems to be deficient in this respect.

Most critics of Walzer's work respond by reasserting "mono-principle" theories of justice. They insist that a theory of justice can, and should, be expressed in terms of one fundamental principle applicable everywhere, regardless of state boundaries. They do so for various reasons, including the belief that morality is a scientific enterprise in which there is a single principle governing and explaining all cases. David Miller, however, responds by *extending*, rather than abandoning, Walzer's call for a pluralistic approach to justice. In *Principles of Social Justice*, Miller argues for plural principles of justice *within* liberal democratic societies. He draws on popular beliefs about justice to argue that the distribution of the benefits and burdens of social cooperation within one society—what he calls "social justice"—should be governed by three principles appropriate for different "modes of relationship." In other words, while Walzer has in mind spheres according to the good distributed, Miller applies a somewhat Hegelian perspective, according to which the level or sort of relationships that are at stake determine the relevant principle of distribution. Within solidaristic communities such as the family, Miller claims, the relevant principle of justice is distribution according to need; within instrumental associations such as the firm, the relevant principle of justice is distribution according to desert; whereas within political communities, goods (such as citizenship) should be distributed in accordance with the principle of equality. Miller supports his theory with extensive empirical research, and he argues that this "multi-principle" approach to justice is more likely to resolve practical conflicts than mono-principle theories of justice. This approach is not only philosophically accurate, but also politically more relevant, he maintains. Miller thus challenges contemporary political theory for being too abstract and detached from real-life cases.

In his book *Citizenship and National Identity*, Miller extends this pluralistic approach to justice to the global realm. Not only are there different principles of justice *within* political communities, there are also different principles of justice *between* communities. This by no means implies that we do not have any social and economic obligations to people living in different political communities. As a matter of fact, Miller's notion of such obligations goes far beyond Walzer's "minimal code." However, Miller insists, these obligations are not the same as obligations owed to cocitizens. Within liberal democratic states, we should strive to realize the three principles of social justice noted previously. National identity plays a crucial role, because conationals are bound by historically embedded ties and commitments. Moreover, they can—and should—deliberate about their common destiny and then be held (at least partly) responsible for the outcomes of those deliberations. Nationality also helps to motivate social justice: by maintaining and sustaining solidarity among citizens in large and diverse states, the well off are more likely to internalize the demands of justice and hence be willing to help needy conationals. Thus, Miller argues for strengthening national identity in various ways, drawing implications for democratic deliberation, national self-determination, secession and minority rights.

Different kinds of principles, however, govern the relations of citizens *between* states. These principles are not as demanding as the principles spelling out obligations of citizens within states, but they set limits to the pursuit of national justice. Miller defends three principles of global justice: the need to secure basic economic rights such as food, shelter, and clothing; the obligation to refrain from exploiting vulnerable communities and individuals in foreign countries; and the obligation to provide all political communities with opportunity to achieve self-determination and social justice.

In short, Miller argues that justice takes different forms, both within and between political communities (hence the title of this book).[1] There are different answers to the question "what is justice?" and different answers to the question "what is the appropriate site for justice?" Within liberal democratic states, there are three principles of social justice, depending on the mode of association. But social justice should also be realized at the global level, and different principles of justice apply in the global realm. In his recent work, Miller spells out the implications of his theory, thus developing the most comprehensive plural theory of justice to date.

This book takes Miller's theory as an organizing focus, but each contributor has been invited to develop his or her own views. The contributors—a group of prominent political philosophers from different parts of the world—met in Nuffield College, Oxford, David Miller's academic home for more than twenty years, to critically reflect upon Miller's theory and propose alternative political visions. Each paper was subject to extensive criticism by other contributors. The final chapter is Miller's own response to his critics.

In part I, the essays address the concept of social justice itself. Adam Swift and Marc Stears reflect on methodological and foundational issues—how do we ultimately justify this or that theory of social justice? Swift recognizes that

Miller's work is distinctive in giving an important role to popular opinion on the subject, but he argues that the strongest and most interesting reason for caring about "what people think" is false. Popular opinion about social justice can be important as food for thought, for reasons of feasibility, and for reasons of legitimacy. But Swift maintains that it cannot be constitutive of the *right* answer about what social justice requires.

Marc Stears contends that the publication of Miller's *Principles of Social Justice* presents an invaluable opportunity for an interdisciplinary reassessment of the social and institutional preconditions for social justice and of the role of the political theorist in shaping them. However, Stears takes issue with Miller's argument that theorizing about social justice must be conducted within the culturally uniform nation-state. While there may be a historical connection between a belief in the centrality of the nation-state and a belief in the possibility of a redistributive welfare system, Stears finds an alternative model in the works of early twentieth-century American progressive philosophers. According to this model, the notion of social justice can be detached from any specific form of political organization, including that of the nation-state. This can support Miller's project because it means that theorists of social justice need not be so vulnerable to the increasing attacks on the nation-state.

The next three chapters deal with what is perhaps Miller's most original contribution to the discourse on social justice—the concept of desert. Andrew Mason follows the first two chapters in the sense that his chapter also relates to Miller's method of comparing theories of justice to popular beliefs about it. However, Mason also relates to the content of Miller's theory. He examines Miller's idea that the best-qualified applicant for a job deserves it. Miller develops two arguments for this claim: (1) the best-qualified candidate deserves the job because he or she is most likely to deserve the rewards (as measured by market-determined income), and (2) the best-qualified candidate deserves the job because he or she deserves the opportunity to obtain the rewards if he or she performs at the level we can reasonably expect. According to Mason, however, neither argument can withstand critical scrutiny. Instead, the justice of appointing the best-qualified candidate should be defended with the argument that there is a failure to respect the candidate's agency when considerations other than qualifications enter into the selection process.

Serena Olsaretti examines the relationship between desert and luck. While luck is viewed to undermine individuals' deserts, Miller argues that the distinction between two types of luck—integral luck and circumstantial luck—can rescue desert on the basis of productive contribution since the latter does not undermine desert. Olsaretti argues, however, that circumstantial luck nonetheless presents a problem for adopting desert on the basis of productive contribution. Admitting this does not result in jettisoning desert, but gives us reason to support desert as a principle that sanctions ambition-sensitive departures from equality.

Daniel Attas's essay is the most radical attack on the idea of market deserts, or, as he puts it, "a persistent popular sentiment that market distributions, at their best, trace individual contributions." Attas argues that desert should not play any role in determining distributions in the economic sphere. He questions the claim that markets distribute rewards that are proportional to participating agents' respective contributions. This claim rests on the notion of marginal productivity and the claim that perfect competition results in a distribution according to marginal contribution, but Attas casts doubt on both contentions. Moreover, Attas argues that marginal contribution is not a measure of contribution to well-being and therefore is not a morally relevant desert basis.

As we have seen in the first chapters, part of the debate about social justice is where to locate it. David Miller argues that the contemporary nation-state is an important site for social justice. In this context, nationality plays a crucial role in the promotion of social justice. Our sense of belonging to a common nation, for example, renders more psychologically plausible the kinds of sacrifices that redistributive schemes require of better-off individuals. But does it really make sense to work with the notion of a common national identity in the contemporary world? If not, what are the implications for social justice?

Chandran Kukathas argues that many states are far more diverse than Miller allows for, and this fact alone shows the conflict between Miller's commitments to social justice and the principle of nationality. Miller points to cultural and ethical diversity to cast doubt on the possibility establishing a single, globally valid conception of social justice, but these same doubts also apply in the case of large, diverse states such as the United States, China, and India. Moreover, the state's historical record as the promoter of social justice is patchy at best. More often than not, the state has been established by and for the rich who have not been particularly inclined to share their wealth with needy cocitizens—not to mention poor refugees from the Third World. Kukathas suggests that those concerned with social justice should think about how to constrain the state's powers and open up its borders rather than emphasizing the need to reinvigorate the state with the principle of nationality.

Miller's idea that citizens must share a common national identity is also the target of Walzer's essay. The claims made on the nation-state by fundamentalist religious communities, aboriginal tribes, and other groups that have "totalizing" ambitions, Walzer argues, pose special problems for the principle of nationality. He accepts Miller's point that such groups cannot justly choose to both withdraw from the obligations of citizenship and make demands on the state on behalf of their group; states can demand that all persons in its territory be educated to make them responsible for the well-being of the political community. On the other hand, liberal states should also tolerate communities that seek to sustain a traditional and total way of life as against the characteristic dividedness of modern life. Walzer is not sanguine about the possibility of a "compromise" between these two desiderata. He points to the difficulty of public education that can both transmit the groups' cultural values and promote a sense of common national identity.

Another question arises, however. If justice is within the state, and if, as Miller for example argues, the guiding principles of justice should reflect, or be sensitive to, public opinion, how should we decide on the principles of justice? Miller believes that "deliberative democracy" is a valuable mechanism to both reveal what the public thinks and, on the other hand, shape public opinion. If democracy becomes deliberative, what are the implications for justice? Avner de-Shalit and Meira Levinson explore this topic. Miller and other theorists have argued that deliberative democracy (1) yields more rational policies, (2) ends in compromises rather than majority decisions, and (3) allows the community to decide upon more innovative policies. However, de-Shalit argues that these claims cannot be empirically supported. He then puts forward alternative reasons to support deliberative democracy, arguing that while it is not clear that deliberative democracy is a good method for deciding about justice, it is very likely to prevent injustice.

Levinson assesses Miller's claim that deliberative democracy is legitimate because it can be structured so as to ensure appropriate involvement and influence of all citizens on the deliberative process. Levinson argues that members of minority groups may be unable to influence debate and policy making within deliberative settings even when their claims are just and should be considered. This may be due to three reasons: incorrect perceptions of minority "extremism" by members of majority groups, blindness to the ways that norms may operate invisibly in majority settings but suddenly seem off-putting or "sectarian" when they are made visible in minority settings, and the well-intentioned but disempowering attempts of individuals to reinterpret what others say in order to make it seem "reasonable." Deliberative forums could be legitimated by means of civic education that includes teaching minorities to speak the "language of power," though Levinson notes that this approach poses significant dangers of its own.

So far, the chapters discuss justice and nationality within the state. What happens, however, when arguments of justice are evoked to support secession? Tamar Meisels assesses the attempt to defend the principle of nationality while allowing for justifiable territorial claims by minority groups in divided societies. Meisels argues that Miller's analysis of the conditions for justifiable national self-determination sheds light on some difficult territorial questions neglected by theorists of "liberal nationalism." However, Meisels suggests an alternative solution to the question of when claims to devolution may justifiably be resisted.

A different approach is taken by Erica Benner and Daniel Bell. They both question the value of Miller's theory for those living outside prosperous liberal democracies. Benner argues that Miller's theory does not travel well outside the relatively stable and secure setting of established liberal democracies like Britain. In fact, although Miller develops his "republican" theory of nationhood to counter the shortcomings of "liberal" individualism and cosmopolitanism, his ideal of republican nationality tacitly relies on those same liberal principles to distinguish it from collectivist nationalism. In places where nationalists and their constituencies cannot be relied on to behave like well-tempered Humeans, theorists of nationalism need to uphold stronger principles of political reason than Miller is prepared to do.

Bell casts doubt on Miller's ideal of nation-based, active, public-spirited citizenship. Not only is it difficult to achieve in the context of Western liberal democracies, but invigorating nationalistic solidarity may have the effect of imposing substantial costs on relatively deprived people in foreign lands. Bell argues that there may be a need to qualify the "active" element of Miller's ideal of citizenship, and he sketches an alternative conception of occasional citizenship that may have better consequences for outsiders.

This leads us to part III of the book, in which the topic of global justice is examined. Stuart White tries to make sense of two of Miller's apparently conflicting arguments: the idea that citizenship is necessarily national in essence, and the idea that we should be held to fairly demanding transnational obligations of justice. According to White, this apparent conflict dissolves upon closer examination of the texts of leading republican theorists. It turns out that nation-based republican patriotism, which involves a commitment to certain universal values, can support transnational solidarities of the kind necessary to achieve global justice. Defenders of global justice can therefore defend both nation-based republican citizenship and meaningful cosmopolitian citizenship.

The next three contributors—Daniel Weinstock, Simon Caney, and Cécile Fabre—all argue against any attempt to comprise international principles of distributive justice with the requirements of "national justice." Weinstock argues that Miller has failed to make his case against transnational norms and institutions of distributive justice. Moreover, aspects of Miller's arguments themselves tell against a restriction of distributive justice to the bounds of the nation-state. Miller has developed a powerful set of tools against conservatism and complacency in the area of distributive justice, and these same tools can (and should) be used to argue powerfully for the extension of principles of global justice to the world's population. Miller is thus an antinationalist globalist *malgré lui*.

Simon Caney and Cécile Fabre both try to rebut Miller's critique of global egalitarianism. Caney examines not only people's rights but also people's duties, among them the duty to secure people's global entitlements. He argues that Miller's account of the type of "bounded societies" to which global comparative principles of distributive justice are meant to apply is implausible, and, in fact, we have some reason to think that comparative principles apply even outside of any associations. Moreover, he argues that Miller's own global noncomparative principles of distributive justice need to be supplemented by two additional principles—the principle of global fair equality of opportunity and the principle of global equal remuneration.

Cécile Fabre makes a case for global egalitarianism grounded in the view that individuals should not be treated unequally simply because they happen to reside in a certain kind of community. Fabre claims that Miller's arguments against global egalitarianism cannot undermine this and related global principles of justice. The reasons she objects to Miller's arguments are partly empirical and partly normative. However, Fabre acknowledges that implementing global egalitarianism may have the effect of undermining democratic self-determination.

Environmental concerns increasingly inform discussions of global justice. However, it is often the case that theorists relate to environmental goods as secondary in importance, or as "nonbasic" goods. Mathew Humphrey challenges this view. According to Humphrey, even though Miller's argument that these goods should not be treated as goods of justice on the grounds that they lack "intrinsic" value may be strong, we still have good grounds to consider some nonbasic environmental goods as goods of justice because the loss of these goods imposes irredeemable costs on present and future generations. This can also be seen as a critique of Miller's metaethical position regarding the conditions that have to be satisfied for a claim to count as a claim of justice.

Finally, David Miller replies to the various arguments raised by this volume's contributors and elsewhere. As indicated previously, Miller's point is that there are forms of justice, not just a single form. Critics of this position have claimed that this position bears two repugnant implications. First, a rather absurd relativism: If every society arranges its principles differently and if in different spheres of human life or different levels of human relationships different standards of justice apply, then there will be as many principles of justice as there are societies and such levels of relationships. Second, theories of justice, in fact the very idea of justice, will lose their critical appeal. All theorists of justice will be able to do is switch to anthropological descriptions of whatever exists in a certain society or in certain levels of relationships. Miller forcefully dismisses these claims and then builds on his argument to reply to the contributors to this volume. The result, he argues, is a pluralistic, critical, and practical theory of justice that navigates between the extremes of complacent relativism and Platonic liberalism.

Much of modern political philosophy grows out of the tension between the different forms of justice. David Miller can be commended for doing more than any other recent thinker to weave the different forms into a coherent and systematic theory of justice. But can it be done, and, if so, does Miller succeed? The essays in this book shed important light on this question and will stimulate interest and debate among political theorists as well as those approaching the subject for the first time.[2]

NOTES

1. The title is also an ironical reference to Plato's argument that there is one "form" of justice.

2. It is worth noting that this book may appeal to an unexpectedly wide range of readers. One of the editors told his then five-year-old son that he was working on a book about justice. His son asked him, "What's that?" The editor explained, "It's like when you say, 'No fair!' What exactly do you mean by that? Does it mean that we have to share all our things? Is it fair when you have so many toys and some children in Africa don't have any? That's what the book is about." The young boy's face lit up, and he replied, "Oh, you're writing a children's book!"

I

SOCIAL JUSTICE

1

Social Justice
Why Does It Matter What the People Think?

Adam Swift

Invited to write something on David Miller's work, I feel spoiled for choice. He and I have worked on a number of similar issues: communitarianism; conceptions of citizenship; complex equality; desert and meritocracy; the relation between social-scientific and philosophical work on principles of justice. Even better, we disagree about lots of them. He thinks that we could have a society in which, because distributive spheres are incommensurable, there are no overall judgments of social standing.[1] I think that this is unrealistic.

> On my account, members of a society can regard one another as equals . . . whilst simultaneously agreeing in their judgments that person X stands higher socially than, perhaps should be deferred to by, and perhaps even should not be expected to marry, person Y. At least I hope so, since I think that equal citizenship matters but am very doubtful that a society in which all have equal social standing is a real possibility.[2]

He thinks that someone's claim to deserve a job rides piggyback on her primary desert claim to the rewards that she will get from doing it.[3] I think something like the opposite: that, if it makes sense at all to say that she "deserves" a job, it is simply because she is the best person to do it, and not at all because she deserves the rewards that the market would give her for doing it.[4] This particular disagreement, of course, results from a more fundamental disagreement about the kind of responsibility that is required to sustain claims to differential economic deserts. He thinks that people can deserve unequal rewards for productively exercising attributes the unequal possession of which is a matter of luck—though he acknowledges that it is unjust if citizenship goods such as medical care and education are also distributed in accordance with people's productive contribution.[5] While agreeing that different desert bases are appropriate for different kinds of reward, I reject the idea that justice permits the resources people have to devote to their life plans to be so subject to factors beyond their control.[6]

Perhaps, rather than regurgitating such differences, I should write about areas of agreement. Maybe this was the opportunity to bring to light the section of my doctoral thesis—"Three Conceptions of Citizenship"—that "inspired" his own typology.[7] Alas, the central thrust of my discussion—that the distinction between liberal and participatory (or communitarian or republican) conceptions of citizenship was not as sharp as many seemed to think, and indeed was hard to pin down with any precision—is by now so familiar[8] and something I have discussed so much elsewhere[9] that even I baulk at the prospect of writing any more about it. Maybe, in that case, I should go for straightforward praise and elaboration. Was this the time to explore his claim about the way in which redistributive principles of the kind favored by contemporary liberals implicitly rely on communitarian—and, as he has developed that thought, nationalistic—premises?[10] Can the feeling of solidarity and identification with others necessary to underpin redistributive liberalism be sustained only through participation in shared practices that go beyond the mere doing of justice to one another? If so, what kind of shared practices? These seem to me among the most crucial questions that political theorists have to confront, and he has done as much as anyone to bring them to the top of the agenda.

In the end, I have decided to say something about an issue—the relation between public opinion and political philosophy—that we disagree about, but one where the disagreement is nested within a broader similarity of perspective. Though I have written on these matters before,[11] my efforts so far clearly have not persuaded him to change his mind. On the contrary, his *Principles of Social Justice* continues to give central place to a claim about the relation between public opinion and political philosophy that I believe to be importantly mistaken. My aim here, then, is to expose the mistake, or at least to show how, in presenting his view, Miller shifts between different positions. There are, to be sure, good reasons for political philosophers to attend to public opinion. But separating these out enables us to see how he trades on these, making it look as if they support a stronger role for such opinion than is in fact justified.

It is because I am generally sympathetic to Miller's approach that I am particularly keen to put these arguments under the microscope. He was the ideal supervisor for my doctoral thesis ("For a Sociologically Informed Political Theory"), and we remain close in overall outlook, because we share a concern to bring empirical, social-scientific work into contact with normative political theory. But we have crucially different understandings of exactly how and why empirical and social-scientific input matters. It is those different understandings that I want to lay out here.

THREE REASONS TO CARE ABOUT
WHAT THE PEOPLE THINK

The kind of empirical input we are talking about is ordinary people's everyday beliefs about social or distributive justice. According to Miller:

> Empirical evidence should play a significant role in justifying a normative theory of justice, or to put it another way, . . . such a theory is to be tested, in part, by its correspondence with our evidence concerning everyday beliefs about justice. Seen in this way, a theory of justice brings out the deep structure of a set of everyday beliefs that, on the surface, are to some degree ambiguous, confused, and contradictory. . . . The evidence helps to confirm the theory by revealing which principles people do in fact subscribe to. The aim is to achieve an equilibrium whereby the theory of justice appears no longer as an external imposition conjured up by the philosopher, but as a clearer and more systematic statement of the principles that people already hold.[12]

These are strong formulations. Although qualified by phrases like "significant role," "in part," and "helps," we are still left with a picture of everyday beliefs being involved in "justifying," "testing," and "confirming" a theory of justice. My suggestion is that when we look at his arguments we find that they support only rather weak versions of such claims. By outlining the three different reasons I can think of why a normative theorist might care about everyday beliefs, and showing how Miller invokes sometimes one, sometimes others, I hope to show that the strong version is less plausible than he makes it seem. In increasing order of strength, they are, first, that such beliefs, and knowledge of their causal determinants, provide food for thought; second, that they constitute feasibility constraints on the realization of the justifiable distribution; and third, that they are constitutive of that distribution itself.

FOOD FOR THOUGHT

The first, so weak as to be uncontroversial, is simply that knowing that others think differently gives the philosopher grounds for caution. Elster[13] observes that "the knowledge that others hold or practice very different conceptions should make him scrutinize his own opinions with extra care" and has elsewhere[14] suggested that Frolich and Oppenheimer's[15] finding that truncated utilitarianism—maximizing total welfare subject to a floor constraint on individual welfare—is overwhelmingly the most popular distribution actually chosen by people in a situation simulating Rawls's veil of ignorance gives philosophers reason to accord it more careful consideration than it has received hitherto. On this account, they may still end up rejecting popular opinion, but at least it will have been treated with appropriate respect.

If descriptive studies can play this cautionary role, then research into the factors that explain why people believe what they do about distributive justice can and should be similarly thought provoking. For example, where sociological research reveals that people are inclined to favor principles that correspond to their self-interest, then philosophers whose own views seem to reflect this process should think again. Of course, they may come to the same conclusions: as Elster acknowledges, correlations of this kind are not sufficient to invalidate arguments.[16] But one does not have time to question all of one's intuitions equally carefully, and empirical research of an explanatory kind can help the philosopher identify those most worthy of suspicion.

Some of what Miller says fits into this category. For example:

> According to Rawls, we must select from among our beliefs about justice those that deserve to be included as "considered judgments." These are judgments that we feel confident about and that as far as we can tell are not affected by our emotions or our personal interests. But can we decide whether a judgment is considered simply by scrutinizing it in solipsistic fashion, relying only on internal evidence to establish how much confidence we should place in it, or whether it has been influenced by one of the distorting factors that Rawls mentions? It is surely of the greatest relevance to see whether the judgments we make are shared by those around us, and if they are not, to try to discover what lies behind the disagreement. Looking at what other people believe about justice, and in particular trying to understand when people disagree and what the grounds of their disagreement are, is integral to the process of deciding which of my own beliefs deserve to be taken as "the fixed points of my considered judgment."[17]

He is clearly worried by the philosopher-as-solipsist: "This evidence should be taken more seriously than it usually is by social philosophers, for it guards us against the solipsistic fallacy that each of us already has a complete intuitive grasp of the requirements of justice."[18] This argument does indeed make the description of what other people think, and the explanation of why they think it, relevant to the normative theorist. And this is a good reason for philosophers to attend to empirical evidence of this kind. But the role remains external. It is in no way constitutive of the right normative answer. There is no suggestion here that what other people think, or even why they think it, can do more than give the philosopher reason cautiously to reconsider her own arguments and intuitions. I could, quite consistently with this argument, find myself to be significantly out of line not only with popular opinion but also with the beliefs of other political philosophers, ponder on why this might be the case, and come to a conclusion that allowed me to continue to affirm the beliefs I started with.

I don't know any philosophers who are solipsists in Miller's sense—who assume that they already have a complete intuitive grasp of the requirements of justice. On the contrary, they seem to me to spend most of their time testing their convictions against the convictions of others—but, typically, the convictions (and, more specifically, the arguments for those convictions) of other *philosophers*. It is true that we cannot rely merely on internal evidence to judge how confident we should be in our beliefs. We assess that by seeing how well they stand up to the things other people say against them, whether our intuitions withstand considerations intended to pull us away from them. But that is precisely what philosophers do. Some of Miller's argument here seems to set up a straw man (philosopher-as-solipsist) and to trade on a false dichotomy between solipsism and attention to popular opinion. For example, I am less confident than I used to be in my belief that conventional desert claims are invalid. There seems to be more to be said in their defense than I had once thought. But this change in the degree of confidence with which I hold that belief has nothing to do with an increased awareness of public opinion. It has much more to do with the arguments of Miller and other political theorists.

FEASIBILITY

The second reason why empirical research might be of interest to the political theorist holds that lay beliefs matter insofar as they constitute the causal field that confronts his or her attempts to guide action. Conceptions of justice that fail sufficiently to correspond to ordinary thinking are doomed to failure, however sound they may be in philosophical terms, for, as Dunn observes, "if historical agents are to be provided with reasons for acting, they must be furnished with reasons which are reasons for *them*."[19] The bounds of political possibility are to a great extent set by popular opinion, so that judging what can be done politically requires knowledge of that opinion. Add to this the claim that it makes little sense to advocate that which it is impossible to achieve, or that there is reason to be concerned with the set of feasible outcomes given the status quo, and one has a variety of moral arguments for why political theorists should take lay beliefs into account. We need not regard those beliefs as making any difference to the truth about justice, for our conclusion may well be simply that justice is unattainable and will remain so while popular opinion remains as it is, but there is reason to take them seriously when offering prescriptions here and now.

Miller invokes this kind of reason more than he does the previous kind. This passage from the preface (x) is also on the back of the dustcover:

> The theory of justice set out in this book has a different character from most theories developed in recent political philosophy. Besides being more sensitive to popular opinion, it also pays closer attention to the social contexts in which principles of justice are applied. This focus gives the theory a less abstract character. It also, I believe, increases its political relevance. I have felt acutely aware, while writing the book, of the huge gap that exists between the conceptions of social justice defended by political philosophers, particularly by those we might describe as egalitarian liberals, and the kind of policy changes it is feasible to propose for the liberal societies of today. Of course social justice always has been, and must always be, a critical idea, one that challenges us to reform our institutions and practices in the name of greater fairness. But it should not be simply utopian . . . theorizing about social justice has become detached from questions of political feasibility.

Miller here identifies three distinct respects in which his theory differs from the recent industry standard. It is (1) more sensitive to popular opinion, (2) less abstract, with greater attention to social contexts, and (3) more politically relevant and less utopian. I will say something about the difference between (1) and (2) shortly. Here, I focus on (1) and (3).

The appropriate response to Miller's claim here is simply to say, "Of course." Of course a theory that starts from people's current beliefs about justice is going to be more "politically relevant" than one that does not—than one, say, that rather seeks correctly to identify true beliefs about justice without regard to the extent to which people currently endorse such beliefs. And of course there are lots of reasons why we might care that a theory is indeed politically relevant—truth is not the only value. We might, for example, care about contributing to the realization of states of the world that are better than those that pertain. (We might even care about maximally contributing—i.e., maximizing our expected contribution.) And doing this might lead us to have little interest in questions of truth at all—at least the kind of precise truth with which political philosophers are so often preoccupied. I don't have any problem with any of this. (Though, if I came across someone who argued against truth seeking on these grounds, I'd want to quiz her about time frames and may emphasize the extent to which what is politically feasible can change over time, partly as a result of people changing their beliefs about justice—which may partly be the result of political philosophers continuing to argue for the truth about justice.) But the obvious point that attending to popular opinion increases political relevance, or feasibility, says nothing in favor of giving such opinion any role in deciding what is true about justice.

Miller occasionally seems to dress up the evident as if it involved some controversial claim. "If we want to describe what social justice means in contemporary debate, then sooner rather than later we must look at what the people themselves think" (ix). Well, yes. If we want to do that, the implication follows. "Is it merely an accident that popular views of social justice have greater political saliency than the theories propounded in the literature of political philosophy? I believe not" (x). Well, neither do I. Indeed, it is hard to imagine a democratic political system in which it was not the case that popular views of social justice had greater political saliency than the theories of political philosophers. (I'll say some more about democracy later.) But, again, such claims in no way suggest that popular opinion tells us anything about what justice does indeed require of us. Such opinion may tell us a lot about what is and is not feasible or utopian, and knowing that may indeed lead us, for strategic reasons, to argue for some conclusions but not others that we also believe to be true. It may even give us strategic reasons to argue for conclusions we believe to be false (if that were judged the most effective way to achieve desired outcomes). It will almost certainly give us reason to frame or formulate our arguments and conclusions in ways that connect or gel with popular opinion. But all this is quite different from regarding popular opinion as any kind of "test" or "confirmation" of the validity of our views about justice.

Perhaps the issue at stake is what a theory of justice is *for;* the proper aim or purpose of the discipline of political theory. According to Miller, "[A]n adequate theory of justice must pay attention to empirical evidence about how the public at large understands justice, and in particular to the way in which different norms of justice are applied in different social contexts."[20]

If "adequate" means "practicable now (or in the foreseeable future)" or "likely to persuade the mass of people on whose persuasion its realization depends," then I agree. But is this what constitutes adequacy in a theory of justice? Contrast Miller's with G. A. Cohen's view: "Facts of human nature and human society of course (1) make a difference to what justice tells us to do in specific terms; they also (2) tell us how much justice we can get, and they (3) bear on how much we should compromise with justice, but . . . they make no difference to the very nature of justice itself."[21]

Such facts include facts about what people believe about justice. Public opinion can crucially influence the likelihood of justice's being realized, or how much of it we can get—it constitutes part of the causal field with which attempts to promote justice necessarily interact—and it may well have strategic impact on what or how we argue. I am all for paying proper attention to such factors and am sympathetic to Miller's impatience with the otherworldliness of some contemporary political philosophy. Perhaps utopian political theorizing—even if correctly identifying what justice requires—has consumed the energies of too many who, had they resisted its seductive charms, might have done more to make the world a fairer place. (Though it is hard to see why such theorists are more culpable than all those others who might work efficiently to bring about a fairer world but choose to do other things with their time. Perhaps the difference is that, unlike some of those others, they seem to care about fairness. The impatience arises from the blatancy of the mismatch between their avowal that fairness matters and their unwillingness to act in ways likely to promote it.) It is frustrating, and to some extent humiliating, to sit in seminars run by think tanks or government agencies and have brought home to one the chasm that exists between the world of cutting-edge journal articles about justice and the real world of practical politics, a large part of which is due to the gap between political philosophy and public opinion. But I also agree with Cohen. If we're thinking about what justice means—*really* means, not "means in contemporary debate"—then it is a mistake to give public opinion any deeper or more constitutive role. Certainly, we should, on occasion, tailor our proposals and policies, perhaps even the presentation of our arguments, to the context. But we must be clear about what precisely is being tailored, and why we are tailoring it. If we do cut our coat (justice-promoting policies and arguments) according to our cloth (what people currently believe about justice), we should not also think that justice itself is made from the same material.

Nor should we tailor justice to what people can be expected to come to believe about justice. At one point, Miller explicitly assumes that political philosophy has "a practical aim: its purpose is not only to get at the truth, but to improve the thinking of those who are not professional philosophers."[22] If empirical research reveals people to be "locked into beliefs about justice that they hold for bad reasons, it may come to seem somewhat pointless to develop a normative theory of justice."[23] I agree with this second claim. If I thought that people could not plausibly be expected to come to believe the truth about justice, I would not waste my time trying to identify it (at least not beyond the point at which I thought they could be brought to agree with it). But it would still be the case that what I was giving up on identifying was *justice*. I see no reason to think that *that* necessarily coincides with "that which people can be expected to come to believe to be justice."

So much for (1) and (3). What about (2)—Miller's observation that his theory of justice is less abstract, and more context specific, than most—a feature he takes to result from its greater sensitivity to popular opinion?

One of the many reasons why social scientists are skeptical about normative theorizing or philosophizing derives specifically from the social scientist's awareness of the extent to which, as a matter of empirical fact, people's distributive judgments are complex and context specific.[24] This is an observation that became familiar to political theorists through Walzer's theory of complex equality, where a methodological injunction to attend to the "social meanings" of goods yielded—contingently, as I read him—a pluralistic conception of justice in which "different goods are distributed for different reasons."[25]

Now, it may be true that philosophers tend to formulate their positions in terms that abstract from complexity and transcend particularity of contexts, to seek the deeper structures of thought, the more general and widely applicable reasons, which ought to guide our concrete judgments. According to Walzer, "the first impulse of the philosopher is . . . to search for some underlying unity: a short list of basic goods, quickly abstracted to a single good; a single distributive criterion or an interconnected set; and the philosopher himself standing, symbolically at least, at a single decision point."[26] Perhaps this is the philosophical impulse. But we should not confuse Walzer's pluralistic substantive theory with the antiphilosophical methodology he claims to use to arrive at it. There is nothing incoherent about the idea of a theory of justice that is pluralistic or contextual, in important senses, but gives little or no weight to popular opinion about how goods should be distributed. Perhaps a plausible theory of justice must acknowledge that one cannot expect to make correct judgments about particular distributive issues without knowing a great deal of detail about the particulars of the situation one is being asked to judge. It may simply be right that what should count as a just distribution depends on various characteristics of the good being distributed, the individuals among whom it is being distributed, the relation between those individuals, and so on. Doubtless, attending to popular opinion can help—may indeed have helped—in providing food for thought, in helping the political theorist come to see how best to think about the demands of justice, including the ways in which different distributive principles are appropriate in different contexts. But the reasons for thinking contextually, in that sense, need not include the fact that this is "what the people think."

The more seriously we take the feasibility constraints of the real world—including popular opinion about justice—the more important it is not to confuse "justice" and "a realistic amount of justice to pursue now." In a piece written six years before it was published, G. A. Cohen[27] has suggested that the endorsement of conventional desert claims in Miller's *Market, State and Community*[28] promotes the kind of adaptive preference formation known as sour grapes. Like the fox who, unable to reach the grapes, decided that they weren't worth having, so socialists, Miller among them, are adapting their conception of justice to what they believe realistically attainable. If we cannot have more justice than would be provided by market socialism, then we had better start thinking that market socialism can give us justice. My view is that Miller's subsequent defense of his view about markets and desert has been an admirable response to that charge. The subtlety of his position suggests that, if it is sour grapes, then he is an expert sour-graper, going to impressive theoretical lengths to shore up his (allegedly adaptive) view. But Cohen alerts us to a more general danger. If we focus too much on "the kind or amount of justice it is realistic to pursue now"—keeping our more controversial views under wraps lest they frighten people away, offering only proposals that are feasible given current constraints—we may start to believe our own rhetoric. Politicians can be relied on to dilute the truth about justice if feasibility constraints require it. The philosophical task is to prevent that truth from slipping out of sight altogether.

CONSTITUTIVE OF JUSTICE

The third reason why popular beliefs might bear on political philosophies of justice is the rather stronger one that the distributive principles that are justified for the society in question may be internally related to lay beliefs themselves. Where the second regards those beliefs merely as constraints upon the feasibility of achieving a just society, and the justification of principles of justice as occurring quite independently of popular beliefs, this third argument claims that such beliefs are in some sense constitutive of a proper understanding of what justice demands. Because they explicitly raise the issue of legitimacy, a concept different from but closely related to that of distributive justice and one that lends superficial plausibility to Miller's position, this section broadens the discussion to look at the work of Walzer and Rawls.

Three versions of this third—constitutive—line of argument can be identified, ranging from the weak and unobjectionable, through the substantial and interesting, to the strong and mistaken. The weak and unobjectionable version says that the philosopher who talks about justice needs to make sure that she is talking about that which is conventionally referred to by the word *justice*. This is indeed an empirical issue, decidable only by attention to the way in which the term and its derivatives are actually used, in particular by attention to those commonplaces that are so commonplace as to be candidates for a priori truths.[29] A philosopher who offers her theory of justice with no claim that it should motivate those to whom it is addressed, or who offers it as a theory of how one should behave to avoid embarrassment, for example, has not understood what the term means. There is, of course, room for philosophical argument as to which commonplaces are indeed a priori truths, but the question of which statements are commonplaces would seem to be an empirical matter. This claim, then, makes popular beliefs about justice constitutive of the philosophically correct view about justice in the sense that they indicate what it is for a belief to be a belief about justice, and not, for example, about charity, or etiquette. One way of seeing how weak and unobjectionable this sense is, is to notice that both Nozick and Rawls, despite the huge differences in the content of their theories, satisfy the requirement to attend to the grammar of justice. They both take themselves to be talking about a subset of moral considerations—roughly that part of morality that is to do with people's rights, duties, and what states are justified in requiring citizens to do to and for one another.

The substantial and interesting version of the constitutive claim notes that principles of justice may give some weight to what people think is just even when the principles themselves have been justified in ways that do not give a constitutive role to what people think. For example, it is plausible to hold, as a principle of justice, that people's legitimate expectations constitute valid claims to reward, or at least that they should be given some weight in judging what distributive outcomes are just. Even someone who regards conventional desert claims as mistaken may acknowledge that the fact that a person's actions have been informed by the belief that they are valid, in a context where all or most other relevant actors believe the same, is pertinent to the question of what she should get as a matter of justice. To the extent that judging a person's legitimate expectations depends on knowing what she and others believe about justice, justice beliefs will clearly be relevant information for anyone deciding what distributive outcomes are just. What people think is just, then, may enter into what justice requires, not via the claim that what they think is constitutive of correct principles of justice but via the claim that there is independent moral reason—a principle of justice (justified independently of popular opinion)—to give those views some weight.

The first two versions of the constitutive claim gives popular beliefs a role, first, in determining what it is for something to be a theory of justice, and, second, when combined with a principle giving some weight to popular beliefs, in making a difference to what justice requires. The third, and strongest (and mistaken), version gives popular opinion a role in determining the content of principles of justice themselves. This is the claim that part of the answer to the question of what principles should govern the distribution of goods in a society is to be found by looking at the way that the people whose society it is think that they ought to be distributed. Walzer and Rawls have both argued something along these lines, so let us examine their methodological positions. My suggestion is that the idea of legitimacy—already touched on in relation to legitimate expectations—is doing much of the work.

When we look at Walzer's justification of his proclaimed method, we find two distinct arguments. One is quasi-conceptual and somewhat relativistic: goods mean different things in different societies, the proper distribution of a good is one in accordance with its social meaning, and there is no cross-cultural basis on which to criticize a society's understandings of its goods. The other is democratic: it is respect for lay beliefs that requires the philosopher to accord them moral weight. If one understands politics and political theory as in the business of responding to citizens' wills, then what matters is not so much the independent philosophical validity (rightness) of citizens' beliefs, but the fact that they are theirs.[30] Although Walzer does not seem to notice this, the quasi-conceptual and somewhat relativistic argument and the democratic argument are quite different. It is one thing to take shared meanings to be constitutive of justice because one lacks a basis for criticism, quite another to give them constitutive weight out of a respect for those who share them.[31]

It is noticeable that in *Spheres of Justice* Walzer puts this second argument somewhat differently. There, he does not mention democracy, but says that what guides his approach is "a decent respect for the opinions of mankind," and he grounds this respect in the claim that it is as culture-producing creatures that we are one another's equals.[32] This change of formulation is significant, for it suggests that Walzer is uncomfortable using an argument familiar from democratic theory in support of a method supposed to yield principles of justice. And uncomfortable he should be, for making the democratic case for respecting the views of one's fellow citizens, or those of another culture, even when those views are mistaken, is surely different from regarding those views as constitutive of justice itself. One may very well accept the democratic legitimacy of distributions that reflect popular opinion without being at all tempted to regard that opinion as constitutive of the right answer as to what distributive justice demands.[33]

We need to be careful. It is consistent with this that popular opinion may be in some sense constitutive of the right answer, where that is taken to be the answer which conforms to the demands of procedural justice. If one holds that what makes a decision legitimate is that it is the outcome of a just procedure, then one will accept the legitimacy of a distribution precisely because it satisfies the demands of this kind of justice. But it remains the case that the decision can be the wrong one in the sense I am discussing. Just as the verdict of a jury has legitimacy even if it judges the case badly, so an ideal democracy might generate decisions on distributive matters that are legitimate (because the outcome of a just procedure) while being quite mistaken about the demands of distributive justice. I take it that we are here discussing beliefs about, and their relation to the justification of, principles of distributive justice *stricto sensu*. But it is crucial to see that people's beliefs about legitimacy—or about what makes a procedure just—can themselves be mistaken. If we have reason to regard citizens' mistaken decisions about distributive justice as legitimate, this is because of a correct analysis of what makes a decision legitimate and not because of what they think makes a decision legitimate.

This line of argument explains why research into public opinion might be important on democratic grounds—the first opinion pollsters conceived their work in just such terms, as do those who advocate more sophisticated methods[34]—and in this way the findings of empirical research (though not necessarily of social surveys) might indeed be of significance to the normative political theorist concerned with legitimacy. But this is not to grant its findings any constitutive role in a theory of distributive justice.[35]

The distinction between justice and legitimacy may also help in the understanding of Rawls's attitude to popular opinion, though here things are yet more complicated—if perhaps less confused—than they were in Walzer's case. Where Rorty interprets Rawls's claim that his theory of justice is political and not metaphysical as showing how liberal democracy can get along without philosophical presuppositions, requiring "only history and sociology,"[36] in fact Rawls adopts a variant of the position that holds that we have moral reason to give weight to the beliefs that citizens hold, or can hold, in common. Rawls's claim is that we should take seriously "certain fundamental ideas seen as implicit in the public political culture of a democratic society," not simply because they represent "the way we live now," but rather because we have reason to value a society that is publicly justifiable to its members. Baldly summarizing a complex argument, what Rawls[37] actually argues is that, since political power is the exercise of power held by free and equal citizens, that exercise is only legitimate when it is used in ways that can be justified by appeal to public reason; the importance of public justifiability leads the political theorist to "society's main institutions, and their accepted forms of interpretation . . . seen as a fund of implicitly shared ideas and principles";[38] the idea of society as a fair scheme of cooperation between free and equal citizens is such an idea, which is articulated by Rawls in terms of the imaginative construct of the "original position"; and from that device of representation emerges a substantive theory of distributive justice.

This, then, is a distinct, and much more fully articulated, variant of the legitimacy argument strands of which we detected in Walzer. It, too, can be thought of as invoking a proper respect for people's beliefs, but here the respect is not shown simply by giving the people what they will—as it is on the democratic view—but by insisting that the use of state coercion is publicly justifiable to them. This is "the liberal principle of legitimacy." As Rawls puts it, "Our exercise of political power is fully proper only when it is exercised in accordance with a constitution the essentials of which all citizens as free and equal may reasonably be expected to endorse in the light of principles and ideals acceptable to their common human reason."[39] Rawls is thus led to espouse a methodology constraining him to the working up of ideas implicit in our public political culture by his distinctively liberal understanding of the proper relation between the individual and the state. And unlike Walzer, Rawls does not confuse the demands of legitimacy with those of justice. That is why he can continue to argue for the justice of justice as fairness, difference principle and all, while recognizing that other liberal political conceptions of justice can satisfy the demands of public reason and hence be legitimate.[40] True, Rawls thinks that views about justice must themselves be argued for in terms that would make them legitimate if they prevailed (i.e., by appeal to public reason). In that sense he gives shared ideas a constitutive role in deciding what justice is. But one need not agree with that further claim. One could accept that principles of distributive justice have to stand in a certain relation to popular opinion if they are to be legitimate while regarding this as a moral constraint on the realization of correct principles of justice (because those principles do not stand in the proper relation to shared values).[41]

So, it may be right to regard the beliefs of a society's members about principles of justice as constitutive of the kinds of principles that may legitimately regulate their society. But that is quite different from regarding those beliefs as constitutive of the right answer as to what principles of justice are correct for that society. This distinction, between principles being justified as legitimate principles to govern the distribution of benefits and burdens in a society and their being justified as correct principles of justice, may seem pedantic, but it is one recognized by all who acknowledge the legitimacy of laws that they themselves regard, and would vote against, as unjust. Walzer veers between a conceptual and a democratic version of the legitimacy argument and seems, mistakenly, to regard both as implying that his method of attending to shared social meanings is a way of justifying principles of justice. Rawls is clearer on the distinction between justice and legitimacy and offers a version of the latter that attends less to what people currently believe than to what can be justified to them in appropriate terms. Though Miller provides an excellent extended discussion of procedural justice and how it may conflict with outcome justice, his index makes no mention of legitimacy.[42] If the reader is sympathetic to the stronger variants of his claim about the significance of public opinion, my hunch is that that is partly because she is confusing distributive justice and legitimacy (or procedural justice).

CONCLUSION

When Gordon Marshall applied for funding for what became the British leg of the International Social Justice Project,[43] his grant proposal received the following anonymous reference:

> Surveys of popular opinion on these topics seem to me of little academic value. . . . The great debate about justice that has been in

progress since the time of Plato has thrown up many difficulties. But we will not be helped in the least in the resolution of these difficulties by a knowledge of the quirks of public opinion. Justice is, one might almost say, a semi-technical notion. It is the topic discussed by Plato in *The Republic*, by Aquinas in *Summa Theologia*, and by Mill in *Utilitarianism*. . . . Someone who knows nothing of this material is hardly in a position to contribute to the resolution of our problems. It would seem therefore a waste of time to survey the views of people who are not in a position to judge the issues.

Despite this, the research was funded (by the Economic and Social Research Council) and was not, I hope, a waste of time and public money. The referee had too specialized and limited a conception of what is and is not "of academic value." (See Kluegel et al. and Marshall et al.[44] to make your own judgment.) But I agree with his or her central claim. Knowing what the people think justice requires contributes little or nothing to our knowledge of what justice requires.

What the people think justice requires is important as food for thought (though not as important as what other normative theorists and philosophers think about justice). What the people think about justice (and what they can reasonably be expected to come to think) matters, further, and very importantly, for reasons of feasibility. If it matters also constitutively, it does so only if and because we hold moral principles that give weight to what they think in deciding what distributions are legitimate (or procedurally just). The principle of legitimate expectations captures this at one level, the principle of democratic legitimacy does so at another. In both cases these principles are not justified by appeal to popular opinion. Popular beliefs about distributive justice are indeed important factors for the political theorist to take into account, but for reasons of feasibility or legitimacy, not because they play any role in the justification of principles of distributive justice. Nor are such principles to be "tested," even in part, by their fit with "our" everyday beliefs about them.

The problem with the view argued for here is that it invites the charge of Platonism. As Miller says: "The notion that philosophers can discover truth by means not available to lay persons is even more difficult to defend today than it was in Plato's time."[45] But that notion has not been defended. The means available to philosophers are also "available" to laypersons. If there is a difference, it is that philosophers have the time and interest to learn and apply them systematically. The problem with Miller's view is that it seems impossible to see how, as a matter of basic moral epistemology, the correctness of a fundamental moral judgment could depend on other people's beliefs as to its correctness.

I do not pretend to have a clear view about the proper method of justification in moral or political philosophy. How precisely we justify our conclusions—to ourselves or to others—and how we come to know some moral claims to be true and others false are, of course, big and difficult questions. My argument has been entirely negative: disagreeing with Miller's stronger claim without any corresponding attempt to defend an alternative methodology. But, though I don't know how to do it, I don't think that it makes sense to do it like *that*. It is revealing that Miller invokes different kinds of reasoning—food for thought, feasibility, and constitutive—and asserts what, on inspection, are quite uncontroversial claims to support his case for attending to what the people think. That suggests to me that he, too, is doubtful about the stronger strand in his argument. Insofar as that strand seems plausible, I would hazard, it is because of a failure to distinguish between distributive justice, on the one hand, and legitimacy (or procedural justice), on the other.

NOTES

1. D. Miller, "Complex Equality," in *Pluralism, Justice and Equality*, ed. David Miller and Michael Walzer (Oxford: Oxford University Press, 1995), 204–209.

2. A. Swift, "The Sociology of Complex Equality," in *Pluralism, Justice and Equality*, in ed. D. Miller and M. Walzer (Oxford: Oxford University Press, 1995), 277–78.

3. D. Miller, *Principles of Social Justice* (Cambridge, Mass.: Harvard University Press, 1999), 167.

4. A. Swift and G. Marshall, "Meritocratic Equality of Opportunity: Economic Efficiency, Social Justice, or Both?" *Policy Studies* 18 (1997): 35–48.

5. Miller, *Principles*, 200.

6. G. Marshall, A. Swift, and S. Roberts, *Against the Odds? Social Class and Social Justice in Industrial Societies* (Oxford: Oxford University Press, 1997), 166–167.

7. D. Miller, *Citizenship and National Identity* (Cambridge: Polity, 2000), 186.

8. For example, R. Dagger, *Civic Virtues* (Oxford: Oxford University Press, 1997).

9. S. Mulhall and A. Swift, "The Social Self in Political Theory: The Communitarian Critique of the Liberal Subject," in *The Social Self*, ed. D. Bakhurst and C. Sypnowich (London: Sage, 1995), 103–122; S. Mulhall and A. Swift, *Liberals and Communitarians*, 2d ed. (Oxford: Blackwell, 1996).

10. Miller, *Principles*; Miller, *Citizenship*, ch. 5.

11. A. Swift et al., "Distributive Justice: Does It Matter What the People Think?" in *Social Justice and Political Change: Public Opinion in Capitalist and Post-Communist States*, ed. J. Kluegel et al. (New York: Aldine de Gruyter, 1995), 15–47; A. Swift, "Public Opinion and Political Philosophy: The Relation between Social-Scientific and Philosophical Analyses of Distributive Justice," *Ethical Theory and Moral Practice* 2 (1999): 337–63. I am grateful to Kluwer Academic Publishers for permission to reproduce parts of the latter.

12. Miller, *Principles*, 51.

13. J. Elster, *Local Justice* (New York: Russell Sage Foundation, 1992), 193.

14. J. Elster, "The Empirical Study of Justice," in *Pluralism, Justice and Equality*, ed. D. Miller and M. Walzer (Oxford: Oxford University Press, 1995), 94–95.

15. N. Frolich and J. A. Oppenheimer, *Choosing Justice: An Experimental Approach to Ethics* (Berkeley: University of California Press, 1992).

16. Elster, "Empirical Study," 94.

17. Miller, *Principles*, 55–56.

18. Miller, *Principles*, 34.

19. J. Dunn, *Political Obligation in Its Historical Context* (Cambridge: Cambridge University Press, 1980), 247.

20. Miller, *Principles*, 42.

21. G. A. Cohen, "Rescuing Justice from Constructivism," (manuscript, Oxford, 2001).

22. Miller, *Principles*, 283.

23. Miller, *Principles*, 60.

24. For some other reasons, see Swift, "Public Opinion and Political Philosophy."

25. M. Walzer, *Spheres of Justice* (New York: Basic Books, 1983).

26. Walzer, *Spheres*, 4.

27. G. A. Cohen, *Self-Ownership, Freedom and Equality* (Cambridge: Cambridge University Press, 1995), 257.

28. D. Miller, *Market, State and Community* (Oxford: Oxford University Press, 1989).

29. F. Jackson and P. Pettit, "Moral Functionalism and Moral Motivation," *Philosophical Quarterly* 45 (1995): 20–40.

30. M. Walzer, "Philosophy and Democracy," *Political Theory* 9 (1981): 379–399.

31. Rorty is similarly ambiguous. Although he argues that there is no way to arrive at principles of justice other than by what he calls "a historico-sociological description of the way we live now," he does so in a paper asserting the priority of democracy to philosophy, which suggests that he, too, can plausibly be read as arguing the democratic, rather than the antifoundationalist, case for heeding the beliefs of his fellow citizens. See R. Rorty, "The Priority of Democracy to Philosophy," in *Reading Rorty*, ed. A. Malachowski (Oxford: Blackwell, 1990), 287.

32. Walzer, *Spheres*, 314, 320.

33. For discussion of the so-called paradox of democracy, see R. Wollheim, "A Paradox in the Theory of Democracy," in *Philosophy, Politics and Society, Second Series*, ed. P. Laslett and W. G. Runciman (Oxford: Blackwell, 1962), 71–87; and D. Estlund, "The Persistent Puzzle of the Minority Democrat," *American Philosophical Quarterly* 16 (1989): 143–151.

34. J. Fishkin, *The Voice of the People: Public Opinion and Democracy* (New Haven, Conn.: Yale University Press, 1995).

35. Two further questions cannot be pursued here. First, what kind of public opinion—how postdeliberation? how philosophically educated?—is relevant for legitimacy? Second, to what extent (and hence by what institutional means) does legitimacy require popular opinion to be accommodated? One might think that conventional liberal democratic processes give sufficient weight to the right kind of popular opinion, with political parties being effectively constrained by their desire for reelection to attend to the findings of opinion polls and focus groups. Or one might argue for a greater role for referenda, or for citizens' juries and deliberative polls, and so on.

36. J. Rawls, *Political Liberalism* (New York: Columbia University Press, 1993), 284.

37. Rawls, *Political Liberalism*.

38. Rawls, *Political Liberalism*, 13–14.

39. Rawls, *Political Liberalism*, 137.

40. D. Estlund, "The Survival of Egalitarian Justice in John Rawls's *Political Liberalism*," *Journal of Political Philosophy* 4 (1996): 68–78.

41. There is another strand of argument in Rawls that emphasizes the importance of stability, and this might seem to give him a further reason to care about popular opinion. The proper role of stability considerations in Rawls's argument is more complicated than can adequately be discussed here (see Mulhall and Swift, *Liberals and Communitarians*, 240–242), but for present purposes it is sufficient to note that to the extent that they constitute a genuinely distinct strand of reasoning they have to do with feasibility, in which case my remarks under that heading apply.

42. Miller, *Principles*, 93–110.

43. Kluegel et al., eds., *Social Justice and Political Change*.

44. Kluegel et al., *Social Justice and Political Change*; and G. Marshall, A. Swift, D. Routh, and C. Burgoyne, "What Is and What Ought to Be: Popular Beliefs about Distributive Justice in Thirteen Countries," *European Sociological Review* 15 (1999): 349–367.

45. Miller, *Principles*, 53.

2

The Political Conditions of Social Justice

Marc Stears

The last three decades have seen the emergence of a remarkable gulf between the aspirations of most political theorists and the concrete developments of practical politics. Since the early 1970s, political theory has been dominated by the pursuit of an ideal liberal theory of justice. Following the publication of John Rawls's *A Theory of Justice,* theorists have spent a large part of their academic effort offering increasingly ambitious amendments to this account of the rightful distribution of social benefits and burden. At the same time, however, politicians, even those on the left, have largely abandoned the pursuit of the widespread redistribution of wealth and opportunity. Acting in response to an apparent revolution in economic relations, social structures, and popular attitudes, even social democratic governments in countries with long histories of radical progressive politics are currently engaged in dramatic programs of "ratcheting down" once ambitious programs of social welfare. Economically appeasing the owners of increasingly mobile capital and electorally appealing to a tax-weary public are now the leading political priorities.[1] Given such mismatch, students beginning classes in normative political theory today and introduced for the first time to Rawls's "difference principle" or Dworkin's "equality of resources" are increasingly to be found thinking that there is an inverse relationship between political theory and political practice. For as the real opportunities for social justice have become more circumscribed, so the aspirations of those who theorize about social justice often appear to have become all the more outlandishly optimistic.[2]

The publication of David Miller's *Principles of Social Justice* marked the beginning of a serious attempt to redress this situation. In this book, Miller consciously sets out to respond to the recent developments in practical politics. He draws "attention to the way in which theorizing about social justice has become

29

detached from questions of political feasibility" and demands that theorists mend their ways.[3] If the realities of politics are changing, Miller contends, so the suggestions of academics interested in social justice have to change, too. Miller is not entirely alone in advocating such a shift, but he does go far further than most. In recent years, a number of other leading theorists have begun to shape practical proposals from philosophical ideals, with Bruce Ackermann and Stephen Holmes acting as exemplars.[4] What distinguishes Miller's approach, though, is that while others have teased out policy guidelines from abstract debates, Miller actually calls the very future of social justice into question. In *Principles,* Miller sets out to identify the structural and attitudinal preconditions that make a recognizable theory of social justice politically viable. He also attempts to ascertain whether there is any role left for progressive political theorists in a world where those preconditions increasingly fail to be met. The very future of social justice, he contends, partly relies on its advocates possessing a better understanding of the social and political frameworks that have supported the ideal and of the popular attitudes that have helped to define it. The result, Miller must hope, is a whole new understanding of the role of the political theorist in modern political debate.

Miller's attempt to recast the agenda of political thought and to reposition the political theorist should be warmly welcomed. Academic political theory and concrete political reality have been out of kilter for far too long and Miller offers an innovative remedy to the problems that has caused. His attempt to reconnect theory with practice, however, does not come without costs. In this chapter, I argue that Miller has gone too far in restricting the political theorist's scope for maneuver. For although he is absolutely right to highlight the need for theorists to appreciate both the structural and attitudinal preconditions for social justice, the particular account of those preconditions offered and the prescriptive guidelines for what theorists should do if those preconditions are not met are both unduly pessimistic. Put another way, while David Miller has undeniably identified the right *questions* as to the future of social justice, he has not yet succeeded in providing a full set of the right *answers.* The role political theorists should play in ensuring that social justice has a future remains to be confirmed. In this chapter, I further suggest that a rather more optimistic account of the possible role for the political theorist can be discovered by paying closer attention to the history of social justice, both as a conceptual ideal and as an empirical reality. History, especially a history that is comparative across both time and geographical location, can often give us a picture of other possibilities. In this particular case, close attention to the period and places in which social justice first emerged fulfills that role perfectly.[5]

This argument is developed here in three sections. First, the chapter outlines both the questions and the answers about the future of social justice and the role of the political theorist in maintaining it as presented by Miller. The second section of the chapter returns to the early days of the modern idea of social justice and examines in particular the work of a group of progressive theorists in the United States. These thinkers and activists faced many of the same problems, asked many of the same questions, but came up with very different answers. Third, the chapter sketches out some of the very general lessons that this story from the past may have for the present. In its most limited form, this section shows how the theorists of the past can still make some contribution to contemporary debates. In its grandest form, it attempts to establish a new agenda for theoretical research in the future.

MILLER'S MODEL:
THE PRECONDITIONS OF SOCIAL JUSTICE

Miller begins *Principles of Social Justice* by identifying a series of usually unstated empirical assumptions regarding the world within which a theory of social justice can both flourish academically and find some resonance in practice. Miller argues that there are "three assumptions" that "have to be made before we can begin theorizing about social justice."[6] In summarizing these three assumptions, he contends that social justice requires theorists to possess "the notion of a society made up of interdependent parts, with an institutional structure that affects the prospects of each individual member, and that is capable of deliberate reform by an agency such as the state in the name of fairness."[7] In order fully to understand Miller's position, it is important to start with each of these three.

The Structural Conditions

The first of Miller's assumptions regards the social environment in which a theory of justice is based. Miller contends that in order to be politically sustainable, theories of social justice have to be situated in a "bounded society with a determinate membership."[8] In order to make meaningful judgments as to the justice of a particular distribution of goods, Miller contends, a theorist must be able to compare the positions of different groups of people so as to assess the relative shares of advantages or disadvantages accruing to them. Given the essentially comparative nature of the enterprise, the relevant groups must have something in common. Miller argues that the appropriate connection is membership of some larger encompassing entity.[9]

Although this idea remains rather vague in *Principles*, Miller has expanded on the need to assume that a theory of social justice is situated in a bounded community elsewhere, notably in *Citizenship and National Identity*. In this work, he suggests that the connections that are forged between people who inhabit the same social environment enable them both to agree on the ideal ways in which goods should be distributed and to make some practical progress toward distributing the goods in that way.[10] Only members of a single—if broadly based—community can be expected to possess roughly the same idea of social justice and, at the same time, be willing to see their resources distributed between each other according to the strictures of that idea. It is because all reasonable theorists recognize that social justice requires agreement and compliance that they must also assume that it requires a strong sense of membership in a community, the boundaries of which are clearly identifiable.

The second assumption suggests that within this clearly bounded community there must exist "an identifiable set of institutions whose impact on the life chances of different individuals can be traced."[11] The idea here is that only if we can identify the impact that different institutions have on an individual's or a group's life chances will it be possible to develop an account of the ways in which these life chances can effectively be shaped so as to ensure that the benefits and burdens of social cooperation are justly distributed. For Miller, this means that theorists must possess the idea that there exists an identifiable "basic structure" of a society or polity which gives shape to a wide range of superstructural phenomena. Theories of social justice rely on the assumption that there is a whole complex of institutions and social forms that together largely shape the life chances of citizens in understandable ways.

The third premise directly follows on from this second. It is that "there is some agency capable of changing the institutional structure in more or less the way our favoured theory demands."[12] This agency is understood as a central authority capable of altering the vast array of institutions and forms of the "basic structure" in line with the recommendations of a theory of social justice. Without the assumption that such an agency exists, Miller contends, theorists of social justice would be unable to imagine that their theories could ever have any real impact on the societies in which they live. A powerful institutional agency is a vital element of any feasible theory of social justice. Without it, any hope of altering the distribution of resources must remain a pipe dream.

If we translate these three premises into preexisting forms, it is clear that Miller is contending that a theory of social justice requires something like an identifiable nation-state. Taking the United States as an example, theorists of social justice can reasonably craft a theory for the United States because the country can be reasonably assumed to be a society that meets each of these three conditions. First, there is an identifiable national community—America—that provides a unit for a comparison and that binds people together irrespective of the important differences between them. Second, there is an identifiable "basic structure" in the United States stretching from the federal, state, and municipal governments through the quasi-governmental agencies of education and charitable organizations to the modern economic corporations that clearly shapes citizens' life chances. Finally, there is a federal government, possibly conjoined with its state and municipal relatives, that constitutes an authority "realistically capable of acting according to intentional and independent instructions in such a way as consciously to shape the other elements of the society and polity of which they are a part."[13] For the time being, therefore, theorists can justifiably begin theorizing about social justice in the United States because each of the three essential assumptions can plausibly be made. Whether these three assumptions will be as easy to make in the foreseeable future is an issue to which we shall return later.

The Role of the Political Theorist

Once the theorist knows that she lives in a society within which it is politically reasonable first to theorize about and then to advocate an ideal of social justice, there is, of course, still much work to be done. In particular, in order to place herself further in context, the theorist must also know what to make of the attitudes of citizens in that society and how they relate to the ideals of social justice she would like to develop. In a later passage of *Principles of Social Justice*, Miller draws a distinction between what he calls a "Platonic" and an "Aristotelian" conception of the role of the political theorist. In the Platonic model, a political theorist's role is to expose the defects of contemporary common understandings of justice and replace them with an alternative vision crafted independently, perhaps even discovered transcendentally, by the philosopher himself. In such an account, the understandings of the public may, at best, provide an inspiration to thought or, at worst, a hindrance to clear thinking. Either way, a *true* account of the ideals of justice is to be found elsewhere: in the speculations of pure logic or in the essence of human nature. The Aristotelian approach to political theory, on the other hand, seeks to understand contemporary common understandings and to render them into a coherent and consistent whole. As such, the Aristotelian approach "seeks to correct common opinion using only methods of argument that common opinion itself endorses." The role of a theorist of justice, on this view, is not to develop an independent alternative to popular opinion but to "correct distortions," to rework prevailing ideas into an account that is internally consistent and coherent.[14] For the Aristotelian, Miller continues, if "popular beliefs about justice are in some respects self-contradictory, for instance, or if they can be shown to rest on factual errors, then the normative theory that we propose as giving the best account of these beliefs may legitimately correct them in these aspects."[15]

In *Principles of Social Justice*, as in all of his mature work, Miller sides firmly with the Aristotelian approach. In defending this preference, he contends that the Platonic vision is beset with moral epistemological problems: "The notion that philosophers can discover truth by means not available to lay persons is even more difficult to defend today than it was in Plato's time."[16] Here the difficulties are of interest to philosophers, but the apparent advantages of the Aristotelian approach are not only epistemological, they are also *political*. Miller explicitly wishes to craft a theory of justice that can have direct practical implications. Yet, abstraction of the sort favored by those who adopt the Platonic approach to political thought simply cannot provide the "practical guidance we need."[17] Theorists who do not firmly root their theories of social justice in contemporary public perceptions are likely to "want to pry justice loose from these moorings and present an entirely context-free theory." The result of such an endeavor can only be a theory of justice either "so abstract that it will give us little or no help in resolving practical disputes" or else that it "will fail to persuade those whose intuitive sense of justice" tells them that it is misplaced.[18] A political theorist interested in persuading the public must start and finish with preexisting public attitudes. The role of the political theorist is to "work the findings of empirical research into a consistent whole." It is only that sort of theory for which "citizens are ripe targets."[19]

Miller's Model

On Miller's account, the role of the political theorist is clearly dependent upon the world in which he/she currently lives. As that world changes, so the possible role for the theorist changes, too. In outlining the three empirical assumptions that theorists of social justice make and placing fundamental importance on the attitudes of citizens in defining the idea of justice, Miller thus identifies the nature of possibilities for the present and the problems for the future. If "we do not inhabit bounded societies, or if people's shares of goods and bads do not depend in ways we can understand on a determinate set of social institutions, or if there is no agency capable of regulating that basic structure," Miller suggests, then "we no longer live in a world in which the idea of social justice has any purchase."[20] Similarly, if we live in a world in which the public's attitudes to issues of justice drift away from the theorists', then the latter are unlikely to make any headway in the political arena, at least in a democratic society. Theorists must reconsider the plausibility of their assumptions and engage in a careful analysis of citizens' preexisting attitudes if their theories are to find any political resonance.

By emphasizing the priority of social and political context over analytic abstraction, Miller's model offers the opportunity for contemporary theories of social justice to engage public debate, a contribution the dramatic gulf between academic aspirations and public attitudes has made exceptionally difficult in recent years. Those who look at the issue within a longer time frame are, however, likely to be a little more skeptical about Miller's conclusions. In particular, they will wish to return both to the structural and the attitudinal assumptions in order to establish whether the first modern theorists of social justice really did believe that they inhabited a world characterized by "a relatively homogeneous political community whose directing agency, the state, ha[d] the capacity to shape its major social institutions," as Miller suggests they must have.[21] On discovering the answer, such scholars will then further ask if earlier generations did not actually think that they inhabited such a world, what did it mean for their approaches to social justice, and what role did it allow them to play as political theorists? It is in this way that a closer look at the historical record may lead contemporary theorists of social justice to other conclusions, and if it does, that might have implications for the present, too. Such an observation takes us back around one hundred years to the beginning of modern social justice.

HISTORICAL ALTERNATIVES: THE NEW NATIONALISM

There was an explosion of writing and theorizing about the principles of social justice at the outset of the twentieth century, and in this regard, if in few others, the United States of America was far from exceptional. Indeed, as Miller points out, the first book to take "Social Justice" as its title was published in America by the Johns Hopkins Professor of Political Science Westel Willoughby in 1900. And Willoughby's text was only the beginning.[22] It was soon followed by a slew of imitators, and within the first two decades of the century, a whole new genre of academic literature had been born. Drawing together the previously disparate disciplines of philosophy, politics, economics, and sociology, American intellectuals joined with their British and European counterparts in taking an "expedition into [academic] territory hitherto not very well occupied," and they presented as a result a whole host of competing accounts of the nature of "social justice."[23]

At the forefront of that expedition in the United States were the progressives: in particular, Herbert Croly, Walter Lippmann, and Walter Weyl, the founders of the leading progressive journal, *The New Republic*, theorists often known now as the "new nationalists."[24] Of all of the works published on social justice in the first two decades of the twentieth century, it was probably Croly's *The Promise of American Life* (1909) and Walter Weyl's *The New Democracy* (1912) that came closest to being the *Political Liberalism* and *Principles of Social Justice* of their day. Walter Lippmann's *Preface to Politics* (1912) and *Drift and Mastery* (1914) and the pages of *The New Republic* then brought the ideas developed in Croly's and Weyl's work to a wider public anxious to build genuine political reform.[25]

The theory of social justice outlined in these works is recognizable in most essentials from those theories that have been developed since the appearance of *A Theory of Justice* in 1971, literary style and contemporary references aside. Like the egalitarian theorists of the Rawlsian variety, Croly, Lippmann, and Weyl all emphasized the fundamental importance of a just distribution of the benefits and burdens of social cooperation. This was, in part, a plea for the guarantee of significant and secure individual rights to self-determination, a plea clearly inherited from classical Jeffersonian or Emersonian liberalism. All of the new nationalists' works, though, also exhibited a distinctively *new* feature: an understanding that the fulfillment of these ideals required access to material resources and that such resources could be provided within the framework of an open, liberal, and democratic society. Forty years before

T. H. Marshall's celebrated essay forged a connection between social, political, and civil rights, Walter Weyl argued that although "you may talk of the equal civil rights of man and all the rest" unless "your man has a secure economic position, a chance to earn his living in honor and dignity, he has no rights whatsoever." "There can be no equality, not any approach to equality," Weyl continued, "except among men economically independent and economically comparable."[26] In this way, the new nationalist thinkers shaped a rounded conception of social justice that committed its exponents to a dramatic redistribution of income, wealth, and economic opportunity.

Striking as the similarities between these early-twentieth-century approaches to social justice and the more modern ones are, one factor sharply differentiates the two. Whereas late-twentieth-century liberal texts before have generally been able to take the essential shape of the governing institutions of liberal democracy and the social structures in which they operated for granted, the new nationalist theorists could not. The new nationalists simply could not assume that their theory of social justice was crafted in a "bounded community" in which the life chances of citizens were shaped in ways that could be controlled by a central institutional agency. Indeed, far from assuming that their society was characterized by the three features Miller describes, the "inadequacy" of American political institutions and social structures for the task of pursuing social justice was a fundamental part of the earlier generations' theoretical vision.[27] As a result, these theorists had to fashion a very different relationship between themselves and practical politics than that which Miller's model anticipates. In that relationship, there was none of the abstraction so roundly criticized in *Principles of Social Justice,* but neither was there the reliance on preexisting forms that characterizes Miller's account of the place of the political theorist. Their account of social justice could not be dependent on preexisting institutional and social structures, as the necessary structures simply did not as yet exist in the United States. To understand the alternative role of the political theorist that the new nationalists outlined, it is important first fully to appreciate the difficulties they faced.

THE STRUCTURES OF GOVERNANCE

The primary problem the new nationalist theorists found with the existing form of governance was its inability constructively to shape the social and economic relations of American citizens. The American system government, these new nationalists complained, was not designed constantly to intervene in, let alone actively to transform, the social and economic order. Indeed, key factors of its institutional design were created precisely to ensure that it did not. "To the early Americans," Walter Weyl wrote, the essential political values were "negative" in character—"an absence of kings, of nobles, of political oppression, of taxation without representation"—and the founding fathers thus crafted an American institutional order marked by a remarkable lack of centralized power.[28] As such, the American constitutional order granted executives, legislatures, and courts "abundant power to prevent others from doing things" but very little power "to do anything themselves."[29] As the demands of any theory of social justice required a central government capable of substantial intervention in social and economic life, the United States seemed to possess a "political system" suitable only for "a totally different civilization."[30]

This was not just special pleading on the part of reformers unable to match their own ideals with workable political programs.[31] From any late-twentieth-century perspective, and indeed from most early-twentieth-century ones, too, the American state was exceptionally weak. The most noted of the factors limiting the possibilities of state activity were, of course, the celebrated separation of judicial, legislative, and executive powers and the equally renowned federal system that largely devolved governing responsibility to the several states. Each of these measures was designed to ensure that temporary electoral majorities would find it difficult to legislate either quickly or effectively. The exceptional weakness of the United States system, though, was due to more than these essential aspects of the constitutional order. It inhered primarily in the lack of administrative capacity of the two major branches of the federal government; there was virtually no central bureaucracy. Politics in the world's first major democracy was dominated almost entirely by local party machines whose role was to dispatch patronage rather than pursue ideology: policy and appointments in such an age were shaped almost entirely by a mixture of "pork barrel" and "log roll."

If there was a single branch of the federal government that exercised any significant sway across the whole nation, it was the Supreme Court. Especially in the immediate aftermath of Reconstruction, the Court, and the nexus of federal and state courts below it, was the only formal institution to hold sway across the entirety of the country. Potentially, then, the Court could have aided the new nationalists in their search for an institution capable of exercising influence over the distribution of social benefits and burdens. Indeed, the role the Court played in kick starting the Civil Rights movement of the 1960s and 1970s demonstrates the sort of authority it could wield. But the case for the possibility of Court activity in the early twentieth century is far from as simple. The Court's own limitations—most of all its lack of a mechanism to enforce the implementation of its judgments—are well documented and would undeniably have restricted its leeway. Far more serious, however, was the fact that the Court continually sought to maintain a constitutional order that it believed expressly prohibited either the federal government or the individual state legislatures from enjoying any significant legislative leeway in the areas recommended by a theory of social justice. As such, throughout the early years of the twentieth century, the Supreme Court acted to restrict the area of governmental intervention in society and economy to its absolute minimum by employing an exceptionally stringent reading of the Fourteenth and the Fifteenth Amendments.[32] The infamous decision in *Lochner* v. *New York* (1905) that prohibited the New York State legislature from regulating the working conditions of bakery workers on the grounds that such regulation posed a "meddlesome" interference in private affairs has become the most frequently cited example of the Court's behavior at the time. It was joined, though, by many more restrictions on the activities of both the federal and the state administrations. As late as 1922, for example, even relatively progressive jurists like Felix Frankfurter were of the opinion that the United States Congress had no right to enact federal prohibitions on the employment of child labor.[33]

The institutional opportunities for introducing reform motivated or legitimated by a modern concept of social justice, especially social justice on a national scale, in the early twentieth century United States, were exceptionally limited. As theorists like Croly, Lippmann, and Weyl outlined their ideals of social justice, there was simply no mechanism in existence to enable them even to contemplate the possibility of the short-term fulfillment of their goals. Even if American politicians had wanted to develop a greater role for the state, the institutional realities of a vigorously localized politics and a shockingly hollow center entailed that such reform was all but impossible. To return to David Miller's stipulated conditions, there simply was no "agency capable of changing the institutional structure in more or less the way our favoured theory demands."[34] There was, furthermore, no reason to believe at the time that these institutional factors would change in the short term, especially not of their own volition. As Stephen Skowronek has suggested, the quest for social justice in the United States "did not entail making the established state more efficient; it entailed building a qualitatively different kind of state."[35]

SOCIAL STRUCTURES AND POPULAR ATTITUDES

Those very same thinkers who were disappointed by the absence of a national system of governance capable of enacting policies demanded by the pursuit of social justice were also concerned that the social conditions did not as yet obtain in the United States. There was, the new nationalists complained, no sense of bounded community and apparently no shared values as to the distribution of goods. Similarly, the attitudes of citizens to social justice differed enormously from the ideals held by theorists.

The first restriction on American communal membership was the United States' renowned culture of "individualism." Writing only three years prior to the publication of Croly's *Promise*, H. G. Wells diagnosed the malady: the "typical American," he argued, has no sense of communal obligation. "I mean," Wells continued, "that he has no perception that his business activities, his private employments, are constituents in a large collective process; that they affect other people and the world forever, and cannot, as he imag-

ines, begin and end with him." "The American," the British novelist and re-
former concluded, had yet to achieve "the conception of a whole to which all
individual acts and happenings are subordinate and contributory."[36] Unflat-
tering as this critique was, Croly, Lippmann, and Weyl all adopted the argument as their own, changing it only insofar as they sought material explana-
tions for the cultural actuality. Weyl blamed the emergence of an American
culture of extreme individualism on the remarkable geographical expanse that
faced the first settlers. "The open continent intoxicated the American," he argued. "It gave him an enlarged view of self. It dwarfed the common spirit. It
made the American mind a little sovereignty of its own, acknowledging no allegiances and but few obligations." Whatever the cause, though, the effect was
the same: the dominant culture in America was a form of "individualism, self-
confident, short-sighted, lawless, doomed in the end to defeat itself."[37] It was,
or so at least Croly thought, this individualism that largely "ensured our
fellow-countrymen neglect or refuse systematically to regulate the distribution
of wealth" according to the precepts of social justice.[38]

In addition to this long-standing cultural peculiarity, Croly, Lippmann, and
Weyl also emphasized the role of two more problems in perpetuating America's
lack of a spirit of national solidarity. As Tocqueville had recognized in the previous century, Americans were not solely driven by a culture of individualism;
they *were* able and willing to craft communal loyalties. Unfortunately for Croly
and his colleagues, though, it appeared that these were loyalties not to the nation but to divisive, sectional interests.[39] The first of new sectional divisions
came from allegiance to ethnic group. Throughout the late nineteenth and early
twentieth centuries, immigrants flocked to the United States from an increasingly disparate series of countries of origin. As they did so, arguments over the
perpetuation of a "hyphenated" citizenry found a central place in American
public debate. Such arguments threw into question the possibilities of any nationwide agreement on either the means or the ends of social justice.[40] Of the
new nationalists, it was Walter Weyl, himself the son of German Jewish immigrants, who expressed the most concern as to the consequences of the new immigration for social justice. He argued that the "babel of traditions" that it
brought to America's shores would "hamper and delay the formation" of the
"national consciousness" essential to social justice. His *New Democracy*
fiercely contended that the danger "of too near a contact" with those fleeing
"European poverty can hardly be overestimated." Only if the immigrants were
"especially selected for their adjustability to American conditions," Weyl concluded, could America "advance in the task of improving the economic, political, and psychological development of the masses as to render inevitable the
progressive attainment of the social goal."[41] As there was little hope of that,
the inevitable segregation of American society looked set to continue.

Nor was this the end of the social difficulties. Ethnic diversity was further
combined with the peculiarities of class relations in the United States in this period. The late nineteenth century was marked by a vast increase in labor unrest,

and as the twentieth century began, vicious "antagonisms between class and class" began to dominate industrial life. "The sword of class consciousness is being whetted," Walter Weyl complained in 1918, "and its sharp edge will cut through the body social, sundering us into two mutually antagonistic groups."[42] The bonds of communal sentiment necessary for forging a sense of social justice were "in danger of being torn to pieces by irreconcilable class enmities."[43] Such class antagonisms could, of course, have been put to good use. In much of Europe the state responded to the increase in social tension by redistributing some wealth and power in accord with the demands of organized labor, moving society closer to the ideal of social justice as it did so. The United States, however, lacked the political mechanisms to channel these demands peacefully into the mainstream. Dismayed by the stranglehold the Supreme Court appeared to have on the legislative process, and distanced by the corruption of the major American parties, the trade union movement in the United States stayed aloof from party politics. Organized American workers, as a result, pursued their demands by the far less socially cohesive root of direct action.[44] What this meant in the short run was that America was engulfed in industrial unrest. In the long run, it entailed that the rise of class unrest intensified social divisions and disagreements and made the possibility of reform for social justice less likely still.

AN ALTERNATIVE ROLE FOR POLITICAL THEORY

Croly, Lippmann, and Weyl were faced both with ingrained institutional limitations and apparently intractable social problems of ingrained cultural individualism and expanding sectional infighting along ethnic and class lines. If their ideas of social justice were to have any impact at all, they could not simply sit back and accept the institutional and social structures of America as they found them. They sought, therefore, to find a distinctive role for themselves that would, in the long run at least, help them to lay the foundations for the future pursuit of social justice. That role, they argued, primarily lay in *institutional design*. The growth and development of strong, organized, national activity, shaped always by the background desire for social justice, was the first building block for a new future. The reason for this priority was straightforward. The new nationalists were certain that there was a direct relationship between the United States' lack of an identifiable national state machinery and the patterns of sectional social relationship and attitudinal commitments that prevailed across the country. Reshaping the nation's institutions would, they believed, help reshape the nation's social structures and its citizens' ideals. Rather than the one being a straightforward precondition for the other, therefore, for Croly, Lippmann, and Weyl, institutional reconstruction and the pursuit of social justice were mutually supportive projects.

The new nationalists believed they could help to get the process of reform started by advancing a series of suggestions for institutional reform. These progressive theorists sometimes attempted to place themselves, or at least their followers, in government so as directly to initiate a carefully orchestrated program of institutional reform from the inside. At other times, they attempted to influence the arguments of a wide range of broader social groups, including most importantly the emergent trade union movement. They offered a series of detailed institutional suggestions to both levels, ranging from arguments for an expansion of the powers of the federal executive to demands for the construction of nationwide democratic collective bargaining for workers' pay and conditions.[45] The underlying ambition was always the same, though. What linked all of these institutional reforms together was a desire to construct new institutional structures which would, in turn, begin to shape the attitudes of the broader American public in ways conducive to broadening national communal sentiment and instilling a greater dedication to social justice. For these progressive reformers, this would act as a sort of virtuous circle. Institutions should be shaped in ways that would help engender the requisite communal sentiments. The broader and deeper the communal sentiments that developed, the more willing citizens would be to redistribute their resources to one another, and the more they redistributed their resources, the broader and deeper the communal sentiments would become. In this way, a culture of social justice could be kick started by an eager and positively reshaped state mechanism.

Such a vision was, of course, not without costs, both conceptual and empirical. Conceptually, the ideal vision of social justice itself had to be adapted to the demands of the time. The new nationalists were not at all interested in utopian theorizing. Rather, they offered a theory of social justice that they believed was potentially attainable in the long term and one that would contribute to its own success. What emerged was a good deal harsher than one with which most latter-day liberal commentators would feel comfortable. Desiring constantly to shape the communal solidarity necessary to build support for redistribution, these theorists emphasized the responsibilities of those citizens who would be net recipients of resources at least as much as they discussed their rights. Indeed, relying on the state to forge the communal sentiments required for social justice sometimes appeared to entail allowing government officials incredible power to direct the lives of those relying on the state. As Croly once summarized, within this approach to social justice it was legitimate to insist that the state must "teach men how they must feel, what they must think, and what they must do, in order that they may live together amicably and profitably."[46]

These theoretical commitments further shaped the theorists' empirical observations. The progressive theorists' obsession with the absence of a powerful state in the United States left them overly prone to see only the good in such administrative mechanisms as did exist and to welcome any extension of their authority as almost inevitably beneficial.[47] Such faith ensured that these thinkers were somewhat blind to the authoritarianism that lurked behind the vigorous state and community-building efforts such as Woodrow Wilson's attempts to encourage nationalistic jingoism through carefully orchestrated state repression during the First World War. This, in turn, led many of these new nationalists' contemporaries to reject their ideals and to try to craft a theory of social justice that did not require such an interventionist state machine. The central dedications, however, remained unchanged. In the aftermath of the war, the new nationalists and their allies tirelessly suggested a range of institutional changes that would in the long run at least enable their fundamental goals to be reached, changes ranging from the nationalization of large swathes of industry through the construction of mechanisms of democratic mechanisms in the workplace to the construction of local schemes of social insurance for workers in sweated industries. What linked them all was a belief that institutional design was a vital precondition to a realistic politics of social justice. "Exhortation to good citizenship is useless" by itself, one ally thus insisted, because we only "get good citizenship by creating those forms within which good citizenship can operate."[48]

RECONSIDERING THE PRECONDITIONS
OF SOCIAL JUSTICE

If reference to the traditions of the past is to be of anything more than historical interest, the comparison of the two periods of time needs to be instructive. This is just such an example. Most important, it shows us that the relationship between institutional, social, and conceptual patterns is far more complicated than we might think. Contrary to Miller's expectation that successful theories depend on preexisting structural forms and popular attitudes, early theories of social justice, especially in the United States, emerged *before* the institutional and social conditions were right for their fulfillment. The task of theorists was not, therefore, to outline a reform agenda that provided detailed policy guidance for potentially well-disposed politicians to follow in a preexistent institutional environment. Rather, these progressive thinkers had to play their part in radically altering the weft of the political and social tissue before their principles of social justice could become a realizable ideal. The lesson for the present (or the future) is thus straightforward in one sense, if undeniably problematic in another. If the institutional and social frameworks and the public attitudes upon which social justice was previously reliant are being undermined, the role of political theorists is not to abandon social justice but to play a role in crafting new frameworks that will, in turn, shape new attitudes.

All of this, of course, contrasts sharply with the position David Miller develops in *Principles of Social Justice*. In the closing sections of that book, Miller returns to his three institutional and social preconditions for social justice and articulates the nagging question that will have been worrying most readers from the outset: is it possible that "our existing world has already passed beyond these circumstances"? Or, to put it in historical perspective, could the early twenty-first century be "witnessing changes in contemporary societies, within and across national boundaries, that spell the end of the era of social justice"?[49] As he presents an answer to this question, Miller rightly identifies two areas of concern, one that emanates from above and one from below the boundaries of the nation-state. From above, it is globalization that provides the challenge. The ever-increasing mobility of global capital, expedited by technological change, appears to be forcing nation-states into a policy of "conspicuous convergence" on a neoliberal economic settlement and all governments' room for policy maneuvre is severely restricted.[50] From below, the challenger is multiculturalism. As many national communities become characterized by ever-increasing ethnocultural diversity, so a host of groups demand that authority should be radically devolved to lower levels. These groups and their advocates contend that power should be removed from a central government that mistakenly seeks to represent a whole nation and handed down to the smaller more homogenous communities where the new social identities and bonds of ethnocommunal allegiance are forged.[51] Again, just as with globalization, such a demand undermines the institutional agency precondition for social justice, but this time the necessary bonds of broadly based social solidarity face a serious challenge, too.

In response to these worries, Miller identifies various ways in which advocates of social justice may proceed. Most important of all, he argues that efforts must be made to shore up the nation-state. In the face of globalization, he concludes, we should recognize that "nation-states have so far been the main instruments of social justice" and we "must look for ways of reinforcing their authority and effectiveness in the face of the global economy."[52] To multiculturalists, the reply is essentially the same: "Rather than taking it for granted that multiculturalism spells the end of the nation-state in its traditional form, we should look at how that institution can be rebuilt to accommodate a more culturally diverse array of citizens."[53] If these efforts cannot work, however, and if the challenges to the nation-state appear too strong, then Miller is not at all optimistic about the future. In the worst-case scenario, he concedes, the very idea of social justice will have to be rethought, and maybe even abandoned. The institutional and social status quo must be protected or the prospects for social justice seem exceptionally "bleak."[54]

There may, of course, be much in what Miller has to say on this issue and his approach may well be the most feasible in the short term. The example of Croly, Lippmann, and Weyl, however, suggests that there is an alternative option available. It suggests that new institutions should be developed in order to develop different patterns of social interaction and to ensure the possibility of attaining social justice remains alive. On this view, the ideational commitment to social justice should inform an institutional reform agenda that, when implemented, should shape the social structures and citizens' attitudes.

The detailed description of such an agenda requires, of course, several articles in its own right. In the light of globalization, it would appear to demand
that particularly serious consideration be given to the construction of new international institutions of governance, institutions that could themselves
come to engender new and broader commitments and communal attachments. Only such commitments, after all, could sustain an attempt to challenge globalization at the level at which it truly operates. This in itself need
not raise the question of the immediate sustainability of a truly cosmopolitan
sense of solidarity and citizenship, a possibility dismissed by Miller. Rather, it
requires only that thoughtful consideration be given to the design of institutions which can already successfully cross national boundaries for *other* reasons but which, in time, could solicit the necessary greater sense of loyalty
and solidarity. Closer connections between European political parties, the increasing interchangeable use of welfare services abroad, and the development
of democratic oversight of European labor law all offer potential ways forward in this regard.[55] The essential point is that they must be designed with
an attitude-shaping agenda clearly in mind.

Beyond worries about the particular institutional forms pursued, though, it
will be more generally objected that political theorists and their ideas can inevitably play only an extremely small part in shaping the course of institutional and social change. The shape of the future is not going to be determined
by intellectuals, no matter how persuasive they are. There is, of course, much
to this. By the 1930s, the American state was capable of engaging in serious
reform in pursuit of social justice, but it took the forces unleashed by a great
depression finally to alter the Supreme Court's opinion of the federal government's legitimate sphere of operation and to transform the government's possible institutional role.[56] Similarly, the leading parts in shaping the new institutional and social structures of tomorrow will no doubt be played by the vast
technological revolution, the continual growth and development of the modern corporation, the reshaping of global capital markets, the erosion of old
class divisions, and the emergence of new patterns of social solidarity. Yet, it
is important not to be overly deterministic about this process. For, as Stephen
Skowronek argued with regard to the New Deal, "whether considered singly
or in some combination," the depression and the war were "only the *stimuli*
for institutional development." The precise nature of the "new institutional
forms and new relations between state and society" that emerge "remain contingent" on how a vast array of political actors respond to those stimuli, drawing on a series of ideas, many of which were inherited from the new nationalists, in the process.[57] Indeed, even Skowronek rather understates the case.
Writing in and of our own time, David Coates has recently reminded us that
such apparently uncontrollable, inevitable developments like the increasing
globalization of trade are themselves only partly a matter of "invisible and inevitable" social or technological evolution. They are also, and perhaps just as
much, the direct and indirect consequences of *intentionally* designed legal and

institutional frameworks and those intentions are more than capable of being normatively informed.

The potential malleability of institutions and social structures is almost always overlooked in the literature on globalization and multiculturalism. Although not surprising, perhaps, such an oversight is deeply dangerous for those committed to social justice. David Miller correctly points out that social justice is a critical ideal and one that demands that individuals and communities behave in ways that they will not necessarily find easy. But although he concedes this much, he holds back from explicitly arguing that social justice demands institutions that can shape citizens' attitudes and that those institutions should themselves be shaped by an ideational commitment to social justice. The reason for this reticence probably lies in two areas. First, there is a hidden economic and social determinism in Miller's model. Both the notion that a concept like social justice is essentially dependent on certain preexisting institutional forms and the idea that there is an internal logic to developments like globalization and multiculturalism that inevitably poses social justice potentially intractable problems overlook the potential influence that ideational commitments can have in shaping governmental, economic, and social trends. Second, Miller's work demonstrates an unwillingness to accept that ideals of social justice have to be crafted at least partially independently of currently prevailing norms, values, or practices. The quasi-Walzerian method by which Miller proceeds, whereby the meaning of social justice itself is derived at least in part from existing social attitudes, makes it difficult for him to accept the need radically to shape citizens' ideals as well as to reflect them. Yet, without such an acceptance there can be little chance of a commitment to radical preference-shaping institutional change. Whatever its cause, though, the institutional pessimism that pervades Miller's diagnosis presents the cause of social justice with serious practical difficulties. The absence of any hope for institutional reform not only leaves advocates of social justice without the immediate means by which to achieve their goals, it also leaves them without a clear agenda for future reform of any sort.

A further possible retort from Miller would emphasize the potential philosophical Platonism and political elitism involved in the new nationalists' model. The first of these criticisms would suggest that the new nationalists claimed to "know better" than their American contemporaries and challenge the rationale for such a view. It might be asked how they developed their own sense of intellectual and moral superiority; if American citizens did not want a politics of social justice, what right did Croly, Lippmann, Weyl, and colleagues have to try to hoist it upon them? Where did they ground their ideals if not in the attitudes and beliefs of actually existing citizens? The only option available to them, Miller might argue, was the unattractive Platonism advanced by so many other reforming idealists. The second component of this critique further suggests that the new nationalists' agenda had, at least implicitly, elitist and hierarchical political implications. For if these ideas were developed without explicit reference to the aspirations of American citizens, were they not likely to serve the interests of others? Or, to put that another way, as the new nationalists designed their institutions it could be suggested that they would likely be institutions that would favor *them* (and not just their ideas) either directly or indirectly.

There is much of value in these criticisms. The new nationalists were prone to a certain intellectual arrogance, and many of their proposed institutions did offer positions of authority to academics, social investigators, and others likely to be of a similar social position to the new nationalists themselves.[58] Yet, neither of these arguments is without a rejoinder. First, the new nationalists did not claim that their commitments to social justice were universal in application, rooted somehow in logic or in the essential and unchanging nature of human beings. Rather, they believed that they were peculiarly suited to the emerging conditions of the modern world. They did hold that certain fundamental aspirations were constantly of value—humans deserved to live worthwhile lives in freedom and community with each other—but they constantly sought to understand the implications of those core ideals in ways that were suited to their particular predicament. It was just that they refused to accept that prevailing social, political, or economic orthodoxies in the United States had all the answers. Alternatives were to be found in a multitude of locations. They could be found partly by examining the experiences of other countries and the arguments that prevailed there, partly by paying careful attention to the aspirations of disadvantaged groups, and partly from a continual process of academic reflection. The new nationalists were no Platonists, but their Aristotelianism recognized fewer boundaries than most.

Second, there is no reason why institutions genuinely designed to foster the development of long-term commitment to social justice should support ideals of elitism or hierarchy. Rather, and directly to the contrary, institutions designed to craft social solidarity and to inculcate a belief in the value of redistribution are more likely to celebrate democracy than hierarchy. The new nationalists were certainly convinced of this; their preferred institutional suggestions—for both federal government and local pressure groups—constantly emphasized the importance of democratic deliberation and decision making, for Croly, Lippmann, and Weyl all believed that the necessary sense of common purpose and of national loyalty could only be discerned and pursued in a democratic polity. "Democracy does not mean merely government by the people, or majority rule, or universal suffrage," Herbert Croly insisted. "All of these political forms or devices are a part of its necessary organization but the chief advantage such methods of organization have is their tendency to promote some salutary and formative purpose."[59] "The end of democracy," Walter Weyl all the more transparently put it, "is thus a social goal." Democratic engagement was one of the chief means by which "the improvement, physical, intellectual, and moral of the millions" who make up the nation could be attained.[60]

CONCLUSION

The publication of David Miller's *Principles of Social Justice* presents an invaluable opportunity for an interdisciplinary reassessment of the social and institutional preconditions for social justice and of the role of the political theorist in shaping them. In so doing, the book draws social science and political theory together and identifies the questions that must lie at the very center of future prospects for social justice. In this chapter, I have attempted to add a historical dimension to that reassessment. A survey of early theorists of social justice leads to the conclusion that a genuinely progressive theory of social justice should not, indeed *cannot*, be narrowly determined by contemporary institutional, social, or attitudinal constraints. If the new nationalists or their American successors, the "New Dealers," had believed that it "is no use setting out principles for reforming the basic structure if in fact we have no means to implement these reforms," then they would not even have begun their project.[61] They faced enormous, and often apparently unconquerable, institutional and social obstacles to the fulfillment of their ideals, but they carried on nonetheless. Moreover, they did not take the practical difficulties they faced to be a license for idle Platonic utopia building. Rather than seeking refuge in the imaginary world of their own ideal theory, the new nationalists continuously sought to construct an academic vision that they believed could help craft the institutions and shape the public attitudes that would allow their conceptual goals to one day be realized. Insofar as the politicians of the New Deal era learned from their predecessors, the new nationalists' task was not in vain.

What all of this should remind us of is that to the generations of theorists, activists, politicians, and bureaucrats that shaped the modern welfare state, the quest for social justice and the search for far-reaching institutional and social change were mutually supportive projects. Given the size of the institutional and social challenges that face progressive theorists in the new century, those projects urgently need to be brought together again. Even if we dislike it, the political and social institutions within which people act *do* shape their political attitudes and social expectations. Is it not better, therefore, to attempt to shape those institutions themselves rather than allow them to emerge without the guidance of ideals of social justice?

NOTES

1. See D. Coates, *Models of Capitalism: Growth and Stagnation in the Modern Era* (Cambridge: Cambridge University Press, 2000), esp. 258–259; and A. Przeworski and M. Wallerstein, "Structural Dependence of the State on Capital," *American Political Science Review* 82 (1998): 11–30.

2. The most striking recent example of this must be the coincidence between the academic excitement that followed Phillipe van Parijs's advocacy of a universal minimum income and the British Labour Party's abandonment of its long-term opposition to American-style workfare. Compare the ideals of P. van Parijs, *Real Freedom for All* (Oxford: Oxford University Press, 1995)

with the accounts of political change in the last chapter of D. King, *In the Name of Liberalism* (Oxford: Oxford University Press, 1999).

3. D. Miller, *Principles of Social Justice* (Cambridge, Mass.: Harvard University Press, 1999), x.

4. See B. Ackermann and A. Alstott, *The Stakeholder Society* (New Haven, Conn.: Yale University Press,1999); and S. Holmes and C. Sunstein, *The Cost of Rights* (New York: W. W. Norton, 1998).

5. The new theorists of globalization often appear to believe that their explanatory and normative theories are qualitatively distinct from their predecessors because "we are now living in a revolution which has so much accelerated the speed of our development that social change can now be directly experienced within a single lifetime." As Karl Popper argued some decades ago, though, careful attention to historical precedent reveals that stories such as these tend to be "sheer mythology." As a reading of Popper powerfully reminds us: "Important revolutions have occurred before our time, and since the days of Heraclitus change has been discovered over and over again" (*The Poverty of Historicism* [London: Routledge and Kegan Paul, 1961], 160).

6. Miller, *Principles*, 4.

7. Miller, *Principles*, 4 (emphasis added).

8. Miller, *Principles*, 4.

9. Miller, *Principles*, 5.

10. See D. Miller, *Citizenship and National Identity* (Cambridge: Polity, 2000), esp. 81–96.

11. Miller, *Principles*, 5.

12. Miller, *Principles*, 6.

13. As Miller puts it: "The main agency here is obviously the state: theories of social justice propose legislative and policy changes that a well-intentioned state is supposed to introduce. I don't mean to imply that the theories in question are exclusively addressed to legislators and other state officials. . . . Nevertheless, given that the theory is meant to regulate the basic structure, and given that the structure is a complex of institutions with its own internal dynamics, an agency with the power and directing capacity that the state is supposed to have is essential if a theory of justice is to be more than a utopian ideal." Miller, *Principles*, 6.

14. Miller, *Principles*, 41.

15. Miller, *Principles*, 53.

16. Miller, *Principles*, 53.

17. Miller, *Principles*, 22.

18. Miller, *Principles*, 35.

19. Miller, *Principles*, 60. For more on these themes, see A. Swift's contribution to this volume.

20. Miller, *Principles*, 6.

21. Miller, *Principles*, 246.

22. See Miller, *Principles*, 4.

23. H. Croly letter to Learned Hand dated March 1909, TS 102-17, The L. Hand Papers, Harvard Law Library, Harvard University, Cambridge, Mass.

24. The name "new nationalists" was derived from a Theodore Roosevelt political campaign speech of 1910 widely reported to have been influenced by Croly. For expert guides to the New Nationalism as both a theoretical and a political phenomenon, see amid a massive literature, C. Forcey, *The Crossroads of Liberalism* (New York: Oxford University Press, 1956) and R. J. Lustig, *Corporate Liberalism* (Berkeley: University of California Press, 1978).

25. For Lippmann, see R. Steel, *Walter Lippmann and the American Century* (New York, 1999).

26. W. Weyl, "Equality," *New Republic* (January 23, 1915): 14.

27. H. J. Ford, "The Promise of American Life," *American Political Science Review* 4 (1910): 614. For an exemplary example of late-twentieth-century liberal theorists' generally unquestioning attitude toward the fundamentals of the prevailing political system, see Rawls, *Political Liberalism* (New York: Columbia University Press, 1993), 212–254.

28. W. Weyl, *The New Democracy* (New York: MacMillan, 1912), 20.

29. H. Croly, "State Political Reorganization," *Proceedings of the American Political Science Association* 8 (1911): 128.

30. W. Lippmann, *Drift and Mastery* (New York: M. Kennerly, 1914), 159.

31. Nor was it simply an inevitable commentary on all Western governments in the pre-welfare-state age. The British government, for example, was in a far more powerful position than its Amer-

ican equivalent. Following the election victories of the Liberal Party in 1906 and 1910, the British government was capable of vastly expanding its responsibilities in line with its vision of social justice without substantial institutional impediment. See M. S. Freeden, *The New Liberalism: An Ideology of Social Reform* (Oxford: Oxford University Press, 1978); and A. S. Orloff and T. Skocpol, "Why Not Equal Protection?" in *Britain and America,* ed. D. Englander (New Haven, Conn.: Yale University Press, 1997), 242–276.

32. The amendments respectively prohibit state and federal authorities from depriving any individual of "life, liberty or property without due process of law."

33. See F. Frankfurter, "Child Labor and the Court," *New Republic* (July 26, 1922): 248–250.

34. Miller, *Principles,* 6.

35. S. Skowronek, *Building a New American State: The Expansion of National Administrative Capacities, 1877–1920* (Cambridge: Cambridge University Press, 1982), 4.

36. H. G. Wells, *The Future in America: A Search After Realities* (New York: MacMillan, 1906), 153–154.

37. Weyl, *New Democracy,* 36. See also Croly, "State Political Reorganization," 127.

38. H. Croly, *The Promise of American Life* (New York, 1909), 409.

39. See Weyl, *New Democracy,* 235–238.

40. For a thorough description of these arguments and trends, see D. King, *Making Americans: Immigration, Race, and the Origins of the Diverse Democracy* (Cambridge, Mass.: Harvard University Press, 2000).

41. Weyl, *New Democracy,* 347.

42. W. Weyl, *Tired Radicals* (New York: B. W. Huebsch, 1921), 24–25.

43. H. Croly, *Progressive Democracy* (New York: MacMillan, 1915), 97.

44. See T. Skocpol, *Protecting Soldier and Mothers: The Political Origins of Social Policy in the United States* (Cambridge, Mass.: Harvard University Press, 1992), 205–243.

45. See M. Stears, *Pluralists and Progressives: Ideologies of Reform in Britain and the United States* (Oxford: Oxford University Press, forthcoming).

46. Croly, *Promise,* 181.

47. Croly, *Promise,* 284.

48. M. Follett, *The New State* (New York: Longmans, Green and Co., 1918), 339.

49. Miller, *Principles,* 6, 245.

50. On which see again Coates, *Models of Capitalism,* and Przeworski and Wallerstein, "Structural Dependence of the State on Capital."

51. See T. Modood, S. Beishon, and S. Virdee, eds., *Changing Ethnic Identities* (London: Policy Studies Institute, 1994).

52. Miller, *Principles,* 264.

53. Miller, *Principles,* 263.

54. Miller, *Principles,* 261.

55. See J. Habermas, *The Postnational Constellation* (Cambridge: Polity, 2001). I thank David Runciman for this point.

56. For an exceptional account of the trials and tribulations associated with that struggle and of the role of ideas and intellectuals in shaping the new American settlement, see M. B. Katz, *In the Shadow of the Poorhouse: A Social History of Welfare in America* (New York: Basic Books, 1986), 206–249. For a comparative perspective, see B. E. Shafer and M. D. Stears, "From Social Welfare to Cultural Values: The Puzzle of Postwar Change in Britain and the United States," *Journal of Policy History* 4 (1999): esp. 333–336.

57. Skowronek, *Building a New American State,* 12. See also A. Brinkley, *Liberalism and Its Discontents* (Cambridge, Mass.: Harvard University Press, 1998), 37–62.

58. For this very criticism, see R. Wiebe, *The Search for Order* (New York: Hill and Wang, 1967).

59. Croly, *Promise,* 207.

60. Weyl, *New Democracy,* 319.

61. Miller, *Principles,* 6.

3

Meritocracy, Desert, and the Moral Force of Intuitions

Andrew Mason

The ideal of meritocracy has enduring popular appeal. My purpose in this chapter is to assess one crucial element of it, namely, the idea that the best-qualified candidate for an advantaged social position deserves to be appointed to it, provided there is fair access to qualifications. I shall focus in particular on David Miller's attempt to justify it since his defense is one of the most sophisticated available.

The idea that the best-qualified candidates for advantaged social positions ought to be appointed to them is firmly embedded in the practices of liberal democracies. Violations of it, whether as a result of racism, sexism, or nepotism, foster anger and resentment. When people object to the candidates' race, sex, or family connections influencing selection decisions, in general they do so not simply on the grounds that this breeds inefficiency, nor simply because they believe that it reduces overall welfare or fails to maximize the prospects of the worst-off group. They seem to believe that appointing the best-qualified candidates is a moral requirement with independent force.

Hard questions arise about precisely what credence should be given to ordinary convictions about the status and significance of the principle that the best-qualified candidates for jobs and educational places ought to be given them. But almost everyone agrees that ordinary moral convictions should be accorded some weight.[1] Indeed the assumption that they should is built into John Rawls's highly influential model of reflective equilibrium, which holds that sometimes at least we ought to modify our principles if they are at odds with our considered judgments.[2] Equally, however, this model accepts that there are occasions when we ought to reject some of our considered judgments, for example, when they conflict with principles that do a good job of explaining a range of other considered judgments more central to our moral outlook.

Let us start with the seemingly innocuous principle that we should not reject widely held convictions unless there is good reason to do so.[3] This principle seems to imply that the onus falls upon theorists to justify rejecting widely shared convictions. They are entitled to do so only if it becomes clear that these convictions are unjustified. Insofar as the idea that we ought to appoint the best-qualified applicants to advantaged social positions has a status and significance that cannot be explained by appealing to considerations of efficiency, utility, or its role in benefiting the worst off, we should explore other possible ways of justifying it. In this respect, the meritocratic ideal warrants serious consideration, for it promises to provide a distinctive moral foundation for the idea that we ought to appoint the best-qualified candidates—that we ought to do so because they deserve to be appointed.

MARKETS, DESERT, AND THE BEST-QUALIFIED CANDIDATE

According to the meritocratic ideal, the best-qualified candidates for advantaged social positions, such as jobs and educational places, deserve them provided there is fair access to qualifications. But why should we think this? The most obvious answer is that the best-qualified applicant under these circumstances deserves to be appointed because of his or her past achievements. According to this approach, jobs reward past performance, providing successful applicants with an appropriate income and various other benefits such as status and the opportunity to obtain job-related satisfaction and self-realization.

On reflection, however, this approach faces considerable difficulties. There is a gap between a person's past achievements and his or her qualifications for a job, which means that the person who has achieved the most in the past, along the dimensions relevant to how well he or she can be expected to do the job, will not always be the best qualified for it. Consider, for example, an applicant for a job who, despite a superb track record, has suffered a serious accident that means he will no longer be able to perform at the same level. His past achievements may be such that there is a real sense in which he deserves the job, but he is no longer the best-qualified for it.

This serves to emphasize the obvious point that selection for jobs and educational places is forward-, not backward-looking; insofar as selectors are concerned with the qualifications of candidates, they are concerned to pick out those who are likely to perform the job well. David Miller develops this point in his analysis of why we cannot justify the idea that the best-qualified candidate for a job deserves it because of his or her past performance: "Jobs are properly rewarded in the course of performing them. . . . When selecting the best-qualified candidate to hold a job, the employer is not in the business of rectifying a shortfall in the rewards that person received in previous employment."[4]

How then does Miller defend the idea that the best-qualified candidate for a job deserves it? His argument has two main parts. First, he maintains that by appointing the best-qualified candidate, "we bring about a situation in which rewards are as closely as possible aligned with deserts."[5] The best-qualified candidate is the person most likely to deserve the rewards, such as the income, which the job brings with it. Second, he argues that the best-qualified candidates deserve the job because they deserve the opportunity to obtain the rewards they will deserve if they perform at the level we can reasonably expect.

Miller's argument makes a conceptual connection between the income that an appropriately designed market assigns to jobs and the deservingness of the best-qualified candidates to fill those jobs when there is fair access to qualifications. His argument is premised on the idea that actual markets can reward contribution, at least approximately.[6] Only if markets can reward contribution, or track it in some rough and ready way, does it make sense for Miller to suppose that the salary that an appropriately designed market assigns a job can properly reward the contribution made in the course of performing it.

We should not underestimate the difficulties involved in the idea that markets reward contribution and therefore desert. Miller is clear that not any old contribution deserves reward; in his view, a contribution deserves reward only if it is connected in the right way to the agent's purposes. If an achievement is simply the result of what he calls "integral luck" so that it is purely accidental, then it does not deserve reward, or at least not the same reward that it would deserve had integral luck not entered the picture.[7] But markets do not, and cannot be designed to, factor out integral luck; they reward achievements regardless of whether they depend upon integral luck.

Market outcomes are also deeply affected by what Miller calls "circumstantial luck." This refers to the kind of luck that affects whether an agent has the opportunity to put in the kind of performance that would make him or her deserving of reward. As Serena Olsaretti points out, market rewards reflect facts about supply and demand, for example, how many others are producing the same kind of goods, or offering the same kind of service, and how many people are interested in obtaining this good or service.[8] Given fluctuations in supply and demand, some of which are in practice wholly unpredictable, those offering a good or service in the marketplace are susceptible to large doses of circumstantial luck, sometimes to their benefit and sometimes to their detriment.

The very idea that actual markets can track desert will seem plausible only if it is assumed that the size of the (economic) contribution a person makes is a function of the demand he or she satisfies. Yet, some product or service might fail to make a real contribution, even if it meets a demand, if that demand is constituted by preferences based upon false beliefs, or it might make a less significant contribution than the demand for it would imply, if people's preferences are distorted by lack of information.

Miller gives little weight to this sort of objection. He insists that actual (or present) contribution, as opposed to potential (or future) contribution, has to be measured by looking at the actual demand that is met by a good, or the actual benefits people receive from it, rather than by making judgments about what the demand for it would be, or how it would benefit people, if it were properly understood or truly appreciated, or immune to the effects of circumstantial luck in general.[9] In short, producing an item or providing a service makes an economic contribution to society if and only if that item or service benefits individuals, and it benefits individuals if and only if it satisfies their desires. But any sophisticated account of well-being must allow that people may want something that does not benefit them, for example, because of false beliefs about it, or which does not benefit them as much as they think because they lack information about the alternatives. Once this point is given due weight, it will be hard to sustain the idea that "the benefit that someone derives from a good or service is measured by the amount she is willing to pay for it,"[10] and it will be correspondingly hard to resist the conclusion that actual markets provide a highly imperfect measure of contribution.

Even if we put aside this particular doubt about the extent to which markets measure contribution, there are plenty of other reasons for denying that markets are likely to secure an exact correspondence between contribution and reward.[11] As Miller seems to acknowledge, there will be many cases in practice where jobs are underpaid or overpaid relative to the contribution they involve. It is not clear, however, that the desert of the best-qualified candidate, or the idea that the best-qualified candidate ought to be appointed, is sensitive to this fact in the way that it should be if Miller were right about the relationship between them. If some job were undervalued by actual markets, then less well-qualified candidates might be as well placed as the best-qualified candidate to deserve the income it provides. In such cases, appointing a less well-qualified candidate would not involve failing to give the best-qualified candidate the opportunity she deserves.

Miller's response is to argue that "it is not possible to move towards a situation of overall justice through a series of such individual decisions. At best, what happens is that one arbitrary injustice is corrected at the expense of creating another."[12] This may be an adequate defense of the idea that hiring the best-qualified candidate is the best way of minimizing the injustices that occur as a result of jobs being overpaid or underpaid relative to the actual contributions they involve. But it is striking that employers do not even entertain the possibility of appointing a less well-qualified candidate to a job in order to correct for the fact that it is underpaid. This is not just because this would be irrational from the point of view of the efficiency of their enterprises. We simply do not suppose that the moral correctness of appointing the best-qualified candidate is affected in any way by whether or not the job concerned receives its proper remuneration. Given his commitment to taking common opinion seriously, Miller ought to be bothered by this counterintuitive feature of his strategy.

DESERT AND EFFORT

Miller emphasizes that desert is a complex notion. For a start, "the basis of desert—the characteristics in virtue of which people are said to deserve this or that—appears to change according to the kind of benefit in question."[13] Moreover, "the range of possible desert bases and the different kinds of benefits that people can deserve depend to some extent on existing institutions and may be expected to vary from place to place."[14]

Notwithstanding these points, it does seem that across a wide range of benefits, desert depends in part upon effort expended (at least insofar as that effort is directed at something worthwhile and not wholly misplaced), not only purposeful achievement. We generally think that effort properly directed at something worthwhile deserves reward even when it does not result in achievement. This is reflected in both the comparative and noncomparative judgments we make. We judge that someone who works hard on a worthwhile project, but through no fault of his own has little of the talent required to complete it successfully, deserves some reward, even if his achievement is negligible.[15] And some would judge that he deserves the same reward as (or even greater reward than) another with more of the relevant talent, who while working on a similar project puts in little effort but completes it successfully. So, whether a person deserves reward depends not only on the contribution he makes but also the effort he expends, even when that effort is unsuccessful. Indeed, turning to the case of employment, we might legitimately suppose that in some cases a less well-qualified candidate for a job will be more likely to deserve the salary attached to it because of the greater effort he will put in, even if we anticipate that he will be less productive or achieve less.

It would be a mistake to assume that effort and achievement are mutually exclusive categories. The effort a person makes can sometimes be a kind of achievement. For example, the effort a severely depressed person succeeds in making despite feelings of despair may in itself constitute an achievement. Furthermore, effort must be directed in some minimal way toward a valuable goal for it to make sense to say that it deserves reward; someone who sets himself the project of counting all the blades of grass in a field but fails to complete that project hardly deserves reward for his efforts. But neither of these observations establishes that effort and achievement do not come apart. When they do, it would seem that effort alone may deserve reward provided that it is directed at something valuable.

To clarify these points it is worth distinguishing some different positions commonly advanced on the relationship between desert, effort, and achievement in the performance of jobs:

1. A person's efforts, and only that person's efforts, deserve reward but only when they are directed at something valuable.[16]

2. A person's achievements, and only that person's achievements, deserve reward. Effort merits reward only insofar as it constitutes an achievement. (This seems to be Miller's position.)
3. A person's achievements and/or that person's efforts may deserve reward when those efforts are directed at something valuable.

Both (1) and (2) have potentially counterintuitive consequences. (1) implies that what a person achieves in the course of performing a job makes no difference to what that person deserves, whereas (2) implies that the effort a person expends in doing a job never makes a difference, in itself, to what that person deserves (unless it constitutes an achievement). But our intuitions seem to me to be wedded to the idea that both effort without achievement and achievement in the course of performing a job may deserve reward.[17] If this is so, our intuitions support (3), not (1) or (2).

There are, of course, a host of questions about what (3) implies. What is the relative importance of effort and achievement? When a person deserves reward for some achievement, do that person's efforts also deserve reward? Consistent with (3), we might coherently maintain that effort deserves independent reward *only* when it does not result in achievement. This would avoid the counterintuitive conclusion that the clumsy deserve more reward than the skillful for making the same object since the effort expended by the former is greater.[18] But any plausible answers to these questions will preclude (3) from giving support to the idea that rewarding solely a person's contribution in a job is equivalent to giving that person what he or she deserves. (If we accept some version of (3), we also cannot avoid the question of whether rewarding desert is practicable, for it is obscure how we could measure effort expended in a publicly checkable way.[19] There will be no reason to think, as Miller does, that it could be rewarded by the market.[20])

Of course, we do employ notions of desert that give no weight to effort except insofar as it issues in achievement; for example, when determining the degree class a student deserves, we look solely at what that student has achieved in his or her coursework and examinations. But these are generally institutional notions of desert that are used to signify a person's legitimate entitlements as a result of performance, judged in the light of the rules of the relevant institution. They are not fundamental, morally speaking, since these rules are subject to evaluation in terms of principles of justice and do not provide content to them. As Miller himself argues, the idea that the best-qualified candidate for a job deserves it cannot be underwritten by an institutional notion of desert of this kind, for institutions might operate with selection procedures that track something other than the qualifications of the applicants.

Miller would of course reply that when we attempt to reward people on the basis of contribution, and give no independent weight to effort, we may still be seeking to reward desert in some preinstitutional sense. Indeed, he would argue that it is precisely this preinstitutional sense that allows us to criticize our institutions and practices for failing to reward people in proportion to the contributions they have made (e.g., when we say that the two different jobs involve equivalent contributions and therefore should receive the same rewards), or failing to track contributions of the right kind (e.g., when we say that excellence in teaching as well as in research should be rewarded by universities).[21] But unless Miller can show that contribution alone deserves reward in these cases, institutions are at best being assessed in terms of some surrogate of desert or one aspect of desert, namely, a person's contributions, not desert itself or full desert.

It is not enough here to argue that rewarding people on the basis of contribution is the best practical approximation to rewarding desert in its ordinary sense. For giving people the rewards they deserve requires tracking the efforts they have made, not just their achievements. Although there is some correlation between contribution and effort, it is so weak that it would be grossly inaccurate to say that when we reward contribution we are rewarding effort and therefore desert.[22]

DESERVING OPPORTUNITIES

Miller might insist that there are some benefits such as prizes that are deserved solely on the basis of achievement (with no further argument being available to justify this idea) and that salaries, when they are set at the appropriate level, are in this respect similar.[23] Effort made in the course of one's employment may deserve gratitude or congratulation when it does not result in achievement, but it does not deserve monetary reward. This would raise various difficulties with brute appeals to intuition that are addressed in the next section of this chapter; for example, can we legitimately appeal to intuitions in advancing an argument when these intuitions are not shared? But even if we were to accept the idea that the financial rewards that are attached to jobs are deserved (when they are deserved) solely on the basis of achievement or purposeful contribution, Miller still needs to explain why the best-qualified candidate deserves the job, rather than simply being the person we have most reason to think will deserve the rewards received in the course of doing the job. Here, Miller offers an analogy: an athlete who is prevented by the petty decision of an official from competing in a race that he has a fair chance of winning deserves the opportunity to compete. This analogy is far from convincing, however.

To see why the analogy is unconvincing we need to fill in some of the details, for it is underdescribed as it stands. The athlete is excluded from the race by "some petty decision of an official."[24] This could be either because the official has decided to prevent the athlete from competing even though strictly speaking he has broken no rules, or because the athlete has broken some minor rule, for example, he has failed to confirm his intention to compete on the day of the event in the way required by the rules. If the former, then the athlete's grievance is expressed most naturally by saying that he is *entitled* to compete, given the rules. If the latter, then we can indeed imagine circumstances in which it would be appropriate to say that the athlete deserves the opportunity to compete, even though he has broken the rule. The logic of desert would require us to cite some desert basis, for desert claims are of the form "A deserves X in virtue of Y."[25] So, we might say that he deserves the opportunity to compete in the final because he has won one of the heats for it, or because he has trained hard for the race, or because he is performing at his best, or because he has a good chance of winning. All these proposals are intelligible at least. What then does Miller suppose to be the basis on which the best-qualified candidate deserves the job (i.e., the opportunity to earn the rewards of contribution)?

Miller claims that the relevant desert basis in this case is the fact that the best-qualified candidate possesses those qualities in virtue of which she can reasonably be expected to perform the job in a way that she comes to deserve the rewards attached to it. But this is obscure. Why should possession of these qualities mean that she deserves the job as opposed to being the person most likely to come to deserve the rewards of contribution? Consider the following principle, which Miller might seem to be invoking. If it is likely (or at least possible) that A will deserve X if A is given the opportunity to be deserving of X, A deserves that opportunity. This is certainly not a general truth, for there are plenty of counterexamples. Rotation and lot can be used as a means of allocating opportunities, in a variety of different contexts where it is implausible to suppose that they violate genuine desert claims. In ancient Athens, for example, lots were used to select councillors. The fact that other more able citizens might have had a better chance of deserving the honors and rewards attached to public office does not show that they deserved the opportunity to earn those honors and rewards. The members of a military task force which is to be sent on a demanding mission might be selected by lot. The fact that other soldiers would have been likely, or more likely, to deserve the rewards for brave conduct had they been selected does not show that they deserved the opportunity to be deserving of those rewards.

Why then should we say that the best-qualified applicant for a job *deserves* it because she deserves the opportunity to obtain the rewards of contribution in virtue of being the person most likely to come to deserve those rewards? In the absence of a persuasive answer to this question, even if we were to concede that the best-qualified applicant for a job is the person most likely to come to deserve the rewards attached to it, at best this would show that we have just reason to appoint her to it, not that she deserves it.

Miller makes some remarks that could be read as a partial response to the objection made in the previous paragraph. He maintains that when jobs, in particular, are allocated on some basis other than qualifications, such as by lot, the people who are appointed become less deserving of the rewards that these jobs carry with them *regardless* of the actual contribution the appointees make in the course of performing them. In the case of lot, in particular, "[m]any could legitimately claim that it was only their bad luck in the draw that prevented them from exercising their talents . . . productively."[26] Although this may provide a good reason for not distributing jobs on the basis of lot, it does nothing to establish the idea that the best-qualified candidate for a job deserves it as opposed to being the person most likely to come to deserve the rewards it carries. (Note also that Miller's remarks imply that people fully deserve the rewards for the jobs they perform on the basis of their contribution only if they came to be appointed to them in the right way. This must also complicate Miller's defense of the desert of the best-qualified candidate; she deserves the job because she is the person most likely to come to deserve the rewards attached to it, but she can fully deserve the rewards attached to it only because she is the person best-qualified for it.[27])

In a survey article Miller distinguishes between indirect and intuitive (or direct) arguments that appeal to the notion of desert. Intuitive arguments rest upon the brute idea that a person may deserve reward simply in virtue of what he or she has done, whereas indirect arguments try to underpin the idea that a person deserves reward by appealing to the way in which the presence of the desert basis contributes to the realization of some other value that justifies the reward.[28] Miller claims that many indirect arguments end up having little to do with desert, properly conceived.[29] It may therefore seem surprising that Miller should try to develop an indirect argument of the kind he does for the idea that the best-qualified candidate for a job deserves to be appointed to it. For it is similarly vulnerable to the contention that it fails to capture the intuitive force of the desert claim under consideration and presents a surrogate of that claim rather than the genuine article.

Should he then simply rest his defense of the desert of the best-qualified applicant on the brute intuition that such an applicant deserves the job in virtue of qualifications? Miller would resist this proposal on the grounds that mere possession of a quality or ability cannot make a person deserving of reward; some "performance" is always required for such claims to be genuine rather than sham.[30] If desert claims that appeal to the possession of a quality or ability are to be considered genuine, they have to be understood as secondary desert judgments, which derive their force from some other desert judgments that are primary. In other words, some indirect desert judgments are legitimate, namely, those properly grounded in primary desert judgments that rely simply on their intuitive force.

So, where does this leave us? We seem to be faced with a clash of primary desert claims, in effect a clash of differing intuitions about desert. Miller's intuition is that in the performance of jobs, contribution and contribution alone provides the relevant desert basis (though a person can fully deserve the rewards for her contribution only if she was the best-qualified candidate at the point of selection). The intuition to which I have appealed is that effort in the performance of jobs may also deserve reward even when it does not result in achievement. (Both positions no doubt find some support in popular opinion, as Miller willingly concedes.)

On my view there is still space for the idea that a person deserves a job for which he or she has applied. Sometimes when we make such claims, we are making noncomparative judgments that are not relevant to the idea that the best-qualified candidate deserves it, for we are not considering the qualities of different applicants (e.g., we simply note the effort our friend has put into obtaining his qualifications). Even when we make comparative judgments, and conclude that some particular individual deserves the job, we may do so on the grounds that he has made the most effort or achieved the most in the past. And here I agree with Miller that this kind of backward-looking approach is unable to underwrite the idea that the best-qualified candidate always deserves the job. This is not simply for the reasons Miller gives. It is also because a person's present qualifications may bear no relation to what he or she has achieved in the past. Consider the case mentioned earlier, of someone who is involved in a serious accident prior to being interviewed for a job. The potential employer might say, quite appropriately: "Given his past efforts and achievements, of all the candidates, he deserves the job. But we shouldn't appoint him because the nature of his disabilities mean he is no longer the best qualified for it."

SOME METHODOLOGICAL QUESTIONS

Miller's arguments in favor of the idea that the best-qualified applicant for a job deserves to be appointed, and the reservations I have expressed about them, raise some difficult questions concerning moral methodology to which I alluded at the beginning of this chapter, regarding the significance that should be given to widely shared convictions. These questions also emerge in Miller's work on nationality, where he is most explicit about his method.[31] There he recommends a method which

> Rather than dismissing ordinary beliefs and sentiments out of hand unless they can be shown to have a rational foundation, leave them in place until strong arguments are produced for rejecting them. . . . [W]e build upon existing sentiments and judgements, correcting them only when they are inconsistent or plainly flawed in some other way.[32]

Miller does not elaborate upon these remarks, but they seem to involve a commitment to the principle with which I began, namely, that we should not reject widely shared views without good reason.

This principle can be understood in different ways, however. How does Miller understand it? Does he take it to imply that there is always a reason for believing that widely shared views are true or justifiably held, perhaps because a view's being widely shared is evidence of its truth or of its being justifiably held?[33] This does seem to be Miller's position; for instance, he maintains that "a theory of justice needs to be grounded in evidence about how ordinary people understand distributive justice."[34] But why should we suppose that a view's being widely held gives it special credibility? The best answer Miller has available is to maintain that there are reliable methods of reaching the truth on moral questions, and that the fact a large number of people have converged upon the same views gives a reason for thinking that they have employed those methods.[35] (This is consistent with acknowledging that in some cases convergence might have occurred for other reasons, for example, because people were disposed to reason in a faulty way[36] or simply because they have all made certain factual errors.[37])

But Miller's version of the principle that we should not reject widely held beliefs without good reason seems to presuppose a further epistemological position that some will find much more contentious: that we are entitled to hold a normative or moral belief that is *unsupported* by reason or argument so long as there is no good reason to reject it. Can this epistemological position be defended?

Consider what a defender of a coherentist theory of justification would say in response to this question. According to a coherentist theory of justification, one's belief that p is justified insofar as p is part of a coherent set of beliefs.[38] Defenders of such a theory will be inclined to argue that even beliefs not directly supported by reasons may receive *indirect* support simply by virtue of being part of a coherent set of beliefs, and thereby count as justified. They can therefore accept that we are entitled to subscribe to a belief that has no direct support provided it coheres with other beliefs we hold.

There is another epistemological position that is also congenial to Miller's position, which some of Wittgenstein's remarks gesture toward. This maintains that one can be entitled to hold a belief (i.e., not be *unjustified* in holding it) even though it is not, and cannot be, justified.[39] This position makes space for the existence of beliefs that are neither justified nor unjustified. This sort of epistemological picture is attractive, but not unproblematic as the following question reveals: Can a belief that rests upon others that are neither justified nor unjustified legitimately be regarded as itself justified? If we answer this question in the negative, then a very large number of our beliefs will turn out not to be justified (though it will not follow that they are unjustified). On the other hand, if we answer the question in the affirmative, we seem to be violating a widely held epistemological principle that "justifying beliefs must themselves be justified."[40]

I do not propose to adjudicate between the coherence theory of justification and the Wittgenstein-inspired alternative I have described, for this is not necessary for my purposes. The idea that there can be beliefs that cannot be given direct support (whether or not they are regarded as justified in virtue of belonging to a coherent set, or as occupying some middle ground between the justified and the unjustified) gives some reason to be cautious, like Miller, in

seeking systematic unity in ethics. The danger of trying to systematize our ethical judgments is that we may misunderstand the basis of our settled convictions. For example, we may suppose that one principle can be derived from another, failing to appreciate that it has an independent basis. If principles and
values are genuinely plural, then our reasons in defense of those principles
and values are likely to run out, fairly quickly in some cases, leaving us with
beliefs that can be given no direct support.

So, Miller can fruitfully draw upon the idea that there may be beliefs that
cannot be given any direct support in defending the idea that the best-qualified
candidate for a job deserves it. As I have already noted, in his work on desert
in general he distinguishes between intuitive and indirect arguments. Intuitive
arguments rest upon brute intuitions about desert of the form that someone deserves X in virtue of possessing some quality Y or performing some action Z.
Indirect arguments, in contrast, try to explain why the possession of some feature Y makes the agent deserving of X by appealing to some further value that
Y realizes or can be expected to realize. Miller is content to allow that some
desert claims may legitimately rest upon brute intuitions about desert that are
not susceptible to any further justification or rationalization. Clearly, this is permitted by the idea that it can be legitimate to subscribe to beliefs that can be
given no direct support.

If I have understood Miller's methodology properly, it seems to me to be defensible.[41] My doubts about his treatment of desert concern not the methodology itself, but how he applies it to ordinary convictions about desert. He
maintains that theories of justice need to be grounded in evidence about how
ordinary people understand distributive justice, yet concedes that common
opinion is "torn between the view that we deserve reward for what we achieve
and the view that we deserve reward only for what is within our control, that
is, our efforts and choices."[42] Miller cannot consistently maintain that theories
of justice need to be grounded in evidence about people's ordinary convictions
yet simply discount part of that evidence, namely, that part which suggests that
many people believe that we deserve reward only for our efforts and choices.
It is not enough in this context to reply that people deserve monetary reward
for purposeful achievement but only gratitude for effort unsuccessfully directed toward the same achievement, for common opinion apparently makes
no such distinction.

RESPECT FOR PERSONS

The prominence in our practices of the idea that justice requires selecting the
best-qualified candidates for jobs and educational places gives us good reason
to search elsewhere for a satisfying justification of it.[43] If that idea cannot
plausibly be underwritten by the notion of desert, how might it be justified? It
seems unlikely that its status as a weighty component of justice could be de-

fended by any approach that saw it as the best means of realizing some independently specifiable conception of justice, or as the most socially efficient means of allocating jobs and educational or training places. There is an alternative strategy available, however, which in my view offers more promise.

In defending the idea that the best-qualified candidates should be appointed, George Sher writes:

> When we hire by merit, we abstract from all facts about the applicants except their ability to perform well at the relevant tasks. By thus concentrating on their ability to perform, we treat them as agents whose purposeful acts are capable of making a difference in the world. . . . [S]electing by merit is a way of taking seriously the potential agency of both the successful and the unsuccessful applicants.[44]

When someone is hired because he is the nephew of the director, or because she is a member of a disadvantaged group, or when hiring that person will bring about better overall consequences for society, the potential agency of the applicants, successful or not, is ignored and they are not accorded respect as rational agents. Candidates are treated "as mere bearers of needs or claims, as passive links in causal chains, or as interchangeable specimens of larger groups or classes."[45] Although Sher claims that this argument is grounded in desert, it is not naturally thought of in these terms. It appeals directly to the idea of respect for persons, and the notion of desert doesn't seem to play any genuine role.[46] (Here, I am perhaps in agreement with Miller, who suggests that many of Sher's indirect arguments fail to underwrite genuine desert claims.)

There does seem to be a way in which the agency (or potential agency) of applicants is not taken seriously when, for example, selectors allow personal connections or prejudices to influence their decisions. But whether a policy or practice treats people with respect surely depends in part on the message conveyed by it;[47] contrary to what Sher implies, ignoring a person's agency is not in itself disrespectful to her. Often the message conveyed by a policy or practice simply derives from its publicly stated rationale or justification or the known intentions of those responsible for it. For example, both prejudice and nepotism usually convey a straightforwardly disrespectful message. When racism overtly influences selection decisions, the applicants receive the message that it is not what you are able to do that matters but the color of your skin, whereas nepotism, when it is transparent at least, conveys the message that it is not what you are able to do that matters but who you know.

Sometimes, however, the message that is conveyed reflects what is, under the circumstances, a natural way of interpreting the policy or practice even though that interpretation ignores or even contradicts the publicly stated justification and the intentions of those responsible for it. In cases of this sort, whether the policy or practice is itself disrespectful depends upon whether the way in which it is interpreted could reasonably be foreseen and countered. So, for example, affirmative action programs may give members of disadvantaged groups the message that the wider society believes they need to be given a head start because they are unable to compete effectively in a fair competition, even if that is not the publicly stated rationale of these programs or the intended message. If this message could be foreseen and countered but no steps are taken to do so, then the policy or practice is itself disrespectful.

This appeal to the importance of the message conveyed by a policy in deciding whether agency is being respected does not reduce the argument to the idea that an established practice of appointing the best-qualified candidate creates a legitimate expectation that the best-qualified candidates will be successful in the future.[48] Rather, it points to the existence of meanings that can transcend the publicly stated rationale for a selection process. The mere expectation that the best-qualified candidate will be appointed could be changed in particular cases simply by announcing publicly that different selection rules are going to apply and that as a result the process may not have this outcome.[49] But even if there were such an announcement, a sense of grievance might arise among unsuccessful candidates because of the message conveyed by the new practice of selection, for example, that what matters is not a person's ability or agency but some other fact about that person.

Indeed, this way of developing Sher's argument is strengthened by being considered in the light of how those candidates who are selected or rejected for reasons that have nothing to do with their ability to do the job well (or their potential to acquire that ability) experience their success or failure. Those who are denied jobs as a result of racial or sexual prejudice generally feel demeaned or insulted at being rejected on this basis because of the message it intentionally conveys. Even those who are the beneficiaries of affirmative action programs in societies that employ quotas for disadvantaged groups sometimes suffer low self-esteem and feelings of inadequacy that can to some extent be traced back to the thought that they owe their positions to membership of a social group rather than their abilities or potential abilities. Those who benefit from affirmative action programs may receive the message: "It is not your abilities that matter but the fact that you are a member of a disadvantaged group." And they may receive that message whether it is intended or not and irrespective of whether it is part of the publicly stated rationale of the program.

These observations do not provide a case against every affirmative action program. Sometimes the intentions of those responsible for these programs, the rationales they give for them, and the efforts they make to avoid misunderstanding may justify the insistence that these programs involve no disrespect to the agency of the applicants. For example, as Sher himself argues, a practice of appointing less well-qualified applicants need involve no disrespect to the agency of the various candidates when it is clear that those who are successful would have been the best-qualified had they not been the victims of past discrimination.[50] Indeed, the idea of respect for persons will itself impose various requirements on access to qualifications, although I do not explore this issue here.

Sher's argument, and the way I have developed it, is likely to face skepticism, mainly because the idea of respect for persons as agents is notoriously vague.

It should be conceded immediately that his argument is, by its nature, inconclusive; insofar as it is successful, its success depends on showing that selecting candidates on some basis other than their qualifications to do the job fails to respect their agency in some way. But there is surely a variety of different ways of taking the agency of candidates seriously other than selecting on the basis of their abilities. For example, it might be argued that a selector takes candidates seriously as agents when weight is given to their needs as well as their ability to do the job. Here, we should concede that attending to people's needs is required if we are to take them seriously as agents, but that the appropriate context in which this should occur is not the point of selection but rather the allocation of resources, perhaps through a system of redistributive taxation that aims to meet basic needs. As Miller himself argues at some length in *Principles of Social Justice*, different principles are appropriate in different contexts.

Doubts about whether even an amended version of Sher's argument could yield the desired conclusion run deeper, however. Richard Arneson, for example, maintains that respect for persons is a purely formal notion:

> One expresses due respect for persons and treats them respectfully by acting towards persons in accordance with the moral principles that are best supported by reasons. In this sense respect for persons looks to be . . . a purely formal idea, neither a clue to what principles are best supported by moral reasons nor a constraint on what principles might be chosen.[51]

But ordinary usage does not support Arneson's contention. It gives respect for persons a narrower meaning; it does not suppose that any failure to comply with the moral principles best supported by reason automatically counts as a failure of respect. It may be possible to construct a moral theory that has as one of its implications the idea that the transgression of a moral demand must always involve some failure of respect. But in the absence of a successful argument for such a theory we should not draw that conclusion.

Rejecting Arneson's position does not commit us to the idea that there is some *independent* idea of respect for persons that permits us to derive a set of moral demands. Rather, we might suppose that the relevant demands express, in a constitutive way, what it is to respect persons. Understood in this way, Sher's proposal is that respect for persons in the process of selection is expressed by considering candidates solely on the basis of their ability to do the relevant tasks.

This sort of appeal to the idea of respect for persons in justifying the selection of the best-qualified candidates is not one that Miller must necessarily find uncongenial. He acknowledges that what it is to treat people as equals, to respect their dignity, varies historically, and from one place to another: for example, it means one thing in an aristocratic society, quite another in democratic societies.[52] He also insists that an aristocratic society, with its hierarchical notion of what it is to treat people with dignity and respect, is not a real option for us, given our commitment to democratic notions of social equality. Similarly, questions might be raised about whether we could become the kind of creatures who did not feel that there had been a failure of respect when we were accepted or rejected on grounds other than our ability to do the job.

The meritocratic ideal's commitment to the idea that the best-qualified applicants should be appointed to advantaged social positions is not only widely shared but also independently appealing. However, it is not adequately grounded in the claim that the best-qualified candidate deserves the position. Instead, we should think of it as justified by the different idea that respect for persons requires us to consider their abilities in selecting for advantaged social positions, not simply because this promotes efficiency or utility or whatever, but because a failure to do so generally conveys a disrespectful message to the candidates.

NOTES

I would like to thank David Owen and participants in the Conference on Justice and Democracy at Nuffield College, July 11–13, 2000, for their helpful comments.

1. The main exceptions here are R. M. Hare and R. Brandt. See especially R. M. Hare, "The Argument from Received Opinion," in his *Essays on Philosophical Method* (London: Macmillan, 1971); R. Brandt, *A Theory of the Right and the Good* (Oxford: Oxford University Press, 1979), 21–22.

2. See J. Rawls, *A Theory of Justice* (Cambridge, Mass.: Harvard University Press, 1971), 19–21, 46–51. For a nuanced discussion of the legitimacy of appeals to intuition in moral argument, see J. Griffin, *Value Judgement: Improving Our Ethical Beliefs* (Oxford: Oxford University Press, 1996), especially ch. I and VIII. See also A. Swift, "Social Justice: Why Does It Matter What the People Think?" in this volume for further discussion of the proper role of people's convictions in assessing principles of justice.

3. I shall suggest later in the chapter that this principle is not as innocuous as it appears.

4. D. Miller, *Principles of Social Justice* (Cambridge Mass.: Harvard University Press, 1999), 160.

5. Miller, *Principles*, 164.

6. See D. Attas, "Markets and Desert," this volume, for further critical discussion of this idea.

7. See Miller, *Principles*, 143–144.

8. S. Olsaretti, "Desert and Luck," this volume.

9. See Miller, *Principles*, 185.

10. Miller, *Principles*, 184–185.

11. For some of these worries, see Nien-He Hsieh, "Moral Desert, Fairness and Legitimate Expectations in the Market," *Journal of Political Philosophy* 8 (2000): esp. 95–99. Hsieh argues that even if we accept the assumptions of neoclassical economics, the equilibrium price of a good or service does not always reflect the contribution made by that good or service because the benefit it provides to an individual is sometimes greater than its equilibrium price. For example, the equilibrium price of a loaf of bread may be $2, but if a baker sells that loaf to someone who would have been willing to pay $10, then his contribution is worth $10 not $2.

12. Miller, *Principles,* 166.

13. D. Miller, *Market, State and Community* (Oxford: Oxford University Press, 1989).

14. Miller, *Principles,* 149.

15. See G. A. Cohen, "David Miller on Market Socialism and Distributive Justice" (All Souls College, Oxford University, 1989).

16. Wojceich Sadurski seems to accept (1), or something close to it, when he says that "effort is the only legitimate basis and measure of desert" (W. Sadurski, *Giving Desert its Due* [Dordrecht, 1985], 116).

17. See also Olsaretti, "Desert and Luck," this volume. Miller discusses some of the empirical evidence and seems to accept that people's intuitions support (3), at least when it comes to contributions to small groups: "People judge that the appropriate reward depends on what each person achieves, but they qualify this to some degree when presented with data about effort so that it is possible for a person who achieves less but tries harder to deserve more than another who tries less but achieves more" (Miller, *Principles,* 66). At times, however, he seems unjustifiably to restrict the alternatives to (1) and (2). For example, he considers the response of Pamela, who invokes compensation, skill, responsibility, effort, and training as justifications for large rewards, but when these criteria clash, maintains that "productivity supersedes effort." Miller's conclusion is that this confirms the idea that "people are torn between the view that we deserve reward for what we achieve and the view that we deserve reward only for what is within our control, that is, our efforts and choices" (Miller, *Principles,* 70–71). But that conclusion is not warranted by what Pamela says, for that is consistent with (3), which says that we deserve reward for both our efforts and our achievements. At the level of theory, Owen McCleod also goes for a hybrid account, but he wants to include a variety of other desert bases, such as moral character, need, entitlement, and being a person. See O. McLeod, "Desert and Wages," in *What Do We Deserve: A Reader on Justice and Desert,* ed. L. Pojman and O. McLeod (New York: Oxford University Press, 1999), 279–280). I'm not convinced that these are genuine desert bases, or that such a position has intuitive support.

18. See Miller, *Principles,* 183.

19. See Rawls, *A Theory of Justice,* 312.

20. See Cohen, "David Miller on Market Socialism."

21. Miller, *Principles,* 142–143.

22. Cf. G. Sher, "Qualifications, Fairness, and Desert," in *Equal Opportunity,* ed. N. Bowie (Boulder, Colo.: Westview, 1988), 118.

23. This seems to be the line he takes against Hayek. He points out that prizes are often deserved purely on the basis of achievement and argues that economic desert also has this character: see Miller, *Principles,* 183–184. I'm not convinced that this is a strategy that Miller can live with, however, given his deference to popular beliefs and his acceptance of the fact that people do often give weight to effort even when it does not result in achievement: see Miller, *Principles,* ch. 3–4, esp. 66–67.

24. Miller, *Principles,* 166.

25. See, for example, J. Feinberg, "Justice and Personal Desert," in *What Do We Deserve?: A Reader on Justice and Desert,* ed. L. Pojman and O. McLeod (New York: Oxford University Press, 1999), 72.

26. Miller, *Principles,* 145.

27. We also have to be careful about phrasing here. Miller cannot without circularity suppose that being the best-qualified candidate is a *basis,* alongside contribution, on which one deserves the rewards attached to a job. He must suppose instead that it is a *condition* of (fully) deserving the rewards for one's contribution.

28. See D. Miller, "Recent Theories of Social Justice," *British Journal of Political Science* 21 (1991): 379–380.

29. See his remarks about the arguments that George Sher presents: Miller, "Recent Theories," 379–381.

30. Miller, *Principles,* 137–138.

31. See S. Caney, "Individuals, Nations and Obligations," in *National Rights, International Obligations*, ed. S. Caney, D. George, and P. Jones (Oxford: Westview, 1996), 125, for criticism of the way in which Miller employs intuitions about nationality in his defense of special obligations to fellow nationals. See also D. Weinstock, "National Partiality: Confronting the Intuitions," *The Monist* 82 (1999): esp. 518–524.

32. D. Miller, "In Defence of Nationality," *Journal of Applied Philosophy* 10 (1993): 4.

33. Could the principle that widely shared views should not be rejected without good reason be derived from the more general principle that we should not reject any view unless there is good reason to do so? If it were derived from this more general principle, then it would not imply that there is any reason for believing that widely shared views are true. Indeed, it would be purely formal and would not imply that there is any presumption in favor of widely shared views being justifiably held. This is not Miller's way of understanding the principle, however.

34. Miller, *Principles*, 61.

35. Is this Miller's reason for endorsing the principle, however? He does maintain that common opinion endorses various methods of inquiry; and he rejects the idea that "philosophers can discover truth by means not available to lay persons" (Miller, *Principles*, 52–53).

36. See G. Gaus, *Justificatory Liberalism: An Essay on Epistemology and Political Theory* (Oxford: Oxford University Press, 1996), 133.

37. See Miller, *Principles*, 53.

38. See D. Brink, *Moral Realism and the Foundations of Ethics* (Cambridge: Cambridge University Press, 1989), 124.

39. Compare, for example, Wittgenstein's claim that "to use a word without a justification does not mean to use it without right" (L. Wittgenstein, *Philosophical Investigations*, trans. G. E. M. Anscombe [Oxford: Blackwell, 1953], sec. 289).

40. David Brink makes use of this principle to argue against epistemological foundationalism: see Brink, *Moral Realism*, 116–122.

41. But see Swift, "Social Justice," for further discussion.

42. Miller, *Principles*, 71.

43. Some of the material in this section is taken from my "Equality of Opportunity, Old and New," *Ethics* 111 (2001).

44. Sher, "Qualifications, Fairness, and Desert," 119–120.

45. Sher, "Qualifications, Fairness, and Desert," 123. Sher's approach here is an extension of one that maintains that selection for advantaged social positions should be done on the basis of relevant reasons. See B. Williams, "The Idea of Equality," in his *Problems of the Self* (Cambridge: Cambridge University Press, 1973).

46. The kind of respect with which Sher is concerned is what Stephen Darwall calls recognition respect, which "consists in giving appropriate consideration or recognition of its object in deliberating about what to do" (S. L. Darwall, "Two Kinds of Respect," *Ethics* 88 [1977]: 38).

47. See T. E. Hill, *Autonomy and Self-Respect* (Cambridge: Cambridge University Press, 1991), ch. 13, for relevant discussion of the way in which policies and practices can convey messages.

48. See R. Goodin, "Negating Positive Desert Claims," *Political Theory* 13, (1985): 575–598, for a defense of the idea that when we say that the best-qualified candidate deserves the job, this amounts to the mere prediction that, ceteris paribus, he or she will get it.

49. Miller, *Principles*, 159.

50. See G. Sher, *Approximate Justice: Studies in Non-Ideal Theory* (Lanham, Md.: Rowman & Littlefield, 1997), ch. 3. This is different from the case when we judge that a candidate from a minority is the best-qualified applicant because we count the effort she has made to overcome various obstacles as a qualification.

51. R. Arneson, "Luck Egalitarianism and Prioritarianism," *Ethics* 110 (2000): 344.

52. Miller, *Principles*, 241.

4

Desert and Luck

Serena Olsaretti

David Miller has long defended the view that, contrary to what many contemporary political philosophers think, desert is a principle of distributive justice and has claimed to find support for it in the fact that it squares up nicely with ordinary attitudes toward desert and distributive justice.[1] One salient difficulty that the adoption of desert as a principle of justice stumbles upon is the issue of the relation between desert and responsibility and the related problem of contingency or luck.[2] To the extent that the justifiable ascription of deserts to individuals—their deservingness—is seen to require some degree of responsibility on those individuals' part, then some presumed desert bases which allow for too great a role of luck in the acquisition of deserts seem to be inadequate. Luck is viewed to undermine individuals' deserts, as illustrated by the standard case of the athlete winning the race by a fluke, thanks to her competitor's tripping right before the finish line. In this case, we would not regard the winning athlete as deserving of the prize.

Since the role of luck, broadly understood to comprise any random event outside individuals' control, is pervasive, accepting that luck undermines desert then requires a careful examination of what role, if any, desert should be given in a theory of distributive justice. This task is especially pressing for those who defend desert on the basis of performance (including desert of rewards on the basis of productive contribution), for performance, unlike effort, is variously affected by factors outside the individuals' control.

In what follows I examine the relationship between luck and desert as a principle of distributive justice that could be put to do the task of justifying market outcomes. In particular, I focus on David Miller's contention that desert on the basis of productive contribution, where the value of one's productive contribution is measured by market prices (what I refer to as the contribution argument), may be defended in spite of the problem of luck.[3] I argue that we should distinguish between two aspects of that problem, regarding the role of contingency on separate individuals' deserts on one hand, and on the distribution of differential deserts across individuals on the other. Luck that undermines an individual's desert clearly also constitutes a problem for making comparative claims about that individual's desert with other individuals' deserts. But there is a further, and independent, problem, regarding the role of contingency on distributions of differential deserts *even when* single individuals' deserts are not undermined by luck. Miller's recent distinction between two types of luck—integral and circumstantial luck— deals with the first of these two problems but fails to address the second, ignoring that it constitutes a problem in its own right. Ultimately, if desert is to be a principle of distributive justice, it requires the elimination of precisely the sort of background luck which, instead, underpins the market, and which Miller tries to reconcile with desert.

I proceed as follows. In the first section, I draw on John Rawls's remarks on desert to illustrate the distinction between the justifiability of single individuals' deserts on the one hand, and the justifiability of a distribution of differential deserts on the other. I then turn in the second section to the problem of luck for the argument that desert on the basis of productive contribution can justify market rewards. In that context, I examine one reply Miller has offered to try and deal with that problem. Miller has suggested that, since desert is not just a matter of good intentions, the fact that individuals' productive contribution is affected by contingencies does not undermine the claim that market prices can, under certain conditions, adequately reflect people's deserts. I argue that, even if it is true that desert isn't simply a matter of good intentions, this is unsatisfactory as a reply to the problem raised by contingency for the justifiability of deserts. The third section analyzes Miller's recent treatment of the problem of luck, which appeals to a distinction between two types of luck—integral and circumstantial—as a way of rescuing desert on the basis of productive contribution as a defensible principle of desert. Miller argues that while integral luck undermines desert, circumstantial luck does not, and that an attempt to eliminate the latter would result in jettisoning desert. I argue, however, that this suggestion overlooks the distinction between the justifiability of single individuals' deserts and the justifiability of a distribution of differential deserts. The presence of circumstantial luck, while not undermining the former, nonetheless presents a problem for adopting desert on the basis of productive contribution as a principle for justifying a distribution of differential deserts. Admitting this does not, I suggest, result in jettisoning desert, but gives us reason to support desert as a principle that sanctions only those departures from equality that reflect people's different choices. Finally, the last section concludes with an assessment of how the problem of luck bears on the view that a differential distribution of market earnings could be justified by desert.

DESERT, RESPONSIBILITY, AND DIFFERENTIAL DESERTS

The problem of luck for desert arises once we acknowledge that desert is in some relation to responsibility.[4] If we think that, for individuals to become deserving, it is necessary that they have control over the bases on which they become deserving, so that they may be held responsible for how deserving they are, then the interference of random events outside the relevant individuals' control renders the ascription of desert inappropriate. The relation between desert and responsibility is a contested point in the desert debate,[5] and I shall not defend that relation here. Instead, I shall assume that desert as a principle of distributive justice does involve a requirement of responsibility, a view I share with Miller, and examine what viewing desert as related to responsibility commits one to. Even if we assume that desert and responsibility are related, it is an open question just how demanding the requirement of responsibility involved by desert ought to be.

In what follows I argue that the requirement of responsibility associated with desert is best understood as a requirement of fair opportunity for the justifiability of differential deserts. I develop this point by examining, and drawing on, Rawls's remarks on desert. This point is of salience for the discussion of the problem of luck, in the following ways.

First, it shows that positing a requirement of responsibility need not have the adverse consequences for desert that some theorists have identified. Some theorists have questioned that desert is related to responsibility, suggesting that if we hold that desert requires responsibility "all the way down," as Rawls is alleged to do, we ultimately undermine the notion of desert. As a reaction, some desert theorists have claimed that, to avoid the conclusion that no desert is possible, only a weak requirement of responsibility is required for desert. I think that neither the attack nor the response is justified. Recognizing the relevance of the problem of luck for desert does not commit one either to rejecting desert altogether or to weakening unduly the link between desert and responsibility.

Second, the following discussion of Rawls's remarks points to the importance of the justifiability of *differential* deserts as a question in its own right, distinct from that of the justifiability of deserts *tout court*. This distinction allows us to gain greater insight into the problem of luck and its consequences for the adoption of desert as a principle of distributive justice.

Let us turn, then, to Rawls's well-known contention about desert, which is as follows:

> It seems to be one of the fixed points of our considered judgements that no one deserves his place in the distribution of native endowments, any more than one deserves one's initial place in society. The assertion that a man deserves the superior character that enables him to make the effort to cultivate his abilities is equally problematic; for his character depends in large part upon fortunate family and social circumstances for which he can claim no credit. The notion of desert seems not to apply to these cases.[6]

If it is true that natural endowments and effort-making ability are undeserved, what follows from this?

On one interpretation of Rawls's remarks, the latter have been taken to support an infinite regress thesis. Rawls is viewed as suggesting that, in order for someone to deserve something, she must wholly deserve the desert grounds.[7] And, since natural endowments and effort-making capacity are not so deserved, we cannot deserve anything on the basis of them. But then we cannot deserve anything at all,[8] since it must be true, for any ground G by virtue of which one deserves, that there is some further ground G_1 by virtue of which G itself is deserved, and then a ground G_2 by virtue of which G_1 is deserved, and so on ad infinitum. No one ever deserves anything.

This antidesert argument crucially rests on the contention, attributed to Rawls, that "the man who deserves something must be able to claim credit (. . .) for the grounds being true of him."[9] That contention, and the argument that it supposedly supports, have been subjected to much criticism, and I will here only mention some main ones briefly. First, it has been pointed out that the fact that Rawls's thesis leads to an infinite regress may be taken as a reductio ad absurdum of the antidesert argument, rather than as a convincing demonstration of that argument.[10] Second, the thesis has been viewed to lead to counterintuitive conclusions, eliminating all room not only for desert but also for related notions of choice and responsibility, and supposedly creating tensions in Rawls's own account.[11] And finally, the thesis, so it is claimed, may be attacked not only for leading to counterintuitive conclusions—that no one ever deserves anything—but also for being hardly intelligible, for we can make no sense of the idea of deserving to deserve to deserve something.[12]

The infinite regress thesis, then, should be rejected. Moreover, the ascription of that thesis to Rawls is mistaken. Rawls's point is a different one, and one that, I think, does have salient consequences for the contention that desert is a principle of justice. It concerns the possibility of people's unequal talents and effort-making capacity giving rise to *unequal* or *differential* deserts, rather than deserts *tout court*. While not denying that people can deserve things, even though the desert bases are themselves undeserved, so that the deserving individual cannot claim credit for them, Rawls's concern is with refuting the claim that the morally arbitrary and differential possession of attributes may justifiably give rise to *inequality* in desert.

Some desert theorists have recognized that the thrust of Rawls's observations is about the justifiability of differential deserts, and, accordingly, they have tried to rescue desert from what they take to be a forceful objection to its capacity to justify inequalities. George Sher, for instance, interprets Rawls as holding that, if some individuals had deserts based on conditions which not everyone possesses, they would thereby have an unfair advantage over others, *unless* they deserved those conditions.[13] Not all desert bases have to be themselves deserved, then, but only those that are differentially distributed among individuals. It is then an open question whether there are any potential desert bases that could justifiably give rise to inequalities in desert.[14]

I think that both Rawls and Sher are mistaken insofar as the former implies, and the latter, in reply to Rawls, explicitly endorses, the view that we would have to *deserve* those desert bases that are differentially distributed. Even where the concern is with the justifiability of *differential* deserts, rather than desert *tout court*, that concern need not take the form of a requirement that the grounds for differential deserts be deserved.

The crucial point, rather, is that a principle that may justify patterns of rewards across persons must not be one that gives unfair advantage to some individuals over others, as a principle justifying inequalities on the basis of unchosen factors would do. For differential deserts to be justified, it has to be the case that individuals have a fair opportunity to acquire differential deserts. Thus understood, Rawls's observations about desert lend support to the adoption of a notion of *active desert*, that is, desert on the basis of the choices people make and the actions they undertake. Desert as a principle of distributive justice is a principle that sanctions inequalities that are the result of individual choices and actions and for which individuals may be held responsible.

So, when Rawls's remarks are understood as a claim about the unfair advantage resulting from the *differential* distribution of talents and effort-making ability, they have considerable bearing on the question of what principle of desert, if any, is appropriate as a principle of distributive justice. Those remarks do not result in the contention that no one ever deserves anything. Nor does the Rawlsian objection properly formulated support the contention that differential deserts should be deserts on grounds that are themselves deserved. Acknowledging that the justifiability of differential deserts constitutes a problem in its own right, distinct from that of the justifiability of single desert claims, points to the fact that desert as a principle of justice is one that would view inequalities as deserved insofar as they are the result of departures from equality that reflect individuals' different ambitions. A configuration of differential desert claims is just insofar as those differential claims arise against a background of fair conditions aimed at equalizing everyone's chances of acquiring differential deserts. In the absence of those conditions, while individual desert claims may well be justified, a differential distribution of them is unjust. When the responsibility requirement is thus understood, as justifying certain background conditions against which differential deserts are just, it is by no means true that it sabotages the whole notion of desert.[15]

THE CONTRIBUTION ARGUMENT, THE PROBLEM OF LUCK, AND GOOD INTENTIONS

With the preceding discussion in mind, let us now turn to consider the problem of luck for the contribution argument defended by Miller. According to that argument, the market is substantively just in as far as it rewards individuals in accordance with their deserts. The incomes individuals reap through the market, the argument goes, are deserved rewards for the value of their productive contribution. Individuals engage in variously valuable social activities, and how valuable those activities are is supposedly reflected by market prices, which measure the value of people's activities in terms of their capacities to meet desires.[16]

There are two aspects of the contribution argument that may be subjected to criticism. The first regards the contention that the value of individuals' productive contribution is adequately reflected by market prices. This is not the sort of objection I will be raising against the contribution argument.[17] I will instead assume that the value of people's productive contribution is its market value and focus on a second aspect of the contribution argument, that is, its claim that desert on the basis of productive contribution is a principle that can justify a differential distribution of earnings. That claim encounters the problem of contingency, or luck, because contingent factors affect individuals' productive contribution in different ways, thus casting doubt on the contention that what individuals receive on the market always matches their deserts. Fluctuations in market prices and changes in market conditions that are due to factors not under the relevant individuals' control affect how much those individuals reap through the market, though it would seem odd to say that their deserts have changed or that how deserving they will be is dependent on external factors over which they have no control.

Both the short-term and the long-term effects of changes in market conditions affect what and how great market rewards are going to be, so that these rewards would not seem to reflect desert. Instances of short-term consequences of changes in market prices include, say, the case in which demand for the good I have been producing and quite successfully trading suddenly goes down, or the case in which the price of a good I produce and currently sell for a given price changes as a result of another supplier entering the market. In both cases, the rewards I reap may diminish, and yet it would seem odd to say that I have become less deserving than I was prior to the change in demand or prior to the appearance of the new supplier. And in the long term, too, the contribution argument seems to imply, oddly, that people's deserts may be affected by contingencies, in that the size of one's market rewards will depend on consumers' tastes and on the willingness of others to meet them. Since the rewards individuals reap on the market partly depend on factors that are outside their control, it is not the case that the differential market rewards will reflect people's differential deserts.

According to Miller, the problem of luck does not present an insurmountable objection to the contribution argument. One reply he has offered to that objection, and which it is worth examining before looking at the more systematic treatment of the relationship between luck and desert developed in Miller's recent work, emphasizes that how deserving one is is inextricably bound up with factors that lie outside of one's control. Desert is not simply a matter of good intentions. Rather, as Miller suggests, "[Desert] also has to do with how much benefit you create for the recipient of your services, and in nearly every case that depends on the configuration of the world outside."[18]

So, Miller claims, since what value one creates is not independent of what others do, it is indeed the case that the service I provide is less valuable if someone else, too, provides it, and perhaps at a more competitive price. Hence, odd as it may seem, it is actually true that my deserts diminish as a result of other suppliers entering the market and outbidding my prices. Similarly, according to Miller, the dependence of an individual's desert on contingencies in the long term is not problematic. In the long term, when equilibrium is reached, an individual's deserts will depend on how she has responded to the contingencies she has faced. So, someone may choose to become skilled at a task that she (rightly) foresees will be much in demand. In this case, Miller remarks, the person "is surely properly rewarded for making that choice."[19] Although various contingencies affect the market rewards a person can reap both in the short and in the long term, a person's deserts are not undermined, and there is no gap between what she deserves and what she gets through the market. The effect of contingencies on how productive individuals are, then, does not threaten the correspondence between market value and desert. To suggest otherwise is to assume, implausibly, that desert is just a matter of good intentions.

This reply, however, is unconvincing. Consider, first, Miller's observations about the short-term effects of market contingencies on a person's deserts. While we may agree that desert is not *merely* a matter of good intentions, the opposite does not follow, namely, that intentions, effort, and commitment do not also count.[20] And yet that is precisely what we need to accept in order to retain the link between market value and desert in the cases I illustrated previously. In those cases, it may well be that, as a result of someone else supplying the same good I have been successfully trading at much more competitive prices, I may not only sell somewhat less, but sell hardly anything at all and quickly go bankrupt. It is undeniable that the value of my goods has decreased, but not obvious that I suddenly become undeserving.

Now, Miller insists that "[i]f desert is based on value created, that value cannot be estimated without taking account of what others have produced; the notion that the service you render has the same value regardless of what others do is absurd."[21] But this observation is both question-begging and mistargeted. It is question-begging because it assumes precisely what is being questioned, namely, that "desert is based on value created." The question under consideration is whether a person's deserts can be based on the market value of her contribution, given that the market value of that contribution can change suddenly and substantially due to factors that are outside of the person's control, whereas it seems that one's deserts do not vary in this way. Further, Miller's insistence that "the notion that the service you render has the same value regardless of what others do is absurd," which presumably characterizes the position he is attacking, is mistargeted. We need not assert that "the service you render has the same value regardless of what others do," where the "value" of a service is its market value. But we may, and must, indeed, assert that, although the market value of a service I provide decreases, the performance of that service is still relevant for how deserving I am, insofar as it reflects my efforts or good intentions. Since desert is also *partly* a matter of good intentions, this means that market value does not appropriately reflect my deserts.

To see this, consider the example Miller adduces in support of his claim. We are to imagine that every month I clean the windows of my elderly neighbor's house, thus deserving "considerable" gratitude. But then, so Miller claims, if one month the neighbor's grandson turns up and does the job before me, I cannot expect to be thanked as warmly as I would have been otherwise. This supposedly confirms that the usefulness of my service, and not my good intentions, is what grounds my deserts.

But Miller draws this conclusion too swiftly. If my neighbor displays considerably less gratitude, I think I may indeed justifiably be disappointed. My neighbor's withdrawal of gratitude would show that he has been failing throughout to appreciate the significance of my willingness to take time off and help him out. My disappointment would be especially justified if the neighbor's grandson turns up unexpectedly, and I carry on with my usual task unaware that I have been forestalled. It may be less justified if, after a while and despite knowing that my service is no longer needed, I keep performing it nonetheless. So, particularly in the short run, it seems odd to say that my deserts have changed, though my deserts may indeed change in the longer term. At any rate, whether or not the neighbor may, in the short term, be justified in not thanking me as warmly as he would do when my service, besides displaying good intentions, was also very useful, he would not be justified in displaying very little or no gratitude at all. But this is precisely what may well happen on the market: my sales may go down drastically and suddenly. The market does not display any concern at all for my intentions; the usefulness of my service is all that matters. That is what market value, standardly, registers.[22]

Miller's remarks about the long-term effects of market contingencies on one's deserts similarly imply that good intentions not only are not the only thing that matters, but that they do not matter at all. The claim that someone who chooses to become skilled at those tasks that he rightly foresees will be in high demand "is surely properly rewarded for making that choice" should not mislead us. The market is inattentive to how certain profitable skills have been acquired. It rewards individuals who have the appropriate skills, whether those skills are the result of deliberate and attentive cultivation, whether they have been stumbled upon, or whether they were forced onto some individual against his will. So, although we may say of Joseph that the high rewards he receives as an information technology (IT) consultant are justified by the fact that he has decided to train in IT skills and forego the pleasure he would have derived from doing philosophy,[23] that justification is not what accounts for Robert's deserts, who was forced by his parents to go into IT, or for Anna's, who became an IT specialist because that was the only course on offer at her local university, without even realizing it would be a potential source of high rewards.[24]

The emphasis on the fact that desert is not solely a matter of good intentions, then, does not rescue the contribution argument from the objection that the presence of luck undermines the correspondence of market value and desert. In his recent work, however, Miller has devoted more attention to the problem of luck, and it remains to be seen whether that treatment provides principled reasons for why certain types of luck do not disrupt desert.

TWO TYPES OF LUCK

There is, Miller claims, a relevant difference between two ways in which luck affects performance:

> On the one hand, the performance itself—what the agent actually achieves—may depend to a greater or lesser extent on his luck. I gave the example earlier of a poor archer who shoots three lucky arrows and wins the competition. I shall label luck of this kind "integral luck." On the other hand, luck may determine whether someone has the opportunity to perform in the first place. The car carrying the athlete to the track may break down so that she has no chance to run. One soldier may be given an opportunity to show courage in battle, while another never gets within the range of the enemy. Luck of this kind can be called "circumstantial luck."[25]

The question under examination here is whether and to what extent an agent can be judged deserving when we know that her performance is affected by luck. The effect of luck of these two different types on desert is, according to Miller, different. Integral luck, he claims, does appear to nullify desert. The athlete who crosses the finish line first because her competitor, who was going to win, trips right before the end did not deserve to win, a desert we do attribute to the unlucky athlete. When we assess people's deserts, we try to factor out the effects of good and bad integral luck. But circumstantial luck is different. If the athlete does not get to the race due to bad luck, then, though we may think that she would have won had she got there, we would still not claim that she deserves to win. "Circumstantial luck always lies in the background of human performance,"[26] Miller remarks, and it does not normally nullify a person's deserts.

The cases, identified earlier, in which market contingencies affect the performance of individuals are then to be seen as cases in which individuals enjoy, or suffer, circumstantial luck, although on some occasions the short-term consequences of some market fluctuations are best seen as instances of integral luck. Miller admits this when he states that an entrepreneur whose product turns out unexpectedly to be a great success does not deserve all his gains, however difficult it would be in this case to factor out the effect of luck from an inspired hunch.[27] But in general, cases in which individuals' performance is affected by underlying market contingencies, as well as by the differential distribution of natural talents, are supposedly cases of circumstantial luck, and, therefore, they are not cases in which the agents' deserts are nullified.

Now, notice that the distinction between integral and circumstantial luck rests, quite simply, on the distinction between the conditions affecting the performance and the conditions affecting whether the performance can occur in the first place. So long as the desert in question is desert for a given performance, circumstantial luck clearly cannot affect desert claims for which the presumed basis is that performance. If performance P is to be a desert basis for getting G, then, unless one engages in P, no desert can be acquired. An athlete who cannot get to the race because of bad luck can sensibly regret not having had the opportunity to participate in the race and can sensibly suggest that she is the best runner and would have won had she taken part in the race. But it would be odd for her to claim that she deserved to win.[28] For someone to make that type of desert claim she must have had an opportunity to display the grounds on which her presumed desert would rest. So, clearly, when we are ascertaining how deserving a particular person is of a particular good or treatment, only integral luck is relevant. If we are interested only in determining what a single individual deserves in isolation, circumstantial luck may be left aside.

The intervention of circumstantial luck, however, does become relevant when we assess people's *differential* claims or make comparisons between different individuals' deserts. The question here is not whether someone who, due to bad circumstantial luck, fails to perform but would have been deserving had he been able to perform is as deserving of the prize or of the reward as the person who has performed in the relevant way and has thereby become deserving. Rather, the question is whether a distribution of differential benefits and burdens matching people's deserts is justified, given that some people did not have a fair opportunity to acquire greater or lesser deserts. This, as I said earlier,[29] is the question raised by Rawls's remarks on desert. When differential deserts are acquired on grounds that are beyond the individuals' control, some individuals have unfair advantage over others, and they may not justifiably lay a claim to getting more than those others.

Insofar as we are concerned with circumstantial luck, then, we are not concerned with its potential role in *nullifying* individuals' deserts, but with the justice of a distribution of differential deserts that are acquired against differential circumstantial luck. Yet Miller's treatment of the question whether circumstantial luck has any effect on how much a person deserves compared with others proceeds as though we were asking the former, not the latter question.

Interestingly, Miller himself at one point considers the relevance of circumstantial luck for making comparative judgments of desert, or judgments comparing different individuals' deserts. He suggests that whether circumstantial luck has any effect on how much someone deserves compared with others will vary according to whether the deserved good is more or less competitive, so that someone's receipt of that good occurs, in a sense, at the expense of others. Hence, the chemistry Nobel Prize winner is said by Miller to be less deserving to the extent that we are convinced that several other chemists would have made the same discovery had they been in a position to do so. This is a situation in which the fact that the deserved good in question is competitive means that a person's receiving it stands in the way of others getting it. So, in this case, barring epistemic problems in ascertaining whether others would have really come to deserve it, too, the fact that those supposed others have not been given the opportunity to come to deserve it is what makes the actual winner less deserving.

Now, this example brings together two different claims that need to be distinguished in order that we may consider carefully the relevance of circumstantial luck for making judgments of people's differential deserts.[30]

First, there is the claim that, insofar as the assignment of the Nobel Prize is an expression of exceptional achievement, the fact that we know that others would have been as deserving of the Nobel Prize means that the actual winner is not really deserving of what the Nobel Prize stands for, to wit, expression of admiration for exceptional achievement. In this sense we would say, indeed, that the actual winner is "less deserving." If there is a competition for who is the best x, and all the potentially good contestants fail to make it to the town where the competition is taking place due to tornadoes except for one, who is local, then, though he may indeed be the best x, the prize he gets becomes less deserved; it fails to express the extent to which it is supposed to select the best x among an adequate pool of contestants.

Second, there is the claim that, since the situation is a competitive one in which one person getting the deserved good precludes others from getting it, the fact that these others are excluded from competing for it on grounds that are beyond their control seems unjust.[31] Notice that this claim does not support the contention that the actual Nobel Prize winner is made *any less deserving* by the existence of these others. Rather, it is fundamentally a claim about the unfairness of excluding others from being potential beneficiaries of a good on grounds that they are not responsible for. But here, and unlike with the first claim, the judgment that the actual prize winner is deserving is unaltered. Just like the athlete who runs well and deserves to win is not made less deserving by the fact that other very good runners fail to get to the race, the Nobel Prize winner who makes an important discovery is not made any less deserving by the fact that other chemists fail to be in the conditions to make that discovery.

We are not here interested in the first claim, which is a claim the pertinence of which is closely related to the fact that the deserved good is a prize that supposedly marks exceptional achievement. Our concern with the effects of circumstantial luck on how much people deserve is captured by the second claim, and its relevance is all the more apparent when, instead of a Nobel Prize, what is at issue is the distribution of income differentials obtained on the market. According to that claim, while single desert claims may legitimately be made against the background of circumstantial luck, the distribution of differential deserts is unjustified, since some will have had unfair advantage over others. As a result, the distribution of differential rewards that match people's differential deserts is unjust.

However, it is because Miller treats the question as one regarding the legitimacy of making isolated desert claims, rather than the justifiability of a distribution of differential deserts, that he states:

> Circumstantial luck may lead us to qualify our judgements about the deserts of those who are its beneficiaries. But if we want to keep the notion of desert and use it to make practical judgements, we cannot compensate completely for luck of the second kind (. . .). Circumstantial luck always lies in the background of human performances, and only when it intrudes in a fairly clear and direct way on what different people achieve relative to one another do we allow it to modify our judgements of desert.[32]

Now, it is true, I submit, that if we claimed that circumstantial luck nullifies people's deserts in the same way that integral luck does, then it would be hard to retain the notion of desert. But that claim, which I do not need to make, is different from the one, which I do make, that if people's differential deserts depend on their differential circumstantial luck, then the distribution of those deserts is not just. Denying the first claim, which would result in sabotaging desert, need not commit us to denying the second, which does not sabotage desert but casts doubt on whether the contribution principle is a principle of desert that may show the distribution of market outcomes to be substantively just.

CIRCUMSTANTIAL LUCK AND THE DIFFERENTIAL DISTRIBUTION OF REWARDS

We can now provide an assessment of how the contribution argument fares in the light of the role of contingency and luck that greatly affect how productive individuals' contributions are. There are two respects in which the distribution of market outcomes seems to be unjust, where *injustice* is defined by reference to a notion of desert that should have application over a distribution of burdens and benefits across persons.

First, some individuals' performance is affected by integral luck, so their deserts are nullified or at least seriously modified, but the market does not register this. An entrepreneur may make a decision that turns out, by fluke, to be extremely profitable, while another may be outbid by the unpredicted marketing of imported goods at competitive prices he cannot afford to charge. When integral luck nullifies some individuals' deserts, those individuals will fail to receive what they individually deserve; some will reap rewards that are higher, and some lower, than what they deserve. The market will not factor out integral luck. As a consequence, the distribution of market rewards will not reflect people's deserts.

Second, the differential market rewards people reap largely depend on differential circumstantial luck so that, even if one insisted that market prices do reflect differences in people's productive performance, the distribution of market rewards for deserts based on productive performance is unjust.

Imagine that someone who defends market rewards as deserved rewards for productive contribution, irrespective of effort, insisted that the differential salaries of doctors and nurses actually do reflect their differential deserts, because, even though nurses work as hard as doctors, their services have less value. This is the contention I suggest we have reason to deny. Circumstantial luck affects those alleged differential deserts in two ways. First, it affects the market rewards nurses reap, in that those rewards are a function of factors that are beyond the individuals' control, such as the actual supply and demand of nurses. And second, it affects in various ways which individuals will be nurses and which doctors, since an individual's career choice is constrained by factors, such as natural talents, which that person has little or no control over. Someone who may have wanted to become a doctor may be unable to do so because she is untalented or was unlucky in other ways, or both. As a result, even if her performance as a nurse may have less market value, her receiving lesser rewards than someone more talented and blessed by good luck who has become a doctor is unjust. We may legitimately say, in one sense, that doctors deserve the high rewards they get, where the judgment is one about doctors' deservingness alone. But the distribution of differential rewards that accompanies differential deserts affected by circumstantial luck is not a just one.

This does not mean that we should factor out that portion of the doctor's performance that is due to circumstantial luck, like we would do with integral luck. Rather, it means that, if desert is to justify a distribution of benefits and burdens across individuals, it must be desert acquired against a background in which circumstantial luck is minimized. Miller himself acknowledges that to the extent that luck is under human control, we have reason to reduce its scope.[33] He then shirks the implications of this suggestion by stating, "Desert is strengthened when opportunities to become deserving themselves depend on the initiative and choice of individuals, and are not artificially distributed by some other human agency."[34]

This seems to me an ambiguous ad hoc qualification, and one that seems to contradict Miller's observations, made elsewhere, regarding the moral irrelevance of the distinction between acts and omissions.[35] For if we are justified in reducing the scope of luck to the extent that doing so is under human control, then we have just as much reason to redress circumstantial luck that is due to the natural lottery, so long as we can do this, as we have to withhold from artificially distributing the opportunities to become deserving when doing so would introduce circumstantial luck.

So long as a distribution of differential market earnings is one that reflects people's differential deserts, where those differential deserts are acquired against a background of circumstantial luck, the contribution argument fails as an argument for the justice of the market. The contribution argument rests on an interpretation of desert that makes true the claim that market earnings reflect people's deserts at the expense of the justice-informing nature of desert. Desert as a principle of distributive justice is a notion of active desert that respects the fair opportunity requirement and should thus have application over a distribution of differential benefits and burdens across individuals. A principle of desert of that sort would require the elimination of precisely the sort of circumstantial luck which instead determines differentials in market earnings, and which the contribution argument tries unsuccessfully to argue is reconcilable with desert.

NOTES

1. See D. Miller, *Social Justice* (Oxford: Clarendon Press, 1976); D. Miller, *Market, State and Community: Theoretical Foundations of Market Socialism* (Oxford: Clarendon Press, 1989); and D. Miller, *Principles of Social Justice* (Cambridge, Mass.: Harvard University Press, 1999). Miller defends the relevance of ordinary attitudes for developing a theory of justice in "Distributive Justice: What the People Think," in *Principles*. For a critical discussion of Miller's stance on the relevance of ordinary attitudes for the formulation of a theory of justice, see Andrew Mason, "Desert and the Moral Force of Intuitions," in this volume. See also A. Swift et al., "Distributive Justice: Does It Matter What the People Think?" in *Social Justice and Political Change: Public Opinion in Capitalist and Post-Communist States*, ed. J. Kluegel et al. (New York: Aldine de Gruyter, 1995), 15–47.

2. Throughout, following Miller, by *luck* I mean any random event outside individuals' control. See Miller, *Principles*, ch. 7. On desert and luck, see also N. Richards, "Luck and Desert," *Mind* 95 (1986): 198–209; and J. Adler, "Luckless Desert is Different Desert," *Mind* 96 (1987): 247–249.

3. Miller, *Market, State and Community*, and *Principles*. A defense of the contribution argument is also offered by J. Riley, "Justice under Capitalism," in *Markets and Justice*, ed. J. W. Chapman and J. Roland Pennock (New York: New York University Press, 1989), 122–162.

4. Hence Jan Narveson does away altogether with the problem of luck by suggesting that anything that is chosen by the potential rewarders as a desert basis is an appropriate ground for desert. On this view, even luckiness can constitute a desert basis. See J. Narveson, "Deserving Profits," in *Profits and Morality*, ed. R. Cowan and M. J. Rizzo (Chicago: University of Chicago Press, 1995), 48–87. I do not examine Narveson's idiosyncratic view here.

5. See, for instance, F. Feldman, "Desert: Reconsideration of Some Received Wisdom," *Mind* 104 (1995): 63–77; and S. Smilansky, "Responsibility and Desert: Defending the Connection," *Mind* 105 (1996): 157–163.

6. J. Rawls, *A Theory of Justice* (Oxford: Oxford University Press, 1972), 104.

7. See, for instance, R. Nozick, *Anarchy, State and Utopia* (New York: Blackwell, 1974), 224.

8. An alternative way of dealing with the Rawlsian claim consists in accepting that the desert basis must itself be deserved, and then in trying to show that this points in the direction of effort-based desert as the only justifiable principle of desert. As later I take issue with the contention that desert bases must be deserved in turn, I do not here consider this, in my view unconvincing, line of argument.

9. A. Zaitchick, "On Deserving to Deserve," *Philosophy and Public Affairs* 6 (1977): 370–388, p. 372.

10. Zaitchick, "On Deserving."

11. S. Scheffler, "Responsibility, Reactive Attitudes, and Liberalism in Philosophy and Politics," *Philosophy and Public Affairs* 21 (1992): 299–323. For an analysis of the rationale behind Rawls's view of the different role desert can play in distributive and retributive justice, see S. Scheffler, "Justice and Desert in Liberal Theory," *California Law Review* 88 (2000): 965–990.

12. Zaitchick, "On Deserving."

13. G. Sher, *Desert* (Princeton, N.J.: Princeton University Press, 1989). According to Sher, Rawls's point is better stated as follows: "If one person does not deserve to have X while another does not [have X], and if having X enables the first person to (. . .) do Y while the second does not, then the first person does not deserve to have or do Y while the second does not" (26).

14. Sher's ambition is to defend the possibility of people having unequal deserts without violating the condition attributed to Rawls. In particular, Sher tries to show that it is not the case that natural endowments and effort-making ability belong with those characteristics that, being unequally distributed, must be deserved in order to ground claims of unequal deserts. I do not think that Sher's argument is successful, but I shall not develop this point here.

15. See Miller, *Principles*, 146, where Miller, in discussing the problem of luck, considers and rejects the possibility of factoring out that part of people's performance that is due to luck on the grounds that it would sabotage the whole notion of desert.

16. See Miller, *Market, State and Community*, 119.

17. For a criticism along these lines, see, however, Daniel Attas, "Markets and Desert," in this volume. The presence of contingency, or luck, is also relevant in questioning the presumed link between market prices and productive contribution, as Attas argues. For further discussion of the difficulties with identifying individual contribution, and with taking market prices as measures of deserved rewards for productive contribution, see also J. Feinberg, "Justice and Personal Desert," in *Doing and Deserving* (Princeton, N.J.: Princeton University Press, 1970); J. Dick, "How to Justify a Distribution of Earnings," *Philosophy and Public Affairs* (1975): 248–272; N. Hsieh, "Moral Desert, Fairness and Legitimate Expectations in the Market," *Journal of Political Philosophy* 8, no. 1 (2000): 91–114. For an argument to the effect that effort-based, as well as contribution-based, desert runs into feasibility problems, see A. Levine, "Rewarding Effort," *Journal of Political Philosophy* 7 (1999): 404–418.

18. Miller, *Market*, 166.

19. Miller, *Market*, 167.

20. For the suggestion that effort, too, is relevant for people's deserts alongside their achievements, see also Andrew Mason's "Meritocracy, Desert, and the Moral Force of Intuitions," in this volume. Note that, by making deserts depend solely on the outcome brought about by individuals, Miller seems to rule out the possibility that the contribution argument is an argument based on the contribution-mirrors-effort view of desert. On the contribution-mirrors-effort argument, see J. Riley, "Justice under Capitalism," in *Markets and Justice*, ed. J. W. Chapman and J. Roland Pennock (New York: New York University Press, 1989), 122–162; J. Lamont, "Problems for Effort-Based Distribution Principles," *Journal of Applied Philosophy* 12 (1995): 215–229; W. Sadurski, *Giving Desert Its Due: Social Justice and Legal Theory* (Dordrecht, Holland: D. Reidel, 1985), 134–135.

21. Miller, *Market, State and Community*, 166.

22. The analogy of the neighbor's gratitude and market rewards is in my view untenable anyway. It stretches credulity to believe that incomes are rewards for "gratitude universalised," as Miller, following Sidgwick, suggests. See Miller, *Social Justice*, 118; and H. Sidgwick, *The Methods of Ethics* 7th ed. (London: Macmillan, 1963), book III, ch. 5.

23. Notice that this justification of Joseph's rewards seems at odds with Miller's general contribution-based account, for it actually appears to rest either on a notion of compensatory desert or a notion of desert as the legitimate expectation to reap the results of one's earlier free choices, both of which interpretations of desert are discarded by Miller.

24. This example introduces the issue of comparisons between individuals' deserts, to which I return later. Here, I just want to underline that the market rewards the value one creates, for which certain skills are crucial. Why or how these skills have been acquired is utterly irrelevant, as far as the market is concerned. As a result, Miller's claim that one is properly rewarded for making the choice to acquire those skills is only going to justify some individuals' rewards and cannot be a general account of why market rewards reflect people's deserts.

25. Miller, *Principles*, 143–144.

26. Miller, *Principles*, 146.

27. Miller, *Principles*, 144. I am uncertain as to whether Miller thereby qualifies his earlier claim by conceding that cases of this sort may be cases of integral luck. If the appearance of another supplier of the good I have been selling occurs unexpectedly, I would seem to suffer bad integral luck, and the decreased rewards would not reflect my (not commensurately altered, in this case) deserts.

28. Note that, oddly, this distinction seems to be elided by Miller himself when he defends the idea that the best-qualified applicant for a job deserves it (*Principles*, ch. 8). There, he claims that the best-qualified candidate deserves the job because he deserves the opportunity to obtain the rewards that he would deserve if he performed at the level at which he can be expected to perform, given his qualifications. There are several problems with this claim that I cannot examine here. See, however, Mason's chapter in this volume.

29. In the first section.

30. There is also a third claim that this example collapses with the two claims I will illustrate. That is a claim to the effect that, since the situation is a competitive one, and since there are other potential prizewinners who are potentially just as deserving as the actual one, the assignment of the prize to one only fails to apportion the relevant benefit to different people's differential deserts. Imagine that A deserves 16 and B deserves 12 units of a given benefit. Imagine further that the benefit is scarce, and only 14 units of it are available. In order for the benefit to be distributed so as to be apportioned to A's and B's deserts, A would have to receive 8 units and B 6 units of the benefit. When the rewards people reap are in part a result of contingent factors, it is unlikely that those rewards will be apportioned to their respective deserts. I do not explore this further issue here, as I am primarily concerned with identifying the problem of the justifiability of differential deserts, rather than the problem of whether, assuming that differential deserts are justifiable, those deserts are met.

31. Since the good in question is the chemistry Nobel Prize, the relevant others are individuals who could compete with the individual for the Nobel Prize, to wit, other scientists. And since we are not concerned about a distribution of Nobel Prizes being just, the claim is a limited one, and we would not extend the same observation to include all wishful Nobel Prize winners who have never had an opportunity to go on to university to study chemistry.

32. Miller, *Principles*, 146.

33. Miller, *Principles*, 145. Miller states, "To the extent that the impact of luck is itself under human control, a decision to allow greater scope to luck will reduce desert." As should be apparent by now, I do not agree with the contention that circumstantial luck *reduces desert*. Rather, I would make the following two claims. First, to the extent that circumstantial luck is in the background, then the distribution of rewards matching people's deserts is unjust. And second, to the extent that we adopt a notion of desert that allows the impact of circumstantial luck to determine people's differential deserts, that notion is not a notion of desert that may lend itself to justify a distribution of burdens and benefits.

34. Miller, *Principles*, 145 (my emphasis).

35. See Miller, *Market, State and Community*, 33. See also D. Miller, "Constraints on Freedom," *Ethics* 92 (1981): 66–86, where Miller comments on some presumed positive obligations we have.

5

Markets and Desert

Daniel Attas

There is a persistent popular sentiment that market distributions, at their best, trace individual contributions. This sentiment has received some academic backing from marginalist economics in the early twentieth century. As a theory of distribution, however, this did not become very influential in economic circles. Criticism mounted against it was mainly based on the unrealistic assumptions of the theory, on the problem of market failures and imperfections, and on the insignificance of marginal contribution as a measure any of real value since it is no more than a sophisticated accounting tool. Nevertheless, at a philosophical level the question remains open. The idea that distribution in markets trace some morally relevant conception of contribution, and that a correlation between contribution and rewards is morally fitting, continues to rally some support.[1]

In line with his earlier work, David Miller articulates this idea in *Principles of Social Justice* and presents perhaps the most sophisticated argument to this effect.[2] There are two parts to Miller's argument. The first concerns the appropriateness of desert to economic justice. It can be summarized as follows: The appropriateness of a principle of distribution to an institution depends on the mode of relationship that characterizes that institution. The mode of relationship that is based on mutual advantage is instrumental association. The proper principle for this mode of relationship is rewards proportional to contribution. That is to say, a principle of desert. The mode of relationship that characterizes the economy is instrumental association. Therefore, the proper principle to govern distribution of income is a principle of desert. I shall begin by discussing the relation between desert and justice and I shall question the premise that desert is appropriate in the economic sphere.

The second part of Miller's argument concerns the relation between the market distribution and the principle of desert. It is claimed that markets (at their best) solve the problem of social value and distribute to the participating agents rewards that are proportional to their respective contributions. This is explained by appeal to the notion of marginal productivity and by the theory that perfect competition results in a distribution according to marginal contribution. Marginal product in this sense is taken to be a measure of the producer's contribution to the consumer's well-being, and so a proportionate reward is something he can be said to deserve. Therefore, nonintervention in the economy results in a distribution that is proper and fitting *to that sphere of social life*. This last qualification is significant since, according to Miller, intervention in the market is required not only to correct for imperfections, but also to cater for requirements of justice from other spheres of life, that is to say, spheres of which the mode of relationship is solidaristic community or citizenship rather than instrumental.

Two questions can be asked relating to this argument. First, does the market really track marginal contribution? Or, to what extent does it do so? There are several substantial and prevalent factors that cast serious doubt on the contention that the market distributes and rewards according to marginal contribution to any significant extent. This much is mostly acknowledged by Miller. I shall therefore set aside this question. Second, is reward according to marginal contribution morally relevant? Particularly, is marginal contribution a measure of contribution to well-being and therefore a morally relevant desert basis? I will argue that it is not.

DESERT AND ECONOMIC JUSTICE

Miller claims that we can best understand the demands of justice in each particular sphere, or area of application, according to the mode of relationship that characterizes that sphere. He identifies three basic modes: solidaristic community, instrumental association, and citizenship. These modes are taken, in a somewhat Hegelian fashion, to characterize three basic institutions in our society: the family, the economy (civil society), and the state. Individuals' attitude to one another within the family, and within any other institution characterized by a solidaristic community mode of relationship, is governed by a sentiment that can be labeled natural sympathy. This sentiment points to need as the proper principle of distribution within the family. We seem to care for other people within this mode, we identify with their pain, or deficiencies, and we are moved to satisfy their wants.

Within the state, the mode of relationship is one of citizenship. Individuals recognize each other as persons worthy of consideration and respect. As such they govern their dealings with each other as equals, and the distributive principle that follows is one of equal rights.

The mode of relationship that Miller calls instrumental association is embodied in the economy. People's attitude to one another is one of prudential reason. Desert, that is reward according to contribution, is the proper distributive principle to such spheres, and, in the economy, income is the fitting reward. Why is desert the proper distributive principle? Presumably because people enter the association for instrumental reasons; and the association is formed for instrumental reasons. If the association is a business enterprise, then, possibly, the purpose of such an organization is profit; and individuals should be paid according to their contribution to profit.

I want to question this characterization of the economy. Is there a parallel between the economic organization, the firm, as an instrumental association and the entire economy, or society, as a whole? Setting *wages* within a firm according to contribution to the organization may be in some sense justified. "The employee who deserves the biggest slice of the firm's profits is the one who has done most to raise its productive output."[3] It is a different issue if we are considering the question of setting *income*, including tax and transfers, according to contribution to society.

As Miller recognizes, contribution to society is not the same as economic contribution.[4] To illustrate the tension between the two, consider welfare services or other functions provided by government or NPOs (nonprofit organizations). A marketization of these functions, that is, running them on a purely profit basis, takes essentially "altruistic" purposes and manages them within an instrumental environment. The individuals—workers and directors—are then taken to participate for instrumental reasons, though their contributions in terms of the purpose of the organization (or society) is perfectionist and nonmonetary. Paying these individuals according to their contributions to profits is, to begin with, a wrong basis for desert; second, it creates incentives to expand profit, sometimes at the expense of the promotion of the perfectionist goal; and third, it tends to change the nature of the organization with the risk that its original purpose be depreciated, and even abandoned in favor of a different objective required by the new internal logic (profit). It is far from evident that as a matter of fact the purpose of the economy as a whole is the maximization of profit. And it is quite implausible that the maximization of profit *ought* to be its guiding principle. The trouble is that if you stick to economic instrumentality as a description of society, then you are left with a false measure of contribution: conduciveness to profit. If you accept, as Miller does, that contribution to society can take many forms, such as health, education, and so forth, then there is no reason to accept income as the proper reward. Moreover, if wages are set by the market, even in its most ideal form, they will be responsive to contribution to profit, not to any more plausible measure of contribution.

The idea that the economy is a form of instrumental association can be further challenged. Instrumental association is a voluntary mode of relationship and is characterized by mutual indifference. As Miller puts it, "people are under no obligation to engage [in these relationships] and can withdraw from them whenever they wish."[5] This again may be true at the particular firm-level, where customers, workers, and suppliers are free to enter an exchange relation or abstain from doing so. But it is not true of the economy as a whole. Individuals in a developed economy, characterized by a division of labor and production for exchange, have no reasonable choice but to sell whatever they have to sell and buy whatever they want or need. That is, they are not really free to abstain from such exchange relations that form the economy. Moreover, although they may be indifferent about the particular person they happen to transact with, they are not indifferent as to what kind of goods and services are produced and consumed (by other people) within their economy, for what purpose, at what price, and so forth. This is so even where there are no externalities. For example, many people object to trade in pornographic material, to buying from firms that produce their goods in countries that don't live up to a certain standard of respecting human rights or that rely on unfair trade and exploitation. It is also not uncommon for people to accept commerce and use of nuclear energy, or biotechnology, but strongly oppose selling such technology to anyone who is suspect to use it for military purposes. Neither voluntariness nor mutual indifference characterize the economy as a whole to such an extent that its mode of relationship can be viewed as an instrumental association.

Now, Miller also presents a positive argument for equality justice. According to this argument, there is a certain mode of relationship from which it follows that an equal distribution of resources provided within it is required as a matter of justice. He says:

> There are certain social groups whose members are entitled to equal treatment by virtue of membership. The claim to equality flows from the very fact of membership. . . .
>   The groups in question may be quite varied in character. At the lowest level you might think of a voluntary association such as a squash club. . . . At the other extreme stands membership in a political community. People who are full members are citizens, and as citizens they can justly claim equal treatment over a wide area—equal legal protection, equal voting rights, equal rights to the benefits of the welfare state and so forth.[6]

Membership (or citizenship) *as a mode of relationship* does not seem to be of the same type as instrumental association or solidaristic community. For membership does not exclude either one of the other two modes. Membership can subsist within an instrumental association—such as the squash club—or within a more solidaristic kind of association such as a nation-state. What purports to be a third mode of relationship turns out to be something that can encompass either one of the first two modes. If distributive principles are implied by the way people within an institution treat each other, then membership does not provide us with any one principle. We need to refer to the purpose of the institution or of the individuals who participate in it to find out what the proper distributive principle that governs this institution ought to be. Of course, we treat people differently when we treat them as members than when we treat them instrumentally or when we care for them. But "membership" is presented here as a basic attitude that follows from the internal logic of the institution and implies a distributive principle of the goods supplied within it. Instead, it turns out to be more directly the principle of equality that is in need of justification. Either we come together and collaborate for some self-interested purpose, or our purpose is in the association itself; "membership," to be sure, requires equal treatment, but this follows from neither of the two basic modes of relationship.

Furthermore, Miller maintains that membership does not dictate what goods will be provided through this institution, only that whatever goods are made available should be made so on the basis of equal treatment. Thus, the state must distribute political rights equally, and it may provide health care, education, or transportation, to any amount so long as these goods are provided equally.

> What matters from the perspective of citizenship is not that each person should enjoy some specifiable amount of "mobility" but that whatever transportation system is adopted should as far as possible treat people equally. . . .[7]
>
> Justice then demands equal treatment for everyone who is a member with respect to the advantages that membership provides.[8]

Now, if votes and transportation, and host of other goods, are provided by the state, why not income? Why is income not a benefit that ought to be distributed equally? If the group has the power to decide which benefits to distribute through membership, couldn't it decide to distribute income? Perhaps there is something about the benefit itself that excludes its distribution through this third mode of relationship. This might have to do with the way the benefit is produced and the object of those who engage in its production. Such a position will take us back to the Walzerian framework,[9] an approach Miller explicitly wants to move away from.[10] Furthermore, I can see no relevant difference between the production of means of public transport and the production of material goods more generally. If the former doesn't dictate a distribution according to desert, neither does the latter. The state, the political community of which we are members, "is the final authority responsible for regulating all other distributive practices."[11] This means that the state has the authority to decide which goods will be distributed through which channels. Indeed, the principle of citizenship is often taken to imply an equal say in the decision of which goods to produce collectively and on what basis to distribute them. This might further imply that the demands of membership, that is, equality, override the demands of need or desert made by other spheres.

There is a meaningful distinction between, on the one hand, the economy— all members of society as participants in economic activity—and, on the other hand, employees or service providers with whom we interact on a self-interested basis that can be viewed more or less in isolation from all other economic activity. The latter may embody an instrumental association mode of relationship and may be governed by a desert principle of distributive justice. The former is not so easily characterized in this manner. Society as a whole has more solidaristic streaks, and these are exhibited in the way it chooses to channel economic activity. The claims of membership may encompass any benefits, including income as a whole. In that case, although wages may require setting them according to contribution, income more generally is the proper sphere for equal distribution.

On the question of the relationship between justice and desert, Miller calls his position the Pluralist View. It is presented as an intermediate position between the view that desert is relevant and exhaustive of justice (the Positive View) and the view that desert is irrelevant to justice because meaningless, not morally obligatory, or although morally required not an obligation of justice (the Negative View).

> Desert is relevant to justice. In deciding what justice requires we should consider what different people deserve. But this is not the only, nor even necessarily the main, relevant consideration. It may conflict with other criteria, such as need, in which case we may have to balance the various criteria against one another in deciding what justice requires.[12]

So, for Miller desert is *always* relevant to justice although it is not the only relevant factor and it can sometimes be overridden by other justice considerations (e.g., need, equality). There is a different possible position on the relation between justice and desert, one that I endorse and that informs much of the discussion in this chapter. Not that desert is meaningless, or morally inappropriate, or not at all a requirement of justice. Such a position would be, I think, implausible. But that in certain contexts desert is inapplicable and therefore in this sense irrelevant. Thus, desert is sometimes but not always relevant to justice. Furthermore, the economic sphere is just such a context where desert is inapplicable.

Let me illustrate the difference among the several sources of irrelevance— meaninglessness, inappropriateness, and inapplicability. (1) A group of people go for a walk in the woods, when they stumble upon a pile of apples which someone has left behind, and they know that person has no intention to reclaim (say, he left a note saying that anyone who finds the apples can have them). Distribution according to desert in this case makes no sense at all. Recall, the kind of desert we are discussing is one based on a contribution principle. None of the group has made any contribution at all to the production of the apples; they simply found them. (2) We produce a drug collectively to cure some of us who have contracted a disease or may contract it in the future. In this case, distribution of the drug according to desert does make sense but is inappropriate. There is a meaningful way we can talk about our different contributions to the production of the drug, and there may be a claim based on justice that each of us ought to get an amount of the drug proportional to her or his contribution. But the reason for our cooperation in the first place and the understanding at its basis was that we were producing to meet an actual or potential need of some of us. Arguably, the drug should be distributed on the basis of need, and desert claims are simply inappropriate. (3) We engage in the production of some other good within the framework of instrumentalist relations. Each of us is in it for what we could get out of it. But then we suffer from amnesia—we have no idea who contributed what. Distribution according to desert is meaningful, plausibly appropriate, but inapplicable.

On Miller's account justice sanctions an equal distribution, *regardless of the particular mode of relationship*, on one of two conditions. First, manna-from-heaven cases, in which no one can advance a claim to any particular part of the benefit to be allocated. This is analogous to the preceding apples example. Second, in cases of uncertainty, particularly uncertainty with respect to contribution, corresponding to the amnesia example.

A principle of desert in the market, I shall argue, is similarly inapplicable. Although we do not suffer from amnesia, contribution in the market context is either unmeasurable or, where we do have a measure, that measure is morally irrelevant from a desert point of view. In other words, even granted that the economy is essentially a mode of relationship of mutual advantage, and that desert is a plausible principle of justice for such contexts, we have no idea how to begin assigning contributions to individuals. In what follows I claim that this is a valid description of the market economy. If I am correct about this, then we have here, on Miller's terms, a situation that calls for equality justice.[13]

THE ARGUMENT FOR MARKET DESERT

Implicit in the argument that markets trace desert—in the sense of reward proportional to contribution—is the following schema:

1. P produces x.
2. x enhances C's welfare.
3. P receives $V(x)$, the value of x.
4. $V(x)$ is a measure of C's increased welfare.

Therefore,

5. P receives a measure of P's contribution to the welfare of C.

Premise (1) implies that x—a physical object or service, or part whereof—is attributable to a particular person's (P's) labor or resources. Premise (2) claims that the consumer of x (C), who freely chose to consume x, derives some utility from this. This isn't a necessary truth: x can be genuinely harmful (e.g., addictive drugs). Nevertheless, it is assumed, quite uncontroversially, that typical market transactions involve increased welfare to both parties in the exchange, in particular to the consumer. Premise (3) states that x has a value and that P receives that value. Marginal Theory of Distribution gives the theoretical backing to this premise, assuring that P receives this value taken as the neoclassical notion of price at general equilibrium in perfect competition. Premise (4) claims that the value of x, which is the price of x at perfect competition, which is what P receives, is proportional to the increased welfare to the consumer C. The conclusion (5) is entailed from the premises in a straightforward manner.

Presenting the argument in this way shows quite clearly its most vulnerable moves. There are, as far as I can see, two main difficulties. The first, which I shall not discuss in length, is the soundness of premise (3), that is to say, whether distribution really traces contribution *as understood by this theory*. This is Offe's point that markets have only a small influence on the distribution of income; and, therefore, there is no basis to presume that remuneration traces marginal contribution.[14] The second difficulty, on which I shall focus, is the soundness of premise (4), that is to say, whether marginal contribution is a measure of the consumer's increased welfare, or whether indeed it has any moral relevance at all. This may be Hayek's point that although—believing as he does that—markets can, should, and do play a substantive role in the distribution of income, marginal contribution is morally irrelevant.[15] Miller presents the Hayekian and the egalitarian critiques—that the market doesn't trace value, and that real income distribution is not affected by market—as incompatible, or at least mutually exclusive.[16] But they can be made compatible in the way I suggested, as applying to the different premises. Both can be true, and the truth of one is sufficient to refute the argument.[17]

There are two principal reasons why we might think that distribution does not really trace contribution as understood by this theory: First, the theoretical idealizations and abstractions. These include the abstractions legitimately associated with any ideal theory, but also unrealistic assumptions about human behavior, and the inattention to market imperfections such as monopoly power. Second, the inapplicability of marginal theory to most of the economy. Services, and particularly state-provided services, are not amenable to marginal contribution theory; moreover, income and price are determined in effect more by political power and socially constructed expectations than by the impersonal forces of supply and demand.

These imperfections and deviations cannot be casually brushed aside. Real markets are not merely corrigible failures or approximations of an ideal model. They are radically and necessarily different. Even if the model can be useful in predicting certain outcomes, there is no basis to attribute the features of the model to the real world. Human behavior diverges from that assumed and predicted by the theory. "Failures" of economic rationality are not the disease, the perversion; they are, in many areas of our lives, the norm. Proponents of the Marginal Theory of Distribution cannot feel untroubled by this fact. A restriction of the theory to "perfect competitive markets" makes it entirely irrelevant to real issues of distributive justice.[18]

THE MORAL IRRELEVANCE OF
MARGINAL CONTRIBUTION

The second problem in the argument that markets trace desert pertains to the meaning attached to "contribution" in this context. Assume that markets are indeed the perfect mechanisms pictured by the theory, and that rewards really are a measure of the marginal contribution (*MC*) of the producer. In other words, let us accept premise (3) that P receives the value of *x* as *MC*. Questions may still be raised about the moral significance of this: Is this the kind of contribution that we want to reward through a principle of desert? Does it follow that the market affords each individual what he or she produced *in the morally relevant sense*? Do prices of commodities and labor, determined by supply and demand, adequately reflect individual contributions from a moral point of view?[19]

Now, premise (4) says that the value of *x* is a measure of C's welfare *(W)*.[20] This is a crucial assumption since without it the conclusion that P deserves his reward would not follow. For if it can be shown that *MC* is not even roughly equivalent to *W*, then the basis for the argument is removed. I shall argue that even in a perfectly competitive market that rewards each producer according to his or her *MC*, such a basis is irrelevant from a contribution-based desert theory perspective.[21]

Whatever it is that could make us think that *MC* and *W* are equivalent has probably to do with the notion of demand. Demand is a significant determinant of *MC*, and it is also quite a good indication of *W*. It might be assumed that, other things being equal, the higher the effective demand for a particular product or service the greater the welfare it engenders and also the greater the *MC* of the producer. There are several reasons why this observed correlation need not hold. I shall present them briefly and then proceed to discuss each of them separately. First, there is a sense in which there is no *x* that can be attributed to a producer P—therefore, any welfare that follows as a result of consuming *x* cannot serve a desert basis for P's reward. Second, demand, insofar as it is concerned with subjective desire or want, steers us clear from any notion of objective contribution to welfare. Yet, we do hold some standards of value that are not subject to market demand. Third, insofar as demand is dependent on willingness/ability to pay, then the outcome is influenced by the distribution of income. Yet, the welfare derived from a commodity or service is not straightforwardly affected by one's level of income. Fourth, the moral relevance of (economic) value is further diminished by the nonuniqueness of equilibrium price. Since income enters at both ends of the explanation, as a determining factor of price and wage, and as a result, it turns out that there is nothing morally immutable about the particular set of prices and the distribution of income it engenders.

THE MIRAGE OF PHYSICAL CONTRIBUTION

It seems fair that what I actually produced, caused to exist, should be mine or at least its value equivalent. But physical contribution as a measure of distributive justice is problematic: the problem is that of comparing different contributions.[22] Of course, if I make two chairs and you make four, then we may say with all plausibility that you deserve twice as much as I do. We assume, that is, that your four chairs have benefited other people twice as much as my two chairs have, that your contribution to welfare is twice as high as mine. Although plausible, this is not evidently true. If I buy four chairs so as to accommodate the occasional guests, this doesn't mean that the welfare I derive from them will be twice as high as I would have derived from the use of two chairs, even though I am willing to pay twice as much for them. Much less does this imply that I derive twice as much welfare as you do from your two chairs. But this is a relatively minor difficulty, the tricky issue is that of comparing different kinds of products; how can we compare one person's contribution in terms of chairs to another's contribution in terms of philosophy lectures? There needs to be a scale in terms of which we can assess both kinds of job. Here, marginal productivity comes in. It assigns a relative value to each kind of work and product. This it does, allegedly, in terms of the contribution one's work makes to the production process.

But how is this relevant at all to moral issues of distribution and contribution to welfare? Consider: Due to a sudden shortage, the tables I make become less replaceable, and therefore my marginal productivity is higher. The price of the table increases, and therefore I get more. But with the rise in price comes a decrease in demand, and therefore of production. In fact, it is possible that I produce less tables and therefore contribute less to welfare, but at higher prices my income will be higher. This example illustrates well the irrelevance of marginal productivity to welfare. But it is supposedly the welfare that morally grounds the deservingness of $MC(R)$.

The separation of MC from contribution to welfare becomes more acute in the cases of joint production. For here, taking MC as a measure of the separate contributions of each individual to a joint product, is even further removed from reality. MC is not determined by the quality and quantity of output, but in terms of the shortage/surplus of labor of this type. The value of an individual's contribution to the work process is not even determined by the supply and demand of *his* particular talents, but by the supply and demand of the skills required by the job. It is certainly not determined by *his* output.

Marginal contribution is affected by many factors, some of which have no bearing on the process of production. Values, essentially determined by supply and demand, can change with changes in tastes, preferences, availability of skills and commodities and with no change in the process of production. The following examples illustrate this point.

By manipulating the supply of labor, management in a particular firm can raise its own marginal contribution without an increase in production (even at the cost of a decrease in production). A Fordist policy imposing a fragmentation of the labor process to segments that reduce the need for training, skill, experience, or special talents reduces the price of labor by raising its supply. The workers continue to produce the same amount as before with no additional help from the managers, but their marginal contribution, their share of the product, has decreased.

An unintentional increase in supply caused by mass immigration or high rate of birth similarly lowers the marginal contribution of workers without the workers producing less (up to a point, even if they produce more). Conversely, in circumstances of diminishing population due to natural disaster or mass emigration, the supply of labor decreases and the marginal contribution of workers increases without the workers producing more (up to a point, even if they actually produce less).

Marginal contribution is not a measure of actual production. There is something very misleading in representing MC as a function of some x. For there is no x that can be attributed to the work of any particular individual in the work process, and a fortiori, no value of that x. The process is reversed: once MC is determined according to the relative scarcity of the skills required to produce a product, then a hypothetical construct, a physical x (as part of the product), is attributed to an individual producer P. But since MC is not determined by *any x*, assigning an x to the individual producer is a conceptual error, and the welfare derived from the mystical x is not a consequence of the production of x, but due to a false association.

TWO MEASURES OF VALUE

Effective demand is the result of two factors: desire or want, and purchasing power or willingness/ability to pay. One problem stems from the former factor, that is to say, from the dependence of demand on desire or wants rather than on needs or some notion of objective interests. Miller takes it that "the benefit that someone derives from a good or a service is measured by the amount she is willing to pay."[23] However, there is a gap between "utility," or contribution as revealed in the actual preferences of the consumers, and the contribution to their well-being as reckoned by some other standard of evaluation. Such a standard is rarely appealed to or articulated. Nevertheless, we do hold a notion of good quality. In some areas this is more formally articulated; in others, less so. But the fact that we have difficulties in formulating objective standards of quality does not mean that they are not there.

Health care is an example of a sphere in which we are less inhibited about invoking objective standards. We know, more or less, what constitutes good health care by the results. At a societal level, we can measure life expectancy, infant mortality, the frequency of diseases, and so forth. These results can signify a higher or lower level of well-being regardless of how much we have paid for them, or how much we are willing to pay for them. Social expenditure on health care in the United States (mostly through market) is high in comparison to expenditure in Europe (mostly government), but in terms of results, Europe is no less successful than the United States. It may follow that not only distributive issues may justify government provision of health care, but also the issue of efficiency. But the efficiency appealed to here is not the economic concept that is neutral about ends, but a notion that takes the ends and desired level of health care as given outside of consumer behavior and aims to minimize the costs.

Although less formalized, I think the same can be true of cultural products or entertainment: imposing these standards might be avoided because freedom may be considered of more importance than welfare or because there is a sense of uncertainty about these standards. People do have an idea of what constitutes good quality, and although they might shun from imposing their evaluations on all of society, nevertheless, it is a common and strongly held belief that the value of culture is independent from its market-determined price. Well-being has objective aspects, it is not merely a matter of tastes. According to Pace Miller, there is no need to invoke a "Marcuse-like theory" of social oppression.[24] In general, I believe, the more we are certain of the formal standard in an area, and the more we value its contribution to well-being in preference to freedom, the less we are likely to let markets decide on the price of the goods and services within that area. Thus, for the case of health care we are both more confident about what constitutes good quality, and we tend to give greater weight to issues of health relative to consumer freedom.

There are several reasons why using value as a determinant of welfare may deviate from economic value. These explain why MC is not equivalent to W and, therefore, not a proper basis for desert. I shall mention just three.

First, manipulative advertising and marketing techniques. By this I don't mean advertising that is straightforwardly deceptive—this would result in consumers believing and acting upon some false information on the quality or relative price of the advertised product and would therefore constitute a case of market failure due to fraudulent action on the part of advertisers. Rather, I am referring to advertising that does not necessarily alter the consumer's beliefs about a product but does affect his or her behavior: repetitive advertising, fear appeals, messages that associate the product with some generally desired state or feature (youth, popularity, sex appeal, power, adventure). The consumer who is exposed to such advertising does not come to believe that purchasing and using the particular brand of aftershave, for example, would really satisfy his sense of adventure or make him more appealing to prospective sexual partners. Yet, he is brought to act as if he believed in these special qualities and to pay a price he would not otherwise pay if he was treating the commodity as just that, stripped of its carefully tailored associative ensemble. Most advertising, particularly TV advertising, is manipulative in one of these senses. High-budget advertising rarely conveys any important commercial information. To the extent that advertising is effective—and I am assuming it is—then MC, which takes preferences as given, diverges from W.

Second, what may be called radical lack of information. This is not merely ignorance as to the quality and price of products and services available on the market; that would be another case of market failure. Rather, it is limited knowledge on the part of the consumer as to what she wants or needs, that is to say, about her very own preferences that economic theory simply takes as given. This problem is most acute in areas such as health care, where the patient–consumer is wholly dependent on the advice of the medical professional, but it equally applies in any professional setting. In the case of professions, we might want to rely on a moral sense and a professional ethic of loyalty to the client to well articulate the client's needs (notice that it is not the wants that the professional has to articulate). But a similar problem exists even beyond the professional setting. For example, in the purchase of commodities that embody complex advanced technology, such as in the purchase of personal computers, the consumer is rarely fully appreciative of the differences between available technologies and of the capabilities, nor is she fully conscious of how well these technologies satisfy her needs. Indeed, it is not unusual for the *seller* to be lacking this information. As a consequence, purchasers of computer hardware and software often buy and pay for capabilities they have no need for. It is not clear in what sense their payment reflects any contribution to their welfare.

Third, cases of weakness of will. There may be kinds of commodities or services consumed in opposition to the consumer's explicit higher-order desires. The availability, the ease, the fact that no effort is required to make this particular consumer decision makes the behavior a bad indication of contribution to welfare. For example: tobacco products may be consumed to the detriment of one's health; unsophisticated, low-involvement television programs may have the quasi-hypnotic effect on viewers, holding them captive for the length of the program.

It is important to stress that these possibilities are consistent with the idea of a perfect competitive market, that is to say, no force or fraud, no externalities, full information on availability and price of goods, rational behavior in terms of optimizing behavior when preferences are given. An ideal market such as this needn't assume that preferences are autonomous, authentic, or rational in some "thicker" sense. If the argument assumes not only an ideal market but also ideal circumstances, then it robs itself of any practical relevance it may still have.

STRATIFIED CONSUMER/PRODUCER MARKET

A further problem in taking price as an indication of welfare stems from the purchasing power factor of effective demand. Demand is dependent on the distribution of income, so that the price paid depends not only on expected welfare but also on one's ability to pay.

Unequal distribution of purchasing power skews the measure of contribution toward products and services consumed by the more powerful. It turns out that diamonds have greater value than bread although it is not at all evident that the welfare that the diamond consumer receives is proportionally greater than the welfare the consumer of bread receives. Thus, the income of those who produce goods and services mainly for the rich will tend to be higher than the income of those who produce for the poor *in proportion to the welfare they create;* MC of producers for the rich will be greater than W, and MC of producers for poor consumption will be lower than W. Not that production for the rich will be necessarily more profitable.

Miller partly accepts this argument and just points out two qualifications. The first is that the more egalitarian a society is, the less likely it is for there to be a stratified consumer market, and therefore, the less force the argument has. Second, the less consumption is stratified, the less relevant the argument becomes. Both these qualifications are surely valid. The question is, what is the force of these qualifications? Miller points out two features of contemporary society that, to his mind, are likely to reduce stratification: "a generally rising standard of living and growing cultural pluralism, which together mean that consumption becomes more homogenous across income groups and less homogenous across subcultures."[25] Now, growing cultural pluralism may indeed make consumption less homogenous across subcultures, but this needn't have any relevance to the issue of the stratification of consumer markets, and, to the extent that it does, it could only make it more acute. For, on the one hand, within each subculture consumption may remain as stratified as before; and on the other hand, if there is a correlation between ethnic background and income level, then the stratification due to income becomes compounded by the effect of culture. As to the generally rising standard of living, there is no reason to suppose that this will result in more homogenous consumption patterns unless this is accompanied by a rising level of equality. True enough, nowadays private cars are not a luxury and almost every family owns at least one car, but not everyone can afford a Rolls Royce or a Mercedes-Benz. And even where there is no gap in quality, marketing techniques split the market so as to receive from basically similar products different prices. One producer will position a commodity as a popular consumer product, another as an exclusive product for the affluent. As to Miller's first point that the more egalitarian a society is the less consumption is likely to be stratified, this is true. However, there are no significant indications that contemporary society is becoming more equal; moreover, there is no reason to suppose that distribution according to MC guided by the market will tend to a more equal distribution. Probably the contrary on both counts.

Marginal contribution is determined not only by how much C is willing to pay for x, but also by how much P is willing to receive for x. Thus, the income accruing to a particular kind of job will depend, as well as on the demand and relative scarcity of a job, also on the expectations of individual workers, on what they take to be a satisfactory level of remuneration. That in turn depends on the standard of living to which they are accustomed or to the reference group to which they compare themselves. How much P is willing to receive for x is not a market-determined factor; it is assumed by the market in a similar way that the preferences of consumers are taken as given. This explains, for example, why income from jobs that are gradually overtaken by workers who have recently emigrated from poorer countries decreases. New immigrants compete with local workforce for jobs for which they are willing to receive lower wages. These lower wages could not possibly reflect a lower level of welfare for the consumer of their products. Now, the job market is more generally stratified, so that there are jobs that go to people of low-income *background*, and jobs that go to people of high-income *background*. Since the latter's expectations will be higher than the former's, their income, that is, their *MC*, will be greater regardless of how much welfare they produce. The two groups are noncompeting: people from more affluent backgrounds will rarely be employed in low-status positions. Several factors sustain this kind of stratification: (1) the general orientation of members of the two groups, their self-esteem, the jobs they consider within their reach; (2) informal networks and the tendency of occupations to reproduce themselves in their own image—choosing persons "of the right type" to occupy these positions; (3) institutional constraints such as training costs and quotas. The wage disparity can then be explained by the different standard of living to which they are accustomed, as well as their differing expectations reinforced by custom, and ideological rationalizations of unequal pay—such as the scholastic notion of "to each according to his status"[26] or even marginal contribution theory of distribution. If this is indeed the case, then remuneration of high-paying jobs will be higher than that of low-paying jobs in proportion to the welfare they produce.

These arguments are consistent with the assumption of a perfect competitive market. Equality is not a necessary feature of this ideal construction; rather, *inequality* is a probable outcome of such a market. Introducing this highly idealized condition, as before, drains the argument of any practical validity.

THE ARBITRARINESS ARGUMENT

The last point I want to make has to do not so much with the equivalence of *MC* and *W*, but concerns the morality of value as *W* or as *MC* as a desert basis. That is to say, even if *MC* is a measure of *W*, we can question the justifiability

of remunerating on either basis. Hayek objects to the notion of "social value"—
that is, value from the point of view of society taken as a whole rather than from
the point of view of a particular individual. He claims that it is a fictitious construction. Due to the incommensurability of goods and services and to the impossibility of interpersonal comparisons of value, such a construction makes no
sense.[27] The problem may be put thus: why would there be any correlation between the *value* of a product taken as equilibrium price and the *individual* consumer *welfare* it engenders? Miller attempts to meet this objection: "Over fairly
large aggregates of people at least, the money they are willing to put up to acquire goods and services provides a reasonable estimate of the value of those
goods and services, and thus a reasonable estimate of the contribution of the
providers".[28]

Miller accepts that there is no "personified-social" value, just an aggregate
of individual value. The method of aggregation adopted is the market mechanism. But the market is just *one* of many possible methods of aggregation, one
of many social welfare functions: the argument of the function being the tastes
and preferences of individuals and their purchasing power; the outcome being
a set of prices. As such a function the market is defined by the weight it attaches to differential tastes *and purchasing power* in its method of aggregation. What justifies the market as *the* method of aggregation? Why is this social welfare function morally superior to any other? Specifically, why is a
political method for determining value—by which the preferences of different
persons carry equal weight and not a weight proportional to their purchasing
power—morally inferior? These questions are simply avoided in Miller's reply.

Allowing the differential purchasing power to determine the prices through
the market would, in effect, doubly reward the more advantaged. Their greater
purchasing power will favor them, first, in terms of how much they can acquire and consume, and consequently in terms of the higher level of *welfare*
they enjoy; and second, in terms of their greater *power* to determine the prices
of commodities, attaching greater weight to the utility *they* derive from different commodities in comparison to the utility derived by their poorer counterparts, and affecting which commodities will be produced at all.

The point is that the market is not merely a method for determining prices,
but also ipso facto, of determining what will be produced. So, even if at the
present production schedule, producers are remunerated according to their
contribution to welfare, we can still question the moral status of the production schedule itself. That is to say, even if we accept that producers deserve the
income they receive and the welfare they consequently enjoy, why does this
also justify the new set of prices and commodities this distribution of income
engenders?

The implication is far more serious than it may at first seem. Given the distribution of talents, the level of technology, and the distribution of tastes, there
is normally more than one possible equilibrium. The distribution of income
enters at both ends of the explanation of value: first, as a factor in the deter-

mination of prices; second, as the outcome of the market prices. This suggests that the distribution of income and the price vector at equilibrium are mutually sustaining. A disequilibrating shock to the system would not necessarily result in a fluctuating reversion to a unique stable point. There is, therefore, no unique value that the producer deserves. So, the value defined as (an) equilibrium price turns out to be completely arbitrary from a moral point of view.

CONCLUSION

In the argument that markets distribute according to contribution, and therefore that people generally deserve their market-determined shares, there are three implicit values. I—the income accruing to the producer; MC—the marginal contribution of the producer; W—the welfare derived by the consumer. The argument depends on an equivalence of the three measures. I have pointed out that I is not equivalent to MC and argued that MC is not equivalent (or proportional) to W.

MC is morally irrelevant as a basis for desert. For one, there is no x presupposed by MC and attributable to an individual producer. Since there is no such x, then there is no sense in which P is said to contribute to the welfare of the consumer of x. Furthermore, market-determined prices do not reflect some standards of value and contribution to welfare. The more significant or important a service or commodity is to our well-being, the less we would be inclined to let the market determine its magnitude. Also, since demand is dependent on willingness and ability to pay, prices and wages reflect a variance in purchasing power. It is implausible that ability to pay correlates with the differences in welfare derived from consumption. Last, even if MC is proportional to W, there is some doubt as to the justice of remuneration on this basis. For the distribution of income and the production schedule for a society are not unique, or in any sense morally privileged.

This is a different though related issue to the question of whether we would be willing to let the market govern production and distribution in society. There may be further reasons why we might think that marketizing a service or commodity is justified; these might be reasons based on efficiency or even on distributive justice. But it cannot be the case that such concerns of justice be grounded on the problematic notion of desert based on contribution. The moral strength of the market, even in its most ideal form, is not in its *equilibrium price*—for that is set not so much by the market as by social psychological factors (power, status, custom, ideology) affecting consumer and producer preferences—but in its *tendency to equilibrate*. The particular point to which it equilibrates needs justification outside of the impersonal workings of supply and demand. Furthermore, both the inapplicability of desert to the economic sphere and the conception of citizenship on Miller's account seem to call for an equal distribution of income.

NOTES

I would like to thank the editors of this volume, Daniel A. Bell and Avner de-Shalit, for their helpful comments. Research for this chapter has benefitted from the financial assistance of the Recanati Foundation.

1. The camp of philosophers who argue for such a conception do not all ride under the same banner. They range from hard-core libertarians to moderate egalitarians. (See, e.g., L. O. Kelso and M. J. Adler, *The Capitalist Manifesto* (New York: Random House, 1958), 55–67; D. Gauthier, *Morals by Agreement* (Oxford: Clarendon Press, 1986); M. G. Velasquez, "Ethics in the Marketplace," in *Business Ethics: Concepts and Cases* (Englewood Cliffs, N.J.: Prentice Hall, 1988), 179–191; R. Ehman, "Market Desert," *Public Affairs Quarterly* 10 (1996): 121–134.) Some are specifically concerned with justifying interest gains from capital (e.g., N. Scott Arnold, "Capitalists and the Ethics of Contribution," *Canadian Journal of Philosophy* 15 [1985]: 87–102), and some discussions of related issues of economic justice simply take it for granted that market-determined wages are a reasonable measure of contribution (e.g., S. White, "The Egalitarian Earnings Subsidy Scheme," *British Journal of Political Science* 29 [1999]: 613).

2. D. Miller, *Principles of Social Justice* (Cambridge, Mass.: Harvard University Press, 1999).

3. See Miller, *Principles*, 135. Though even here it is not clear from Miller's account whether rewards should be *equivalent* to contribution or *proportional* to it. (Compare with *Principles*, 28 and 29.)

4. See Miller, *Principles*, 29, 37–38, 185.

5. Miller, *Principles*, 30.

6. Miller, *Principles*, 236–237.

7. Miller, *Principles*, 237.

8. Miller, *Principles*, 238–239.

9. See Michael Walzer, *Spheres of Justice* (Oxford: Blackwell, 1983), 6–10.

10. Miller, *Principles*, 25.

11. Miller, *Principles*, 241.

12. Miller, *Principles*, 133.

13. Miller, *Principles*, 233–236.

14. C. Offe, *Industry and Inequality: The Achievement Principle in Work and Social Status* (London: Edward Arnold, 1976).

15. F. Hayek, *Law, Legislation and Liberty, ii: The Mirage of Social Justice* (London: Routledge and Kegan Paul, 1976).

16. Miller, *Principles*, 182.

17. Although in *Mirage of Social Justice* (73ff) Hayek's position is somewhat ambivalent, the point he actually makes in *The Constitution of Liberty* is that value, as the benefit conferred on the users of the product, is distinct from merit as the effort and pain suffered in the production. Markets do not and should not reward merit, only value. But this is substantively Miller's point and the issue seems to boil down to semantic inconsistencies. In *Mirage*, Hayek goes so far as to say that markets lay beyond the scope of social justice.

18. J. S. Mill calls attention to the fact that the distribution of income is "the result of two determining agencies: Competition and Custom." He criticizes English political economists for exaggerating the influence of the former and almost totally neglecting the influence of the latter. *Principles of Political Economy and Chapters on Socialism* (Oxford: Oxford University Press, 1994), 50–51.

19. Milton Friedman, *Capitalism and Freedom* (Chicago: Chicago University Press, 1962), 168, supports a distribution according to contribution to product, but offers an instrumental justification for such a practice.

20. Ignoring the problem of consumer surplus, Nien-he Hsieh, "Moral Desert, Fairness and Legitimate Expectations in the Market," *Journal of Political Philosophy* 8 (2000): 95–99, argues that consumer surplus makes contribution to welfare diverge from reward for all but the con-

sumer consuming the last unit of a particular good. For reasons I cannot expound on here, I think the problem is real but practically insignificant.

21. This is a different point from those raised by Andrew Mason and by Serena Olsaretti. Both authors criticize the proposition that market rewards reflect desert-based justice. Mason ("Meritocracy, Desert, and the Moral Force of Intuitions," this volume) claims that desert essentially depends also on effort and not only on contribution. Since market rewards completely ignore effort, the market distribution is unjust. Olsaretti ("Desert and Luck," this volume) argues that desert (even contribution-based desert) is just only against a background of minimized circumstantial luck. Since rewards in a market are contaminated by humanly controllable circumstantial luck, they are unjust.

22. Daniel Hausman, "Are Markets Morally Free Zones?" *Philosophy and Public Affairs*, 18 (1989) 323–24, points out that the producer P is not wholly responsible for the value of x, since that value is mostly determined by factors beyond the producer's control, to wit, the impersonal forces of supply and demand. This is, of course, true. But Miller need not deny this, for his notion of desert does not require responsibility "all the way down." P is assumed to be responsible for the production of x and produced it within a social-economic context expecting to be remunerated in proportion to the value (MC) of the product.

23. Miller, *Principles*, 184ff.

24. Miller, *Principles*, 184–185.

25. Miller, *Principles*, 188.

26. Michael Fogarty, *The Just Wage* (London: Chapman, 1961), 267–273.

27. Hayek, *Law, Legislation and Liberty* (Chicago: University of Chicago Press, 1982), 75–78.

28. Miller, *Principles*, 186.

II

NATIONAL JUSTICE

6

Social Justice and the Nation-State
A Modest Attack

Chandran Kukathas

MILLER'S THINKING

Social justice, David Miller tells us, must always be a critical idea, one that challenges us to reform our institutions and practices in the name of greater fairness. These words from the preface (and the dustjacket) of *Principles of Social Justice* pick out the concerns that dominate not only his latest work, but also his thinking of the past three decades. A good political community is one that tries to discover and implement the principles of social justice that all can share. David Miller's approach to the defense of these ideas has been dispassionate rather than shrill, his style sober rather than excited. There are no unkind remarks about recalcitrant opponents (such as the present writer),[1] or denunciations of the excesses of uncongenial ideologies—capitalism, libertarianism, Thatcherism, to mention just three of the usual culprits. There have been no fireworks—only the relentless march of a growing body of argument, defending a position carefully crafted and not easily cracked.

Yet, it would be a mistake to think that the absence of pyrotechnics is the result of Miller having chosen the easy path, or the road well traveled, to defend what is commonplace or uncontroversial. Far from it. For in developing his view of social justice, he has not lost sight of the fact that there are other political values that are important competitors for a limited amount of moral space, and that it is not enough simply to defend one value without explaining what is to happen to other concerns which might have no less powerful a claim on our support. To be specific, the claims of justice can run up against claims of community and, more particularly, national community.

The position Miller takes is a very hardheaded one: social justice is to be pursued within the confines of the nation-state. These entities called *nation-states* have a special standing, he argues, "because where a state is constituted in such a way that its citizens share a common national identity, the resulting political community has three features that make the application of principles of social justice feasible and fruitful."[2] First, because national identities tend to create strong bonds of solidarity, the community thus formed "becomes a natural reference group when people ask themselves whether the share of resources they are getting is fair or not."[3] Second, national political cultures include a range of shared understandings that is essential for principles of social justice. And third, nation-states can help provide an assurance to each that others will show a similar restraint in following fair principles and procedures of social justice. Indeed, Miller argues, the absence of these features "at world level" means that global justice cannot (yet) be understood on the model of social justice.[4] Thus, thinking about global inequalities, for example, should be guided not by comparative principles such as the principle of equality, but by the noncomparative ideas of protecting basic rights and preventing exploitation.[5] Global justice involves an obligation to respect basic human rights, an obligation to refrain from exploitation, and an obligation to "provide all political communities with the opportunity to achieve self-determination and social justice."[6]

It is worth asking what lies behind this stance and, in particular, what values motivate Miller's arguments for the national pursuit of social justice and the international search for a just world of nations, each capable of securing social justice within its boundaries. There are several commitments that appear to be centrally important. First, there is a strong sense of the importance of community: a good society, for Miller, is one in which people engage together in pursuing collective ends—even though such a society must also be one which gives some weight to individual freedom to pursue separate, or personal, goals. Second, the political community is accorded a special weight, for a good society is to some degree one in which people relate to one another as citizens who engage in determining their common future together. Third, justice is a very important consideration, for a good society cannot be one that is indifferent to the distributive outcomes its institutional arrangements foster. And finally, what might best be described as straightforwardly humanitarian concerns run through Miller's thinking: that poverty and suffering are evils, and that the purpose of social institutions is in part to address these evils.

Miller's thinking is an effort to address these humanitarian concerns within a realistic moral framework. And that means not moving unguardedly from convictions about the importance of social justice and the alleviation of suffering to a doctrine of global social justice. It means taking a modest course, albeit a course that is no less controversial than any of its alternatives.

A SKEPTIC'S RESPONSE

How defensible is this position, combining a modest nationalism and social justice? If the issue were the coherence of the view in question, the matter would easily be resolved in Miller's favor. A commitment to social justice and to a principle of nationality is entirely consistent. Nonetheless, this position is open to challenge on at least three counts. First, in spite of Miller's attempts to find ways of addressing problems of global justice, the commitment to nationality may turn out to run counter to important humanitarian concerns—not simply because it is inegalitarian but because the protection of nationality requires the closing of borders (not literally, perhaps, but at least to the extent that the movement of people is seriously impeded). Second, the argument for the national pursuit of social justice may rest on unwarranted assumptions about the workings of the state and about politics. Third, Miller's own arguments about the difficulty of pursuing social justice at the global level point to similar problems pursuing it at the national level. In the remainder of this chapter, I want to present these three challenges. My intention, however, is not to suggest that Miller is mistaken in rejecting the idea of pursuing global justice or global equality, but rather to argue that we need to be wary of national enterprises, particularly when they come with moral notions like justice attached.

INTERNATIONAL JUSTICE AND NATIONAL BOUNDARIES

A serious problem confronts anyone hoping that some of the worst problems of human suffering will be addressed by states. This is that states, by and large, will look first to their own interests and not only decline to help alleviate suffering but obstruct the efforts of others trying to aid the disadvantaged in an attempt to protect their own national interests. Nowhere is this more clear than in the international arena.

That the great majority of people in the world are very poorly off is a commonplace. As David Miller points out, tables of world development indicators such as those issued by the World Bank show the gulf between countries like Tanzania, with a per capita GNP of about $140 per annum, and Germany, with a per capita GNP of $25,000.[7] How should we think about this issue, and what should we do? In Miller's view, our thinking should be governed, first, by a recognition of basic rights. For one thing, "My recognition of others as human beings like myself implies that I have a duty to safeguard them against conditions which would unavoidably blight their lives"; and while I am not obliged to help an unknown person X build a temple in which to worship, "I am bound to refrain from disabling X or to feed X when he is starving, because I must recognize disablement and starvation as conditions that impair any human life I can conceive of."[8] Responsibility for ensuring that such rights are properly distributed, however, in Miller's view, falls first upon the particular political community within which the rights need to be upheld. In cases where the political community is unwilling or unable to do this, the obligations of outsiders are limited. In cases where the political community is dominated by elites oppressing or impoverishing the people, outsiders have some obligation not to collude with the rulers by, for example, offering safe haven for stolen wealth. Outsiders might also make economic cooperation conditional on policy change. But direct intervention is ruled out as not only infeasible but also wrong to the extent that it takes responsibility for righting injustice away from the people themselves.[9] On top of this, international arrangements ought perhaps to be reconfigured so that a greater share of wealth goes to poorer countries, and development aid ought to be given to build up the resource bases of the less developed societies.[10]

The second thing that should govern our thinking about global injustice, according to Miller, is the need to avoid, and eliminate, exploitation. There are three ways to address the problem of exploitation. The first, which Miller rejects, is to sever all economic relationships between rich and poor countries. This solution would do the poor no good, since poor countries may still be gainers from exploitative relationships, and the badly off may be better served by having an exploitative paymaster than by having no paymaster at all. "The only escape route from absolute poverty is to gain access to the capital and consumption goods held by the rich countries."[11] The second option is to require massive resource transfers from rich to poor countries. This, however, is not only politically unfeasible but, in Miller's view, would not guarantee an end to exploitative trade and investment on the part of rich countries. The third option, therefore, is the best bet: to create an international regime that constrains the actions of potential exploiters—say, by breaking up trading monopolies and dismantling tariff barriers.[12]

While Miller is right in his assessment of the feasibility of the different alternatives, however, what he does not take sufficient note of is the extent to which the obstacle to the alleviation of human misery is the nation-state itself. To see this, we should begin by considering the fact that some of the most serious problems confronting the modern world are not problems of poverty per se but problems of human displacement. According to various United Nations organizations and international human rights groups, there are more than 40 million displaced people in the world. These people live in appalling conditions with little security, having been forced to leave their homes because of civil or international war, political conflict, "ethnic cleansing," human rights violations, natural disasters, or economic development projects.[13] The problem for a large proportion of these people (possibly half or more of the numbers in question) is that, as refugees fleeing war or persecution, they are unable to have their "basic rights" addressed by their own political communities, either because those communities are in political disarray or because they are themselves the victims of the regimes in power, from which they are now trying to escape. The obvious question to ask is: what should be done to help these people?

One equally obvious answer is that these people should be resettled (if they so wish) in countries wealthy and stable enough to accommodate them—at least until they are able to return safely to their homes, but if necessary, permanently. In fact, the UN Convention Relating to the Status of Refugees adopted in 1951 requires that its signatory states (now numbering over 120) do precisely that: resettle within their borders those fleeing persecution. A brief look at the history, and the contemporary politics, of refugee resettlement, however, reveals that what states will agree to in principle is a long way from what they will do in fact. Many countries, like Australia, while willing to fulfill their obligations when they are inescapable, devote a considerable amount of their resources to efforts to discourage refugees from coming to seek asylum. In Australia, those arriving by boat are detained in camps in remote desert locations while their cases are assessed.[14] In Britain the number of asylum-seeking arrivals has prompted demands, and political promises, for tougher or less hospitable treatment for persons. And within the European Union, refugees are regarded by governments as unwanted persons who are to be passed on to other states when possible, even as border controls are tightened and policies to deter people from seeking asylum are put in place. In general, states are reluctant to cooperate when asylum and permanent resettlement are at issue, though their efforts are more readily coordinated when restrictive measures are to be devised to reduce the influx of the desperate and destitute.

Much of this is, perhaps, not particularly surprising. Governments of rich nations confronting problems of unemployment and social unrest coupled with fiscal pressures are unlikely to want to increase their own burdens—even if it is true that the financial problems posed even by 40 million displaced persons don't amount to a hill of beans when set beside the combined wealth of the handful of countries that make up North America, Australasia, and Western Europe. But it is revealing nonetheless. The nation-state is not, if it can help it, going to be hospitable even to the worst-off if they reside outside its borders; and for large numbers of people this simply means that their sufferings have no prospect of being alleviated.

The problem here, in part, is that governments are political actors who are wary of doing anything that might be expensive or electorally unpopular. And measures like admitting refugees may be both expensive and unpopular.[15] But the deeper problem is that the nature of the state makes it unlikely that such matters as human displacement will be addressed if solutions run against the interests of the state. And there is no doubt that solutions involving admitting people within borders do so run. They require not only a sharing of wealth and opportunities but also embracing elements that threaten to water down, if not undermine, the solidarity that states are eager to foster—not least in the interests of preserving their legitimacy.

Here, some important values come into conflict. In particular, the value of political community and national social solidarity come up against the claims of humanity. To defend the interests of the nation-state as an ethical institution is to concede that great human suffering—leave aside inequality—has to be accepted.

It is worth noting that this is before one has even begun to consider the cases of people who are not fleeing war or persecution—whether by the Taliban or by Saddam Hussein—but are fleeing poverty and looking to improve their lot in life and would, if permitted, emigrate to wealthier nations to improve their circumstances. A Tanzanian eking out a living on $140 per annum, but unmolested, has no case he can make before any national or international tribunal to allow him to try to improve his lot elsewhere. To my mind, these things weaken severely the case for placing such importance on the nation-state as a value. The idea that the state as a political community becomes a "natural reference group," within which people can ask themselves whether or not the share of resources they are getting is fair, does not seem like a compelling reason to offer our Tanzanian, who wants to join in and take a share himself, for excluding him from this opportunity.

But the nation-state, unfortunately, does not stop at excluding would-be immigrants. Not only is our Tanzanian likely to be turned around at the border, but many of his goods are as well, so that even if he tries to improve his lot by selling his wares to wealthy Europeans, his path may be blocked by protective trade barriers—protecting some of those within. Miller has quite rightly pointed out that one of the most important ways of helping those in poorer countries is to develop a regime of free trade. Yet, the most important obstacles to this are states, few of whom have clean hands on this issue. Indeed, the problem may be that the greater the extent of national solidarity, the less likely are states likely to accept free trade, for they will look even more firmly then to their own interests. France is not going to reverse its strong protectionist policies, enforced within its own borders and promoted successfully within the EU, because the interests of the Third World might hang in the balance.

Now Miller might argue at this point that all I have done here is point out a fact about realpolitik: that our Tanzanian cannot make a case to improve his lot elsewhere before any national or international tribunal. But he could surely make a case according to Miller's principles of global justice. These principles place us under an obligation to provide all communities with the opportunity to achieve self-determination and social justice. This implies that there is a case to answer if this principle is not honored: our Tanzanian does have a case he can present drawing on Miller's theory. The problem with this, however, is that it offers an answer that does not answer the Tanzanian's immediate concerns: it denies him the opportunity to help himself. Moreover, by maintaining that the preeminent value is protecting the integrity of the national community, Miller's principles entrench the interests of those existing communities that are well-to-do in preserving their advantages. According to

Miller's theory, the French to whom the Tanzanian complains that restraint of trade is harming his prospects can rightly reply: but this is merely the consequence of our doing what we need to do to preserve our nation.

The problem, in the end, is that the two goals Miller advocates—building up nations as sites of solidarity and social justice and reshaping international institutions so that a greater share of wealth goes to the poorer peoples of the world—go against each other. If the lot of the international poor improves in these circumstances, it will not be because of the state but in spite of it. If the nation-state is to be defended as an important moral construct, it ought to be conceded that the implications from a humanitarian point of view are very troubling. This is not to deny that there are cases in which nationality and humanitarian considerations are quite compatible. There are undoubtedly cases of nations with a strong sense of national solidarity, and yet also traditions of humanitarianism. The problem arises at the margin. It is when the transfer of wealth through the reshaping of international institutions starts to impinge seriously on (or even threaten) the economic interests of people in wealthy countries that wealthy countries will begin to wobble in their commitment to reform.

This difficulty is perhaps well illustrated by the tortuous process through which a regime of free world trade has had to be pursued. The Uruguay Round of the General Agreement on Tariffs and Trade (GATT) negotiations took eight years, at the end of which was formed a World Trade Organization which has struggled to obtain generalized support. Those who argue for free trade tout its long-term benefits and have generally been able to persuade policy-making elites of different nations to agree. But one consequence of this that they have not been able to conceal is that such agreements reduce the sovereign powers of national governments. All international agreements, to varying degrees, tie the hands of sovereign states and limit their capacity to act as they would wish in matters of domestic policy. Unsurprisingly, many domestic interests (notably agricultural ones) in Western countries campaign vigorously against such agreements because they recognize that they mean a decline of sovereign authority—and a decline in their capacity to pursue their sectional interests. Globalization undermines rather than supports national solidarity. National solidarity is necessary to resist globalization.

The idea that the humanitarian problem might be better addressed through wealth transfers in the form of development aid is not compelling because it is unlikely to address the humanitarian problem. There are several reasons for this. First, it is very much a second-best solution, since the volume of wealth transferred is going to be small; and the impact of development programs, while not negligible, is not great in view of the magnitude of the problems of poverty and displacement. Aid budgets are never going to be large, in part because wealthy democracies with their own problems of poverty will struggle (electorally) to justify spending money abroad that could just as well be used for charity at home. And the budgets of international humanitarian agencies are stretched. In the UN High Commissioner for Refugee office in Pakistan the waiting time for a refugee to have his or her claim for asylum addressed is 122 weeks, as the camps overflow with people.[16]

Second, much of the money and resources made available as aid does not reach its intended beneficiaries, since aid from state to state enters not the pockets of the poor but the coffers of governments, which distribute it under pressure from various political interests. This may not always bespeak high levels of political corruption—although this is certainly rampant in many parts of the world—but simply reflects the nature of politics.[17]

Third, given that in so much of the world human misery is the product of tyrannical and exploitative governments, the combination of foreign aid and borders closed to migrants and refugees serves to sustain bad regimes. Their citizens can neither emigrate nor flee and, so, find it difficult to undermine the regime or to challenge it. The poor are thus often kept at the mercy of their dictators and exploiters. At the same time, foreign aid might simply boost such a regime's own strength.[18] In these circumstances, the emphasis on the sanctity of state boundaries seems not just to ignore social justice but to contribute to its suppression.

THE POLITICS OF SOCIAL JUSTICE

It is not only in the international arena, however, that the state pursues its own interests. The state's primary interest is in its own survival, which it cannot ensure without protecting its legitimacy—although in extreme cases, such as that of Iraq under Saddam Hussein, the use of force and terror may also play a significant role in suppressing dissent and crushing any incipient challenge to the ruling regime. If the nation-state is a political association with interests of its own to protect, we have to be wary of making it the means through which social justice is reached.

The picture David Miller presents of the nation-state is one of an entity made up of citizens sharing a common identity. Here we find, he contends, a community in which national identity has created strong bonds of solidarity and the national culture has developed a range of shared understandings essential for social justice. Within, and through, such an entity, people can acquire a measure of confidence that if they abide by certain fair principles and procedures (of social justice) others will, too.

This picture, I think, needs to be challenged on a number of counts. The first question that ought to be raised is the question of the need for social solidarity at the level of the nation-state for the pursuit of social justice. At one level, Miller seems clearly on the right track insofar as his point is that some kind of shared understanding is needed if people are to cooperate. The more extensive this cooperation, and the more there is at stake, the deeper the level of mutual understanding or ethical agreement necessary. At the same time, however, it is not clear that this agreement has to be bounded—or shaped—by the nation-state. Many kinds of communities and associations operate or are sustained across state boundaries, and contractual arrangements of all kind are made by people coming to the bargaining table from different parts of the globe. When I buy a book through Amazon.com, or join the American Political Science Association, or live my life guided by the authoritative pronouncements of the Pope on matters of personal morality, my behavior is governed less by what my compatriots think than by the understandings shared with strangers abroad. When distributive matters are at stake, there is no reason why communities formed by religious commitment, for example, rather than by territoriality, cannot have as deep a shared understanding—one which might act as the basis of distributive arrangements accepted within the group.

Equally, it seems implausible to think there is something natural or obvious about the nation-state as the community within which questions of distribution must be addressed. Miller describes it as a "natural reference group" when people ask themselves whether they are getting a fair share of resources. But states are anything but natural entities: they are political entities, often created by war, conquest, or the arbitrary judgments of colonial powers. The world is teeming with people (and peoples) who resent having been placed on the wrong side of imaginary lines, subjugating them to one ruler or another. Miller himself recognizes this in his discussion of "nested nationalities."[19] Equally, it is surely remarkable that this thing that is the site of social justice can be so variable in geographical size, population, and wealth. Australia, with a population of 19 million, a land area of 7.7 square kilometers, and a GDP of $410 billion, is as much of a state as Qatar, with a population of 0.7 million, a land area of 11,747 square kilometers, and a GDP of $8.3 billion, and India, with a population of 980 million, a land area of 3.3 million square kilometers, and a GDP of $444 billion. India could just as easily be a dozen nation-states, as indeed could Australia. That either is a single nation-state is less because either forms a natural reference group for its inhabitants but because those political interests seeking to create a larger union were successful. (In the Australian case, New Zealand's refusal to become a part of the federation was accepted without demur, while in the Indian case, Pakistan broke away after a violent and bloody conflict.)

The point of all this is not to argue for the elimination of the state (or to predict its imminent demise) but simply to show that it is not a natural reference group and to suggest that it is a mistake to think either that people caught within it share special obligations to one another by virtue of membership. To be sure, in many countries people do have attachments and feel loyalties to their nations, and this cannot be discounted altogether. But equally, it should be recognized that this is in good measure a manufactured sentiment, encouraged and fostered by states themselves. And in many states large numbers of people are considered members of states to which they feel no attachment even in spite of decades (of centuries) of governmental efforts to assimilate them.

The peoples of West Irian do not regard themselves as a part of Indonesia; the people of Bougainville do not regard themselves as a part of Papua New Guinea; and many Kashmiris do not see themselves as belonging to India.[20] In many, many countries it is hard to see how all of the groups of people that comprise them could form a whole with shared understandings that might act as the basis of institutions of social justice.

Moreover, it is important to recognize that the pursuit of national integrity, at its extreme, can have terrible consequences. On occasion it leads to conflicts of the sort that have disfigured the history of the Balkans, where what Noel Malcolm has described as "bogus theories of racial-ethnic identity" have dominated national politics.[21] Where local sentiments of belonging or community are strong, they are also attractive to political elites looking to mobilize support for their own particular interests.

Even if we discount the problem of accounting for the state as a community of people who share a common identity, however, there remains the problem of viewing the state as the site of social justice. Assuming that there is general agreement about what social justice requires, there seems to be little reason to think that states are going to be especially good at promoting it. One reason for skepticism is that there are many regimes in the world that are simply repressive: North Korea, Libya, Cuba, Zimbabwe, Haiti, and Belarus, to name just a handful. But even if we focus only on the stable liberal democracies, it is hard not to be struck by the great disparities in wealth and life chances. Some of the disparity in wealth can undoubtedly be accounted for simply by the fact that the scope for inequality is much greater in rich societies than in poor ones since the range of levels of income and wealth extends higher. (It is hard to be a billionaire in Belize, which has a GDP of only $650 million, though it is possible to be destitute both in Belize and in America.) Nonetheless, the differences in wealth in rich liberal democracies like Britain and the United States are considerable in spite of extensive government activity. In Britain, government expenditures equalled 40.1 percent of GDP ($1.2 trillion) in 1998, and in the United States, government expenditures that year equalled 30.5 percent of GDP ($8.5 trillion).[22] Accounting for the differences in wealth is a complex matter, and I do not propose to rush to any particular conclusions in these cases. But the persistence of poverty and of great inequalities in the face of significant government expenditure and the great resources available to the state raises a serious question about the capacity (or interest) of the state in pursuing social justice.

One general explanation of this phenomenon is intimated in the writings of Rousseau in his essay on "The Origins of Inequality." For Rousseau, society and law, by their nature, served the interests of the rich. Indeed, it was the rich who first hit upon the idea of establishing institutions to protect their property. Having realized that physical strength alone was not going give them the security they desired against the claims of the masses, they saw the solution to their problem in the turning of all claims of property into matters of right.

"Let us join," said [they], "to guard the weak from oppression, to restraint the ambitious, and secure to every man the possession of what belongs to him: let us institute rules of justice and peace, to which all without exception may be obliged to conform; rules that may in some measure make amends for the caprices of fortune, by subjecting equally the powerful and the weak to the observance of reciprocal obligations. Let us, in a word, instead of turning our forces against ourselves, collect them in a supreme power which may govern us by wise laws, protect and defend all the members of the association, repulse their common enemies, and maintain eternal harmony among us."

Such, suggested Rousseau, may have been the origin of society and law, "which bound new fetters on the poor, and gave new powers to the rich; . . . converted clever usurpation into unalterable right."[23]

What is implausible about Rousseau's analysis is the implication (intended or otherwise) that there could be a society without law or property—or that human beings could live other than in society. But what is powerful and compelling about the analysis is the observation that those who have most to gain by the establishment of power—collecting society's capacity to exercise force—are the rich; and that the rich are unlikely to put up with laws that do not protect their interests first. In the global scheme of things, rich nations are unlikely to agree to arrangements that do not bring them advantages. In the realm of the nation-state, the rich will support—and use their wealth to promote—laws and state powers, which ensure the security of their own interests.

No doubt, this analysis could be made considerably more sophisticated, since the exercise of power is often more subtle than this, particularly in liberal democracies. Yet, Rousseau's analysis retains its importance for two insights: first, that the well off will seek to protect their advantages by controlling the power of defining right; and second, that the masses will be manipulated until they come to believe that their chains will secure their liberty.[24] In the modern state the well off protect themselves by trying to define rights so that others cannot enter markets and compete for a share of the rents to be gained.

The modern state, in this regard, is not readily recognizable as the site of collective deliberation to settle and address questions of social justice. It is the site of political competition, in which every important political player claims to be a champion of the poor. Now, in the end, we may not be able to do much better than this. But we ought not be seduced by the hope that nation-states will serve us well because they make the achievement of social justice possible.

TRADITIONS OF SOCIAL JUSTICE

One of the most important elements in Miller's theory of social justice is his contention that principles of justice "are always, as a matter of psychological fact, applied within bounded communities." The integrating power of national identity, he thus argues, enables us to "make the national community our primary universe of distribution."[25] We might sometimes be able to make judgments of justice, he observes, by approaching issues in smaller communities, such as workplaces, where our sense of justice can effectively be engaged. But it would be difficult to do this in units larger than nation-states. "A Spaniard who feels that he is being underpaid may be comparing himself with other Spaniards generally, or with other workers in his factory or village, but he will not be comparing himself with Germans or Americans, say."[26]

This is an important argument, which sits neatly with Miller's critique of principles of global equality. Here, Miller's argument is that the difficulty with pursuing equality at the global level is that it runs up against the problem of value. Questions of value can only be settled by examining the range of background conditions that give resources their worth. Uranium in the ground is of no value to a society that does not know how to exploit its particular properties; and good wine-growing soil is of no use to inhabitants whose religion prohibits the production, sale, or consumption of alcohol. If, for any reason, these resources remain unexploited, their value remains indeterminate, for we cannot say what they are worth until they are developed sufficiently for their market value to be assessed.[27] So, distributive principles seeking to determine how such resources should be divided up across different communities will struggle even to establish the values that have to be distributed. This problem, Miller also shows, becomes even more difficult once we recognize that different communities may have quite different views and practices with respect to the resources they control. Every community will make different trade-offs when determining how much to consume, how to value or care for the environment, or what population numbers to sustain. It would be difficult, if not entirely unreasonable, for one community to demand a share of another's resources on the basis of its own assessment of how the other community ought to have managed its resources and what those resources are properly worth.[28]

These arguments against adopting a global standpoint are very powerful, and indeed the preceding summary barely does justice to Miller's insightful analysis. Yet, if these arguments work against the global standpoint, they also work to a considerable degree against the standpoint of the state. If we consider, first, the issue of how effectively we might engage our sense of justice when the unit within which justice is considered grows in size, it is not immediately clear why many nation-states are not simply too large. Miller thinks that when considering, say, comparative wages, Spanish workers may compare themselves with their fellow workmates, or villagers, or Spaniards more generally, but not with people around the globe generally. But Spain is a very big and diverse place, with 40 million people occupying more than half a million square kilometers. There are important regional variations in custom, attitude, and spoken language. How could this vast land be thought to share a single conception of social justice? But even if Spain looked plausible, how could one think that a state like the United States or China or India could be ruled by a single conception of social justice? The United States is home to a great diversity of peoples, including, for example, the people of Hawaii, which only became a state of the Union in 1959. It also contains numerous ethnic and cultural groups with very different conceptions of social justice, from Mormons in Utah to the Amish in several Midwestern states, to Native American peoples, to the poor whites of the Appalachians. China is no less diverse, but is even more populous, her people making up one-fifth of the world's numbers. If China can be one state, why not look to create a world state? China is made up of many regions, embracing different cultures, religions (many now suppressed), and languages. It stretches from capitalist Hong Kong, to rural Singkiang, to occupied Tibet, to "renegade" Taiwan. If these 1,200 million people can make one state, under one conception of social justice, a world state does not look as implausible as one might think. The same point can be made as easily about India. All of Miller's observations about the difficulty of establishing a single, globally valid, conception of social justice would surely apply to arguments for establishing a single conception of social justice for *at least some* nation-states.

Now, it might be argued here that in each of the societies just described—Spain, the United States, China, and India—a common ethos can be, and indeed has been, established. Indeed, what is important about the nation-state is that it can in fact be the site for establishing such ties that might bind people together. Yet, if one-fifth of the world's population can be so bound in a single unit, why not the whole world?

Equally important, if the argument is that a shared ethos can be created, the case for viewing the state as somehow a natural unit ceases to be relevant to the issue. But Miller's original point is that the state should be regarded as a natural reference group rather than an artificial one. To be sure, "naturalness" here may be a matter of degree, and the argument may be that some form of social engineering is needed sometimes to solidify and regularize understandings and mutual commitments that exist in incipient form. This, however, does not take into account those many societies in which the incorporation of minorities is not welcomed but resisted.

In this respect, there is also plenty of reason to be wary of the state and its claims to be the appropriate site of social justice. Large states, and even many small ones, are made up of many different communities. The conceptions of value and the ideas of social justice informing these societies within the state often vary considerably. The inclination of the state is to try to standardize the thinking of these different groups because this diversity does not usually suit its purposes. Over time states have tried, and often succeeded, in enforcing single standards of measurement, or particular patterns of settlement and land use, or acceptable systems of money. It is in its interest to know how many people it controls, where they are, what resources they can exploit and make available, and how quickly it can all be mobilized.[29] The concern that dominates the state's activity is not social justice but its own security. But to the extent that states—and particularly large and diverse states—do address the question of social justice, they are not generally inclined to be sensitive to the varieties of social understandings and forms of social solidarity, and especially not if they run up against the interests of the state.

David Miller has put up some convincing arguments against the pursuit of social justice at the global level. But these arguments also tell against at least some states—particularly large, diverse states. The question is, where does all this leave us? We cannot, Rousseau tells us, return to the forests to live with the bears; and the state is with us now, for good or for ill.

SOME MODEST CONCLUSIONS

In general, criticism, even when well conceived, is easy, while theory building is hard. The artist who labors mightily can have her works airily dismissed by the critic who feels under no obligation to put forward an alternative offering of his own—sometimes, one suspects, because that critic has no capacity to do anything of the sort. In this particular case, however, it would be remiss of the critic not to at least remind the reader of the significance of the work he has targeted. And a few words about the direction from which the criticisms have been launched would not go astray either.

The position David Miller defends is a complex one—not because it is difficult to understand but because it tries to develop a consistent position while at the same time showing how different contexts (local, national, and global) call for different ethical responses. This demands not only a theory about what justice requires in general terms and in particular circumstances, but also a theory of how and why distinctions should be drawn between different ethical spheres. In building a philosophical position, Miller has explored numerous issues, only a few of which have been addressed in this chapter, which has focused on (what I take to be) the central problems in his theory.[30]

The standpoint from which this position is criticized in this essay is in some ways sympathetic to Miller's enterprise (hard though this may be to believe). I think Miller is right to be critical of the idea that a single standard of social justice may be applied globally, and right to think in terms of how the diversity of ethical traditions should constrain our reflections on what political arrangements are appropriate. Equally, I think Miller is right in his assessment of the postmodern response offered in the work of writers like Iris Young and Nancy Fraser, that a turn to identity politics simply evades many important questions.[31]

But Miller's aim, in the end, is to show that we should not be spooked either by the forces of globalization or the threats posed by multiculturalism into abandoning the quest for social justice, which is still best secured by the nation-state. He is looking to sail the ship of state between the Scylla of globalization and the Charybdis of postmodernist multiculturalism.

The standpoint from which this modest attack on Miller is launched is one that questions the very idea that we should look at the politics from the perspective of the ship of state. Miller wants to defend a theory of social justice that applies "within the borders of a well-defined political community."[32] The assumptions he makes are that political institutions can be devised to secure social justice within these borders, and that these borders have a very considerable ethical significance. Like a ship, the state has its members—passengers and crew, presumably a captain, though undoubtedly one who is merely first among deliberative equals—and it is up to them how they arrange the rights and duties all must share if the ship is to run smoothly. But the modern state, from this critic's point of view, is not a ship, and its borders are not closed, or even well defined. More important, assuming that they are is ethically dubious because it justifies diminishing the claims of outsiders to a share of wealth and security and elevates the standing of an institution—government—whose record as a moral actor is patchy at best.

From this point of view, the challenging task confronting us is to work out not how to secure the sovereign state but how to constrain its exercise of its powers and open up its boundaries. To embark upon that task one could do worse than to begin by grappling with David Miller's political ideas.

NOTES

1. This might be a good point at which to acknowledge my personal appreciation of David Miller's warmth and generosity as friend, supervisor, and colleague. He has repaid my criticisms of his work, and my unending efforts to persuade him of the merits of libertarianism, with only kindness and hospitality.

2. David Miller, *Principles of Social Justice* (Cambridge, Mass.: Harvard University Press, 1999), 18.

3. Miller, *Principles,* 18.

4. Miller, *Principles,* 19.

5. Miller defends this view in detail in his "Justice and Global Inequality," in *Inequality, Globalization and World Politics,* ed. Andrew Hurrell and Ngaire Woods (Oxford: Oxford University Press, 1999), 187–210.

6. See Miller, "National Self-Determination and Global Justice," in *Citizenship and National Identity* (Cambridge: Polity, 2000), 161–179, at p. 177.

7. Miller, "Justice and Global Inequality," 187.

8. Miller, "Justice and Global Inequality," 200.

9. Miller, "Justice and Global Inequality," 201–202.

10. Miller, "Justice and Global Inequality," 202–203.

11. Miller, "Justice and Global Inequality," 208.

12. Miller, "Justice and Global Inequality," 208.

13. See, for example, Janie Hampton, ed., *Internally Displaced People: A Global Survey* (London: Earthscan, 1998). Hampton estimates 20 to 22 million internally displaced persons in the world in 1998. The United Nations High Commissioner for Refugees estimates 21 million displaced persons outside their own countries.

14. Periods of detention have varied, with some asylum seekers let out within four months, but many unable to secure their own release in less than one or two years. Conditions within the

detention camps have drawn considerable public criticism, particularly in view of the number of cases of detention-induced mental illness and suicide. For a recent treatment of the issue, see Peter Mares, *Borderline: Australia's Treatment of Refugees and Asylum Seekers* (Sydney: University of New South Wales Press, 2001).

15. There is no reason in principle, however, why admitting asylum seekers as refugees need be especially expensive unless they are entitled to extensive welfare services. The problem is that it may not be easy to have differing entitlements for some residents—or, for that matter, desirable.

16. I am grateful to William Maley for this statistic, accurate in July 2001.

17. This is, of course, a highly contentious area. I make these arguments because I have been persuaded by the writings of development economists such as Peter Bauer and, more recently, Deepak Lal. See Peter Bauer, *Dissent on Development* (London: Weidenfeld and Nicolson, 1972); Bauer, *The Development Frontier: Essays in Applied Economics* (Cambridge, Mass.: Harvard University Press, 1991); Lal, *The Poverty of Development Economics* (London: Institute of Economic Affairs, 1991).

18. It is interesting to note in this regard that a number of declarations of human rights by Third World nations have taken pains to emphasize the overriding importance of national sovereignty and the right of governments to govern without outside interference. See, for example, the Bangkok Declaration (1993) and the Kuala Lumpur Declaration (also 1993).

19. Miller, *Citizenship*, 127–141. This section reveals a sophistication in Miller's analysis that my arguments here may appear to overlook, but I think my criticisms of his assumption that the state is a natural reference group hold in spite of his recognition that devolutionary measures may sometimes be necessary or wise.

20. Somewhat perversely, perhaps, the only way to disentangle oneself from a state is often to try to form a new one. My concern here, however, is not to advance a case for secession but simply to draw attention to the moral arbitrariness of state membership. This would be even more abundantly clear when one considers how often secessionist movements themselves reflect not so much popular desires for separateness as political opportunism on the part of the advocates of a new state.

21. Noel Malcolm, *Bosnia: A Short History* (London: Macmillan, 1996), 1.

22. Figures from G. P. O'Driscoll, Kim R. Holmes, and Melanie Kirkpatrick, eds., *2001 Index of Economic Freedom* (New York and Washington, D.C.: Wall Street Journal and Heritage Foundation, 2001), 375–378.

23. Both quotations come from "A Discourse on the Origin of Inequality," in Jean-Jacques Rousseau, *The Social Contract and Discourses*, translated and introduced by G. D. H. Cole, revised by J. H. Brumfitt and John C. Hall, updated by P. D. Jimack (London: Everyman, 1993), 98–99.

24. "All ran headlong into their chains, in hopes of securing their liberty; for they had just wit enough to perceive the advantages of political institutions, without experience enough to enable them to foresee the dangers." Rousseau, *Social Contract*, 99.

25. Both quotations from Miller, *Principles*, 18.

26. Miller, *Principles*, 18.

27. Miller, "Justice and Global Inequality," 193.

28. Miller, "Justice and Global Inequality," 193–196.

29. For a thorough investigation of this aspect of the state, see James Scott, *Seeing Like a State* (New Haven, Conn.: Yale University Press, 1998).

30. Arguably, one aspect of Miller's position that ought to have received careful consideration is his theory of deliberative democracy, which is at the heart of his account of the political process through which social justice is to be secured. This issue is taken up by other chapters in this volume.

31. See Miller, *Principles*, 253. This is another aspect of Miller's argument that I have not addressed in detail, though again other contributors to this volume have done so.

32. Miller, *Principles*, 246.

7

What Rights for Illiberal Communities?

Michael Walzer

I

What is the meaning of the "cultural rights" demanded by so many minority religious and ethnic communities in the modern world? And how far can liberal democratic or social democratic nation-states go in accommodating communities of these kinds? These seem to me the crucial questions raised by recent arguments for "multicultural citizenship"—they point to the conflicts that erupt in actually existing pluralist societies and to the likely political firestorms.[1] In his book *On Nationality* and again in *Citizenship and National Identity*, David Miller addresses some of these questions, but he focuses only briefly on what seems to me the hardest of them, which has to do with cultural reproduction.[2] I want to take up this question in a way that roughly follows his line of argument, but with a somewhat higher level of anxiety than he displays.

For my purposes here, I shall take Miller's "nationality principle" to articulate a strong version of citizenship, holding that citizens must share a common history and political culture. How then should they deal with minority communities whose members don't quite share, or don't acknowledge sharing, either of these, or who don't attribute importance to them? How should people who are, so to speak, citizens first, relate to people who are members first? Before answering this question, however, I need to say something about the kinds of communities and the kinds of membership that are at issue here. If we are to argue usefully about the political culture of a pluralist democracy, we have to pay attention to the sociology of group life.

The strong version of citizenship that I take Miller to defend (which he distinguishes from one stronger still) would raise no problems with "cultural rights" of a certain sort. It would accommodate rights to voluntary self-organization by minority communities, and to the free and open use of a communal language in ritual or domestic settings and (perhaps) in some political settings, and to some degree of public recognition of the community in museums and monuments and even in the state calendar—so long as the priority of the culture of citizenship was not thereby challenged.

But the core meaning of *cultural rights* has been shaped in response to the problems many communities have, because they are small and relatively powerless, in reproducing themselves. Their members look for protection, maybe also for help, and this is the claim they make on their fellow citizens (whom they may or may not acknowledge as "fellows"): that all ethnic and religious and, maybe, political and ideological communities have a right to reproduce themselves or, at least, to try to do that—which means, they have a right to raise and educate their own children. They may also claim a right to state assistance in this project, since they will often be hard-pressed to fund it on their own.

"The right to try. . . ." If that sounds like an easy right, readily acknowledged, uncontested, it isn't. It isn't easy, above all, because in so much of the modern world people belong to more than one community, and so "cultural reproduction" is likely to require that their children be taught more than one culture—crucially, for our purposes, the culture of the minority community and of the democratic state. But the teachings may be inconsistent, even contradictory; and there are sure to be conflicts over which teaching takes precedence and over who, finally, is in control of the educational process. These conflicts can be wrenching for individuals, and when they are acted out politically they can significantly divide the country (any country). Still, given certain sorts of communities, the conflicts are not unmanageable.

Imagine a case from my own country: a set of parents who are U.S. citizens, Catholics, and Italian Americans. At every level of the educational system, these parents will have to make difficult or potentially difficult choices between public/secular and parochial/religious schools. These are parental choices exclusively, but they are shaped, and their financial consequences determined, by decisions made within the Church, by the governments of the several states, and by thousands of cities and towns (schooling is the most decentralized of governmental functions in the United States) about their educational budgets. It is an important and disputed political question whether the cultural reproduction of Catholic Italian Americans should be funded, wholly or partly or not at all, with public money. If public funding is provided, then it seems obvious that the body of citizens has a right, if not a duty, to attend to its own reproduction, if only so that its agents can go on collecting taxes and providing the funds. The easiest way to do that is to require that certain subjects, having to do with the state and its legitimacy, be taught in the parochial (religious) schools that the state is paying for. In the United States, indeed, state governments claim such a right to ensure their own ongoing legitimacy, even though they don't pay for but only license and certify the parochial schools: they commonly require courses on American history and democratic politics. And isn't it a justifiable practice for democratic citizens, exactly as it is for strongly identified Italians or faithful Catholics, to try to reproduce their values and commitments in the next generation?

Yes, it is justifiable, and it is also possible, most of the time, to arrange for the simultaneous enactment of these different reproductive/educational activities . . . because each of the three communities I am now considering is prepared to accept the divided loyalties of its members. The United States has long acknowledged the pluralism of American society and the resulting hyphenated identities of its citizens (it even permits, in practice if not in law, dual citizenship and the twofold allegiance that this entails). So, "Italian American" is fine with other Americans—as it is, also, with Italians-in-America, whose community is very loosely structured, ready to accommodate the participation of its members in American politics and in American society generally, and to accept, however unhappily, the consequences of this participation: namely, members who come and go, who move away from Italianess and then, sometimes, return, often with non-Italian husbands or wives in tow. In similar fashion, American Catholicism has gradually accommodated itself to the practices and even to the values of democratic debate and decision (despite its own hierarchical character)—so that faithful Catholics can also be Democrats and Republicans, liberals and conservatives, socialists and defenders of laissez-faire. These three communities, then, have been pluralized from within, and as a result the claims they make to reproduce themselves are already qualified by a recognition of similar (but different) claims made on behalf of some or even all of their own members.[3]

These different claims have to be, and can be, negotiated. Of course, it isn't difficult to imagine the negotiations temporarily deadlocked or suspended in anger—as negotiations over the funding and regulation of parochial schools have frequently been in the United States since Catholic immigrants began arriving in large numbers in the 1840s. But once Catholics recognize that their children are also future citizens of a democratic secular state, and once all the other Americans recognize that some of their fellow citizens are faithful Catholics, and once Italian Americans recognize that their children may marry non–Italian Americans, the hardest questions have been settled. The key to the settlement is that these communities have effectively given up any claim to the total loyalty of their members. No doubt, they still hope for a substantial part of the time, energy, and available wealth of those same members, but they don't demand everything.

This is exactly the situation that Miller describes with a different example, arguing that there is no conflict between an Arab ethnic identity and a French national identity.[4] That's right, so long as the two, so to speak, make room for each other—as some militant Muslims and some modern-day Jacobins are not entirely willing to do. So, what about "identities" that claim all the possible room?

Some years ago, the sociologist Lewis Coser published a book called *Greedy Institutions*, in which he examined groups and organizations that did in fact demand everything their members could give.[5] Most of the groups discussed in Coser's book recruited their members as adults (the Communist Party–as-it-once-was is an obvious example). But there are also greedy or totalizing communities into which people are born and bred. And it seems to me that it is these groups whose "right" to cultural reproduction is most problematic. I mean, problematic for a liberal and democratic state, but it is only in liberal, democratic states that claims are commonly made and regularly adjudicated in the language of rights. So, this is my question: do totalizing communities, like fundamentalist or ultraorthodox religious groups (the *haredim* in Israel, evangelical and pentacostal sects in the United States) or like traditionalist ethnic groups (the aboriginal tribes of Canada or New Zealand), have a right to reproduce themselves—that is, to do whatever they think necessary to pass on their way of life to their children, who are also future citizens of a democratic state? And should the state subsidize the exercise of this right?

The right is problematic for (at least) two reasons:

- First, because these groups generally don't recognize the individual rights attributed to their members by the democratic state and so won't be inclined to teach their members about such rights. Above all, they won't want their members to understand the full extent of their liberal right of exit—the right to leave, resign, walk away, become an apostate—which holds for any and all groups, including the religious community (and, in principle at least, the state too).
- Second, because these groups are unlikely to teach their members the values that underlie democratic politics: the equality of citizens, the need for free and open debate, the right of opposition, and above all the commitment to a "commonweal" or general good that extends to all citizens of the nation-state, including nonmembers of the parochial community—heretics, apostates, infidels, "foreigners," and so on.[6]

Assume now that the descriptive statements I have just made are accurate; totalizing groups will in fact behave in these ways. That means, first, that the education they provide won't produce individuals who are capable of acting autonomously in the world; and second, that it won't produce citizens who are ready to take responsibility for the well-being of a political community that includes "the others." It may well be that the reproductive project of totalizing groups depends upon these two results: the project won't succeed, I mean, won't prosper over time, unless new members are taught not to seek autonomy and not to pursue the general good. And then, should the democratic state support, should it allow, that success?

II

The first issue raised by this question is the extent of parental rights over children—when these rights are contested not by the children themselves but by other people who claim to have an interest in the future values and behavior of the children. In this case it is the nation-state, or better, the body of citizens, that claims this interest. I suppose that the usual claim is limited: the citizens have an interest that exists alongside the parental interest and modifies it to such and such a degree; their aim is to "add a national identity to an ethnic identity," as Miller says.[7] Only if the state were itself a totalizing community, only if it were a totalitarian state, would it claim a superceding interest or try to impose a singular identity.

Let us try to imagine a group of citizens explaining their interest to skeptical or hostile parents. "You can raise your children (or try to raise them) to be whatever you want them to be," they would say, "with this qualification: that if they are to be citizens, if they are to participate in the public life of the wider community, join in debates about domestic and foreign policy, vote in our elections, then they must be taught something about the history of the country, the meaning of citizenship, and the values of democratic politics. As citizens, they are not simply your children; they are, so to speak, the children of the republic, which means that together with our children, they are going to make critical decisions about the shape of our common life, perhaps even about the survival of this political community. And they have to be taught to understand and acknowledge their responsibility so that we can be reasonably confident that they will attend to it—because what is at stake is of critical importance to all of us."

That is, I think, the minimalist position of the citizens; note that it doesn't specify the extent of the educational role they are claiming. But even if the extent is modest, they will probably have more to say than I have just imagined them saying. For I imagined the citizens speaking only about democratic citizenship, not about personal autonomy. (Compare Miller's statement that he will not consider the issues that education raises about "individual rights and autonomy, but look at the problem from the perspective of nationality."[8]) Though citizenship and autonomy are certainly connected, the argument that I want to make is more easily grounded in the first of these. Still, if some of the children of the parochial group lay claim to the rights that go with autonomy and that are guaranteed to all citizens—the right of escape, say, from the discipline of a religious court or the patriarchal control of ethnic elders—this right (and others too) would certainly be enforced by the officials of the democratic state. "Among us," the officials will say, "all men and women are equal before the law, and this equality must be upheld by the state and enforced by the magistrates, whatever the consequences for particular parochial groups. Above all, individuals can leave these groups without any civil penalty—indeed, without costs of any sort so far as the state is concerned."

III

But this brings us immediately to the second issue that groups of this sort pose—and that is the extent to which we really are prepared to tolerate difference. Liberal advocates of toleration sometimes assume that they are being as tolerant as they can possibly be, as tolerant as anyone could possibly want them to be, when they recognize a very wide range of individual choice. Virtually any imaginable life plan, short of a plan to rob or murder one's fellows, is legitimate, and people are free to associate freely in support of any plan that requires their cooperation. Many plans, many associations: what more could anyone ask?

In truth, however, the life plans that people form under these conditions of individual freedom turn out to be remarkably similar to one another. At least, they are similar relative to the actual range of difference revealed in the historical and anthropological record. People who plan their lives, who make their lives into personal projects, who are entrepreneurs of the self, are people of one sort among many possible sorts. I know them intimately, and so will most of the readers of this essay; nonetheless, they have made a rather late appearance in human history; it is only in the last couple of centuries that they have come to dominate Western societies. Today, they are us (or most of us), and so we have to ask ourselves: Are we prepared to tolerate the others, men and women who are differently connected to their own lives, who have inherited rather than chosen their lives, for example, or whose lives are collectively rather than individually determined, or who bear the yoke of divine command?

I am inclined to worry more about this question than Miller seems to do. For only if we are prepared to tolerate people with lives of that kind can we call ourselves tolerant of *difference*. And then we have to imagine what such people, members of a total community that isn't (in their understanding of it) a voluntary association, would say to a group of liberal/democratic citizens who claim an interest in their children. "But if you mean to tolerate us," they would say,

> [I]f you mean to recognize our right to live in our own way and to raise our children to value and sustain that way, then you must allow us full control over their education. For our way is an integral whole, complete in itself, leaving no aspect of personal or social life without guidance and constraint. It can't be compromised; it can't be combined with a little bit of this and a little bit of that. Perhaps in the course of their working lives, many of our sons will be forced to move into the larger world and adapt to its manners and mores. But that makes it all the more important that we control their education for as long as we can and that we control even more completely the education and upbringing of our daughters. For it is the daughters who bear the burdens of continuity; they guard the home even when our sons wander; they give to our infant grandchildren their first words and earliest inclinations. In any case, we can't compete for the allegiance of our chil-

dren, for until we have taught them the value of our ways, the outside world is sure to look more exciting; its gratifications come more quickly; its responsibilities, for all your talk of citizenship, are much easier to live with than the responsibilities we impose—to God, to our ancestors, to one another. We simply can't survive as a voluntary association of autonomous individuals, each with his or her own life plan.

Groups of this sort may or may not be internally democratic, but they are obviously hostile to the values of the democratic state whose toleration they are seeking. Nor is it likely that such a state, or its regime of toleration, would survive if a single totalizing group became demographically dominant. Nonetheless, there is a strong argument in favor of tolerating such groups, even in favor of providing some degree of state support for their cultural reproduction. This argument provides the grounding for (a modest version of) what is today called "multiculturalism," and what it holds is, first, that human beings need the support and nurturance of a cultural community (not necessarily of only one but at least of one) if they are to live decent lives; second, that cultural communities are highly complex entities, created over many generations, with the effort and devotion of many people; third, that though these communities are unchosen by their members, the members are, most often, deeply committed to them; and fourth, that these communities embody values that can't be rank ordered on a single scale (which doesn't mean that they can't be criticized).

Most members of communities of this kind, as I have already suggested, are members of more than one. But some men and women—most obviously, the adherents of fundamentalist religious sects—hold fast to a singular membership and value precisely its singularity. And though they would have no trouble ranking their community, and all the others, on a single scale, it seems to me that the rest of us should avoid doing that. At any rate, for those singular members, the four points about community hold, just as they hold for pluralist members of more liberal groups: they are indeed supported and nourished; they stand in a tradition and continue the efforts of their predecessors; they accept communal responsibilities; and their way of life cannot be located in a single hierarchy of value. And we have to find some way to accommodate that way of life . . . at least to some significant degree. Even if the values of the democratic state take precedence over those of the parochial community *for certain purposes*, they can't come first in every case.

But it isn't easy to determine the precise extent of legitimate state purposes and so of the demands that citizens can make on members. The number of purposes is potentially large, but disputed at every point: does the state have an interest in the economic competence of its future citizens? in their understanding of modern science? in their military training? in their acceptance of public health measures? in equal opportunity for their boys and girls? I have a strong inclination to say yes to all these questions (and I suspect that Miller would have the same inclination), but that can't be the right answer, for it would turn the body of democratic citizens into something much too close to a totalizing community.

Consider the problem that I have already hinted at: political participation, where interesting questions arise that relate both to the gender hierarchy and to the everyday meaning of democracy.[9] The democratic state recognizes the political equality of men and women, grants them the same rights to vote, hold office, join in campaigns and policy debates, and so on. The different parochial communities cannot then deny these rights, as many of them would be inclined to do, to their women members. But what if the women are taught to defer to their fathers and husbands in such matters and either not to vote at all or, since their numbers are useful, to vote only as they are told? I doubt that democracies can tolerate that kind of inequality, though I also doubt that they can avoid it.

But the male members of the community are commonly taught much the same thing: to defer, say, to religious leaders and vote only for approved candidates. So, the most immediate outcome that totalizing groups produce is not disenfranchised women but bloc voting of a sort alien to a democratic society—for in well-functioning and well-integrated democracies, group members routinely disagree, and ought to be able to disagree, about how to vote. Even in such a highly polarized community as contemporary Quebec, for example, the Liberal party manages to challenge the Nationalists for the support of francophone voters. There is a general truth here: given a politics of argument and opposition, any claim to know the one right way for members of a community to respond to its difficulties is sure to be disputed—and disputed within the community itself. In the United States, similarly, if 65 percent of unionized workers vote Democratic, that is considered a remarkable instance of class discipline; no one imagines that American workers could have a single and unanimous or even near-unanimous view of their situation. By contrast, when 85 percent of blacks vote Democratic, that is taken as a sign of their radical alienation from the political mainstream; if they were more integrated, they would be more divided. But totalizing groups, when they are politically mobilized, are likely to deliver even higher percentages of their votes to a single party or candidate (as ultraorthodox communities routinely do in Israel)—a sign of even more radical alienation. The give-and-take of democratic politics simply isn't part of the experience of these voters; it is, in fact, wholly alien to them.

Should it be part of their experience? And if it should, what can their fellow citizens do to make it so? These questions require, it seems to me, highly qualified answers. Democracy should indeed be *part* of the experience of all citizens, but not necessarily a large part, and not, as it were, the same part for everyone. And the citizens as a body can do something, but not everything, to make it so. Earlier on, I imagined citizens claiming a say, without specifying how much of a say, in the education of the next generation. They might well allow a religious community to control its own schools and shape a large part of the curriculum—but subject to limits and controls. The state could, as I have suggested, require that certain courses be taught; it could send teachers into the parochial schools to teach them; it could set examinations that students must pass before being certified as high school graduates; it could take students out of the parochial schools for fixed periods of time, for national service, perhaps, or simply to show them something of the world outside their own community.[10] I can readily imagine Ministry of Education officials doing these sorts of things with a heavy hand and with perverse effects. But given some sensitivity and a readiness to negotiate the arrangements in detail, it's not impossible to imagine the officials doing their job well or reasonably well.

But the programs would have to be coercive—legally mandated and compulsory. Since they challenge the totalizing claims of the religious or ethnic community, they are sure to encounter fierce opposition. Their aim is to allow or encourage the community's children, as many of them as possible, to accept another identity (I am speaking now only of citizenship, still bracketing the question of autonomy). The citizens can honestly say, as Miller says, that they want these children to *add* citizenship to their religious or ethnic self-understanding, not to replace the latter with the former. But there is in fact a replacement here: a singular and undivided (ethnic or religious) traditionalism is being replaced by the characteristic dividedness of modern life. If we advocate and then actively pursue that replacement, are we abandoning toleration?

IV

I do advocate that replacement, and I don't want to abandon toleration (hence the movement of this chapter, around and around a dilemma that I can't cut my way through). I believe that parents have a right to (try to) sustain a traditional and total way of life and that citizens have a right to (try to) educate the young men and women who will soon be responsible for the well-being of the political community. It is the coexistence of the two rights that makes the difficulty—which is to say that it's democracy that makes the difficulty. Democratic citizenship is an inclusive status, and it is an official status, a kind of political office that carries with it significant responsibilities. If the members of the total community were not citizens, if their children were not future citizens, there would be no problem. In a multinational or multireligious empire, where all the members of the different nations or religions are imperial subjects whose only responsibility is obedience, the emperor has little reason to interfere in the different projects for cultural reproduction carried on in communal schools (though he may want his portrait to hang in every school building). He can even allow the existence of parochial courts with fairly extended jursidictions, alongside the imperial courts—as in the Ottoman millet system. There is no common life for which his subjects need to be trained; it is probably in his interest that no common life emerges. But democracy requires the common life of the public square, the assembly, the political arena, and certain understandings must be shared among the citizens if what goes on in those places is to issue in legitimate laws and policies. Citizens, as Rousseau said, "give the law to themselves."[11] But they can't do that if different groups among them are bound to other, wholly encompassing laws that demand total commitment.

Or rather, they can't do that unless these groups, like the Amish in the United States, live entirely on the margins of the political community, claiming none of the benefits, exercising none of the rights, of citizenship. "They may choose," says Miller, "to withdraw from citizenship and live . . . as internal exiles within the state."[12] Marginalization is one way of dealing with totalizing groups; I think that it is Miller's preferred way, so long as the groups are relatively small. If it is successful, they won't be required to give the law to themselves (a good thing, since they believe they can't do that; they have already *been given* the law), and what is even more important, they won't be allowed to give it to the other citizens. They will live in a corner of the democratic state as if they were living in a vast empire.

But most totalizing communities, including some fundamentalist religions, aren't in fact . . . total. Totality may be an idea they cherish, but their everyday practice falls short. They make more radical claims than the American groups with which I began, but they still leave room for political maneuver and prudential decision making. Hence, some sort of negotiation is possible between members and citizens, between the parochial groups and the democratic state—and if it is possible, it is probably necessary. Still, I can't see a principled resolution of the conflict between them. Miller seems to believe that democracy can resolve the conflict, in principle if not always in practice. Imagine a country, he suggests, where all formal education is secular in character. Then "the claim [which is sure to be made] that Islamic schools [are] essential to Muslim identity would have to be assessed on its own merits, and might well be rejected in a democratic forum." To call the rejection illegitimate, Miller argues, is to deny the very essence of republican citizenship.[13] Well, maybe. But how would the Muslims know whether their fellow citizens were deciding that Islamic schools were not, as a matter of fact, essential to Muslim survival or that Muslim survival itself wasn't essential? I am not sure that the first question can be decided democratically; I am sure that the second question shouldn't be. What the citizens can and must decide is what sort of education, what course of study, is necessary for citizenship. If they are wise, they will set a minimalist standard, even if they hope for additional courses, say, in political history or theory. But whatever they do, they are posing a problem for the members of parochial communities, not resolving the problem.

From the standpoint of the two parties, citizens and members, there are only better and worse positions along a spectrum of possibilities, none of them likely to be stable. The two can only coexist in antagonism, for the democratic state demands some significant part of the attention and commitment of the group's members, especially its youngest members—and the group feels, probably rightly, that any concessions on this point are the beginning of the end. I mean the end of the wholly encompassing way of life, for alternative, more modest or more liberal, versions of the way can probably be saved.

Of course, there is another possibility that I have not yet considered; I have been assuming that the totalizing groups are minorities, but that isn't necessarily a correct assumption. The group may grow, as fundamentalist religious movements have grown in many parts of the world in recent years. Then we have to consider the possible takeover of the state or of major state institutions by the totalizing group, which is likely to mean the end of democracy. Again, I mean the end of liberal democracy, for some modified version of democratic politics can probably be sustained (as it is in Iran today). Imagine the conflict now as a power struggle. Perfect equilibrium is unlikely; the balance will tilt one way or another. So, the questions that I have been asking can be given a new form: which way would we tilt the balance (if we could)?

Now it seems to me that there is a principled position: if political power is at stake we should tilt decisively against the totalizing groups. The reason for this is simply that their view of "the others" is much harsher than the democratic state's view of group members. No doubt, the conflict can produce ugliness on both sides, but liberal democratic toleration, even if it is finally intolerant of totalizing religions and ethnicities, is gentler, less humiliating, less frightening than the alternative is likely to be. Liberal democracy has managed to include fundamentalist religions and chauvinist nationalities, even if it has also modified, even transformed, them in the process. Fundamentalism-in-power and chauvinism-with-an-army are far more likely to exclude than to bring in, and if this is in a certain sense more respectful of difference (since it acknowledges the actual depth of the differences), it has often been far less respectful both of human dignity and of life and limb.

But this liberal democratic tilt is simply a guideline for decision making in a political crisis. It doesn't solve, or even address, the problem of day-to-day coexistence. For that there is no theoretical solution, no deduction from a set of principles, not even from Miller's nationality principle; there are only compromises that have to be made and remade endlessly and that are sure to leave both democratic citizens and community members unhappy. Bad compromises maximize unhappiness, on one side or the other; better compromises minimize and equalize it. But the citizens and the members are unhappy *with each other*, and they can't escape each other. When we write about these questions, we must never hold out to either one the hope of such an escape. So, maybe happiness just can't be the main subject or primary aim of politics—or of political theory.

NOTES

1. See Will Kymlicka, *Liberalism, Community, and Culture* (Oxford: Clarendon Press, 1989) and *Multicultural Citizenship* (Oxford: Clarendon Press, 1996); and Charles Taylor, *Multicultur-alism and "The Politics of Recognition"* (Princeton, N.J.: Princeton University Press, 1992) for ar-gument with which I am, with reservations, sympathetic. For the full range of views, see Kym-licka, ed., *The Rights of Minority Cultures* (Oxford: Oxford University Press, 1995).

2. David Miller, *On Nationality* (Oxford: Clarendon Press, 1995), 143–145; *Citizenship and National Identity* (Cambridge: Polity, 2000), ch. 3.

3. On the character of ethnic and religious communities in the United States, see my *What It Means to Be an American* (New York: Marsilio, 1992).

4. Miller, *Nationality*, 144.

5. Lewis A. Coser, *Greedy Institutions: Patterns of Undivided Commitment* (New York: Free Press, 1974).

6. On the necessary content of an education in democratic values, see Amy Gutmann, *Dem-ocratic Education* (Princeton, N.J.: Princeton University Press, 1987; revised ed. with an epilogue, 1999); the new epilogue directly addresses the issues discussed here.

7. Miller, *Nationality*, 143.

8. Miller, *Nationality*, 145.

9. For a fuller discussion of the gender issues than I can provide here, see Susan Moller Okin, "Feminism and Multiculturalism: Some Tensions," in *Liberalism and Its Practice*, ed. Dan Avnon and Avner de-Shalit (London: Routledge, 1999), 81–105; also Anne Phillips, "Democracy and Difference: Some Problems for Feminist Theory," in *Rights of Minority Cultures*, ed. Kymlicka, 288–299.

10. A wide range of possibilities is considered in the articles collected by Yael Tamir, ed., *Dem-ocratic Education in a Multicultural State* (Oxford: Blackwell, 1995).

11. Jean-Jacques Rousseau, *The Social Contract*, Bk. One, ch. viii: "Obedience to a law which we prescribe to ourselves is liberty."

12. Miller, *Nationality*, 145.

13. Miller, *Citizenship*, 57.

8

Deliberative Democracy
Guarantee for Justice or Preventing Injustice?

Avner de-Shalit

David Miller's egalitarianism leads him to support deliberative democracy. His egalitarianism is also reflected in his discussion of justice. In fact, Miller ties the two together, claiming that there is a very strong connection between them. More precisely, Miller seems to claim that if we have deliberative democracy we are likely to have justice. We shall have justice, in the very democratic sense of the term, because we shall be able to find out what people think of justice and what principles of justice they want to have. I want to argue that the connection is a weaker one: deliberative democracy may help to prevent arbitrary injustice, but it cannot guarantee justice. The reason for this, I shall argue, is that the expectation, that deliberation will bring about better information and therefore more rational decisions, is far-fetched.[1]

But first let me say a few words about deliberative democracy. In her review essay on books on deliberative democracy, Emily Hauptmann asserts that "as recently as twenty years ago, no one would have identified himself or herself as a 'deliberative democrat.'"[2] Nowadays, however, it is quite common to declare that this is what you are. Deliberative democracy remains to achieve a final definition due to the range of definitions that abound. In this chapter, I plan to focus on David Miller's notion of deliberative democracy, namely, that a democratic system is "deliberative" "to the extent that the decisions it reaches reflect open discussion among the participants, with people ready to listen to the views and consider the interests of others, and modify their own opinions accordingly."[3] My argument, however, relates to the work of other scholars as well, and my reading of Miller's defense of deliberative democracy is influenced by arguments raised by Gutmann, Habermas, Dryzek, Joshua Cohen, Elster, and others.[4]

Miller and others claim that deliberative democracy can help in (1) forming decisions that are more rational; (2) forming "justified" agreements; and (3) initiating and legitimizing Promethean, or more radical, policies. These are possible because deliberations expose the participants to (1) more and more accurate information; and (2) thoughts and feelings of other people. The participants therefore become more flexible and ready to revise and modify their positions. However, I would like to raise doubts concerning the empirical veracity of such claims. To do this, I offer the analysis of the findings of two empirical research studies. The case I would argue is that when deliberation characterizes all public institutions, that is, the deliberation is general and concerns ideological matters, as in the context of a debate on the good life, it then addresses a heterogeneous, broad, mixed package of issues and questions. In such understanding of deliberation, I argue, indeed it has the capacity to contribute greatly to the process of decision making. I call this "multi-issue" deliberation. However, "ad hoc" deliberations, that is, public debates on particular policies, taking place within specific bodies, as we recently saw in citizen-based consensus conferences (CBCC) or "citizens' juries," fail to produce what political theorists including Miller suggest they would. Indeed, in such test cases, the preceding descriptions of deliberation appear nothing more than a mythology.

Having said that, I have no wish to challenge the fourth expectation of deliberation, namely, its ability to contribute to people's self-esteem, and thereby to their sense of community. I see this expectation as well founded. Moreover, I end this chapter by suggesting an alternative argument in favor of deliberative democracy, namely, that it may help prevent arbitrary injustice. (It is at this point that my discussion of democracy relates to justice.) Thus, this critique of deliberative democracy theory is put forward with much sympathy. It is a critique of the justifications, rather than the practice of deliberative democracy.

EXPECTATIONS

Advocates of deliberative democracy claim that it is morally superior to any other form of democracy. Perhaps Jean-Jacques Rousseau was the first theorist to claim so when he argued that in such a democracy, the individual is not motivated solely by self-interest, but also by an interest in the well-being of the community.[5] Rousseau believed that the more people participate, the more their preferences would be guided by the general will. His expectations, however, were rather different from those of contemporary theorists in the sense that he had in mind a small-size political community.[6]

Basically, we can divide the expectations of deliberative democracy into two groups. The first set of expectations involves the benefits of the information to which those involved in the deliberation are exposed; they have more information and a better understanding of the issue, and hence, it is assumed, they will tackle the issues at hand more rationally and arrive at better decisions. Second, there are the benefits deriving from the actual involvement in such a social process. People have to rephrase their positions in such a way that others will accept them; hence, they are forced to consider the other's perspective, point of view, even rhetoric. They thus tend to empathize with the other and learn to understand other positions. Eventually, they become more flexible and more able to compromise. Decisions will become "*justifiable* agreements," and what is more, since decisions reached after deliberation have far greater legitimacy, it is easier to promote and decide upon innovative, timely, or novel policies. John Dryzek, for example, argues that deliberation also relies on "practical" (rather than instrumental) reason, involving purpose as well as means, and is pedagogical and communal rather than instrumental.[7] Dryzek claims that deliberation therefore entails the "collective cultivation of virtuous behaviour rather than administration of people or things."[8]

So far, however, these expectations are about the decisions we reach in the democratic process. Arendt and Mill suggest that deliberation offers a fourth benefit, namely, that it can help to create better people. Those who become involved in politics develop their capacity for judgment and their "power of agency" by being confronted with other opinions.[9] Miller also seems to go along with this optimism, which, admittedly, might have a sound empirical footing. His idea is that deliberation is part of socialization because it has the effect of turning a collection of separate individuals into a group.[10] I shall argue that this is indeed the case when people take part in multi-issue, ideological deliberations about politics, and sometimes—but not always—when they are engaged in ad hoc deliberation. (While discussing this, I raise another question: why should we accept that deliberation "has the effect of turning a collection of separate individuals into a group? Isn't it the other way around; that is, that "separate people" don't engage in deliberation because they are "separate," whereas only people, who already consider themselves a group, become engaged in deliberation? I say more about this later.)

First, however, I should mention that Miller dismisses a fifth expectation, that deliberation can be helpful in reaching a "true policy." He distinguishes between deliberative democracy and what is called "epistemic democracy."[11] In the latter, one of the main hopes of democratic processes is that a "correct answer to some question facing the political community" will be reached. A distinction should be drawn here, between those who claim that moral disagreements should be discussed through deliberation[12] and those who think that moral disputes can be solved in terms of finding the right answer. Gutmann and Thompson, in fact, openly declare that "deliberative democracy has no problem saying that what the majority decides, even after deliberating, need not be right."[13]

In similar vein, Miller writes that the goal of epistemic democracy is an "unrealistically high standard of political decision-making," although he does claim that "deliberation tends to improve the quality of decisions."[14] This enhanced quality, Miller argues, may be reached by agreeing on a certain "substantive norm," which "all concur in thinking is the appropriate norm for the case in hand." This is, of course, different from reaching the truth. Miller is skeptical about whether we should even be aiming at the truth. For example, he writes that "republican citizenship [that is based on deliberation] is actually better to respond to cultural diversity than other versions [of democracy], by virtue of its ability to draw groups who initially have very different priorities into public debate, and to find *compromise solutions* to political issues that members of each group can accept."[15] Thus, deliberation is not about deciding who is right; at most, it is about *finding out* the norms we all share and which qualify as substantive norms. In those cases where we do not share the same norms, deliberation will help us to reach the "fairest compromise between competing points of view."[16] To conclude: If deliberative democracy is about finding compromise solutions, it is not about finding out the truth; and, therefore, epistemic democracy is self-contradictory.

But let me return to the more widely shared expectations, namely, those concerning the status of decisions that follow deliberation. How does the magic work?[17] How do people with competing viewpoints reach a compromise through deliberation? Moreover, can deliberation be helpful in overcoming disagreements, or does it help one side to accept decisions when it finds itself the minority? According to Miller, the compromise mechanism works as follows: individuals enter the deliberation process with preferences that are defined and explained in terms of narrow interests. Knowing, however, that these terms could never persuade others to accept their position, these individuals seek alternative ways of putting forward their proposals. They do so "under the rubric of general principles or policy considerations that others could accept."[18] Consequently, these individuals begin to think as citizens and internalize the perspective of a citizen; that is, they begin to sympathize with others. And why? Because in order to persuade the other, they need to understand his or her motives, in other words, "put themselves in the other's shoes."[19] Now, the others, being exposed to more reasonable arguments, learn more about their fellow citizens' perspectives. Thus, a mechanism of republican citizenship[20] rather than a bargaining is born. Thus, although in our personal lives commitments may be very different, we are all equally citizens, and it is as citizens that we advance claims in the public realm and assess the claims made by others.[21]

What is the status of a decision taken following deliberation? Miller argues that "in a deliberative democracy the final decision taken may not be wholly consensual, but it should represent a *fair balance* between the different views expressed in the course of the discussion, and to the extent that it does, even those who would prefer some other outcome can recognise the decision as legitimate."[22] At the same time, Miller is open to the possibility— indeed, he thinks this is the whole point of deliberation—that people will "modify their opinions," or "alter their political preferences."[23] Therefore, "the final decision reached is likely to represent the majority will, at least of the participants."[24]

This belief in the fairness of deliberation (giving equal chance to all voices) and the spontaneous emergence of a wide majority is the background to the claim of deliberative democracy theorists that deliberative democracy is a precondition for introducing novel policies and making them legitimate. Moreover, this is the reason politicians have recently begun to encourage and even rely on citizen-based consensus conferences (CBCCs) to legitimize new policies, mainly in the sphere of environmental policies.[25]

EMPIRICAL RESEARCH: A METHODOLOGICAL COMMENT

However, if deliberation is about all these expectations, shouldn't these therefore be examined empirically?[26] One might wonder whether my aim here is relevant: political theory is normative, and so there is no need to stop and examine whether it ties in with what people think and how they behave. I therefore intend to pause here and argue that it is relevant to ask what people think and how they behave. Since I developed this argument elsewhere,[27] I will just summarize it here.

(If the reader agrees with me, he or she can skip ahead.)

Miller concurs with this view, though for different reasons. He rightly claims that a theory that also relates to what people think is more politically relevant.[28] But above all, he argues that if political theory relates to what the public thinks, then it will acquire increasing accuracy.[29] His motives, then, are mainly academic.[30] I would like to suggest that, in addition, when philosophers and theorists try to develop a political theory, they are often motivated by the will to change reality. This would entail the application of a mechanism of "public reflective equilibrium," which would require weighing people's opinions and behavior.

It is widely accepted that moral exploration involves a process of "reflective equilibrium." Basically, *reflective equilibrium* means "that we 'test' various parts of our system of moral beliefs against other beliefs we hold, seeking coherence among the widest set of moral and non-moral beliefs."[31] We find coherence, which involves "more than logical consistency," but also simplicity, by constantly moving forward and then retracing our steps, by continuously revising and modifying our theories and intuitions. These revisions are crucial. Reflective equilibrium means that if a theory is very appealing in that it fully explains and justifies a number of intuitions, but at the same time contradicts some other intuition, it is often the case that we will change the other intuition—the "instinctive belief"—rather than modify the theory. Failing to do so implies dogmatism.

There is the question, of course, of whose intuitions and whose theories should be weighed against one another, and two models of reflective equilibrium have been suggested in response. One was offered by John Rawls,[32] who argues that reflective equilibrium is private, in the sense that both the intuitions and the theories are those of the philosopher. As Miller puts it, "the reflective equilibrium that emerges is an equilibrium only for the person who has engaged in the thought-process Rawls describes."[33] How do we know that this process is a success? The answer is that success is when the philosopher can offer a consistent and coherent theory, which ties in with his or her intuitions. Sometimes these intuitions happen to be shared by many others, but the point of the "private" reflective equilibrium is not to convince the reader of a philosophy that a theory fits the reader's intuition, but rather to convince the reader that the philosopher has managed to develop a very accurate theory whose principles of morality harmonize with philosophical intuitions that are themselves reasonable. In other words, a successful theory meets the condition that if the reader shares the author's intuitions, he or she is also likely to accept the moral principles put forward, and consequently the theory.

An alternative and more promising (in the context of politics) model of reflective equilibrium—what I would like to call "contextual reflective equilibrium"—is suggested by Michael Walzer in three of his books.[34] Although, to the best of my knowledge, Walzer has never claimed to be using a mechanism of what I call here contextual reflective equilibrium. I nevertheless think this is a proper reading of his suggestions regarding political philosophy. Walzer argues that social criticism is applied to a particular community and its morality. This is what I would call "contextual" reflective equilibrium. The philosopher understands and examines the values of a society and then proceeds to theorize about them. This is an interpretative[35] rather than inventive process. The philosopher examines the behavior and expressed views of the individuals who make up the community and interprets them in terms of what he or she understands the community's values to be. The philosopher does not invent morality, but holds up a mirror to his or her community. The mirror is a critic as far as it holds up a standard of "profound social idealism."[36] The philosopher serves to reveal all of the lies that a society tells itself. This is a "reiterative" activity[37] in the sense that the philosopher is not interested in having the last word, but sees the theory put forward as providing fresh input into the moral discourse, pending reevaluation. "The critics who aim to get things right aim at a rightness that is relative to their critical occasions. They want to produce a strong argument and a local political effect, but also . . . an object of reflection and debate."[38]

In Walzer's model, however, the intuitions considered are those of the philosopher's and the community's intellectuals, while the theories are those of the philosopher alone. It is at this point that I put forward a third model, namely, the model of "public" reflective equilibrium, where the theories considered are also those of the public, and where the philosopher engages in and conducts the process of finding a reflective equilibrium. I suggest, in other words, that a theory of political philosophy should relate to real cases and be relevant to real life. To do this, it should also arise from cases of practice. The best way to do so would be to start with the general public, activists and individuals who are engaged in moral reasoning and political activism and their dilemmas. Hence, a theory of political philosophy should be derived from wider sources, that is, not only the laid-back philosopher or anthropological explorer, but the public as well. It should be a theory that reflects the actual philosophical needs of the public, of people who seek to convince others by appealing to practical issues, and not necessarily the philosophical needs of the philosopher, who convinces colleagues by appealing to consistency and simplicity. Naturally, the philosopher should not take the value of the public's propositions for granted. People's intuitions, arguments, claims, and theories should also be scrutinized. However, the fact that they need to be critically examined does not affect the main point: that people's intuitions, claims, and theories should be the starting point for a political philosophy of democracy that seeks policy change. This is why I allow myself to ask whether the theory of deliberative democracy suggested by Miller and others actually works and actually reflects the way people think and behave. For this reason, one might argue that if a theory does not tie in with the way citizens behave and think, it might (although this is not necessarily the case) be telling us that the theory needs to be modified.

THE EMPIRICAL RESEARCH: ANALYZING RESULTS

Now that I have justified this approach, I would like to examine the results of two empirical research studies. The first is an examination of a citizen-based consensus conference that took place in Israel in early summer 2000.[39] The second is a research I conducted at the Hebrew University of Jerusalem.[40]

The subject of the first citizens' conference that took place in Israel was "the future of transportation in Israel." It addressed, among other questions, two of the most debated questions in Israeli politics: (1) Should the government follow the citizens' preferences to use private cars and pave more roads and motorways, or should public transportation be developed? (2) Should the government invest in trains? The conference was organized by a nongovernmental organization (NGO) with the financial and organizational support of the Israeli parliament. The conference had three stages: The first round of meetings was devoted mainly to discussing the participants' opinions and deciding about what they would like to ask the experts. In the second round of meetings, the participants met experts. Following those meetings, the citizens met at the parliament for two days to discuss the issue and reach decisions. The goal of this conference was defined as "producing an informed and agreed document" about transportation policies in Israel. The information reported here is based on a report that was prepared by two social psychologists hired to evaluate the process.

Let us now see whether the target—informed and agreed decisions—was met. First, then, did the participants know better following those meetings? Did they understand more following the conference? Was there a difference between the first and the second meeting? What was their attitude toward the experts who were interviewed during the conference?

Naturally, it is difficult to know whether objectively the participants' knowledge of the subject matter improved. However, we do have information about their subjective reflections about their knowledge and understanding of the matters discussed.

According to the report, most of the improvement in knowledge was after the second meeting, but before meeting the experts. In fact, following the meeting with the experts there was very little sense of advancement in terms of knowledge and understanding. It is revealed that the initial expectations to learn from the experts were much greater than the final degree of subjective feelings about what had been learned from them.[41] Some of the participants claimed, after meeting the experts, that they actually did not think they ought to be considered "experts" in the field.[42] The authors of the report suggest, though, that following their internal meetings most of the participants had constructed fixed opinions and were much less open than before to information from the experts. We can learn that the knowledge that these people claimed to have was "popular" knowledge, or in the report's language, "naive knowledge"[43] rather than scientific, and that their motive to know more was mainly their wish not to appear ignorant in their meetings with the other participants.[44] This is important, because as we shall see also from my own research later, it is not the case that people become more flexible and open when they are engaged in such deliberations; instead, many of them become more stubborn. An interesting note is that in some fields, for example, the impact of governmental policies on road accidents and development of inter-city roads, the participants reported that they had less understanding in the final stage of the conference.[45] This may suggest that the meetings actually confused them. They had their own opinions, but now that they were faced with new information, they did not want to change their minds, even though they sensed a cognitive dissonance.

The main question, though, is not whether they had more knowledge, but rather whether whatever knowledge they did have helped them reach "informed and agreed" decisions. Surprisingly, most of the participants reported that if they did change their views and were influenced by any knowledge, it was due to "authorized" knowledge that was found outside the conference.[46] In other words, a by-product of this conference was that people searched for information and perhaps then shaped their positions. Barne'a and Melech claim, though, that most participants did not change their opinions but "reshaped" them, perhaps because they felt that they could better base their original positions.[47] Most of the knowledge and understanding reported was directly linked to literature read at home.[48]

Now, the conference was meant to lead not only to "informed" decisions but also to "agreed" ones. However, a question is raised: what do people in such groups agree upon? Barne'a and Melech are quite explicit about it: "The agreements were about specific issues; they were never about basic values or political standpoints."[49] In the case of the first Israeli citizens' conference, such a debate was never taken.[50]

This is a very important observation. If it is true, this may be a blow to the deliberation theory. The whole approach is based on the assumption that politics is not instrumental only; it is about thinking as citizens and about deliberating our values. However, as it seems in those ad hoc deliberative groups, moral and general political issues cannot be discussed. There is pressure to reach a decision, and when such pressure exists there is no time to discuss the more profound, and naturally more controversial, issues. When facing deadlines and pressure to arrive at a consensus, people seek agreements precisely by pushing aside and bracketing their disagreement, especially the more fundamental ones, for example, morality.

And yet, one should not come to the conclusion that no agreement or change in people's standpoints and understanding was possible. In fact, the participants became much more sophisticated with regard to the causes of problems in transportation. For example, while after their first meeting many participants thought that the cause for traffic jams was technical, after the second meeting they agreed that it was mainly lack of cooperation between different political and municipal bodies.

Nevertheless, those understandings were mainly with regard to the problems, not necessarily with regard to solutions. This is bad news for the advocates of such deliberative mechanisms because they count on these meetings to help people put forward suggestions for—indeed, reach—"better" solutions.

Now, supporters of CBCC and other such deliberative institutions may concede at this point but argue that if the process of deliberation does not improve the participants' knowledge and understanding of the issue at stake, at least it sustains their sense of community. As I suggested previously, this may be true. However, it may also mean that the first goal of reaching "better" and "more informed" solutions is even more remote. The reason is in the participants' reports that they had a sense of belonging to the group, which was very important for them. All the same, they also reported that—partly because they did not want to harm this sense of togetherness and community—many disagreements and conflicts were not discussed as they should have been.[51] Moreover, the participants reported that the price of disagreement was high in the sense that it was very frustrating.[52] Apparently, sustaining the sense of community became a goal: the community was a good that the participants did not wish to give up by having to decide this way or another.

Thus, from this examination of the CBCC we can learn that indeed community formation becomes a key goal of deliberations, especially in small groups. (Later I argue that this is one reason why deliberation should be understood and practiced differently, in larger scales.) Hence, I conducted a research that aims at the question of information and reaching "informed" agreements. In March–April 2000 I asked political science students to answer a questionnaire. Each student received 30 shekels (approximately $6) for answering it. This attracted many students who were happy to take part. The questionnaire posed a series of questions involving novel policies. Some policies had to do with matters the students already knew about, other policies were completely new and unfamiliar. After describing each policy, I asked the students to grade their support for the policy (ranging from 0 for complete rejection to 10 for full approval). I then showed them a synopsis of a deliberation that had taken place. The function of showing them what was argued in the deliberation was to better inform them about the policy and make them feel they were hearing the pros and cons and the various interests involved. After receiving each piece of new information or hearing one of the sides in the deliberation, the students were again asked to grade their support for the policy. Let us recall that I was interested in examining the following:

Whether a long and more in-depth deliberation (which implies more information) is likely to yield broader consensus to innovative policies. It also explored whether the degree of correspondence between the additional and the original information affects people's doubts concerning accepting the new policy.[53]

Whether hearing the other side's argument in ad hoc deliberations produces agreement and compromise and whether people become more flexible.

Whether people behave more rationally and pay more attention to information when required to take a decision within a framework of deliberation, compared to cases when they must decide without a deliberation.[54]

The first point that the questionnaire explored was whether people are more likely to agree and accept the other's views when they deliberate about political issues.[55] Let us start with a general question that was put to the students.

Q1: Imagine yourself engaged in a debate with an ultraorthodox Jew in Israel. He is straightforward and describes his position openly. How would you react?[56]

He convinces me, and I agree with him: 0 percent

I become more moderate and see his position as legitimate: 10 percent

I see where my arguments are weak and revise my positions: 32.5 percent

I am ready to accept his position as legitimate, but not to revise my position or compromise: 47.5 percent

I see that he does not want to compromise and accept my position. Hence, I am strengthened in my position: 2.5 percent

Actually, I can't even see myself considering compromise in such matters: 7.5 percent

It is interesting to note that 42.5 percent of the students reported that they would revise their position. However, while they saw themselves as flexible people, perhaps also as open minded and liberal, in practice they did not change their minds.[57] This was clear from their responses to a series of questions.

First, students were asked to grade their support for a certain environmental policy.[58] After deciding whether and to what extent they supported this policy, they were told that they would read a script in which the two sides of the deliberation were represented. They were asked whether they thought they would be flexible and might change their minds. Next, after reading each of the arguments in the script, they were asked to regrade their support for the policy after each argument read. Finally, they were asked to reflect upon their responses and attitudes as they followed the debate, and especially about whether they had indeed been flexible. Let us start with the students' answers to their potential openness:

Q2: Now that you will see both sides' views, would you say that after hearing the other's point of view you might have more empathy toward his or her position, and that you could agree to compromise?

The results were rather impressive: 17.5 percent thought that they were going to be flexible; 57.5 percent felt that they would be at least slightly flexible; and only 25 percent thought they would find it difficult to compromise.

But the students' actual positions during the debate itself reveal a different picture. They were first asked to mark their support for the new motorway on the scale of 0 to 10 (5 indicating neutrality). Those who opposed the motorway (those whose level of support was less than 5) were then shown arguments in favor of the road and were asked to regrade their support. Those who favored the road were shown arguments against it and were asked to regrade their support. Finally, everyone was asked to read all the pros and cons and regrade their level of support. Our interest was to learn how many actually did change their views, and what was the average change on a scale of 0 to 10.

The initial average support for the road was 4.775
The average support after hearing the other side's arguments was 4.45
The average support after the whole deliberation was 4.575
The average absolute move on the scale (either in favor or against) from the initial position to the final one was 0.3

The students were then asked to reflect on their own experience in this experiment and to estimate whether their final positions were more or less the same as their initial positions or whether they were clearly different. This time, after being engaged in the process, the students were less optimistic about their openness and flexibility: 97.5 percent admitted that their final positions were more or less the same as the initial one.

We can thus say that not only did they not change their minds during or following the debate, but also that subjectively—although they had thought of themselves as rather flexible—upon reflection and following the experience itself, the students acknowledged that they had not revised their positions. These results may show that with regard to ad hoc deliberations, we cannot expect deliberation and more information to strengthen people's flexibility.

At this point, one could claim that the function of deliberation is not to change people's views, but to open their minds to the other, so that whatever is decided upon is seen as a compromise and an agreement. But then, as we see clearly, the students did not believe that they came to terms with the other side, or that they had compromised as a result of deliberation. To reexamine this point, I offered the students an ideological case not directly relevant to their everyday lives. I was under the impression that the students' self-image had been a far cry from their actual behavior because when they portrayed themselves as open minded they were thinking in terms of multi-issue deliberation, or ideological debate, rather than ad hoc deliberation. Thus, the additional case I gave them, since it was far from being a matter of private interests, allowed them to consider it as part of a general debate, which, I have argued, provokes greater flexibility in people.

The question was about social processes in the kibbutz. The students were told that the dining room services in a certain kibbutz had been privatized. I then asked them whether they thought this was all right.[59] The results were 71 percent in favor and 29 percent against. In the next stage, the students were informed of all arguments put forward by those in favor of privatizing the kibbutz dining room, for example, economic and social arguments. They were also told that a majority of the kibbutz favored privatization. This time 83 percent supported the move and only 17 percent objected. Then the students were told that during the debate in the kibbutz, it turned out that 85 percent of the kibbutz members who were above 65 years old resented the change. Those elderly people claimed that the reform conflicted with their values and expressed fears that it would alienate them from the community. The students were then asked to reflect on the case again. This time only 62 percent supported and 38 percent voted against.

In this case we find that people did change their minds and that they demonstrated flexibility and responsiveness to reasoning and arguments. Also important is that the information they were given appears to have been relevant and effective. The reason for this is apparently that the information was not only about impersonal interests. Instead, the students had to confront the question of their own general (one dare say ideological) attitudes to privatization and the social cost. This perhaps suggests that if deliberation is general and ideological, rather than about certain policy, then it will be effective.

Another benefit ascribed to deliberation is that it is more likely to yield a broad consensus for Promethean policies. My hypothesis was that additional information, even if consistent with previous information, may result in skepticism and flight toward what is already known and familiar. To examine this, I told the students that the university and the student union had decided that by 2001, 70 percent of the food in the cafeteria would have to be organic and that by 2002, all of the food in the cafeteria would be organic. I asked whether they agreed with this. The result was that 22.5 percent supported strongly, 45 percent supported, and 32.5 percent were against this decision. I then added new information. I told the student that the reason for the university's decision was the detrimental effect of chemicals and additives on the fertility of young men and women and the fact that 64 percent of the students eat or drink at least twice a day in the cafeteria. Now the total support was 80 percent with 30 percent strongly supporting; 7.5 percent opposed it, and 2.5 percent strongly objected; 10 percent said they could not decide!

This is interesting, and on the face of it rather promising, for deliberative democracy advocates. The level of support when more information is provided and when deliberation occurs is 80 percent (in contrast to the stage 1 level of 67.5 percent support) with only 10 percent against (stage 1 was 32.5 percent). This may also imply that people do change their minds as a result of more information. Unfortunately, the next stage was less promising. Next, the students were told that the cost of this arrangement would be high. This organic food would cost students an extra 9.14 shekels (about $1.87) a day. People say, I added, that as a result, students will be reluctant to buy food at the cafeteria and will therefore buy nonorganic food outside the university. Support dropped to 42.5 percent with 35 percent opposing and 22.5 percent who could not make up their minds.

Now we find that 22.5 percent were completely confused. If we add those who opposed the food reform, we find that a majority of 57.5 percent did not accept organic food in the cafeteria, in contrast to stage 1, when 67.5 percent were in favor. One might claim that this is indeed an example of deliberation working, and of people consequently changing their minds. However, the point is not only that a quarter of the people could not decide; a very interesting piece of data is that 70 percent of those who could not make up their mind had initially been supporters of the policy. Thus, the policy supporters became those who could not make up their mind, while the remainder of the people remained more or less true to their original opinions. This may suggest that ad hoc deliberation does not make a serious impact, or that if it does, the impact on the chances of promoting a new idea or policy may be a negative one.

In this question, however, the additional information was negative or contradicted the original information. This might explain why people started to hesitate. I therefore added a series of questions in which I offered more supportive information every round. Due to lack of space I shall not review each question here. The bottom line was clear: support for innovative policies dropped dramatically the more information I added. This is so even though the information was positive. Most of those who originally supported the policy changed to "can't make up my mind," whereas those who objected remained in their opposition. In general, almost half of the students could not decide.

Again, advocates of deliberation could point to these figures and claim that this proves that deliberation does have an impact. Alas, when we analyze the moves in positions we see that almost all those who changed their positions changed them to "can't make up my mind": 33 percent did not change their minds; 67 percent did. However, among them, 75 percent changed to "cannot make up my mind." So, we see that people do not change their minds to become more flexible and agree with the other side, but that they become more indecisive. Moreover, among those who opposed the suggested reforms, only 10 percent became supporters due to the new information. This may indicate that the flexible ones are those who initially support novel policy: their flexibility is "negative" from the point of view of a society interested in promoting Promethean policies. They will be the first to withdraw their support upon receipt of new information. This may imply that it is very difficult to promote novel policies through ad hoc deliberations. The more conservative people are not likely to change their minds, whereas those who are willing to try the novel policy may get cold feet as soon as they are exposed to more information.

The results of this research, namely, that very radical and innovative policies are not likely to be accepted in an ad hoc deliberation, should not surprise us. Theorists of deliberative democracy claim that for a deliberation to be successful, individuals must shift from using the terminology of private interests to discussing the general interest. Miller himself deduces that "in all cases the success of any particular demand will depend upon how far it can be expressed in terms that are close to, or distant from, the general political ethos of the community."[60] If this is so, then we cannot expect Promethean, or radical policies, to be legislated or agreed upon in the process of deliberation. By their very nature innovative ideas and policies represent a departure from mainstream political views, from the patterns in which mainstream people think, or from "the general political ethos of the community"; otherwise we would not refer to them as "innovative." In other words, innovative policies will rarely be agreed upon in a process of deliberation because deliberation is aimed at reaching a consensus: those involved in the deliberation have a prima facie "obligation" to reach a "justified agreement." In other words, they must seek the widest possible majority and construct their decision in vague and mainstream terms so that as many people as possible can accept it. By virtue of aiming to construct a sense of agreement, ad hoc deliberative democracy could become a rather conservative idea, instead of a radical one.

At this point I should modify my argument. If continuing the status quo would seem to a large group of the citizens very bad, they *are* likely to push toward a more radical change. In other words, if there is a consensus that the status quo is worse than any suggested reform, radical reforms may be agreed upon. (However, we know that these situations are rather rare.)[61]

It is also not surprising that the more information people have, the less they are likely to support the policy. More information does not necessarily make people more confident about their actions or decisions. In fact, it is often the case that the less one knows about an issue, the more one feels confident about one's positions because the full picture is missing: a one-side picture makes people confident that they are in the right (even where moral dilemmas are at stake). However, when both sides of an issue are known, the individual becomes doubtful and even perplexed.[62] This is not to suggest that we should oppose making information available. On the contrary, democracy means openness and transparency, but this does not imply we should expect people to become more confident in this process.

In fact, it is not quite clear how information about specific cases is relevant to the way people decide. It seems that people like to make their decisions based on their general ideology rather than by relating to a specific issue, hence information and deliberation are not very relevant for them. Indeed, this last point leads me to suggest that deliberation is important when it is heterogeneous, broad, and includes mixed subjects: that is to say that when there exists a wide, open, and egalitarian deliberation about a package of issues and political questions, rather than when the form of deliberation is ad hoc. Thus, the preceding criticism of the way in which deliberative democracy, especially ad hoc deliberation, has been promoted does not imply that deliberative democracy is bad for us. I therefore now turn to the last section of this chapter and to defending deliberative democracy.

DELIBERATIVE DEMOCRACY AND (IN)JUSTICE

My first argument is that the political function of deliberation should be clarified and modified. The question is how do we regard the relationships between deliberation and decision making. There are two possible answers (apart, of course, from denying any connection): we could either see deliberation as a necessary condition for the decision-making process to be legitimized, or we could want the deliberation to actually replace the formal decision-making process. In the first model, the citizens who take part in the deliberation are thought to constitute (in the sense of legitimization) policies. The emphasis in this model is on the citizens' legal and moral status in a democracy, and therefore on the necessity of letting them become involved in democratic processes. In the second model, however, the citizens, by deliberating, replace (or limit the role of) officials and politicians. Thus, the emphasis in this model is on the citizens as a democratic institution and on deliberation as a mechanism of constructing (envisioning and composing) the state's policies.

Miller and deliberative democracy theorists believe that true democracy means that the citizens *constitute* policies. In other words, citizens, by participating in deliberations, legitimize policies. Although many theorists agree with this position, some go a step further and suggest that the citizens should also *construct* policies. These theorists, I would like to argue, are wrong. Let me explain.

Early deliberation theorists put forward two arguments, which, I am afraid, do not live in harmony. First, they advocate what I have called the idea of "multi-issue deliberation." This was an open and egalitarian debate about a heterogeneous *package* of ideas, policies, and positions. Hence, deliberation was to take place *before* decisionmakers decide upon policies. This, they claimed, represented democratic sovereignty, and only when such multi-issue deliberations took place could policies be legitimate.

At the same time, however, the motivation to discuss deliberative democracy was those theorists' uneasiness with democracy, according to which politicians were failing to represent the people. Moreover, they claimed, politicians did not necessarily know better. The conclusion was that new and more direct mechanisms of governing were to be introduced.[63] Active participation in the form of deliberation was thus the cure to modern democracy's disease. However, by suggesting this role for deliberation, those theorists changed deliberation's function from legitimizing and constituting policies, perhaps complementing decision-making procedures, to actually constructing policies, thereby limiting the role of politicians and bureaucrats. In fact, deliberation was no more preceding decision making, but actually replacing it.

Now that deliberation was to construct the policy, the idea was that citizens would even decide by themselves, or discuss things in a manner that would limit the politicians' options when they come to decide. But how will these discussions take place? The political agenda is too dense. Therefore, the theorists suggested, citizens should be engaged in discussions only about a sample of subjects: some citizens discuss one matter and others discuss another.[64] This way deliberative democracy theorists have come to emphasize CBCCs and ad hoc deliberations rather than general, multi-issue deliberation. They have seen those bodies as an alternative to representative democracy.

In other words, these theorists think that CBCCs can become the body of a new form of direct democracy. This is the second model mentioned previously, where deliberation constructs policies. I would like to suggest that on the basis of empirical studies this description of the citizens' role in politics is far-fetched, and in fact, not necessarily healthy for democracy. I shall first acknowledge that deliberation partly constitutes policies, but, I shall then argue, this is done by taking place *after* decisions have been made, or to be more precise, by reacting to the many political decisions. In that sense, the citizens cannot be directly involved in constructing policy. Deliberations do constitute the policy, but they do not and should not construct it.

As seen earlier, citizens cannot devote their entire energy and time to participation. Moreover, as seen in the first sections, even when they do participate, they do not necessarily fully comprehend every aspect of the issue at stake. When reflecting upon their participation in deliberations they also come to the conclusion that they do not necessarily become more flexible or "rational" due to the deliberation, and they are skeptical about their professional contribution. Thus, if deliberative democracy theorists wanted us to deliberate in order to save democracy from its politicians and bureaucrats, ad hoc deliberations and CBCCs are not going to help. Moreover, it is empirically not true that by participating in deliberations the citizens can construct policies. At the end of the day all they can do is suggest, put forward ideas, and assert their positions. Most of them lack the capability of shaping those positions in terms of policies.

However, this does not mean that citizens have no role to play and that deliberations should not be a crucial part of democracy.

Suppose that decisionmakers know in advance that their decisions would be subject to public scrutiny in a process of open and egalitarian deliberation *after* decisions have been made. The decisionmakers would refrain from making arbitrary decisions, or from suggestions that only represent a minority's interests or their own private interests. Instead, they would do their best to suggest policies that are likely to be accepted by the general public, not only for the obvious reason of increasing their own popularity and chances of reelection, but also because of economic reasons. (Economic here may be in terms of time, energy, pressures on the political agenda, as well as public money.) In fact, the former (aiming at being reelected) applies only to politicians, who are subject to reelection. Alas, most decisions concern regulations and are made by bureaucrats who have no fear of not being reelected. However, if decisionmakers, including bureaucrats, are aware that their decisions will be followed by critical public deliberation, then they will take the public's potential positions and interests into account, at the very least for economic reasons. To better understand this mechanism, let me emphasize that according to this model of decision making, policies are seen as just another input to the system, since after decisions are made, even after implementation, they become known to the public and are subject to critical review by the media, the state comptroller, intellectuals, the general public, and so on.

Now, if a certain policy provokes strong opposition, it will need to be reexamined. Thus, from the point of view of decisionmakers, there is an economic need to reduce the number of times that policies are reevaluated, or else they will collapse under the burden of work. The less controversial and confrontational policies are, the more time, money, and effort decisionmakers are likely to save for the system (and themselves). Alas, as argued earlier, and since novel ideas are always controversial, this also implies that innovative, Promethean policies are unlikely to be implemented in deliberative democracies unless the changes are gradual and systematically undertaken.[65]

This implies that while deliberation often takes place after decisions, and in that sense legitimizes (and also in an indirect manner constitutes) the policy decision, if we are looking for radical reforms and novel policies, deliberative democracy is not likely to produce it. However, an argument that is likely to support deliberative democracy does not necessarily relate to efficiency. Instead, I draw on David Miller's work and develop his argument to show that deliberative democracy, which takes the form of a multi-issue deliberation, has the potential of preventing injustice.

Miller argues that the meeting point between democracy and justice lies in their being essential components of community. He believes that deliberation—here in the sense of multi-issue deliberation—helps in creating "chemistry" between people. He envisions majorities and minorities being able to sympathize and identify with one other through deliberation.[66] Perhaps the term should be *empathy*, not *sympathy*. Sympathy means sharing the feelings of the other, or harmony in feelings. This is a heavy demand: many people cannot *share* other people's feelings or positions because they cannot accept those feelings or because they disagree with their positions. Empathy, however, stands for the intellectual identification with the feelings, thoughts, and experiences of the other, without necessarily agreeing or sharing those feelings. Thus, we can have community where people discuss their thoughts—including their disagreements—but where it is not necessary for them to share similar ideas in the sense of thinking along similar lines. Community exists when people debate and discuss issues; they do not necessarily have to agree. So, I would suggest using *empathy* here. However, the lesson from Miller's theory is that community in the sense of a higher form of human relationships is built through and sustained by deliberation.

What circumstances will tend to fortify such empathy? Justice enters the picture because, in order for people to entertain such empathy toward the values expressed by others, they must feel they belong to a *just* community that has equal respect for all its members' values.[67] Miller argues that the more just a society is, the greater the sensitivity and attentiveness that citizens develop for others' conceptions of the good. Miller assumes that caring and community are latent human qualities; we just need to expose them and remove the layers that hide them. A sense of justice can do this. For Miller, therefore, deliberation is the road to community, and justice will secure a healthy form of deliberation. In other words, where justice prevails, deliberation can flourish and will thereby enhance community.

A question arises: why should deliberative democracy expose caring? And what if there is no justice? Imagine a situation in which a person fails to develop a sense of caring and empathy. Suppose this person thinks her society is *not* just. She might lose her good will and empathy toward others.[68] In other words, subjective evaluations of injustice may prevent a sense of community.

Unless, that is, this person believes that she has a good chance of changing this injustice. When people feel they have the power to influence matters, they feel less alienated and tend to empathize with others more easily. Even though they feel their society is not completely just, they will not become alienated or give up hope since they still feel they can make an impact and help to improve things. Needless to say, one such mechanism of impact is the deliberation that takes place within a society. In other words, deliberative democracy which takes the form of a multi-issue deliberation will contribute to its members' willingness to work harder to achieve justice and prevent injustice because they do not believe that their efforts are futile.

Let me elaborate. First, deliberation does not automatically lead to justice. Miller himself points this out when he argues that not every call for democratization is a call for greater justice,[69] and that claiming that justice and democracy are one and the same is wrong and prevents one from choosing between these values.[70] Indeed, even when deliberative democracy flourishes, not all policies are just. For example, in Israel there is a lively and serious multi-issue deliberation taking place, characterized by intensive and broad participation. Nevertheless, it cannot be said that justice prevails. For example, the allocation of money to local municipalities is extremely unfair: for various reasons, it is likely that towns populated by Arab Israelis will receive much less funding per person than towns with Jewish Israeli populations. Thus, deliberation itself is not a sufficient condition for justice. Nevertheless, the deliberation that has taken place since this discrimination was revealed several years ago has served to impede any further injustice. As a result of demonstrations, strikes, and citizens' petitions, parliament and the government have been working on curbing this injustice. However, and more important, the deliberation that this injustice has sparked has sent warning signals to decisionmakers that have an impact on many other decisions affecting both Arabs and Jews in Israel. Let me put it this way: just as lawyers often claim that a particular policy will not stand the test of an appeal to the Supreme Court, it could also be argued that where persistent, multi-issue deliberative democracy exists, certain policy proposals or legislative bills will fail the test of deliberative democracy. Hence, politicians and those responsible for policies will tend not to put forward ideas that discriminate sectors or individuals in society, if they know that the postdecision deliberation is likely to raise well-grounded objections. So, the very fact that multi-issue deliberation exists may prevent injustice.

However, notice that for this to happen, we must have deliberation not only preceding decision making, but also following it. Thus, we can relate to any decision as a yet another input to the ongoing deliberation about political questions. Indeed, only in democracy is it legitimate to keep debating and criticizing policies even after decisions take place and the policies have been announced. Thus, we can see that the merit of deliberative democracy lies in the fact that it takes place also after decisions have been made, as a preventative measure against injustice and arbitrariness. In fact, each item and issue does not actually have to be deliberated. Suffice it that decisionmakers are aware of the possibility of there being wide-ranging and persistent critical deliberation, for them to avoid taking arbitrary action and making discretionary decisions.[71]

CONCLUSION

I have argued that of late, deliberative democracy theorists—who first had in mind multi-issue deliberations about packages of ideas, policies, and values—are now tending to regard the essence of deliberation as debates that take place in CBCCs and ad hoc situations. At the same time their expectations of deliberation have remained the same, that is, that it will yield more rational decisions, help form agreements, and legitimize Promethean policies. I have argued that these expectations do not match the way people behave. All the same, deliberative democracy is to be promoted because when it is multi-issue, that is, about a package of positions and ideas, it might have the capacity to prevent arbitrary injustice. Miller claims that when there are relations of domination and oppression, and when there is uncertainty regarding "precisely what it means to be someone's fellow citizen," that is, when democracy is absent, then the "basic structure" is unjust.[72] I have added that when multi-issue deliberation is vigorous, free, and egalitarian, thereby creating a sense of what it means to be someone's fellow citizen, then injustice is less likely to prevail.

It now remains to be seen how such deliberations are to be promoted and sustained, how to outreach a larger section of society, how to create a culture of debating and listening, and how to attract people to this mode of democracy.

NOTES

1. However, Miller is right about deliberation sustaining a sense of community.

2. Emily Hauptmann, "Deliberation = legitimacy = Democracy," *Political Theory* 27 (1999): 857. John Dryzek's view is that the turn from democracy as collective decisions through voting and representation to deliberative democracy took place around 1990. See John Dryzek, *Deliberative Democracy and Beyond* (Oxford: Oxford University Press, 2000), 1–7.

3. David Miller, *Citizenship and National Identity* (Cambridge: Polity Press, 2000), 3.

4. Amy Gutmann and Dennis Thompson, *Democracy and Disagreement: Why Moral Conflict Cannot Be Avoided in Politics and What Can Be Done About It* (Cambridge, Mass.: Harvard University Press, 1996); Amy Gutmann and Dennis Thompson, "Why Deliberative Democracy Is Different," *Social Philosophy and Policy* 17 (2000): 161–180; Juergen Habermas, "Three Normative Models of Democracy," in *Democracy and Difference*, ed. S. Benhabib (Princeton, N.J.: Princeton University Press, 1996), 21–31; John Dryzek, *Democracy in Capitalist Times* (New York: Oxford University Press, 1996); John Dryzek, *Deliberative Democracy and Beyond* (Oxford: Oxford University Press, 2000); Joshua Cohen, "Deliberation and Democratic Legitimacy," in *The Good Polity*, ed. A. Hamlin and P. Pettit (Oxford: Blackwell, 1989); Jon Elster, ed., *Deliberative Democracy* (Cambridge: Cambridge University Press, 1998). Gutmann and Thompson define deliberative democracy differently. "Democracy is deliberative to the extent that decisions and policies are justified in a process of discussion among free and equal citizens or their accountable representatives. . . . Its fundamental principle is that citizens owe one another justifications for the laws they collectively impose on one another" (Amy Gutmann and Dennis Thompson, "Why Deliberative Democracy Is Different," 161). This definition focuses on general processes in the society rather than on ad hoc groups. The latter, much the focus of many deliberative democracy theorists, is the object of my critique. However, there are more radical consid-

erations of democratic deliberation, such as the one recently put forward by Robert Goodin, "Democratic Deliberation Within," *Philosophy and Public Affairs* 29 (2000): 81–109, among others. This is what Goodin calls "democratic deliberation within." The idea is that we should "ease the burdens of deliberative democracy in mass society by altering our focus from the 'external-collective' to the 'internal-reflective' mode, shifting much of the work of democratic deliberation back inside the head of each individual" (Goodin, "Democratic Deliberation Within," 83). However, this seems to me a suggestion that follows the general mood of virtual worlds rather than a genuine deliberation. Goodin himself is quite aware of this potential criticism, and he suggests this internal deliberation as second best (Goodin, "Democratic Deliberation Within," 99ff.)

5. Roger Masters, "Rousseau, Jean-Jacques," in *The Blackwell Encyclopedia of Political Thought*, ed. D. Miller (Oxford: Blackwell, 1987).

6. Nowadays some theorists offer that there should be many small-size groups deliberating, thereby forming a web of deliberations. Goodin writes that this idea (which, he attributes to Aristotle [Aristotle, *Politics*, 129a13]) will not work. Rather than forming a web in which all citizens are linked to as many other citizens as possible (say, if each citizen participates in five such groups), in the real world, argues Goodin, too many people are "socially excluded," and they will therefore participate in no such group. In other words, Goodin is rightly cautious about such an arrangement because it will lead to a situation whereby only the elite participates in the deliberations.

7. John Dryzek, "Representative Democracy and the Environment," in *Democracy and the Environment*, ed. J. Meadowcraft (Edward Elgar, 1997), 120.

8. John Dryzek, *Rational Ecology* (Oxford: Blackwell, 1988), 200. Interestingly, while Dryzek believes that if such practical reasoning is applied, then the legitimacy of the majority's support is not required (because the action is supported by the best reason), David Miller believes that if an issue is deliberated, the majority will consequently support the consequent decision. Though it could be argued that the two positions do not contrast each other, Miller's argument is descriptive, whereas Dryzek's argument is normative.

9. M. P. d'Entrèves, "Hannah Arendt and the Idea of Citizenship," in *Dimensions of Radical Democracy*, ed. C. Morffe (London: Verso, 1992), 146; Hanna Arendt, *Between Past and Future* (New York: Viking Press, 1968).

10. Miller, *Citizenship*, ch. 1

11. Joshua Cohen, "An Epistemic Conception of Democracy," *Ethics* 97 (1987): 26–38.

12. For example, Gutmann and Thompson, *Democracy and Disagreement*.

13. Gutmann and Thompson, "Why Deliberative Democracy Is Different," 169.

14. Miller, *Citizenship*, 10 and fn. 9. See also the discussion of Walzer's similar position in Stephen Mulhall and Adam Swift, *Liberals and Communitarians* (Oxford: Blackwell, 1996), 135.

15. Miller, *Citizenship*, 3 (my emphasis).

16. Miller, *Citizenship*, 22.

17. I call this a magic because I accept, as an assumption, that political disagreements are, as Andrew Mason, *Explaining Political Disagreement* (Cambridge: Cambridge University Press, 1993), 2, writes, "pervasive and intractable."

18. Miller, *Citizenship*, 9.

19. Miller writes:

> By giving these reasons, I am committing myself to a general principle, which by implication applies to any other similarly placed group. Thus I am forced to take a wider view, and either defend the claim I am making when applied not only to my group but to groups B, C, and D which are like A in the relevant respects, or else to back down and moderate the claim to something I am prepared to accept in these other cases too. (Miller, *Citizenship*, 10)

And: "The first requirement of deliberation is that the reasons behind the proposal must be elaborated. . . . Beyond that it would be necessary to connect the reasons given to more general reasons that others were likely to accept" (Miller, *Citizenship*, 55).

20. Miller's notion of a good citizen is "Republican." A Republican citizen is "actively involved in shaping the future direction of his or her society" (Miller, *Citizenship*, 3; and ch. 3).

21. Miller, *Citizenship*, ch. 3. Mark Sagoff is right to claim that such a position distinguishes between the individual as a "consumer" and the individual as a "citizen" (Mark Sagoff, *The Economy of the Earth* [Cambridge: Cambridge University Press: 1988], 93–95).

22. Miller, *Citizenship*, 4 (my emphasis).

23. Miller, *Citizenship*, 4.

24. Miller, *Citizenship*, 4.

25. The first citizen-based consensus conference was practiced in Denmark by the parliament in the late 1980s, and since then there have been many such gatherings of laypersons in ten other countries—recently in Israel as well (see the following)—to discuss environmental, biotechnology, genetic engineering, telecommunication, and transportation policies. These conferences are sponsored by the states.

26. Miller (*Citizenship*, ch. 1) does relate to an empirical research about deliberation and what people think about which verdict a jury should reach. However, this is a case of court. It is far from being a case of politics.

27. Avner de-Shalit, *The Environment: Between Theory and Practice* (Oxford: Oxford University Press, 2000), ch. 1.

28. David Miller, *Principles of Social Justice* (Cambridge, Mass.: Harvard University Press, 1999), x.

29. Miller, *Principles*, 51–59.

30. He therefore presents a similarity between why political scientists need political theory and why political theorists need political science. For further discussion of Miller's methodology, see the papers by Stears, Swift, White, and Mason in this volume.

31. Norman Daniels, *Justice and Justification* (Cambridge: Cambridge University Press, 1996), 2.

32. John Rawls, *A Theory of Justice* (Oxford: Oxford University Press, 1973).

33. Miller, *Citizenship*, 54.

34. Michael Walzer, *Interpretation and Social Criticism* (Cambridge, Mass.: Harvard University Press, 1987); Michael Walzer, *The Company of Critics* (New York: Basic), 1988; Michael Walzer, *Thick and Thin: Moral Arguments at Home and Abroad* (South Bend: University of Notre Dame Press, 1994).

35. Walzer, *Interpretation*, 1–33.

36. Walzer, *Thick and Thin*, 42.

37. Walzer, *Thick and Thin*, 52–53.

38. Walzer, *Thick and Thin*, 52–53.

39. Based on a report by Marina Barne'a and Gilah Melech, "Ve'idat Erazchim Reshona Be'Isarel—The First Citizens Conference in Israel," (report, in Hebrew, 2000). I would like to thank Mr. Ronen Gofer, chief organizer of this conference, for allowing me to see this report.

40. I should like to thank the Schein Center for Research in the Social Sciences at the Hebrew University for a generous grant received for this research. Many thanks to Ms. Tal Tamir for conducting the research and her comments on the results. In doing this research, I was inspired by Jyrki Aakkula, from the Agricultural Economics Research Institute at Helsinki, and his research into interaction between attitudes and information. Technically, since this research was done among students who had known each other (unlike the case of CBCCs), and since (1) I wanted to prevent the goal of community formation, and (2) there was a risk of people adjusting their opinions to what they thought I would want them to claim, or to charismatic students, I did not conduct it as an actual deliberation. Instead, people read scripts of imagined deliberations and were asked to enter the deliberation in several stages. In doing so, I overlooked the personal benefit one finds in participating in an actual debate. However, this research is not interested in this matter, because it is assumed that this benefit is indeed true, and yet, it applies to a general, rather than only to an ad hoc, deliberation as well.

41. Barne'a and Melech, "Ve'idat Erazchim," 23.

42. Some of them even declared that "they were not going to compete with the experts," as if

the experts were there to challenge the participants.

43. Barne'a and Melech, "Ve'idat Erazchim," 13.

44. Such motive is suggested also by James Fishkin, "Deliberative Polling" (lecture given at the Israeli parliament, May 2000).

45. Barne'a and Melech, "Ve'idat Erazchim," 14.

46. Barne'a and Melech, "Ve'idat Erazchim," 17, 13, 23.

47. Barne'a and Melech, "Ve'idat Erazchim," 17, fn. 4.

48. Barne'a and Melech, "Ve'idat Erazchim," 13, 23. I should add that one possible reason for people to report that the more they were involved in the process of learning the less they felt competent about the various issues discussed is that in general the more people learn about an issue, the more they realize its complexity, thereby feeling they know very little about it. However, Marina Barne'a and Gilah Melech ("Ve'idat Erazchim," 16) suggest that it could be that the dynamics of sitting together and deciding about important issues caused these people to close themselves to new information. They felt that they already "knew enough."

49. Barne'a and Melech, "Ve'idat Erazchim," 18.

50. Barne'a and Melech, "Ve'idat Erazchim," 19.

51. Barne'a and Melech, "Ve'idat Erazchim," 2, 18–19.

52. Barne'a and Melech, "Ve'idat Erazchim," 21.

53. It seems that politicians suspect that people's hesitation would increase the more information they get even when the new information is consistent with the original. For example, in 1999, when it seemed that Israel was about to sign a peace agreement with Syria, the government agreed to public demands that a referendum be called before the agreement was approved. Several ministers among the Labour party agreed to this on condition that the debate preceding the referendum be as short and minimal as possible and that very few details from the peace contract be revealed. They feared that the more information that was revealed to the public, even if this information was "positive," the more people would vote against it. For example, if the public learns that the United States will guarantee Israel's security after the agreement is signed—which is consistent with the government's claim that a peace treaty implies more rather than less security—people might start raising questions such as why we need American guarantees if we are talking about peace. This, so these Labour ministers feared, would make people change their minds from supporting to rejecting the peace agreement.

54. Irrational behavior here would be sticking to one's general ideology regardless of the benefits involved in compromise on the specific issue.

55. While admittedly the experiment did not include actual deliberation (see preceding), those students were given written responses to their answers and were allowed to ask questions and comment.

56. This situation is very common in Israel and involves bitter debates. Religion is a key component of identity in Israel. In addition, bitterness among secular Jews arises due to the release from compulsory military service (of three years and then twenty days a year of military reserve service) that the ultraorthodox enjoy, due to political arrangements.

57. However, as I argue later, flexibility rises tremendously when general ideological matters are discussed, as opposed to specific policies and ad hoc matters. So, people viewing their self-image as flexible could be explained as relating to such cases.

58. Regarding the Trans-Israel Highway, a highly controversial and very expensive project.

59. I also gave them the option to not answer because this issue was not interesting, but very few (only two) preferred not to answer.

60. Miller, *Citizenship*, 56.

61. I thank Jo Wolff for this comment.

62. Amos Tversky, "The Psychology of Judgement and Decision-Making," *Economic Quarterly* 44 (1997): 327–337 (in Hebrew).

63. For example, James Fishkin, *Democracy and Deliberation* (New Haven, Conn.: Yale University Press, 1991); and James Fishkin, *The Voice of the People* (New Haven, Conn.: Yale University Press, 1995).

64. Miller does write that ideally the same persons will discuss many issues, but that this is not

very likely to happen. Miller, *Citizenship,* 205, fn. 25.

65. A good example was a decision made in 1993 by the then Israeli prime minister, Mr. Rabin, and his chancellor. Being social democrats, they decided to tax income from the stock market. However, following their decision, which was presented as a regulation, there was a collapse in the stock market and severe criticism by journalists, other politicians, and many among the general public. The result was that they treated their decision as input into a public deliberation, not so much about the specific decision, but rather about the Israeli society and its positions on distributive justice. It turned out that following more or less fifteen years of uninterrupted rule of the right-wing party, it was too difficult and unpopular to put forward such innovative policies. So, finally, Rabin and his chancellor regretfully canceled their decision.

66. Miller, *Citizenship,* introduction.

67. Miller, *Principles,* ch. 11, esp. 237–238.

68. Miller seems to assume that this possibility is not plausible when justice is done to the vast majority, as if one should realize that, say, in the given circumstances this is the best that could be done. However, it should be noted that this sense of being a member of a just society is subjective. For example, an outsider might wonder why it is that members of kibbutzim often feel that their society is not just enough even though this outsider can compare the kibbutz with other communities and find it egalitarian and just. And yet, many kibbutz members have a subjective feeling of uneasiness about how just their kibbutz is, presumably because their moral standards are very high. So, even if the society is just, it could well be the case that many people will not feel it is.

69. Miller, *Principles,* 15.

70. Miller, *Principles,* 17.

71. See also Avner de-Shalit, "On Behalf of the Participation of the People," *Res Publica* 3 (1997): 62–75.

72. Miller, *Principles,* 17, 40.

9

Minority Participation and Civic Education in Deliberative Democracies

Meira Levinson

In his thought-provoking book *Citizenship and National Identity*, David Miller makes a concerted case for the desirability of deliberative democracy (or republicanism, as he sometimes terms it) as a governing political norm and practice. According to Miller, deliberative democracy promotes a process by which politics proceeds "through an open and uncoerced discussion of the issue at stake with the aim of arriving at an agreed judgement."[1] This is in contrast to what he terms *liberal adversarial democracy*, which he suggests aims merely at a "fair and efficient" aggregation of preferences.[2] In adversarial democracy, people give reasons to support their position and convert people to their side, but they also try to win adherents by bargaining, airing attack ads, making alliances, and so forth. In deliberative democracy, on the other hand, people give and listen to reasons in order to reach a consensus; alliances and bargains are not made because decisions are not made through majority voting but through deliberation and compromise until all members of the deliberative body agree. Deliberative democracy thus has many attractive elements: it fosters cooperation and mutual understanding, rather than winning and losing (as adversarial democracy seems to); it purports to give to all citizens a "voice" rather than just to the most powerful or the most numerous (as tends to occur in majoritarian democracy); and it encourages citizens to make decisions based on "public reasons" that can be supported through deliberation rather than on individual prejudices that thrive in the privacy of the voting booth.

To achieve deliberative democracy in practice is, of course, difficult. As Miller clearly understands, aspiration and realization are two very different things. Even if it is desirable that decisions are made through deliberative rather than liberal adversarial processes, certain social and political conditions must be present if deliberative democracy is to live up to its promise. Crucially, Miller points out, the *ability* (as opposed to merely the right) of all groups to partici- pate equally is central to deliberative democracy's rationality and legitimacy:

> Deliberative democracy may be formally inclusive, in the sense that everyone is permitted to enter and speak in democratic forums, but if the debate by its very nature favours some groups at the expense of others, it is not inclusive in a sub- stantive sense. Similarly if the reasons that prove to count in deliberative settings are not reasons for everyone, but only reasons for particular groups or coalitions of groups, then the outcome cannot be described as rational in a sense that tran- scends group membership. If the rationality claim falls, so does the legitimacy claim, for why should the disadvantaged groups accept as legitimate a procedure that relies upon methods of argument and reasons that they cannot share?[3]

As a result, it is essential to Miller's argument that he be able to show that deliberative democracy does enable members of all groups to participate on an equal basis, not only in the sense of their simply being present at the discus- sions, but also in the sense of their speaking out, being listened to and under- stood, and influencing the debate where appropriate.

Miller therefore starts by arguing that members of all significant groups should be "present in legislative assemblies and other political forums"[4] so that the entire range of opinions and perspectives within the community will be voiced. He leaves it frustratingly unclear how he would ensure such a range of participation, since he rightly comes out against quotas or other means of institutionalizing group identity and participation (i.e., establishing a "politics of recognition"), but does not give a positive political program of his own. He does argue in favor of continuing "the battle to free the public sphere of sym- bols, practices and unstated assumptions that prevent the members of some groups from participating as equal citizens,"[5] and he suggests that national identities should be remade "in a way that is more hospitable to women, eth- nic minorities and other groups without emptying them of content and de- stroying the underpinnings of democratic politics."[6]

This is admirable, but hardly a straightforward means of increasing minor- ity participation in political institutions. But he does (indirectly) make it clear, I think, that deliberative institutions would certainly be no worse than current liberal political institutions at fostering widespread participation, and might in fact be better, so I won't press him on this issue here.

In addition to arguing in favor of minority presence, Miller addresses the is- sue of minority participation, especially in relation to minority groups' appar- ent discomfort at speaking out in deliberative and other political settings. He considers the evidence given by Iris Marion Young and Lynn Sanders that men and women, and whites and blacks, participate unequally in verdict-driven jury deliberation and in adversarial settings such as courts or parliaments— and thus presumably in other adversarial deliberative settings such as a delib- erative democracy might institutionalize.[7] In response, he argues (persuasively, if extremely idealistically, I think) that other models of deliberation and of deliberative institutions are available, such as evidence-based jury deliberation and nonadversarial lawmaking bodies, which do foster more equal participation by women and men and blacks and whites.

The lesson for deliberative democrats, therefore, is not that they should throw up their hands in dismay when it is pointed out that members of disadvantaged groups tend to participate less in collective deliberation, but that they should look for ways of ensuring that deliberation takes a form that corresponds to an evidence-driven jury, which means that instead of trying to move quickly to a yes/no decision, the arguments for and against different options should be explored without individual participants having to declare which they support. This, it seems to me, is what good political deliberation would in any case require.[8]

Thus, properly structured deliberative institutions present a kind of "win-win" situation: they reduce or eliminate inequalities in people's comfort in contributing to the deliberations, and they improve the overall quality of political deliberation. Furthermore, as Miller later argues, deliberative institutions such as these are the best—and really the only—way of rationally reaching political solutions to common problems, and thus members of all groups, and especially minority groups, are well served by participating in them.[9]

So far, so good. What Miller does not consider carefully enough, however, are the other aspects of participation that matter for deliberative democracy to be rational and legitimate: namely, all participants' being listened to and understood, and their thereby actually influencing the debate where appropriate. Again, the preconditions of a legitimate set of deliberative democratic institutions are as follows:

> Deliberative democracy requires that political debate should be structured in such a way that, first, as wide a range of relevant views and arguments as possible should enter the debate, so that the ensuing discussion should genuinely reflect the concerns, interests and convictions of the members of the deliberating body; and second, that as the body attempts to move towards a solution to the issue that they confront, it should be the weight of the reasons offered in support of the different positions that counts.[10]

We have seen that Miller hopes to encourage a wide range of groups, views, and arguments to be present in deliberative settings (even if we're not quite sure how he would achieve it). And we have seen how Miller would reorient deliberative institutions to make them more conducive to all participants' having a "voice." But Miller seems to assume a direct causal relationship between "relevant views and arguments" "enter[ing]" the debate and the "ensuing discussion" "genuinely reflect[ing] the concerns, interests, and convictions" of the participants. This causal inference is wrong, I believe, for reasons that I will give in the first part of this chapter. As I will explain, even if members of groups from across the political and social spectrum are present in a deliberative body, and even the participants all "enter" their ideas by speaking up, not everything that is said is likely to be heard and understood in such a way as to be appropriately reflected in the deliberations. It is possible that a certain type of deliberative civic education can help individuals overcome these deliberative disjunctions, and I discuss this in the second section of this chapter. Ultimately, however, deliberative civic education introduces as many problems as it solves; these concerns, their implications for deliberative democracy's legitimacy, and the potential superiority of liberal adversarial democracy and civic education provide the focus for the last section of this chapter.

THE CHALLENGE OF DELIBERATIVE EQUALITY

There are three reasons that equal participation in deliberative bodies, even when coupled with the best of intentions and good will by all participants, may nonetheless result in unequal and inappropriate disjunctions in influence on the deliberative process. These reasons include incorrect perceptions of minority "extremism" by members of majority groups, blindness to the ways that norms may operate invisibly in majority settings but suddenly seem offputting or "sectarian" when they are made visible in minority settings, and the well-intentioned but disempowering attempt of individuals to reinterpret what others say in order to make it seem "reasonable." I will address these one at a time.

Minority "Extremism"

The first reason that equal participation (or at least "vocalization") does not necessarily translate to equal appropriate consideration within a deliberative setting is that minority groups may have such different experiences from the majority group that they come to understand how the world (or the nation) works in a way that is significantly different from, and even incomprehensible to, members of the advantaged majority. As a result, a member from the minority group may put forth arguments within a political debate that rest on premises about the world that are generally accepted by all of the other members of his group but are rejected as bizarre or crazy by the majority of the deliberative body. In this case, the deliberation is unlikely to be substantively inclusive, and therefore unlikely to be legitimate from the minority group's point of view. This lack of legitimacy would be further increased if the contributions of a number of minority groups were regularly viewed this way by the majority of the deliberants, or if the group that was viewed this way constituted a substantial (albeit still minority) share of the population, or if the group whose ideas were regularly rejected were constituted by something other than belief (i.e., ethnicity, race, gender, etc.). For although it is true that there are some groups in the world whose ideas really are crazy across the board, these groups are rarely very large, presumably not numerous within any one deliberative setting (city, district, or nation), and almost inevitably formed around the crazy beliefs they espouse. If we discover, therefore, that the contributions of blacks, or women, or Muslims (of a range of stripes, not just the most extreme) are consistently viewed in this way in deliberative settings, then we would be right to conclude that such deliberations are not substantively inclusive.

It is important to emphasize that this problem may arise even when the claims that the minority group makes appeal to common interests of all citizens rather than to the group's own interests only, and when the norms behind the appeals are also generally shared among all citizens, minorities and others alike. I mention this because of Miller's comment:

> Very broadly we can separate two kinds of claims that may be advanced in [republican] political debate. On the one hand there are claims that appeal at base to an interest common to all the citizens of a particular country, such as an interest in security from attack. On the other hand there are claims that reflect the interest of a particular group and whose satisfaction would typically impose some costs on other groups. In the second case but not the first, in order to reach agreement an appeal has to be made to a norm of justice, such as a principle of equal treatment. However this does not necessarily mean that claims in the second category are more difficult to advance than claims in the first. The norm itself may be relatively uncontroversial: the problem may be to convince hearers that the group in question really does have a case under the norm, which may be a matter of drawing attention to facts that have hitherto gone unnoticed. *In both cases the degree of difficulty will depend on how extreme (relative to others in your political community) your views are.*[11]

In a certain way, Miller is right. The degree of difficulty in convincing the deliberative body as a whole will depend on how extreme your views seem to be. But as I mentioned previously, because of different life experiences or other cultural differences, members of a minority group may put forward claims about a common interest (such as community protection through policing) that appeal to common norms and that seem totally mundane from that group's perspective, yet seem absolutely extreme from the majority group's perspective. This problem cannot necessarily be solved by "drawing attention to facts that have hitherto gone unnoticed,"[12] as it is the facts themselves that may be a matter of debate.

For example, many American blacks remain extremely suspicious of government health care policy in the United States as a result of revelations that for over fifty years, the federal government sponsored doctors to observe but not treat black men who suffered from syphilis in the now-infamous Tuskegee syphilis study. This lack of trust has led to significant suspicion within the black community of state-mandated childhood immunizations and even of the antiretroviral drug "cocktails" now used to combat HIV and AIDS.[13] A smaller but still surprisingly significant number of blacks also believe, or at least seriously entertain the idea—again stemming from the Tuskegee experience—that the CIA developed and spread AIDS in inner cities and Africa and developed and sold crack cocaine in the inner cities in the 1980s.[14] A further example of what might seem like "extremism" to many white Americans but which is well entrenched in many American black communities is the belief that blacks who rise too high in America other than in sports or entertainment, and especially in politics, are inevitable targets for (possibly government-sponsored) assassination. As a middle school teacher, teaching American history and English to thirteen- to fifteen-year-olds, I am frequently confronted by questions from my students in this regard. During the Republican presidential primary season in 1999, my students in Boston asked me if I thought that Alan Keyes, a black candidate, would soon be assassinated.[15] Similarly, my students in Atlanta and my (black) colleague there who taught American history were sure that Ron Brown, the Democratic National Committee chairman and Clinton's cabinet secretary who died in an airplane crash in the Balkans, was killed on governmental orders. Just a few years before that, it was widely reported that celebrated Persian Gulf War general Colin Powell did not run for president because his wife was afraid he would be assassinated. And finally, probably the most celebrated recent example of vast disparities in white and black interpretations of "the facts" was the O. J. Simpson case, in which blacks and whites arguably subscribed to the same norms of justice but tended to be 180 degrees opposed in their beliefs about the justice of the verdict.

These examples remind us, I hope, of the crucial disparities in how many blacks and whites in America experience and interpret American life, and therefore of the often incredibly different interpretations of how "facts on the ground" relate to governmental policy or political decisions more generally. (I have used examples about whites and blacks in the United States because I am most familiar with them; I would suggest, however, that similar examples could be found in most heterogeneous societies, including Protestants and Catholics in Northern Ireland, Southeast Asians and whites in England, Palestinians and Jews in Israel and the occupied territories, East and West Germans, and so forth.) It is unlikely that blacks and whites disagree about the desirability of good-quality low-cost health care, of improving the prospects for terminally ill patients by developing new drugs, of free and open elections, or of proper channels for procedural and substantive justice. But blacks who subscribe to the beliefs related previously may have surprising—and possibly even incomprehensible or just crazy—things to say as far as most whites are concerned about public policies in these areas. (Blacks are unlikely to be as surprised at white perspectives on these matters, since majority perspectives are better expressed in the media, etc.) Assuming that whites would make up the majority of deliberative institutions, therefore, which would presumably be appropriate or at least acceptable since they currently make up the majority of the population, they may end up consistently rejecting blacks' contributions to the debate as irrelevant or insupportable—despite every intention to foster a mutually respectful deliberative forum that is focused on finding common solutions rather than "winning."

Now it may be too quick to say that blacks' impotence in influencing debate under such conditions is the fault of deliberative democracy. It may simply be up to black Americans to make the case to white Americans that their understanding of the "facts on the ground" is true. They need to prove that politically powerful blacks are being targeted for assassination, for example, as slow and painful a process as that proof may be, just like whites in America are finally accepting the idea that being harassed or arrested for "Driving While Black" is a real phenomenon, now known as "racial profiling." After all, white Americans have no reason to accept the idea that there are sinister government forces targeting politically powerful blacks just because many black Americans think this is true. (I was never convinced by my colleague that Ron Brown was assassinated, despite our discussions about the topic, and I therefore disagreed with him on policy issues that related to our beliefs in this matter.) This may be the time for "personal testimony" to enter the deliberation, [16] as blacks try to help whites understand the experience of being black in America, and thus to understand also why they believe that black politicians are subject to government attack, federal agencies are spreading disease and drugs in the inner cities, and so forth.

In the meantime, however, it strikes me as being very unlikely that blacks, who make up 12 to 13 percent of the American population, should necessarily accept the rationality and legitimacy of the deliberative democratic process and of the political decisions that are made prior to white America's acceptance of black America's descriptions of its experiences. Furthermore, to the extent that similar disconnects could be found between women and men, religious minorities and Christians, and poor people versus wealthy people, deliberative democracy becomes increasingly untenable. To take an example driven by class rather than race, many of my students—Puerto Rican, Cape Verdean, Jamaican, Irish, African American, Dominican, but all essentially poor—are convinced that rents are going up in their neighborhoods because of a conspiracy on the part of wealthy Bostonians to exile poor people to the suburbs (!) and get rid of all subsidized housing now that poor people have cleaned up the neighborhoods for them. Although my students undoubtedly hold these beliefs in part because of predictable adolescent confusion about complex economic forces, my students are not alone in their convictions. Many of their parents subscribe to the same conspiracy theories, and similar views are articulated by community newspapers and local activists. Whether or not they are right, many middle-class residents of Boston who are searching for decent housing in good neighborhoods will reject their arguments as absurd or paranoid—not out of ill will, but because their views seem extreme. To the extent that this pattern of mutual incomprehension—especially on the part of majority group members who listen to but don't "hear" minority group members—replicates itself across racial, ethnic, religious, class, gender, or other lines, deliberative democracy suffers real problems with legitimacy. Furthermore, I suggest that this remains true despite Miller's brush-off of "realist" criticisms of deliberative democracy, since these problems would surface in any real community, no matter how idealized the structure and content of the deliberative practices.

Unacknowledged Norms and the Sectarian Reasons

A second reason that minority groups may end up having an inappropriately small effect on deliberation despite having representatives who appropriately voice their concerns and ideas in deliberative settings is that members of the majority group may live by certain norms, or benefit from experiences of the world, that they deny when these are articulated by members of minority communities. For example, studies of identity development in the United States have shown that white children are the only ones who generally do not use race to describe themselves.[17] Black, Hispanic, and Asian children consistently describe themselves from a fairly young age as being black, Hispanic, or Asian (as well as being tall, having brown eyes, etc.). White children, in contrast, generally do not describe themselves as being white. It is clearly a white privilege to see oneself as not having a race, or as not being even partially defined by race. But this differential experience of race (the experience of its not seeming to matter, because it is taken as a default assumption—being white is "normal" in a way that being anything else is not) is very hard for whites to acknowledge. Thus, in response to a black person's invocation of race in a political debate, whites in America (and I expect in many other countries) will often complain, privately at least, "Why do blacks talk about race all the time?" They have listened to the black person's reason or idea, but they do not "hear" it or allow it to influence them appropriately—despite having the best of intentions—because of their inability to acknowledge that their own experiences have been shaped by race—in their case by the privilege of white race.

A second example, one that occasionally comes up in the cafeteria of the school where I teach and that was a very live issue when I was a college student, concerns apparent minority self-segregation. At Yale in the late 1980s, fierce debates raged about the appropriateness of "heritage houses" and separate freshman orientations for minority students. Furthermore, in the college dining halls (as sometimes in the school cafeteria now), the question would quietly be raised, "Why are all the blacks sitting together?" As Beverly Daniel Tatum points out in her book, *Why Are All the Black Kids Sitting Together in the Cafeteria?* whites ask these questions because although the process of building a racial identity involves similar activities and experiences for both blacks and whites, including the experiences of interacting with same-race peer groups, it is again an invisible process in the white community, since whites are almost always "naturally" surrounded by other whites. (Notice that the question is rarely asked, "Why are all the whites sitting together?"—and that's not because all-white groups don't form.) This same process will be quite visible for minority students in a majority setting, however, because they will have to (visibly) seek same-race peers.

A third and final example takes the discussion out of a solely racial context and may shed further light on how good arguments may end up being excluded from deliberation for bad reasons, thereby putting the legitimacy of the deliberative process itself into question. In *Citizenship and National Identity*, Miller discusses the case of a Muslim parent who tries to argue in favor of the establishment of Muslim schools. In his example, the parent starts out by saying that "it is vitally important that a child's religious background be supported by his or her school," but this argument gets nowhere as "many people held precisely the opposite opinion." The parent thus switches to arguing that "Muslim children would in many cases not flourish academically unless they were sent to schools where the teaching reflected their cultural values," which invokes the more acceptable norm of the "principle of equal opportunity," and which therefore ends up (possibly) being successful.[18] Miller concludes from this: "The search for agreement will itself act as a filter on the kinds of reason that prevail in the discussion, sectarian reasons being weeded out precisely because it becomes apparent to their supporters that they are not going to command wide assent."[19] In other words, Miller interprets the Muslim parent's arguments as representing a movement from unpalatable sectarian values (that are permitted in debate but will gain no purchase and will therefore naturally be filtered out) to desirable common norms.

I suggest, however, that the Muslim parent might have been drawing on common norms in both cases, but that in response to the first argument the presumably Christian majority weeded out a norm to which they unknowingly subscribe in practice and benefit from themselves, but are unwilling or unable to acknowledge. In other words, a norm that was so well entrenched as to be invisible in the mainstream, Christian context became "sectarian" as soon as it was applied in a nonmainstream (e.g., Muslim) context. After all, this example was rooted in the British context, and most British schoolchildren do have their religious background supported by their schools. Bland Christianity is part of most Britons' culture, and as such is supported by the religious education curriculum, school assemblies and holidays, and other aspects of the school calendar and curriculum. But because they are in the majority, and because British Christianity is in general such a mushy thing, Christian parents in Britain don't think about the fact that their children daily benefit from the application of the first norm in their schools. They don't have consciously to subscribe to it, and even have the luxury of consciously rejecting it in non-Christian contexts as inappropriately "sectarian," because the Christian state educational establishment already subscribes to the same norm for them, much to their children's benefit.

Again, it's possible that in a properly respectful deliberative setting, these unacknowledged norms and experiences will be exposed and understood by all participants because whites and Christians would feel comfortable articulating their complaints and questions ("Why are you always obsessed with race?" "Why do you have to put religion into everything?") and blacks and non-Christians would feel comfortable answering them. If so, then blacks' claims about the importance of establishing certain segregated settings such as "heritage houses," and Muslim's claims about the importance of schools' supporting children's religious background, would likely be "heard" as well as listened to. But there is a question as to how ideal we can envision deliberative democratic institutions as being without our losing purchase on positive, applicable political theory and action. Even in a solution-oriented (rather than victory-oriented) setting in which people interacted according to principles of mutual respect, it may be too much to hope that participants will expend the time and energy to engage in what is an inevitably slow and painful process of self-discovery. As a result, I suggest that often, even in a mutually respectful deliberative setting, it's likely that whites/members of majority groups will shy away from claims that seem too racially focused or self-segregating. They will listen to but then reject them, and these reasons may therefore wrongly—and illegitimately, from minority groups' perspectives—not gain purchase on future deliberations.

"What You Really Mean to Say Is . . ."

A third way in which minorities' influence on democratic deliberation may be illegitimately limited is by members of the majority group's unintentionally but pervasively reinterpreting what minorities say in order to make minorities' claims make sense to them. This may be done unconsciously, or may be done as a misguided extension of respect—they may think that by saying or thinking, "What you're really trying to say is . . . ," they are doing a service to the minority group. Miller himself provides an example of this, I believe, in the following comment:

> If we take, not militant Islam . . . but Islamic religious identity of the more usual kind, it is perfectly possible for a Christian to value this identity while holding to Christian values. There is likely to be sufficient overlap in the virtues embodied in the two ways of life for the Christian to endorse the Muslim identity, even while recognizing that this is not an identity he or she would wish to embrace.[20]

This claim misses the point, I think, about what it means to value other cultures (and highlights the difficulty of really "hearing" the claims made by members of other cultures). Valuing the overlaps between one's own culture and somebody else's means that one simply values other cultures to the extent that they replicate or mirror one's own (with sufficient, "open-minded" discount for superficial differences). This is not the kind of respect or "valuation" that Iris Marion Young (to whom Miller is responding) means, and it's not sufficient respect for a deliberative democracy to work without privileging majority groups over minority groups. For an individual's "concerns, interests and convictions"[21] really to count in and appropriately influence deliberation, the *differences* between his position and others' must be recognized and taken into account; otherwise, he might as well not participate. Similarly, efforts to rephrase a person's position ("What she's really trying to say is . . .") often have the outcome, whether intended or not, of neutralizing her claims; in the process of rephrasing, the "weight of reasons"[22] often is shifted to fit comfortably into the other discussants' already-present understanding of the matter at hand, rather than forcing people to grapple with an idea that is new or challenging. As a result, dissenting individuals, especially if they come to an issue as outsiders whose views and experiences are different from the mainstream, run the risk of having their positions seemingly assimilated into the deliberations without their actually exerting influence in the appropriate way.

DELIBERATIVE CIVIC EDUCATION AND THE "LANGUAGE OF POWER"

Even within well-designed and well-intentioned deliberative contexts, therefore, the differential experiences of majority and minority group members can result in a loss of deliberative equality, and thus in a delegitimizing of deliberative democracy itself. If deliberative democracy nonetheless remains a civic goal, as it does for Miller, then civic education must be structured so as to overcome these liabilities as much as possible. How it might do so is the focus of this section.

For people who teach members of majority groups—and this description includes not just teachers in the formal sense of the word but also members of mainstream media outlets, politicians, public thinkers, and so forth: in other words, all people who help to shape and influence public opinion—their (our) goal as deliberative civic educators should clearly be to help members of majority groups "hear" the claims of minority co-deliberators without automatically rejecting them as "extreme" or "sectarian" or rephrasing them to fit more familiar beliefs and experiences. This is hard. It is hard to teach and hard for others to learn. "Hearing" the claims made by people who seem very different from us requires a real exercise of thoughtful imagination combined with complex historical knowledge and understanding, and as those of us who teach know, it is extremely difficult to help students reach this point. As a teacher of English and American history to early adolescents, I am thrilled if once per quarter students really seem to grasp a complex set of ideas from the inside and to be able to rethink and reimagine their own experience in that historical context. It's possible that I set my goals too low, but I don't believe I do. This kind of thoughtful, historically, culturally, and politically informed imaginative work is difficult and can even be painful. Although I advocate it strongly, therefore, we cannot trust that this type of civic education will on its own equip citizens to engage and fully "hear" each other in deliberative democratic settings.

On the other side, minorities can make themselves more comprehensible to majorities by adopting the language of the majority in setting forth their claims. For those of us who teach members of minority groups, therefore, it is our responsibility as civic educators to teach our students how to express themselves in terms that others will naturally understand. To put it baldly—as baldly as I put it to my students each year—in every country and in every community, there is a language of power, and if one wants to be effective through political dialogue (as opposed to through direct action, boycotts, radical street theater, etc.), one must master and use that language.[23] For members of the majority group(s) (whether these are based on class, race, religion, ethnicity, other features, or some combination), this language is usually easy to master because it is their own language. It is spoken at home, reinforced in the books they read, and repeated in the TV and movies they watch. Members of disadvantaged groups, however, have a harder row to hoe. They have to learn to express themselves in language that makes sense to the majority group—in the language of power—and this may require minorities to shift their grammar, vocabulary, and narrative or expository form, as well as their cultural, political, and experiential referents, in order to be understood and respected. When members of minority or disadvantaged groups do not make this switch, then it is easy for even well-intentioned majorities to reject, misunderstand, or misinterpret their arguments, as I discussed in the first section of this chapter. If they are able to make this switch, however, then they may be able to reduce or eliminate one of the barriers to effective cross-cultural communication.

Just as it is difficult for majority listeners to learn fully to "hear" the claims of others, it is also difficult for minority speakers to learn to master the language of power, particularly if they attend all-minority schools, which is the case for students in many urban schools. When I taught English in Atlanta, for example, my students attended an all-black school in which 87 percent of students lived at or below the poverty line; they lived in all-black neighborhoods, traveled on public transportation that was used almost exclusively by blacks, visited mostly black rap sites on the Web, watched black-oriented TV, and listened to black-oriented radio stations. Almost none of their daily experiences, therefore, other than those explicitly designed and directed by their teachers in school, exposed them to or encouraged them to use and master Standard American English—the "language of power" in the United States. Most of my students wanted to learn to "speak right" and "write correctly" anyway, and we focused on that throughout the year. But these circumstances present a huge challenge for both teachers and students. Students have to master so much vocabulary to which they have never been exposed (two years in a row, the second story we read in September caused confusion because my eighth graders didn't know the words *ditch, wade, peasant, monarch, shore,* etc.), as well as learn grammatical constructions that are simply different in Standard American English from Black English. This is not to mention the skills they have to learn in structuring an argument, dressing appropriately, speaking convincingly (my students had explicitly to practice looking at the person they were trying to convince, because one of the continuing legacies of slavery is that in black culture in the American South, looking somebody in the eye is a sign of disrespect), and so forth.

It was also a challenge—but no less important from a civic perspective—to teach them all that they needed to know about mainstream—in this case, white and middle-class—culture, history, and politics, so that they could learn to couch arguments intended for a mainstream audience in that context. When we studied Martin Luther King Jr.'s "I Have a Dream" speech, for example, we focused on how many of his allusions were to Shakespeare, the Bible, Abraham Lincoln—not to Langston Hughes, Phyllis Wheatley, Frederick Douglass, or Sojourner Truth, as important as those black Americans are to American history and culture. To students whose exposure to mainstream culture and history is slim (they could all recite Maya Angelou's poem "Still I Rise," but none had heard of Robert Frost or Walt Whitman; and, on a lighter but I think no less telling note, they lost a quiz bowl round against a mostly white team from the northern part of the city because they had never heard of Kurt Cobain, Nirvana, or grunge, but were disbelieving when I told them the other team had probably never heard of Master P or Mia X)—to students whose exposure to mainstream culture and history is slim, mastering the language of power is a daunting task, even with rhetorical masters such as Martin Luther King Jr. to guide us.

This is not to say that this isn't a worthwhile task. It absolutely is. Frost, Whitman, Lincoln, Emerson—and yes, non-Americans such as Shakespeare, Milton, Dickens, Shelley—are part of *all* Americans' cultural heritage or "birthright," and it massively disserves black Americans or other minorities if they are taught otherwise. Likewise, Angelou, Hughes, Douglass, Zora Neale Hurston, Ralph Ellison, and James Baldwin are equally part of American culture and should thus be taught to and embraced by all Americans as well. Americans' heritage is America; I do not believe it divides down the color, class, religion, or any other line. But to say this is not and cannot be to minimize the vastly different exposure of and experience with—the "social capital" possessed by—members of majority and minority groups in America to these cultural, historical, and experiential norms. Furthermore, America is not alone in this level of social and cultural division; examples of privileged access to and exclusion from the language and experience of power can be found across most societies, and thus should be of concern to all deliberative democrats.

CIVIC EDUCATION FOR DELIBERATIVE DEMOCRACY

To educate future citizens to be effective members of a deliberative democracy, therefore, is a heavy task. It requires that children learn how to listen to each other in such a way that they actually "hear" the import of claims that on the surface may seem bizarre, irrational, unappealing, or confused. It also requires that children learn to express themselves in ways that other citizens find palatable and easier to "hear" and understand, by changing their modes of speech, dress, vocabulary, cultural referents, and so forth. Neither of these lessons is easy to teach or to learn, and they bring challenges in their wake.

I wish in this section to focus more specifically on the implications and challenges of the second lesson—that minority students should learn to speak and use a "language of power" that is not intrinsically their own. This aspect of deliberative civic education is of special interest to me—and should be of particular concern for Miller—for a few reasons. First, as I will show later, this model of civic education implicates the school in partially defining a student's personal identity and then attaching that to his or her civic identity—both actions that Miller deplores. Also, by emphasizing their outsider status to minority students, the school potentially fosters an oppositional attitude—one intended to enable deliberative cooperation, of course, but one that in the meantime might seem to undercut the trust that Miller believes is crucial for deliberative justice. These issues (and others that I discuss later) cut to the heart of Miller's republican project, and thus should be of foremost concern.

Second, I concentrate on minority deliberative civic education because it is important to recognize that many minority students will have to learn the language of power as an explicit educational task, rather than more "naturally" through regular interaction with students from majority groups. This is because so many minority students attend predominantly or all-minority schools. While it is true that integrated schools may foster mutual understanding and the development of cross-cultural communication skills through students' natural interactions in the classroom and on the playground, many minority students, even in liberal democracies such as Britain and the United States, attend schools that are virtually or totally segregated. The United States is perhaps most shocking when one considers segregation by race: fully one-third of black and Latino students attend schools that are 90 to 100 percent minority.[24] But it is important to remember that just as *majority* and *minority* refer not just to race, but also to ethnicity, religion, national origin, class, sexual orientation, and possibly gender, so should *segregated schools* be taken to apply to these various aspects of identity. In the United States, many students attend schools that are effectively segregated by race and class; in Britain, Australia, and even France, many schools are effectively segregated by class, religion, and/or gender; in Canada, schools are purposely segregated by religion and, in Quebec, language; in Israel, virtually all public schools are intentionally segregated by religion and ethnicity. Thus, minority students (and, correlatively, majority students) are likely to attend segregated schools in many democracies. This situation is unlikely to change, even in Miller's idealized deliberative democracies, because democratic states (especially those that are republican rather than liberal) cannot force children to attend integrated schools, and empirical evidence shows that full integration will not happen naturally. Gary Orfield, in fact, provides compelling empirical evidence that school segregation is actually increasing in the United States, now that many integration-oriented court orders are being lifted and districts are free to set policies on their own again.[25] In any democracy it is extremely unlikely that citizens would decide to approve the kind of heavy-handed intervention into educational institutions, property rights, local taxation, and so forth that the state would have to take in order to foster truly integrated schools. Thus, unless we undemocratically (although in my view, more liberally[26]) legislated new patterns for integrated children's education as a sort of paternalistic preparation for future entry into a new deliberative democratic order, then integrated schools will be unlikely ever to be sufficiently prevalent to solve the problem of cross-cultural communication barriers on their own. As a result, it is important to consider the political and personal implications of deliberative civic education that is specifically designed for minority students.

A final reason that I choose to focus on civic education in minority settings is because that is the context in which I have experience as a teacher. My primary teaching experiences have been in Atlanta, at an all-black school, and now in Boston, at a school that is 85 percent minority and composed primarily of first- and second-generation immigrants. In both schools, about 90 percent of my students live near or under the poverty line, so they are outside the mainstream in terms of class as well as race, ethnicity, and/or residency status, and although my students in Atlanta were overwhelmingly Christian—members especially of the Southern Baptist, AME, or sometimes Pentecostal Churches, and thus members of the religious mainstream in the South in that respect—many of my students in Boston are either religiously unaffiliated or members of minority religious groups: Hindu, Buddhist, Jehovah's Witness, Seventh Day Adventist, even Wicca. My experience as a teacher, therefore, is firmly rooted in schools that serve minority populations, whether measured by class, ethnicity, race, or to a lesser extent, religion, and it is in this context that I started thinking seriously as a theorist-practitioner about civic education.

Taking all of this into account, it is clearly important to consider the implications, if any, of my argument that civic education for a deliberative democracy requires explicitly teaching minority students to master a language of power that is not, at least initially, their own. I suggest that there are at least five difficulties posed by this conception of deliberative civic education.

First, from both a pedagogical and a more broadly civic standpoint, it is obviously extremely troubling to teach citizens (or future citizens) that they are "outsiders" of a civic community. The school's goal, of course, is to teach minority children (and all others as well, of course) that they are all civic beings who can and should function like insiders in deliberative settings: i.e., they should join, speak up, vote, etc. In order to teach them to function *effectively* as insiders in the deliberative process, however, the school must simultaneously teach minority students that they are outsiders in the sense of having to learn and use a language of power that is initially not their own. This places the school in a bind—as it places society in a bind. It runs the real risk of reinforcing many students' already-strong sense of being excluded or discriminated against.

Of course, this may also be a more honest way of teaching. Many minority students, at least whom I teach, *do* feel excluded from and/or discriminated against by American history and American society—and I'm sure that many Asian students in England, Mahgrebi students in France, Sephardic and Arab students in Israel, and aboriginal students everywhere feel similarly about their countries. It does them and us no good, therefore, to pretend otherwise. To admit this explicitly, however, and especially to adopt this as a model of civic education, is to abandon the cherished notion that contemporary citizenship is a common right and experience. Let me explain. Almost all discussions of citizenship, including Miller's, emphasize the common heritage of citizenship. To be a citizen, almost by definition, is to have the same bundle of rights and obligations, to "share the same legal status,"[27] and even the same civic identity (*qua* citizen), as all other citizens. As Miller comments, "Citizenship is supposed to provide [a common] reference point. Our personal lives and commitments may be very different, but we are all equally citizens, and it is as citizens that we advance claims in the public realm and assess the claims made by others."[28] Consequently, it is to be expected that civic education would also be a common experience of all future citizens within a community. Regardless of individual, personal differences, children would all learn equally about their rights and obligations as citizens, and would develop the same citizenship skills. As I made clear earlier, however, this is not necessarily the case, neither in reality nor even possibly as an ideal (within the real world, that is). Because of the different status and life experiences of members of advantaged and disadvantaged, majority and minority groups, children from one group may need to develop different skills from children in another group in order to become equally effective citizens within a republic. As I argued before, children from disadvantaged backgrounds may need to learn to translate their experiences, both literally in terms of language and figuratively in terms of the references and contextual descriptions they use, in order to ensure that other people properly understand and pay attention to what they are trying to say. Children from advantaged backgrounds just don't need to learn these skills to the same extent, because these skills are not relevant to their becoming effective citizens of a deliberative democracy.

Furthermore, even if teachers' approach to the curriculum were the same for all students, students' responses to the curriculum—and their experiences of citizenship in general—would vary dramatically, in part due to their identity and group membership. This is true even if Miller's (extremely improbable) dream comes true of reconstructing national identity so as to be less historically or culturally tainted. Miller argues:

> I want to reply to [the argument that national identities are always in practice biased in favor of the dominant group] first by conceding that it is descriptively true in many historical cases—national identities have very often been formed by taking over elements from the group culture that happens to be dominant in a particular state—but then adding that it is not integral to national identities that they should be loaded in this way. . . . Although in standard cases a national identity is something one is born into . . . there is no reason why others should not acquire it by adoption. . . . Although *a priori* a nation might define itself tightly by descent, in practice nations extend membership more or less freely to those who are resident and show willingness to exhibit those traits that make up national character.[29]

Thus, Miller would like for nations to redefine themselves along nationally specific but non–culturally specific lines. This would have the virtue, he believes, of negating the need for identity politics, because all citizens, no matter what their cultural background or identification, would be able to identify equally with the conditions for and character of national membership and would therefore also feel comfortable participating as equals in the civic sphere.

This is a nice idea, but it is problematic on a number of levels. Even if national identity is not culturally biased, there is inevitably cultural bias within the citizenry who make up the nation, and in order to be effective politically, one has to be able to play to that bias, or be comprehensible within that culture. It would be inefficient, to say the least, to try to participate in political deliberation in England but not couch arguments in terms that whites and Christians are likely to be sympathetic to. Also, even if a gradual re-creation of a national character is possible—for example, even if England or Britain were to find or create symbols of nationhood that are inclusive and could be adopted by anyone who is resident and wishes to become a citizen (i.e., not the Union Jack, fox hunting, "English gentleman," servant of empire, etc.)—one still has to deal with the history of the nation as it stands. England could not simply ignore the downsides of its colonial history in its program of civic education, even if its history and experience as an empire no longer were central to English identity. After all, the lives and histories of most ethnic minority families in England—whether Indian, Pakistani, Bangladeshi, Afro-Caribbean, African, Irish, Arab, Chinese, or other—have been directly shaped by English colonialism, missionarism, racism, and the "white man's burden." The fact that England has (according to this counterfactual example) reconstructed its national identity in a non–culturally biased way is good, but it does not and cannot remove the sense of distance, exclusion, and/or ambivalence about citizenship and subjecthood that many minority students who are aware of its history are likely to feel.

Likewise, America has some powerful symbols of nationhood that are unifying and to some extent can be adopted by all citizens as a common heritage:
the Constitution, Declaration of Independence, flag, "American Dream," and
so forth. But it, too, cannot thereby simply ignore the parts of American history that contradicted these more desirable aspects of American nationhood:
slavery, the destruction of Native American tribes and their land, isolationism
and anti-immigrationism, segregation, and so forth. As a result, despite the
common heritage of the Constitution and the American Dream (for example),
a black person's civic identity in America is extremely likely to be different
from a white person's American civic identity. Acts of civil injustice—from
slavery through Jim Crow through Tuskegee—have partially shaped the family history of every black person whose family has lived in America for longer
than a few decades (as well as more recent immigrants, realistically speaking).
White children's family histories rarely show the scars of racial injustice in the
same way; generally, parents, grandparents, and other ancestors benefited
from the white privilege bestowed by these laws, even if they were personally
opposed to them, or even if they ignored politics altogether. (Their histories
may also have been marked and stunted by prejudice against ethnic whites or
anti-Semitism, but that is separate from anti-black hatred.) This is not to say
that entrenched civil injustice and racism did not harm whites; it did certainly
on psychological and moral grounds, and potentially in other ways as well.
(Some psychologists argue that the current antisocial and violent behavior of
some white adolescent boys and men derives from anger resulting from having been raised with an implicit sense of entitlement that is no longer fulfilled.)
But it harmed them differently from how it harmed blacks.

It does not require educating children to be explicitly race-conscious, therefore, to have black children react to American racial history in a significantly
different way (with an added personal sense of injustice, say) from how white
children might. Both black and white children might be equally appalled when
they learn about the Jim Crow laws or about white resistance to school desegregation orders. How that sense of horror is channeled, however, may differ for whites and blacks. White children may feel a sense of shame that blacks
will not feel. Blacks may feel alienated from a country that would do these
things, whereas whites may simply feel relieved that their country has grown
up and become more overtly just. Furthermore, the connections students draw
to their own lives may well be different. This is especially likely to happen in
segregated schools, where teachers and the students themselves both often re-
inforce racialized readings of history and literature.[30]

What does this mean for our conception of civic education in a deliberative democracy? In addition to the first problem of reinforcing minorities'
sense of alienation by stressing their "outsider" status, a second, related
problem arises that it is likely to be harder to build the kind of trust that
deliberative democrats such as Miller correctly argue is required for deliberative democracy to function effectively and justly, since minorities will be

consistently aware of working in a world that is partly not their own. Miller comments:

> For deliberative democracy to work well, people must exercise what we might call democratic self-restraint; they must think it more important that the decision reached should be a genuinely democratic one than that it is the decision that they themselves favour. This depends in turn on the level of trust that exists in the deliberating body: people will tend to behave in a democratic spirit to the extent that they believe that others can be trusted to behave likewise.[31]

Although Miller is right about the importance of trust, it is easy to see how minority citizens might find it hard to put trust in mainstream deliberative institutions, given the tainted history of so many liberal democracies.

Third, this model of civic education implicates the school (and almost always the state school, since most minority children, with the possible exception of religious minorities, attend state schools) in partially interpreting the relationship between personal identity and civic identity. In some sense, the school at least temporarily "fixes" what a minority student's identity means in the civic context by stressing the knowledge and skills particular to minority membership in a deliberative democracy. Thus, black students are consciously and intentionally introduced to a civic education curriculum different from that taught to white students, and within that curriculum they are explicitly taught that *as blacks*, they must develop particular skills in order to be successful *as citizens*. This is again extremely problematic for Miller, who opposes institutionalizing in any way a politics of recognition:

> It is also clear that having a particular female or gay *identity* is to a large extent within the control of the individual [just as is the case for individuals' ethnic identities]. . . . [A] politics of recognition, if it were successful, would fix the answers to these questions [about personal identity within groups]. It would generate a distinct sense of what it means to be a woman, what women's basic demands are, and so forth. What is now fluid and uncertain would become clearly specified for all those who chose to accept the politically defined identity.[32]

Despite Miller's (probably appropriate) opposition to such an outcome, however, it is hard to see how it can be avoided if minority children are to learn how to participate most effectively in deliberative political institutions.

Two additional problems with this conception of deliberative civic education are unrelated to "outsider" versus "insider" status. One of these is the problem of translation. Merely learning the language of power does not mean that every good idea can necessarily be expressed within it. This may be especially clear if we consider the cultural, political, and social referents implicit within majority dialogue. A religious conservative, for example, may be against pornography for religious reasons but know that these reasons will not be "heard" by a secularly oriented majority. She may choose, therefore, to translate her arguments into secular terms—arguing not that pornography desecrates God's sacred vessel, for example, but that it promotes violence against women. While this act of translation may allow her to promote her ultimate goal of banning pornography, however, it also distorts her position in the meantime. This is not the reason that she is against pornography (she may in fact be more convinced by research showing that soft-core pornography reduces violence against women by giving men another outlet), and she would not be satisfied by a ban simply on violent, hard-core pornography. Furthermore, in contrast to the notion that deliberative democracy promotes mutual communication and understanding, this woman is reduced virtually to lying to her fellow citizens; she is promoting an action based on reasons to which she does not necessarily subscribe and cannot give the reasons that she truly believes in. Members of other minority groups—blacks, the poor, recent immigrants—may feel the same way in other situations. Thus, teaching students to translate their ideas, thoughts, and concerns into language that members of mainstream groups will understand does not guarantee that they will feel free and able to express themselves honestly and openly, free of distortion.

Finally, learning the language of power may in some, even many, cases extract the ultimate cost of permanently altering students' personal identities. Short-term accommodations, made over and over again, can have transformative long-term consequences in the form of assimilation and loss of original language. Being effective in a deliberative setting in many ways is a function of "fitting in," of seeming reasonable rather than radical, an insider rather than an outsider. To what extent can we expect individuals to fit themselves into mainstream dialogue, repeatedly and completely, without expecting that they will eventually fit permanently into the mainstream—that they will assimilate? If this is a goal of civic education—and it certainly has been one historically in many societies—then well and good. There is no problem with this model of civic education for a deliberative democracy. But if assimilation into the mainstream is not an explicit goal of civic education today, then we may be led to question a model of civic participation—that of deliberative rather than adversarial democracy—that requires so many individuals to shed their own languages, their own experiences, their own cultural or social referents, at the door of the polis.

One possible response to these problems is to abandon a deliberative model of democracy for a different democratic model—probably adversarial democracy. Insofar as adversarial democracy requires that individuals master the technologies of power—building alliances, gaining media exposure, lobbying effectively, voting strategically, and so forth—rather than only the language of power, it would enable a form of civic education that might be less problematic than what I have described so far.[33] In an adversarial democracy, for example, Hispanics or Muslims or gays may exert influence and power not by convincing politicians of the *reasonableness* of their positions, but by convincing those politicians that their positions must be *treated* as reasonable if they want to earn the Hispanic/Muslim/gay vote in their (re)election bids. Thus, for example, almost nobody in mainstream American society in 1999 thought that six-year-old Cuban refugee Elian Gonzales should be forcibly kept in the United States or that his Cuban father's custody claims should be rejected. But because of the strategic voting power of Miami Cuban Americans, many mainstream media outlets and politicians (including Al Gore, who was even then acutely aware of Florida's potential importance in the 2000 presidential election) treated these claims seriously nonetheless. Cuban Americans in Miami did not have to *convince* anyone of their position, as would be required in a deliberative democracy; rather, they used their power as a voting bloc to compel people to treat their position as reasonable despite their apparent extremity. Applying this example to the design of civic education, this suggests that in a liberal adversarial democracy, all students might learn the same skills of employing the technologies of power, regardless of their identity or minority status, and be encouraged to use these technologies to influence politics, achieve their political aims, and strive for liberal justice. All students under this model can be taught to think of themselves as insiders of various groups—as well as learn how to organize communities or interest groups and to build coalitions in which they will be insiders—as a means of helping them achieve appropriate political power and influence. As a result, liberal adversarial civic education would seem to free the state school from distinguishing among students based on its perception of their personal identities and group membership, and also free students from having to learn that they must both acknowledge and overcome their outsider status in order to succeed in the political realm.

Despite the attractions of this approach, however, it is clear that adversarial democracy—which is essentially what exists now in most modern liberal democracies—does not solve everything. After all, the pedagogical dilemmas that I have described throughout this essay stem from my experience as a teacher now, teaching in the context of adversarial democracy, not just as a teacher educating for deliberative democracy. Adversarial democracy still requires that individuals master the language of power if they wish to be politically efficient and effective. Also, even if the school under this model is not implicated in "fixing" students' identities, the technologies of adversarial democracy—bloc voting, building strategic alliances, keeping people "on message"—would seem to promote group identification and identity politics above a sense of common citizenship and a shared political mission. The Elian Gonzales case illuminates how much turned on group loyalty and narrow interest politics; this cannot be what we, and certainly not Miller, hope to foster in developing liberal democracies. Finally, even if all students can equally benefit from learning how to master the technologies of power in a liberal democracy, it will be patently clear to children and adults alike that these technologies are not equally distributed or effective.[33] Teachers will still have to confront the pessimism and frustration of minority students who feel that the majority will always have the upper hand in employing the technologies of power in gaining access to the nightly news, financing campaigns, lobbying the right people, even using the police to intimidate other groups in subtle but effective ways. Certainly students' study of history and culture in many liberal nations will not dissuade them from this conclusion. As a result, teachers and schools will still have to grapple with students' feelings of being outsiders and will have to find ways to convert disaffection and cynicism into activism and involvement. In these respects, teachers, schools, and states face similar challenges in adversarial and deliberative democracies alike.

Hence, the questions still remain: Is there a single sense of civic identity that children can adopt and sustain even in the face of the divisiveness of past and recent civic history and students' inevitably different reactions to it? Likewise, even if minority children do have to learn to think of themselves as partial outsiders in order to improve their capacity to function as insiders in civic life, can this be taught in a way that doesn't alienate them from civic life altogether? Can a school successfully teach minority children that they are full civic beings who should try to function like "insiders" in deliberative settings (i.e., they should join, speak up, vote) while simultaneously teaching them that they are "outsiders" in the sense of having to learn and use a language of power that is not their own? The answers to these questions are crucial to Miller's work, both because of their centrality to the deliberative process and republican ideals that infuse *Citizenship and National Identity*, and because of the fine line they walk between fostering civic egalitarianism and promoting an identity politics of recognition. I must confess that I don't know the answers to these questions—they are some of the reasons that it remains interesting to be a teacher. But I hope that the answers to both of these questions are (or can become) "yes," for the sake of national unity within liberal democracies and because we want all future citizens ultimately to view citizenship positively, as an opportunity to participate in political deliberation and to enact positive political change. These are dilemmas in such quasi-liberal states as America and Britain today and would be dilemmas in the deliberative democracies of tomorrow, as well.

NOTES

1. David Miller, *Citizenship and National Identity* (Cambridge: Polity Press, 2000), 9.
2. Miller, *Citizenship*, 9.
3. Miller, *Citizenship*, 144.
4. Miller, *Citizenship*, 79.
5. Miller, *Citizenship*, 79–80.
6. Miller, *Citizenship*, 80.
7. Miller, *Citizenship*, 142–147.
8. Miller, *Citizenship*, 146.

9. See Miller, *Citizenship*, 147–160, for a spirited and convincing argument against the idea that "greeting," "rhetoric," or "personal testimony" should replace the deliberative ideal, and against the idea that some minority groups are culturally unable to present solutions supported by reasons in a deliberative forum.

10. Miller, *Citizenship*, 146.

11. Miller, *Citizenship*, 56 (italics mine).

12. Miller, *Citizenship*, 56.

13. See M. E. Guinan, "Black Communities' Belief in 'AIDS as Genocide': A Barrier to Overcome for HIV Prevention," *Annals of Epidemiology* 3, no. 2 (March 1993): 193–195; S. B. Thomas and S. C. Quinn, "The Tuskegee Syphilis Study, 1932 to 1972: Implications for HIV Education and AIDS Risk Programs in the Black Community," *American Journal of Public Health* 81, no. 11 (November 1991): 1498–1505; K. Siegel, D. Karus, E. W. Schrimshaw, "Racial Differences in Attitudes Toward Protease Inhibitors among Older HIV-Infected Men," *AIDS Care* 12, no. 4 (August 2000): 423–434.

14. An excellent website, essentially structured as an annotated bibliography, that details the history and media coverage of black Americans' suspicions about connections between the CIA and drugs is "Central Intelligence Agency, 1995–2000: San Jose *Mercury News* Story on Nicaraguans, Crack, and the CIA," intellit.muskingum.edu/intellisite/cia1990s_folder/cia1995-96crack.html. See also "Nation of Islam Investigates Possible CIA Crack Connection," CNN, www.cnn.com/US/9610/13/farrakhan, October 13, 1996; Kathleen Koch, "CIA Disavows Crack Connection; Many Skeptical," CNN, www.cnn.com/US/9610/23/cia.crack, October 23, 1996; and Daniel Brandt and Steve Badrich, "Pipe Dreams: The CIA, Drugs, and the Media," www.pir.org/news16.html.

15. I didn't answer them directly, although I did tell them that he was (objectively) such a kook that he would never get far enough to become a significant target.

16. See Miller, *Citizenship*, 156.

17. Beverly Daniel Tatum, *Why Are All the Black Kids Sitting Together in the Cafeteria?* (New York: Basic, 1997). For a partially dissenting view, see Marguerite A. Wright, *I'm Chocolate; You're Vanilla: Raising Healthy Black and Biracial Children in a Race-Conscious World* (San Francisco: Jossey-Bass, 1998).

18. Miller, *Citizenship*, 151.

19. Miller, *Citizenship*, 151. I should note that even if these reasons are "heard," they won't necessarily decide the debate in favor of "heritage houses" or Muslim schools. Considerations of racial identity development do not trump all other arguments, just as one may acknowledge the role that self-segregated minority groups play in fostering adolescents' development of racial or religious identity without necessarily favoring any particular self-segregation proposal.

20. Miller, *Citizenship*, 74.

21. Miller, *Citizenship*, 146.

22. Miller, *Citizenship*, 146.

23. I am indebted here and in the discussion that follows to Lisa Delpit's phenomenal book, *Other People's Children* (New York: New Press, 1995).

24. See Gary Orfield and John T. Yun, "Resegregation in American Schools," www.law.harvard.edu/groups/civilrights/publications/resegregation99.html, June 1999. See also Gary Orfield, Susan E. Eaton, and The Harvard Project on School Desegregation, *Dismantling Desegregation: The Quiet Reversal of Brown v. Board of Education* (New York: New Press, 1996).

25. See Gary Orfield, Susan E. Eaton, and The Harvard Project on School Desegregation, *Dismantling Desegregation: The Quiet Reversal of Brown v. Board of Education* (New York: New Press, 1996).

26. See Meira Levinson, *The Demands of Liberal Education* (Oxford: Oxford University Press, 1999) for an extended liberal argument in favor of forcible school integration policies.

27. Miller, *Citizenship*, 41.

28. Miller, *Citizenship*, 41.

29. Miller, *Citizenship*, 35.

30. *Racialized* should not necessarily be interpreted to mean prejudiced or discriminatory. When I reflected on my teaching in Atlanta, where I taught English in an all-black school, I was stunned to realize how racially oriented I was (and also certainly my colleagues were) in selecting course materials, in approaching the texts, and in drawing connections for our students to modern life. None of us was prejudiced, I believe; we just oriented all aspects of the curriculum, possibly too much, to the African American context in which we were teaching.

31. Miller, *Citizenship*, 22.

32. Miller, *Citizenship*, 71.

33. I am grateful to the conference attendees, and especially to Marc Stears, for pushing me on this point.

34. Miller makes this point well in *Citizenship*, 159.

10

Territorial Resolutions in Divided Societies

Tamar Meisels

David Miller's *Citizenship and National Identity* contains, among other things, a refreshing insight into the territorial aspect of the national phenomenon that is commonly neglected by authors on "liberal nationalism." In this chapter, I argue that Miller's defense of the principle of nationality and, more specifically, his analysis of national self-determination, secession, and particularly of nationality in divided societies sheds light on some of the difficult territorial questions that plague our contemporary international arena. Moreover, I argue, it does so in a way that no other theoretical account of national self-determination has done so far. Notwithstanding this, however, I shall also offer some comments on Miller's evaluation of some of these issues.[1]

NATIONAL SELF-DETERMINATION
AND TERRITORIAL DISPUTES

Contrary to what might be assumed, the principle of self-determination does not in and of itself take us very far along the way to resolving the kind of territorial disputes we are familiar with in contemporary politics. As will become apparent, the shortcomings of the former leave theorists on nationality with ample work to do on the territorial front. Although it is difficult to achieve a canonical definition of the principle of national self-determination, a small sampling of its most prominent interpretations reveals the deficiencies that I have in mind and that, I suggest, Miller's recent work goes a long way toward overcoming.

One such definition of national self-determination has been suggested by Joseph Raz and Avishai Margalit, who interpret this right as equivalent to the right to secede and form a separate state. For them, the core content of national self-determination is "a right to determine whether a certain territory shall become, or remain, a separate state."[2] Later in this joint article, they speak of allowing an "encompassing group that forms a substantial majority in a territory to have the right to determine whether that territory shall form an independent state."[3] Since this definition clearly links the principle of self-determination with the right to secession, it might appear at first glance to be particularly sensitive to territorial issues or at least to supply an answer to the question of whom should determine the destiny of disputed territories.[4] It, however, does not. For one thing, this interpretation of the self-determination principle does not even indicate any solution for the many cases in which the territory in question is to a significant degree nationally mixed. It tends to imply, quite implausibly, that a territorially concentrated encompassing group has the right to secede and form an independent state regardless of whether or not other members of that group have already established a self-determining state (or several states) elsewhere.

A related worry with the Raz–Margalit definition concerns its implicit endorsement of endless acts of secession resulting in the Balkanization of our territorially finite world. In contrast, in David Miller's recent book, the practical problems involved in adopting a free-for-all secessionist policy are raised explicitly and addressed directly.[5] Far from being avoided or downplayed, answering these concerns, and the objections to the principle of national self-determination stemming from them, form a central part of Miller's project throughout chapters 7 and 8.[6]

As for some other problems with the Raz–Margalit thesis, most important perhaps is the vagueness of the key phrase in their interpretation of self-determination, which grants the majority of "a certain territory" or "a territory" the right to secede. In many real-world territorial conflicts, talk of "a given territory" may be largely indeterminate and will consequently, in and of itself, reopen all of the relevant territorial questions it might purport to answer. In contested cases, the question of whether or not the disputed territory is in fact a separate unit, a "given territory," with its own relevant majority and minority is often itself the crucial point.

The problem of determining the relevant jurisdictional unit for holding a plebiscite on the question of secession has not gone unnoticed by writers on self-determination.[7] Miller, who has already in the past criticized the idea that majorities' consent to secession suffices to justify it,[8] returns to make precisely this point toward the end of his chapter "Nationality in Divided Societies," though he refrains from mentioning Raz and Margalit specifically in this connection.[9] Miller pays serious attention to the fact, which Raz and Margalit just barely acknowledge, that majority decisions as a democratic procedure apply only when we have already settled who belongs within the political community and who does not.[10] And this question is a central and essential one that Miller tackles throughout the two aforementioned chapters of his *Citizenship and National Identity*.[11]

Granted, Raz and Margalit do appear to recognize this problem with their theory when they discuss the question of the relevant majority involved in their proposed decision-making procedure and pose the question "'what is the relevant democratic unit?'"[12] They admit that the answer to this question cannot be achieved on the basis of majoritarian principles and must instead rely on other background principles. But they do not supply conclusive answers to the questions this raises. What are the appropriate criteria for resolving territorial disputes within divided societies? This, I suggest, is one of the most central questions of contemporary political debates and one that Miller explores at length in his chapter "Nationality in Divided Societies."[13] It does not receive an answer from the principle of self-determination as formulated by Raz and Margalit, or by anyone else for that matter.

Israeli philosopher Yael Tamir offers an innovative approach to national self-determination that she contrasts with the kind of definition cited previously, namely, Raz and Margalit's thesis.[14] Tamir argues that the right to national self-determination "stakes a cultural rather than a political claim, namely, it is the right to preserve the existence of a nation as a distinct cultural entity. This right differs from the right of individuals to govern their lives and to participate in a free and democratic political process."[15] She classifies this right as an individual right, which is "merely a particular case of the wider right to culture."[16] According to Tamir, the full realization of this individual right to self-determination entails the existence of a shared public sphere within which individuals' communal cultural identity can find full expression.[17] However, it does not necessarily entail a right to an independent state.[18] Independent statehood is viewed as the optimal form of realizing this right, but not as the only possible form.[19]

Quite clearly, this cultural (as opposed to any political) approach to national self-determination does not by its very nature even purport to resolve any territorial issues. Some have even read Tamir's cultural-individualistic view of the right to self-determination as a totally nonterritorial one. If, in Tamir's view, the right in question is a right to culture, then, one might assume, her account must take territory to be relatively incidental.[20] This, however, need not be the case. Particular territories often constitute central components of the national cultures Tamir is so eager to protect.[21] Nevertheless, she does not pursue the territorial aspect of self-determination along these lines and to a large extent avoids tackling the political-territorial issues involved in particular demands for national self-determination.

In contrast, Avner de-Shalit presents his theory of national self-determination as political rather than cultural.[22] Bearing Tamir's view in mind, de-Shalit argues that, as a rule, the appropriate way of meeting such demands, at least in cases of antagonistic ethnic groups, is to redraw the territorial boundaries in the disputed region so as to enable those claiming self-determination to establish their own independent state. In arguing along these lines, de-Shalit places his theory in line with Raz and Margalit's aforementioned view. Accordingly, satisfying the claim to national self-determination is understood in terms of territorial separation and the formation of a new state. Consequently, his argument also retains many of the territorial indeterminencies of the Raz–Margalit thesis, which were pointed to previously.[23]

Finally, one further example of the variation on the self-determination principle that is no more illuminating on the issue of territory can be found in Thomas Baldwin's article dedicated specifically to the territorial aspect of states.[24] Baldwin recommends we adopt "a principle of self-determination to the effect that political communities which seek autonomy should, as far as practicable, be allocated a territory within which they can become autonomous states."[25] This account of the "territorial state" surprisingly leaves even more territorial questions open than the previous theses did. Here, despite the territorial focus of the article, the most basic questions concerning what territory should be allocated to whom are not even acknowledged.

The admittedly limited attention focused here on various interpretations of the principle of national self-determination suffices nonetheless to illustrate my point that many important territorial questions are left open by them all.[26] When taken on its own, David Miller's definition of national self-determination might not appear to present an exception to this rule. However, as I indicated at the outset, the way in which Miller develops this notion, and the implications he draws from it, serve to advance our understanding of various territorial conflicts and the stand we ought to take with regard to them in an invaluable way, as yet unmatched by any other account of this doctrine.

MILLER ON NATIONALITY AND SELF-DETERMINATION

David Miller's earlier book *On Nationality* offers a somewhat different account of the concept of self-determination than the ones suggested by the authors cited previously. According to Miller, "national communities have a good claim to be politically self-determining."[27] Thus, the third element of his principle of nationality holds that "where the inhabitants of a territory form a national community, they have a good claim to political self-determination."[28] In his earlier book, Miller explains that "as far as possible, each nation should have its own set of political institutions which allow it to decide collectively those matters that are the primary concern of its members."[29] And, though Miller recognizes that the optimal vehicle for achieving self-determination of this kind may well be independent statehood (historically, he says, it has certainly been so), he also states that this may not in the present always be a feasible option.[30] Furthermore, as far as independent statehood is concerned, Miller's remarks imply that each nation should, when possible, have *one* such state, whereas Raz and Margalit's aforementioned definition suggests that a group that forms a majority in a given territory has a right to secede and form an independent state whether or not that group already has a nation-state in some other place.

In his "Nationality in Divided Societies," Miller articulates his definition of the principle of national self-determination more precisely when he states that the principle of national self-determination is "the principle that where a body of people form a national community, they should be allowed to control their own affairs through institutions of self-government."[31] He realizes, however, that this principle in and of itself does not dictate any particular territorial solution in all specific cases of rival national claims over land.[32] On the other hand, Miller's wider idea of nationality does supply us with some further guidelines for determining the territorial question.[33]

The Problem

As the previous section asserts, recent liberal literature on nationalism and self-determination contains a curious void as far as any delicate territorial questions are concerned. As early as in his first book "On Nationality," Miller observed: "People of liberal disposition . . . will throw up their hands in despair when asked to resolve the practical problems that arise when . . . two nationalities make claim to the same territory as, for instance, in the case of the Jews and the Palestinians in Israel."[34] In his recent book, he turns some of his attention to rectifying this state of despair.

As is often the case with remedies, the first step toward this cure is recognizing the existence of a problem and identifying the deficiency in need of repair. In chapter 7 of his *Citizenship and National Identity,* Miller spells out the need for a theory of secession in a way which pinpoints precisely what is lacking in much of the modern-day literature on nationalism. As regards a theory of secession, Miller states that such a theory should be viewed as political, that is, as "one that articulates principles that should guide us when thinking about secessionist claims."[35]

Such guidance is necessary not only with regard to secessionist claims, but also for the evaluation of various other types of territorial issues. For all the vast literature on nationalism in general, and "liberal nationalism" in particular, we still lack any systematic, well thought out method of approaching a variety of territorial issues consistently. We are in need of some form of mechanism, some general orderly guidelines, that will enable us to reflect upon our views on specific territorial conflicts and form opinions when we are confronted with new situations. What criteria should apply when trying to form an opinion in a case where the Xs and the Ys are involved in a dispute over a piece of territory T? What guidelines should we adopt for settling such disputes?

In connection with secession, Miller observes that in any adequate theory thereof secession must be multicriterial, raising a variety of questions concerning, among other things, political authority, historical identity, economic justice, and the rights of minorities. These various criteria will often pull in different directions, and thus reaching a conclusion in any concrete case will necessarily involve the balancing of conflicting claims.[36]

Miller proceeds—not only in his aforementioned chapter on secession, but also, and to a greater extent, in his eighth chapter on "Nationality in Divided Societies"—to offer considerable guidance on these matters concerning territorial conflict. Thus, he enters the relatively unexplored realm of national disputes over territory into which liberal nationalists have so far feared to tread.[37] In what follows, I shall depart somewhat, though not entirely, from the narrow context of secessionist claims and concentrate on Miller's chapter on "Nationality in Divided Societies," which includes the issue of secession but is not limited to it alone. This chapter, I argue, alongside the author's comments on secession, constitutes a significant contribution to the territorial aspect of the national phenomenon. They, however, also involve several noteworthy assertions, which I believe deserve further discussion.

Miller's "Nationality in Divided Societies"

Demands for national self-determination, Miller tells us, and the territorial claims that usually accompany them often surface within nonhomogenous territorial entities, whereas, he observes, if the entire world were like Iceland, implementing the principle of national self-determination would presumably be nonproblematic and relatively uncontroversial.[38] In reality, however, this principle often involves competing claims to a single territory, and, in such cases, things tend to get a bit sticky from a liberal point a view.

In response to various liberal dilemmas often resulting in (albeit reluctant) willingness to do away with the principle altogether, Miller argues in several places that culturally mixed territories can, and should, be categorized into roughly three ideal types, each warranting a different, and politically feasible, territorial arrangement vis-á-vis self-determination.[39]

First, there are ethnically divided states, as opposed to multinational ones, in which each group, despite its distinct culture, is nonetheless able to participate in a common national identity.[40] An *ethnic group* is defined as "a set of people with a distinct set of cultural values and a shared language, who recognize their cultural kinship with one another, and engage in practices that set them apart from outsiders (e.g., Italians in the United States, Ukrainians in Canada, Jews and Muslims in Britain).[41] Ethnic groups, according to Miller, characteristically lack two distinct features embodied by full-fledged national groups. "The first is that ethnicity is not an intrinsically political identity, in the sense that ethnic groups do not aim or aspire to become self-governing political communities."[42] Second, "there is no territory which the group claims as its own"[43] that is at least not within the boundaries of the political community they inhabit. Consequently, a society divided along ethnic lines can have a common national identity and enjoy national self-determination in a relatively straightforward manner. Since ethnic identities are essentially cultural ones, whose field of expression is civil society, they can be combined with an overreaching national identity. The latter should therefore be forged, or remade, in such a way as to enable all groups to take part in a collective project of self-determination, leaving no need to resort to any separatist means.[44] In more territorial terms, ethnic groups have no claim to acquire separate control over parts of the territory they inhabit, nor would they be justified in doing so if they had.

The second ideal type of culturally mixed territories that Miller discusses is that of states inhabited by "rival national groups." In this second case, "we find groups with mutually exclusive national identities each seeking to control all or part of the territory of the state" (e.g., Israelis and Palestinians in Israel; Catholics and Protestants in Northern Ireland; Serbs and Croats in Bosnia).[45] Despite the different possible configurations of this second case, what all have in common is that they involve cohabitant groups whose mutual relationship will, virtually inevitably, be an antagonistic one that, combined with the territorial conflict, prevents an overreaching national identity from emerging across the various national groups.[46]

For this reason, Miller's principle of nationality will in such instances quite often point toward separatist territorial solutions such as secession or the redrawing of borders.[47] Certainly, his guidelines indicate that, where members of each group are territorially concentrated and, for the most part, physically separated from those of the rival group, the appropriate solution will often be a separatist one. When, on the other hand, members of the rival groups are physically intermingled, achieving full national self-determination for members of each group (or the closest approximation thereof) will often require elaborate constitutional arrangements, rather than separation.[48]

Finally, the third configuration of nonhomogenous territorial entities is that which Miller dubs the case of "nested nationalities."[49] Here, "the members of each community typically have a split identity. They think of themselves as belonging both to the smaller community and to the larger one, and they do not experience this as schizophrenic, because their two identities fit together reasonably well."[50] While focussing on the Anglo-Scottish case as a paradigm thereof, Miller adds several further illustrative examples. These include Catalans, Basques and Castilians in Spain, Flemings and Walloons in Belgium, as well as the Welsh and the English themselves, in Britain,[51] all of which are taken to be cases of split-level national identities in which both identities exist simultaneously, on different levels as it were.[52]

According to Miller, in the case of nested, as opposed to rival, nationalities, "full independence or secession from the existing state are not appropriate solutions."[53] The reasons being, first, that "where people have nested national identities, their higher level identities also demand recognition through institutions of political self-determination."[54] Therefore, Miller's proposed arrangement for such cases is a constitutional one that will give recognition both to the overall identity and to the difference between the two lower-level cultural identities. Moreover, according to Miller, when taken together the members of the higher-level identity establish over time a valid claim to control over the whole of the territory inhabited by the members of the various nested nationalities, which together compose their common national identity.[55]

NESTED VERSUS RIVAL NATIONALITIES—THE CASE FOR RESISTING POLITICAL SEPARATION

Thus far I have concentrated on illustrating my first claim, whereby Miller's understanding of the principle of national self-determination tells a far greater part of the territorial story involved in applying this principle than any other liberal-nationalist account has done so far. In the remainder of this chapter I am interested in calling the reader's attention to two interesting points in Miller's argument on nested nationalities which struck me as potentially relevant to cases of rival nations as well.

The bulk of Miller's chapter on "Nationality in Divided Societies" is dedicated to those cases in which the territorial disputes arise in societies, such as Britain, that are made up of several so-called nested nationalities. The features that, according to Miller, differentiate the case of nested nationalities from that of rival ones include the emergence of an overarching common national identity, overlapping cultures, mutually advantageous economic cooperation, and an interwoven history.[56] The existence of a split-level identity, as well as the other identifying features of nested nationalities as described by Miller, sets these cases apart from cases of rival nationalities in which he advocates separation as the desired solution.

The thrust of Miller's argument is that, in the case of nested as opposed to rival nationalities, it will often be justified to oppose, and even resist, secessionist demands.[57] This is, first, because "where people have nested national identities their higher level identities also demand recognition through institutions of political self-determination."[58] And such recognition can naturally be obtained only within the wider political unit. Furthermore where, in spite of these unifying features, one subcommunity (say, the Scots in Britain) wishes nonetheless to sever its connection with the larger state and voices this preference in a referendum, the larger group may be justified in denying this request on the grounds that it is misguided. For one thing, the demand may be insincere, that is it may be motivated by considerations such as perceived economic advantages, rather than by a sincere expression of a separate political identity. Furthermore, according to Miller, even when a majority vote favoring secession expressed in a referendum is indeed a sincere expression of political identity (as in: "the way we now understand ourselves as a people requires that we should form a separate state"), it can nevertheless legitimately be judged as a mistake in self-understanding and subsequently ignored.[59]

Aside from the need to recognize the overarching higher-level identity through institutions of political self-determination, Miller's second justification for resisting the secession of nested national groups concerns the territory involved in the potential secession. In most cases, all groups within the overarching community have an important stake in the territory inhabited by the would-be secessionist subgroup.[60] This joint stake in the disputed territory is attributed to the existence of those shared identifying features that were listed earlier as characterizing nested, as opposed to rival, nationalities (i.e., a common national identity stemming from a joint history, overlapping cultures, mutually advantageous economic collaboration, nonexploitation). In the British (Anglo-Scottish) case, Miller believes that his arguments throughout point to the conclusion that the English majority have a right to resist unilateral secession and are justified in exercising this right.[61]

While Miller's precise characterization of nested nationalities does indeed set them apart from rival nationalities, I argue that some of the reasons he states as justification for resisting unilateral secession may be applicable in principle to some cases of rival nationalities as well. And, in these latter cases, the antisecessionist considerations that Miller points to tend to get a bit trickier from a liberal point of view. Note that I do not deny that Miller may ultimately be correct in prescribing different solutions in each of the cases. He may be justified in doing so because, in the final analysis, the differences between competing territorial claims arising among nested national groups, as opposed to those existing among rival national groups, may prove to outweigh the similarities between the two cases. Miller may also be politically correct in guiding us toward different solutions in each of these cases for purely pragmatic reasons, that is (as he himself argues), due to the plain fact that political arrangements that might work in communities' territories divided along the former lines simply won't work for one inhabited by rival nationalities. The point I wish to make, however, is that if one accepts Miller's reasoning for resisting secession in the Anglo-Scottish case, one cannot totally ignore similar argumentation in connection with resisting the secession of rival groups. In particular, two main points that Miller makes in his argument against the unilateral secession of nested subgroups (such as the Scots) struck me as potentially applicable to this second category (that of rival nationalities) as well. The first point concerns the possibility of error in a group's self-perception; the second concerns the interests of the wider community in holding on to the entire territory of its original state.

As for my first point, recall Miller's controversial assertion whereby it is sometimes justified to question the sincerity, as well as the authenticity, of demands for territorial partition.[62] Miller argues, initially, that such demands are often in need of interpretation in order to determine whether they honestly represent an expression of political identity, or whether they are instead primarily motivated by the perception that secession would result in economic, or other, advantages.[63] Second, Miller maintains that even if we treat a majority vote for secession "as an expression of political identity, it is still possible that the majority verdict is on this occasion wrong."[64] The vote expresses a judgment: it says, in effect, "the way that we now understand ourselves as a people require that we should form a separate state."[65] And, according to Miller, we are entitled to pass judgment on such statements and conclude that they are wrong "just as we might say of an individual who tries not merely to reinterpret but to jettison the identity he has been brought up to have that he probably doesn't 'understand himself.'"[66] In the Anglo-Scottish case, Miller holds that "we can say that for Scots to renounce their higher level British identity would in one way to be to fail to understand who they are, what makes them the people they are today."[67]

In voicing this position, Miller takes a strong stand (and in my view a brave and welcome one) against that body of opinion within liberal nationalism that views the national identity of a group almost entirely as a subjective matter concerning the will and self-perception of its members.[68] The possible drawback of this view, however, must be acknowledged as well. It clearly cannot be confined to assessing the demands of nested groups alone. If a group's perception of itself as a separate nation can be contested on objective grounds in the case of nested nationalities, then surely it can, in principle, also be contested in the case of rival nationalities. And in these latter cases, the legitimization of attacks on peoples' self-understanding may prove more problematic than in the former. At the very least, Miller is suggesting that a group's perception of its own identity, as well as its assessment of the means necessary for the fulfillment of that identity (e.g., secession), can be called into question on objective grounds.

I have in mind the case of the Israeli-Palestinian conflict that Miller classifies as belonging to his second category.[69] Until relatively recently, it was not uncommon for Israeli nationals to question Palestinian demands for self-determination on the grounds that the latter do not honestly constitute a free-standing nation. Of course, no one argued that the Palestinians form a nested nation within the wider Israeli community in the way that Miller argues for Scottish nestedness within Britain. However, some Israeli politicians have argued that the Palestinians are in fact no more than a diaspora ethnic group whose national identity is no different than that of other Arabs who already enjoy national self-determination in several independent states, and that they therefore have no legitimate (territorial) claim against Israel. As in Miller's argument, this view holds, first, that Palestinian territorial demands are insincere. That is, that they do not represent an honest expression of an independent political identity (i.e., independent of the rest of the Arab world), but are rather a ploy designed by the Arab nations as a whole to extract territory from Israel. Second, it holds that, even if this is a sincere expression of political identity, it is misguided. These arguments are usually backed up with a list of objective historical facts, quite reminiscent of the historical cameo Miller gives in his eighth chapter on "Nationality in Divided Societies" concerning Scottish identity.[70] Thus, it is often pointed out that there was no Palestinian nation as such, even by their own account, until roughly twenty or thirty years ago.[71]

Such arguments are echoed (critically) and rejected by Yael Tamir in her work on self-determination, which implies that we cannot resist national fragmentation on objective grounds and that what counts ultimately is the group members' collective self-understanding. She says of the Palestinians, "They share many objective features with other Arabs, and it might well be the case that from a historical, cultural, linguistic and religious point of view, Palestinians have more in common with Jordanians or Syrians than a native Israeli has with an Ethiopian Jew. Yet the Palestinians *feel* that they belong to a distinct nation,"[72] and ultimately, for Tamir, this subjective feeling is all that seems to count.

Now, however admirable Tamir's political motivation for holding this subjective approach may be, Miller's demand for objective evaluation clearly holds the higher theoretical ground. It appears patently absurd to maintain that any variant of an existing nation can declare independence of the wider group and demand a separate right to national self-determination and territorial sovereignty on the basis of their *feelings* alone. Could American or British Jews make such a demand of Britain or the United States on the basis of feelings that allegedly separate their group identity from the Israeli one?[73] This would be totally out of step with our everyday treatment of people's feelings and their subsequent claims (e.g., I may believe I am descended from the house of Windsor, but I doubt the British royal family would grant me any financial privileges on the basis of my feelings). In short, whatever one's reasons for supporting the Palestinian cause, these need not (and indeed cannot reasonably) rest on a theoretical commitment to accepting every national claim on its say-so alone, as Tamir would have us believe.

In some of his earlier comments on national identity, Miller himself appears to endorse a more subjectivist approach, one based on belief, which would be more in keeping with Tamir's line of thought. Thus, Miller might wish to deny the implications I have attributed to his later argument.[74] Perhaps he would claim that his Anglo-Scottish argument does not imply that a group's perception of itself as an independent nation can be put to the test, but rather that we can legitimately question the belief that its identity necessitates secession. While this more modest proposition may represent Miller's intent (indeed, it is more in keeping with some of his previous comments), the stronger assertion does emerge clearly from his text. Toward the end of his "Nationality in Divided Societies," he explicitly asks whether "Scottish identity has become detached from British" and raises doubts as to whether a majority vote on this matter constitutes "decisive evidence" to that effect.[75]

Naturally, opening up these questions of national identity does not amount to accepting any particular assertion of misperception as necessarily correct. Often we can be mistaken in accusing someone of misunderstanding himself or herself, and we may equally misjudge the self-perception of a national group. In the Palestinian case, for instance, the aforementioned accusation whereby they misunderstand, or misrepresent, their collective identity as a national one may reasonably be contested on objective grounds. Most obviously, it can be argued the Palestinians' sense of uniqueness has been reinforced by being subject to military occupation and that this justifies their demands for an independent state. The fact that the Palestinians share a joint history (as do the Scots) and that (unlike the Scots) it is one of subjection to military occupation is an objective factor indicating separateness from other Arabs who do not share this particular biography.[76] Moreover, the Palestinians themselves claim that, far from constituting a new nation, they are in fact the descendants of one or another of the Canaanite peoples whose collective existence predates that of even the ancient Israelites.[77] Correspondingly, they claim to have preceded the latter's inhabitancy of the disputed territories. Just recently, Palestinian archaeologists claimed to have uncovered Canaanite houses in the territories now under Palestinian authority, allegedly dating back approximately to the year 3000 B.C. "This strengthens our historical right to the land," they claim.[78]

Nevertheless, the point remains that the principle whereby there is an objective matter of fact on questions of independent nationhood and group identity does open the door to conflicting interpretations among rival groups, as well as among nested ones. And in the case of rival groups, this may often serve to further complicate an already difficult situation and at times may be at odds with the prevailing liberal view that Miller would presumably wish to endorse.

To sum up this first comment then, while I believe that Miller's objectivism vis-á-vis national identity is theoretically preferable to the subjectivist approach advanced by Tamir, I do not see how it can be restricted to cases of nested nationalities alone. If Miller is correct in principle (as I have argued that he is) in maintaining that a group's self-perception can legitimately be contested on objective grounds, this inevitably loosens the leash on such arguments of collective misperception in cases other than those of nested nationalities. While Miller's view on Scotland does not commit him to denying nationhood in any other specific case (indeed, the specific reasons for favoring his conclusion in the British case do not apply to cases of rival groups—such as the Jews and Palestinians), it does pave the way for the legitimization of such contentions in other cases, including rival ones. Nevertheless, bearing in mind the grave stakes involved in recognizing nationhood (primarily, its implications for territorial sovereignty), I believe that Miller is correct in advocating an objectivist approach to identifying a nation, but, again, he cannot hope to confine this approach to the relatively peaceful context of nested national groups.

The grave stakes involved in demands for territorial separation bring me to my second comment on Miller's analysis of cultural division and territorial conflict.

As Miller notes, separation and the subsequent redrawing of borders involve not only people, but also territory. In his chapter on "Secession and the Principle of Nationality," he points out that "secession does not only involve a political separation, but also a partition of territory."[79] And, as is often the case with dissolving a marriage, the separation parties may be only too happy to see each other go, but far less eager to part with half of their communal property.[80] In the British case, that is, in the case of nested nationalities, Miller attributes conclusive weight to the fact that all groups within the overarching community have an important stake in the territory inhabited by the would-be secessionist subgroup.[81] Thus, his second consideration for opposing Scottish secession is as follows:

> The British People taken together have established a valid claim to control the whole territory of Britain, and this claim would be infringed by a unilateral secession. Claims to exercise territorial authority arise when people sharing a common national identity form a political community and occupy territory over a substantial period of history. Thus the English now have a stake in Scottish lands, a stake that arises from . . . the emergence of a common national identity from overlapping cultures, mutually advantageous economic co-operation, and an interwoven history.[82]

The factors listed do not, at least for the most part, exist in the case of rival national groups, and consequently Miller's conclusion does not apply to the latter.[83] On each of these scores (i.e., "the emergence of a common national identity from overlapping cultures, mutually advantageous economic co-operation, and an interwoven history"), the differences between nested nationalities and rival ones warrant Miller's conclusion that they should be treated differently, as well as the strong divide he draws between endorsing separation in the one case and denying it in the other. Nevertheless, the emphasis that Miller places on the interests of members of the remainder group in potentially seceding territories ought not to be overlooked in cases of national rivalry either. Some of these interests will be the same (both in kind and in intensity) regardless of whether the groups involved are nested or rival ones. This point concerning the interests of the larger group in the seceding territory is one that Miller himself clearly recognizes in his previous chapter on secession[84] but which he does not take seriously enough with regard to rival groups.

In the case of nested groups, Miller willingly acknowledges that the demands of the would-be secessionists (henceforth, "the Xs") have to be set against the equally legitimate demands of the larger group ("the Ys") "not to be deprived of part of the territory which they and their ancestors have helped to shape, and which they quite naturally think of as theirs."[85] And he states that consequently, "in a non-economic sense, the Y's will be poorer if the X's secede. If no compromise is possible the Xs' demand may finally prove the stronger, but in such a case there is powerful reason to find a solution which gives the Xs a form of autonomy that falls short of independence."[86]

In light of this statement, Miller's swift and unhesitating conclusion favoring the physical separation of rivaling nations who inhabit a joint territory is strikingly surprising.[87] Clearly, in many cases involving rivaling groups, as well as in cases of nested ones, both groups will have a significant interest in the territory in question. In many such cases the remainder majority group will also have a vested (noneconomic) interest in the disputed territory whose nature and appearance they will have helped to shape. They, too, as well as the would-be secessionists, will have fostered a strong attachment to that land as a result of their historical connection to it.

What precisely are these noneconomic interests, claimed here to be ethically relevant to rivaling cases as well as to nested ones? The scope of this chapter does not enable (nor do its limited objectives require) me to spell out a detailed independent argument outlining the appropriate guidelines for the just adjudication of rival territorial claims. I confine myself to describing what I take to be the two most central features of the relationship between individual nationals and the territories they value, both of which I believe are embedded in Miller's own argument against devolution in nested cases.

Recall that in the case of nested nationalities, Miller tells a story about the occupation and transformation of territory that is supposed to explain why, for instance, all Britons now have a relevant interest in Scottish territory.[88] But remainder rival groups, and not only nested ones, will often have had a hand in settling the territory that they are being asked to sacrifice—building it, shaping it, and molding it in light of their national culture by making and implementing significant culturally dependent decisions with regard to it in the course of time (e.g., choosing particular modes of architecture, specific agricultural techniques, certain ways of cultivation and construction). Here, too, then, the concession of territory will constitute not only a financial loss but, far more significantly from an ethical point of view, will often result in the loss of a portion of land (or parts thereof) whose landscape and architecture largely reflect the cultural identity of the remainder nation. If the territory in question has indeed been labored upon and transformed by members of the remainder nation at least partly in light of their culture, then sacrificing a portion of that land inevitably represents not only a deprivation of the fruits of their labor, but also a loss to that aspect of their respective personal identities that is constituted by their national-cultural affiliation and that liberal nationalism has made so much of over the past decade. Such interests, which I believe are akin to those Miller attributes to nested groups, may attach themselves with equal force to the members of various rival groups as well. In both cases, such interests, as well as their normative force, arise as a result of the effect that nations and their cultures have on the development of the territories they occupy and settle (the imprint and manifestation of their members' identity culture on the territories they inhabit) and from the identity-related implications thereof.

A second, distinct type of identity-related interest in territory that can apply equally to rival (as well as nested) groups concerns the constitutive role that a nation's territorial homeland plays in the formation of that nation as a historic entity and in shaping its specific historic identity. It relies on the suggestion that, in some instances, a disputed territory is of primary importance in forming the historical identity of the remainder group (as well as the seceding one) and that, as a consequence thereof, these "formative territories" are likely to be perceived by the members of that nation as bearing deep and significant ties to their very essence.[89] Note that this historical type of interest is not a version of original occupation arguments, which constitute quite a different kind of historical claim whose ethical significance is admittedly questionable. Not unlike Miller's own reference to history in connection with nested groups,[90] it relies on the impact a particular territory has on a nation's history and consequently on forging that nation's culture and the cultural identity of its members.

Both of the territorial interests I have outlined can be comprehended, and should be respected, within liberalism. Assuming one accepts this (and Miller appears to), they generate equally good liberal reasons to consider these interests in our normative evaluation of territorial conflict among rival groups as among nested ones. If one concedes the basic liberal-national assumption invoked here, whereby national cultures form an essential component of their individual members' identities; and if these same national cultures are both partly defined by their connection to certain territories and manifest themselves in those territories, then those territories are of unarguable significance to the personal identity of (at least most of) the individuals composing that nation, and therefore yield normatively significant (though admittedly nonconclusive) reasons to oppose their forfeiture whether in favor of a nested or rival national group.

Considering the strong emphasis Miller places on remainder-group interests in opposing the devolution of territories inhabited by nested groups, it is unreasonable for him to ignore or downplay the normative weight carried by similar interests in cases of potentially seceding rival groups as well.

Moreover, any attempt to form opinions on particular territorial disputes (and, in the case of world leaders, even an attempt to adjudicate them) while totally dismissing the particularistic, nationalist arguments voiced by either side may ultimately bear grave consequences for our actual ability to achieve the very goal toward which it strives. Given the tremendous force that nationalism has proved to be—for better or for worse—in the modern world, and the central role that territory has played in the history of nationalism, I doubt very much that the outright dismissal of the noneconomic, national interests of one of the rival parties is likely to be very helpful in reducing regional strife. Quite the contrary. The lack of a clear understanding of the nature and possible normative force of these claims (which, in the eyes of the members of the remainder group, are thought to represent the very factors entitling them to the seceding territory) may actually prove detrimental to their final adjudication.

Once again, this is not to deny that Miller's conclusion, whereby resisting secession might be justified in cases of nested nationalities but not in the case of rival ones, is totally coherent. There are, as Miller points out, significant differences between the various kinds of nationally divided communities, which make his threefold typology both theoretically illuminating and practically useful. Nevertheless, if one accepts Miller's justifications for resisting devolution in the case of nested nationalities, one must acknowledge and attribute some (though by no means necessarily conclusive) normative force to similar reasons in evaluating territorial disputes among rival national groups. One cannot accept these reasons for resisting devolution as conclusive, in the one case, and remain totally unsympathetic to similar interests on the part of those opposing secession in the other case.

Miller's neglect of these interests in the case of rival groups seems to imply that, where the fierce antagonism between rival groups hampers the possibility of continued cohabitancy, the interests fostered by the majority remainder group do not count for anything at all.[91] In contrast, I argue that we must acknowledge these interests even in those cases where they are ultimately outweighed by conflicting claims, or where they cannot be accommodated for practical reasons. For one thing, even where separation is judged to be the appropriate solution, the interests of the remainder group might still play an important role in determining the extent of the territory that ought to be removed by the seceding nation. For another thing, even when the interests of the remainder group are totally outweighed by competing factors, a clear appreciation of these interests, and a sincere attempt to accommodate them, can significantly help along the difficult process of achieving a peaceful solution to a prolonged rivalry.

Thus, concluding my second comment, I maintain that the interests of the remainder group in the potentially seceding territory warrant greater attention and more serious consideration within the framework of Miller's discussion of rival nationalities. Moreover, I hold this to be true regardless of the final conclusion on the appropriate destiny of any specific territory. Focusing greater attention on these interests in the case of rival groups would be beneficial both for the internal consistency of Miller's argument and for advancing successful political solutions.

CONCLUSION

The purpose of this chapter was to take a brief look at the territorial implications of David Miller's most recent work on nationality. Within its limited scope, I could not hope to do more than supply the reader with a taste of the complicated territorial issues tackled in this book and a flavor of the guidance it offers on this rarely addressed aspect of the national phenomenon. Toward the end of the chapter, I have pointed out several steps in Miller's argument that, I argue, may have further implications in cases of international rivalry over land.

NOTES

1. See David Miller, *Citizenship and National Identity* (Cambridge: Polity Press, 2000).

2. Joseph Raz and Avishai Margalit, "National Self-Determination," in *Ethics in the Public Domain,* ed. Joseph Raz (Oxford: Clarendon, 1994), 125–145, 126–127, 139.

3. Raz and Margalit, "National Self-Determination," 141.

4. Note that for Raz and Margalit, "the right to self-determination answers the question 'who is to decide?', not 'what is the best decision?'" Raz and Margalit, "National Self-Determination," 139, 140, 143.

5. Miller, *Citizenship,* 36–38, 110–111. See also Avner de-Shalit, "National Self-Determination: Political, not Cultural," *Political Studies* XLIV (1996): 906–920, 916–917.

6. Miller, *Citizenship,* 111–112, 124, 125–126.

7. See for just three examples Brian Barry, "Self Government Revisited," *Democracy and Power* (Oxford: Clarendon Press, 1991), 162; Margaret Moore, "Introduction: The Self-Determination Principle and the Ethics of Secession," in *National Self-Determination and Secession,* ed. Margaret Moore (Oxford: Oxford University Press, 1998), 1–12, 2; and Margaret Moore, "The Territorial Dimension of Self-Determination," in *National Self-Determination,* 134–157, 134–135.

8. David Miller, *On Nationality* (Oxford: Clarendon Press, 1995), 111–112, where he criticizes Beran's consent theory of secession and argues that it is both potentially chaotic—as it can legitimize an infinite number of secessions within secessions—and that it is often ineffective in solving the problems of minorities, as secession will often result in a new majority-minority relationship. The point is reiterated in Miller, *Citizenship,* 118, 139.

9. Miller, *Citizenship,* ch. 8, 139; and, with reference to Margaret Moore's *National Self-Determination,* see Miller, *Citizenship,* 202, n. 34.

10. Miller, *Citizenship,* 139.

11. Miller, *Citizenship,* ch. 7 and 8. I refer here to Miller's distinction between the various types of groups that may coexist within a given territory (ethnic, rival, and nested) and to the implications concerning the future of the political community that he draws from this distinction.

12. Raz and Margalit, "National Self-Determination," 140–141.

13. Miller, *Citizenship,* throughout ch. 8. Once again, I refer here primarily to the introduction of Miller's tripartite distinction between the different types of divided societies and the guidelines suggested by this distinction for determining when it is, and when it is not, justified to break up an existing state. When, as in the case of rival nationalities, such a breakup is viewed by Miller as justified, his principle of national self-determination offers further guidance concerning the appropriate territorial solution depending on the precise configuration of the communities involved. Miller, *Citizenship,* 129.

14. Yael Tamir, *Liberal Nationalism* (Princeton, N.J.: Princeton University Press, 1993), ch. 3, 57–77, 57; and Yael Tamir, "The Right to National Self-Determination," *Social Research* 58, no. 3 (fall 1991): 565–590, 565.

15. Tamir, *Liberal Nationalism,* esp. on 73–74; and Tamir, "Right to National Self-Determination," 566, 586.

16. Tamir, *Liberal Nationalism,* 73; and Tamir, "Right to National Self-Determination," 586.

17. Tamir, *Liberal Nationalism,* 73–74.

18. Tamir, "Right to National Self-Determination," 587.

19. Tamir, *Liberal Nationalism,* 74–75; and Tamir, "Right to National Self-Determination," 587.

20. In fact, Tamir is a bit unclear about the territorial aspect of her interpretation. On the one hand, she has been interpreted as suggesting a totally nonterritorial conception of self-determination. Thus, Judith Lichtenberg goes so far as to claim that Tamir's argument, whereby "'it is the cultural rather than the political version of nationalism that best accords with a liberal viewpoint' severs the connection between nation and territory." And she quotes Michael Ignatieff, who also interprets Tamir in this manner and subsequently criticizes her on this allegedly

nonterritorial note. See Judith Lichtenberg, "Nationalism For and (Mainly) Against," in *The Morality of Nationalism*, ed. Robert McKim and Jeff McMahan (Oxford: Oxford University Press, 1997), 158–175, 165. On the other hand, Tamir's lifelong commitment to Zionism, alongside her support for Palestinian territorial demands on Israel; her repeated reference to a group's need for what she has termed "a public sphere" that must take on some form of territorial dimension; and her implied grading of independent statehood as the optimal form of enjoying this public sphere, with various forms of autonomy as possible "second-best" options, all indicate the existence of a strong territorial element in her thesis. All this leaves the precise attitude of her strand of nationalism toward territory open to interpretation. For the reasons stated previously, I believe that it would be a gross exaggeration to interpret Tamir's thesis on national self-determination as totally nonterritorial or indeed as severing the connection between nation and territory. In any event, her account, however interpreted, certainly does not address (nor is it intended to address) the kind of territorial questions that occupy me here. Lichtenberg's own account of the right to national self-determination is no more illuminating on these matters; see her aforementioned "Nationalism For and (Mainly) Against," 162–164.

21. This is a point pursued in depth by Chaim Gans, "Historical Rights—The Evaluation of Nationalist Claims to Sovereignty," *Political Theory* 29, no. 1 (February 2001): 58–79. Though Tamir does not consider this possibility in any of her early work on liberal nationalism and national self-determination, she does seem to have acknowledged it more recently in Yael Tamir, "Theoretical Difficulties in the Study of Nationalism," in *Rethinking Nationalism*, ed. Jocelyn Couture, Kai Nielsen, and Michel Seymour (Calgary, Alberta: University of Calgary Press, 1998), 65–92, 73. There, she addresses the issue of territory and the possibility that a nation may demand sovereignty over a particular piece of land on a historical-cultural, identity-related basis. Thus, she comments: "The demand that the national home is to be established in a particular place is also influenced by the history of a nation. Hence the demand to establish the Jewish state in the land of Israel rests on the constitutive role of this territory in the history of the Jewish people."

22. Avner de-Shalit, "National Self-Determination: Political, Not Cultural."

23. Note that this need not be viewed as a shortcoming of de-Shalit's thesis, which deliberately focuses solely on the analysis and reinterpretation of the claim for self-determination and examines possible forms of addressing it (e.g., autonomy) in light thereof, rather than on any questions of precise boundary demarcation.

24. Thomas Baldwin, "The Territorial State," in *Jurisprudence—Cambridge Essays*, ed. H. Gross and T. Harrison (Oxford: Clarendon Press, 1992), ch. 10, 209–230.

25. Baldwin, "Territorial State," 228.

26. For just one among many other accounts of national self-determination that do not advance us any further toward solving territorial problems, see David Copp, "Democracy and Communal Self-Determination," in *The Morality of Nationalism*, ed. Robert McKim and Jeff McMahan (Oxford: Oxford University Press, 1997), 277–300. See esp. pp. 278–279, where the principle is defined. Copp's interpretation of the principle is not only unhelpful territorially, but is also, as he puts it, nonnational but rather societal and amounts to the right to hold on to, or form, an independent state.

27. David Miller, *On Nationality*, 81.

28. See Miller, *Citizenship*, 113, 125, 140.

29. Miller, *On Nationality*, 81.

30. Miller, *On Nationality*, 81. And Miller, *Citizenship*, ch. 2, 27, and ch. 7, 113. These are views he shares with Yael Tamir; see Tamir, *Liberal Nationalism*, 74–75, and Tamir, "Right to National Self-Determination," 587.

31. David Miller, *Citizenship*, ch. 8, 125. See also p. 140 where he reiterates the same idea.

32. Miller, *Citizenship*, 129.

33. See Miller, *Citizenship*, 129.

34. Miller, *On Nationality*, ch. 1, 1–2. Similar thoughts are voiced also toward the end of that book, ch. 7, 183.

35. Miller, *Citizenship*, ch 7, 112.

36. Miller, *Citizenship*, ch. 7, 113.

37. This is not to deny that considerable attention has been, and is, focused by various theorists of nationalism on the issue of secession specifically. Still, relatively little exists in the way of well thought out general guidelines for solving territorial disputes of a variety of types—secession being only one such variant. As Allen Buchanan has himself pointed out recently, "at present, systematic liberal thinking about the making and unmaking of boundaries is in its infancy (or perhaps gestation). Hence, there is no characteristic liberal view on the topic." See A. Buchanan, "The Making and Unmaking of Boundaries: What Liberalism Has to Say" (conference paper for *Ethickon*, June 1999), 2. Furthermore, as illustrated by the preceding, territorial issues have rarely, if ever, been adequately addressed within a theory of national self-determination.

38. Miller, *Citizenship*, ch. 7, 113, ch. 8, 125–126.

39. Miller, *Citizenship*, 127–129.

40. Miller, *Citizenship*, 126.

41. Miller, *Citizenship*, 127.

42. Miller, *Citizenship*, 127.

43. Miller, *Citizenship*, 127.

44. Miller, *Citizenship*, 128.

45. Miller, *Citizenship*, 128.

46. Miller, *Citizenship*, 128–129.

47. Miller, *Citizenship*, 129.

48. Miller, *Citizenship*, 129.

49. Miller, *Citizenship*, 129.

50. Miller, *Citizenship*, 129.

51. Miller, *Citizenship*, 129. This category also includes, for example, the Quebecois and English speakers in Canada and the Macedonians and Greeks in Greece.

52. Miller, *Citizenship*, 129–130.

53. Miller, *Citizenship*, 131.

54. Miller, *Citizenship*, 131.

55. This is the generalization that arises out of Miller's conclusion on the Anglo-Scottish case, on Miller, *Citizenship*, 139.

56. Miller, *Citizenship*, ch. 8, 132–136, 139.

57. Miller, *Citizenship*, 139.

58. Miller, *Citizenship*, 138.

59. Miller, *Citizenship*, 138–139.

60. Miller, *Citizenship*, 139.

61. Miller, *Citizenship*, 139.

62. Miller, *Citizenship*, ch. 8, 138–139.

63. Miller, *Citizenship*, 138.

64. Miller, *Citizenship*, 138.

65. Miller, *Citizenship*, 138.

66. Miller, *Citizenship*, 138.

67. Miller, *Citizenship*, ch. 8, 138, see also 202, n. 30: "As with all beliefs, these may be true, false, exaggerated, distorted, etc. Someone who says: 'the Scots should separate from the U.K.: they have nothing in common with the English' is supporting his demand with an unwarranted assertion." Miller makes this point about the objective appraisal of groups' self-perception in a more brief and general form in ch. 7, "Secession and the Principle of Nationality" as well (p.115). Though he never says so explicitly, the latter context would indicate an implicit recognition of the applicability of this idea to cases other than nested ones. Earlier in chapter 7 he also addresses the question of what these objective criteria for nationhood might be (pp. 113–114), a fuller account of which is given in chapter 2 of his earlier *On Nationality.*

68. Miller quotes Renan in this connection and his famous description of a nation as "a daily plebiscite." See Miller, *Citizenship*, 202, n. 30. A more explicit articulation of the view that nationality is primarily a subjective matter that can rarely, if ever, be contested on the grounds of

objective fact can be found in Yael Tamir's *Liberal Nationalism*, 66. In his defense of nationality (ch. 2), Miller himself is somewhat vague on this matter. When noting several points on national identity, he even implies an endorsement of the subjectivist view thereof. See Miller, *Citizenship*, 28–30, in particular the first and last points he makes.

69. Miller, *Citizenship*, 128. It is worth noting, if only as a point of law, that the Israeli-Palestinian case is not strictly speaking a secessionist issue. As Lea Brilmayer points out, "'secession' is not really the right word to describe it. . . . Because the occupied West Bank does not now lie clearly within the recognized borders of Israel, one cannot call the Palestinian argument 'secessionist.'" Notwithstanding this legal observation, Brilmayer herself points out: "The structure of the demand is similar." See Lea Brilmayer, "Groups, Histories, and International Law," *Cornell International Law Journal* 25: 355–363. Thus, this case is usually discussed in connection with the general debate on secession.

70. Miller, *Citizenship*, 132–136.

71. It is sometimes pointed out here that at one time, *Palestinian* was actually the term used to denote all the inhabitants of British mandatory Palestine, most definitely including its Jewish ones. Another trivial fact which often surfaces in this connection concerns the origin of the name *Palestine*, which is Roman, rather than Arab.

72. Yael Tamir, *Liberal Nationalism*, ch. 3, 66.

73. Cf. Miller, *Citizenship*, ch. 7, 113, where, as he puts it, if "someone were to propose holding an independence ballot among the Jews of Montreal, we would immediately recognize this as a not-very-serious proposal and react accordingly." See also Avner de-Shalit, "National Self-Determination," 910, his example concerning the Jewish orthodox community in Brooklyn.

74. Miller, *Citizenship*, 28–30, 113–114.

75. Miller, *Citizenship*, 138.

76. This argument raises the question of whether even physical persecution can, in and of itself, create independent nationhood, where other attributes are lacking. Homosexuals were persecuted by the Nazis, but this is not taken to constitute grounds for granting them a nation-state. The fact that European Jews were persecuted in the Holocaust does not separate them as a distinct nation from other Jews, warranting a separate state for each group.

77. See Avishai Margalit, "Historical Rights," *Iyun* (Hebrew) 35 (1985): 252–258, 256, where he mentions viewing a documentary on Jordanian Television that presented the Palestinians as descendants of the Jebosites, who preceded the Jews in Jerusalem. I am grateful to Karma Nabulsi for her enlightening comments concerning the last 2,000 years of Palestinian history.

78. *Ha'aretz*, August 4, 1998.

79. Miller, *Citizenship*, ch. 7, 116.

80. Miller refers to the example of divorce both in Miller, *Citizenship,* 116, and also in chapter 8, "Nationality in Divided Societies," 139; and I have borrowed this analogy from him here, though I also tend to accept his observation that there is something of a disanalogy between it and the national case.

81. Miller, *Citizenship*, 139.

82. Miller, *Citizenship*, 139.

83. I say that they do not exist "for the most part" in the case of rival nations because some of these conditions may obtain in some cases of rivalry as well. Mutually advantageous economic cocooperation for one is not limited to nested (or otherwise friendly) national groups, but can exist (admittedly often alongside some degree of exploitation) between rival groups as well. The same will often be true to some degree as regards the other factors as well. Ironically, long-lasting rivalries will often result in some cultural overlap. Less ironically, perhaps, the mere fact of physical proximity will do the trick. Prolonged national rivalries will almost necessarily result in a type of interwoven history, though here I am inclined to join Miller in doubting whether this is the relevant type of historical relationship that is pertinent to the present purposes.

84. Miller, *Citizenship*, 116–117.

85. Miller, *Citizenship*, 117.

86. Miller, *Citizenship*, ch. 7, 117.

87. Miller, *Citizenship*, ch. 7, 117, and ch. 8, 129, where Miller expresses little, if any, hesitation in prescribing territorial partition as the best solution for all cases of rivaling nations in which this is a politically feasible option.

88. Miller, *Citizenship*, 117, 139.

89. This is an argument originally formulated and best explored by Chaim Gans, "Historical Rights: The Evaluation of Nationalist Claims to Sovereignty," see n. 21 earlier. As I noted there, Tamir touches on this same idea as well, in Tamir, "Theoretical Difficulties."

90. Miller, *Citizenship*, 139.

91. Miller, *Citizenship*, 117, 129.

11

The Liberal Limits of Republican Nationality

Erica Benner

David Miller defends nationality, not "nationalism." The distinction is important because, as Miller points out at the start of *On Nationality*, "Nationalism is thought to have a wide range of unwelcome connotations which can be avoided by using some other term . . . for the defensible position, and abandoning 'nationalism' to the opposition."[1] To be sure, the word *nationalism* has a strongly negative sense in most European languages today.[2] Many people think of nationalism as a conservative doctrine that often veers toward the far right. Benign forms of conservative nationalism have sought to preserve existing states or to set up new ones grounded in older collective identities. These identities are based on allegiance to traditional institutions and social relations, not on popular sovereignty and aspirations for social reform. Conservative nationalism may also assert that "cultural" differences from other nations, particularly differences in language or religion, constitute fundamental moral divisions between peoples. These ideas are pushed further to the right when nationalists claim that the traditional bonds of community face some sort of mortal threat. Everyday efforts to maintain national integrity are cranked up, emergency measures to save the nation are proclaimed. Cultural bonds are presented as natural, and natural bonds as sacred, thereby placing national claims beyond reasoned political discussion.

David Miller wants to distance himself from both these forms of nationalism. He assumes that most of his readers are "people of liberal and pacific disposition."[3] If such people are to be persuaded that nationality deserves a philosophical defense, they need some assurance that this defense does not have illiberal and aggressive implications. Unlike moderate conservative nationalists, Miller calls on the "principle of nationality" to promote solidarity, social justice, and participation in public decision making. But while these values may appeal to many readers of a "liberal disposition," Miller does not see them as liberal values, nor does he want to defend a liberal "theory" of nationality. The kind of nationality he favors is linked to "social democratic" or "republican" values, labels Miller picks to signal his disagreement with mainstream liberal views about nationality.

Liberals have always supported some national movements, especially those directed against authoritarian rule and colonial oppression. But they have also insisted that national claims should be restrained by more fundamental moral and political requirements. Two such requirements have been seen as especially important. One is that states and political movements should respect the personal autonomy of subjects. This principle protects the rights of individuals against collective claims made in the name of the nation. The other requirement is set by the idea of equal human dignity. On a strong reading, this idea implies that nationalists should show an active concern to seek justice for all of humanity, and not just for their own part of it. On a weaker reading, it says that moral duties to human beings as such are at least as compelling as particular duties to conationals, and that particular duties should not be discharged in ways that lead to the humiliation or oppression of other human beings. Both requirements have been expressed in a variety of phrases, and not all liberals would accept the terms "respect for personal autonomy" and "equal human dignity" as expressions of their own principles. Nor, for that matter, have all the major liberal writers on nationality embraced them.[4] Nevertheless, they are an adequate shorthand for the principles that define a distinctive liberal position on nationality.[5]

Other political theorists have argued that these constraints were applied too strictly in the past, and that many liberals therefore failed to appreciate the strength and legitimacy of national sentiments. Their response has been to modify liberal principles so that they give a wider berth to national claims.[6] Miller's argument takes a different tack. He questions the basic principles themselves and denies that they form a higher standpoint for assessing national claims. Indeed, his key arguments about nationality are developed in contrast to positions he describes as liberal. Miller is especially critical toward liberal doctrines of "individualism" and "ethical universalism," which he associates with a demanding Kantian moral theory.[7] Whereas other liberals have seen individualist and universalist values as restraints on national collectivism and ethnocentricity, Miller sees them as the source of some of modern society's gravest ills. Individualism leads to political apathy and a reluctance to share material benefits in a cooperative economic scheme. Universalism leads well-meaning people down the path of naïve idealism, urging them to try to solve insoluble problems abroad—often dirtying their hands in the process—while neglecting real concerns close to home.[8] Miller's defense of nationality is meant to counteract these failures of individualism and universalism. Instead of calling for an improved version of liberal nationality, he marries a robust national principle with a republican theory of politics and argues that this union underwrites social justice better than liberal values.

The terms *liberal* or *republican* are not, of course, what matters here, and my aim in this chapter is not to question Miller's use of labels. Instead, I want to ask how far Miller succeeds in charting a middle way between nationalism and liberalism that avoids the shortcomings of both. In particular, I ask whether the benign national values Miller defends are likely to remain benign if they are not constrained by the same individualist and universalist principles that Miller criticizes. The next section sketches the main arguments behind Miller's defense of a strong national principle. The remaining sections assess these arguments.

I

Drawing on the books *On Nationality* and *Citizenship and National Identity*, it seems to me that Miller's defense of nationality consists of three main, interconnected elements. These are, (1) first, an empiricist *moral epistemology*; (2) second, a *constitutional ideal* of politics based on republican values and deliberative democracy; and (3) third, a *constitutive ideal* of nationhood as the main principle of political and international order. I explain each of these elements in the following.

(1) The deepest layer of Miller's argument lies in what Adam Swift calls his "moral epistemology."[9] Moral epistemologies answer two related questions: What kind of knowledge can people have of themselves and the world? And in the light of this knowledge and its limits, what principles are most likely to promote the good and limit the bad? Miller's answer to the first question is that experience, including everyday experience, is our most reliable source of knowledge. Experience and commonsense observation are also reliable sources of moral knowledge and should be consulted when we frame our moral principles. This robust empiricism is the touchstone for much of Miller's reasoning about nationality. He claims that it has a Humean pedigree and invokes it to criticize mainstream liberal moral theories. His approach to national values diverges from that of idealist or rationalist liberalism in three key respects.

First, Miller takes people's avowed preferences and beliefs as the starting point of moral reasoning. His defense of nationality is based on "a philosophy which, rather than dismissing ordinary beliefs and sentiments out of hand unless they can be shown to have a rational foundation, leaves them in place until strong arguments are produced for rejecting them."[10] This down-to-earth approach is meant to replace the demand for "universal and rational" moral foundations "such as Kant tried to provide with the categorical imperative."[11] The everyday judgments of real people are more important sources of morality than idealized human capacities for thinking and acting better. Miller's antiperfectionist reasoning is reflected in his decision to treat deep national attachments "simply as a psychological fact" and to accept this fact as a valid, though not sufficient, reason for treating nationhood as morally important.[12] We should, Miller says, "start from the premise that people generally do exhibit such attachments and allegiances, and then try to build a political philosophy which incorporates them" as constitutive elements of justice.[13]

The second feature distinguishing Miller's approach from standard liberal theories is his Humean emphasis on "sentiments" as a source of justice. Miller sees national identities as "sentiment-based" and argues that national sentiments are a primary basis for political obligations. That is, peoples' feelings of national attachment and distinctness are among the main criteria that determine the boundaries of justice. As Miller puts it, "The duties we owe to our fellow-nationals are different from, and more extensive than, the duties we owe to human beings as such."[14] This is by no means a purely sentimentalist ethics. Other criteria such as need, desert, or entitlement may supplement or correct conclusions based on sentiment, and Miller stresses that we have duties to human beings as such, even if our feelings of humanitarian commitment are far weaker than sentiments of national partiality. Still, Miller thinks that national sentiments *should* limit the application of other "universal and rational" criteria in dispensing justice beyond national boundaries, as a matter of morality as well as feasibility.[15] Miller's position should not, moreover, be confused with the romantic antirationalism of some nationalists. His recent work outlines ideal procedures designed to make people reflect on their current sentiments and adjust them in the light of public deliberation.[16] Yet, sentiments remain the bedrock of justice in Miller's theory, and national sentiments appear as the main source of social and political—as distinct from personal or family—obligations.

Third, Miller's moral empiricism leads him to question the "ethical universalism" that he sees behind much liberal thinking on nationality.[17] The trouble with universalism, according to Miller, is that it fails to supply an adequate motivation for justice. He cites "research undertaken by social psychologists which shows that the boundaries of the moral community within which people are willing to apply principles of justice to fellow-members are affected by perceptions of similarity and common identity." Other philosophers might want to criticize the self-regarding attitude reflected in these "psychological facts," or to suggest that the perceptions they involve are wrong. Miller does neither of these things. He accepts the moral authority of current "perceptions of common identity," concluding that "there is a strong correlation between identification and justice, even among subjects whose political attitudes are generally liberal."[18] Although Miller's main antiuniversalist argument concerns motivation, however, he sometimes expresses a more general worry about the likely psychological and social consequences of putting universalist ideals into practice. Without national loyalties, Miller declares, "we would be cast adrift in a region of great moral uncertainty" since justice as he conceives it is shaped at the deepest level by national identities.[19] Such passages highlight Miller's anxieties about the darker sides of moral universalism and "globalisation."

They also support the argument that strong forms of national identity are needed to avert these consequences.

(2) The second main element in Miller's theory of nationality is a constitutional ideal based on republican values and on decision-making procedures that Miller describes under the heading "deliberative democracy."[20] Three central values seem to lie at the heart of Miller's republican ideal: participation, solidarity, and particularity. Again, each of these values sets Miller's politics apart from what he describes as mainstream liberal ideals. Republicans value participation because they have a "thick" rather than a "thin" conception of citizenship. Republican citizenship is a role, not just a legal status. It requires citizens "to behave and act in a certain way" and involves a willingness to "take active steps to defend the rights of other members of the political community."[21] Miller's ideal citizen participates, moreover, not just to promote his or her own interests or to check political abuses, but rather "as a way of expressing . . . commitment to the community."[22]

Social and political solidarity is among the ends of participatory politics. For Miller, the call for solidarity involves two main things. First, it demands that "people acting in public forums should adopt an inclusive identity as citizens which transcends their sectional identities as women, members of ethnic minorities, etc."[23] This inclusive identity sets limits on the individual and subnational claims that can be pressed against the civic community as a whole. Second, the call for solidarity supports Miller's argument that the "regulative ideal" of republican politics is agreement or "consensusote," rather than mere compromise or competition among individual and sectional interests.[24] Miller suggests that a politics aimed at solidarity in these senses demands a substantial moral effort from both state and citizen, whereas the liberal values of rational interest balancing, cultural neutrality, and toleration of differences fail to promote any sense of the common good. Republican values ask citizens to look hard for common ground where it is not easy to see, inspired by a sense of public virtue and a belief in the intrinsic value of civic life.[25]

Finally, although he doesn't expressly designate particularity as a core republican value, its importance is implied in the way Miller connects republican values to his particularist moral theory. He states clearly, "The practice of citizenship must . . . be confined within the boundaries of national political communities," since the values of participation and solidarity cannot be realized where sentiments of nationhood are absent.[26] Miller also presents this argument as a key point of difference between his position and that of typically universalist liberals. While republicans may share liberal concerns to promote individual freedom and what Mazzini called "duties to humanity," they have usually argued that these values must be advanced first of all within bounded nations or states.[27] Moreover, republican patriots see these units as moral communities, not just pragmatic associations or the accidental artifacts of history. Miller thus builds on a long tradition of republican thought to defend moderate particularist values against universalist objections.

Many "liberal-minded" readers will have some sympathy with these repub-lican values. But some may wonder just how Miller proposes to elicit partici-pation, solidarity, and consensus when these are not readily forthcoming. As Avner de-Shalit points out in this volume, consensus may be too demanding a political goal for complex modern societies, especially those with large cultural or religious minorities.[28] Here, the call for consensus or "solidarity" may ac-tually encourage majorities to adopt repressive practices, though these may not be officially sanctioned. Readers might well worry that in practice, Miller's full-blooded republican values require centralizing, *etatist* cultural policies, and justify the cultural marginalization or coercion of dissenters and minori-ties. This has, in fact, been a common criticism of the centralist-republican models of nationhood developed in countries like France and Turkey.

Miller admires the "French model," but he also wants to ward off suspicions that his call for solidarity and his trenchant critique of multicultural pluralism in the earlier book *On Nationality* justify the tyranny of national majorities.

In his most recent writings, therefore, Miller takes pluralist concerns very se-riously. He addresses them in *Citizenship and National Identity* through a carefully refined conception of "deliberative democracy," which now appears as a procedural model of decision making designed to limit the ways in which republican ideals may be pursued. This later Miller is willing to meet plural-ists half way. He concedes that a final decision reached through open public discussions "may not be wholly consensual, but it should represent a fair bal-ance between the different views expressed in the course of the discussion."[29] He also develops more clearly defined constraints on suffocating cultural cen-tralism, and tries to reassure readers that minority concerns do not get short shrift in his republican ideal.[30]

(3) The third major element of Miller's defense of nationality is his argument that nations are the best available *constitutive* units of political and interna-tional order. Miller hints at a difference between the constitutional ideal just outlined and what I call "constitutive" national values in the opening pages of *Citizenship*. His aim, he says, is to "reassert the underlying values of republi-can citizenship as a form of politics and nationhood as a form of identity.[31] The republican "form of politics" and national identity correspond roughly to my distinction between the "constitutional" and "constitutive" dimensions of political life.[32]

The concerns Miller discusses under the heading "republican politics" are es-sentially constitutional: they have to do with the just distribution of powers and entitlements within the state and with the procedures most likely to promote just and stable government. Miller treats these concerns as at least partly dis-tinct from the questions about members' "political identity," although in prac-tice they are bound together. The questions of political identity that nationhood addresses are constitutive in that they ask how a viable and legitimate polity should be constituted, especially in relation to other polities. Criteria for decid-ing a polity's boundaries and membership—that is, exclusive as well as inclusive criteria—are thus among the core constitutive issues. Although national answers to constitutive questions are extremely diverse, at least two core values are central to the idea of nationhood in its "civic" and "ethnic," cultural and political forms. One is the value of strong, continuous identity among all the members of a nation, cutting across classes and regions.[33] The other is the value of distinctness or particularity. This is often regarded as the necessary counterpart of strong identity: we identify strongly with our own nation only insofar as we see it as distinct from others, and endow this distinctness with value. The core values of strong, continuous identity and particularity set nationality apart from other constitutive doctrines such as city-statehood, empire, federalism, transnationalism, and globalism. While nationhood usually overlaps with these other constitutive arrangements in practice, the basic values behind them are quite different and clash when they are asserted strongly.

The distinction between constitutional and constitutive issues should not, of course, be drawn too sharply. Debates about devolution, secession, and other such relations between regional or local and central powers are usually described as constitutional and cut across my distinction between constitutive and constitutional questions. Nevertheless, the distinction does help us to see why Miller thinks that republican politics *needs* the support of "nationhood as a form of political identity." If you want a republican constitution, the argument goes, you first have to constitute the republic by ensuring that it has boundaries and terms of membership that support republican values. Participation, solidarity, and particularity cannot get adequate support from looser federations, transnational organizations, let alone fashionable notions of cosmopolitan citizenship. By the same token, units smaller than the nation will not be viable if they cannot command the resources needed to sustain modern levels of welfare provision. Nations, then, are the best constitutive option we have for promoting republican values, and hence social justice. This is why Miller thinks that "the practice of citizenship must . . . be confined within the boundaries of national political communities."[34]

We have also seen that for Miller, the distinct identities of such communities come from belief, sentiment, and history, not from specific cultural attributes or political institutions. What matters above all is that members "are believed to share certain traits that mark them off from other peoples." This sense of distinctness, "over and above the fact of sharing common institutions," is what allows observers to say that a certain group constitutes a nation. And it is these basic constitutive features of nationality, not political criteria alone, that Miller sees as essential to any well-functioning democracy. One might even say that Miller's constitutional political ideal cannot be realized outside the constitutive frame of nationhood. As he writes in *Market, State and Community*, "Nations are the only possible form in which overall community can be realized in modern societies. . . . Nationality gives people the common identity that makes it possible for them to conceive of shaping their world together."[35]

II

At this point, we might raise some initial questions about how Miller relates republican political values to the constitutive values of national identity. Miller wants to create the impression that these two sets of values are bound inextricably together, so that you can't have one without the other. Republican politics comes virtually built into nationality, and vice versa, as a sort of package deal.[36] But although Miller tries to anchor his defense of national identity in a theory of political justice, many passages imply that the connection is unequal. Having the right kind of republican politics depends on having strong national identities, but these identities may be strong and enduring without any connection to republican values. In *Citizenship*, for example, Miller defends the independent value of the "real cultural unity" achieved in some nations regardless of whether this was achieved through power politics and violence, and without reference to how cultural unity might contribute to republican ideals.[37] He then goes on to argue that both the obligatory force of national attachments and the content of social justice derives from the bonds and ways of life expressed in a particular "public political culture," not primarily from independent or quasi-independent principles of republican justice.[38] Miller does gesture toward these principles when he says that each public culture may be variously interpreted, and that some interpretations come closer than others to meeting standards of justice. But the argument still implies that the "real cultural unity" and "special sentimental ties" of nationality are the core foundations of justice in general, with a moral significance that precedes and conditions that of specifically republican justice. Republican values are inescapably dependent on nationhood, but the dependence is asymmetrical.

Moreover, Miller sometimes gives questions of boundaries and membership an importance that is quite independent of the republican values he wants nationality to serve. For example, the argument that citizenship must be "confined" within national boundaries suggests that nationality is logically and practically prior to republican justice, since it supplies the necessary framework for justice to work. The same practical priority is implied by his claim that the limits of distributive justice are " set by the bounds of a community whose members recognise one another as belonging to that community."[39] The main reason Miller gives for setting such boundaries is that solidarity, participation, and identification will thereby be strengthened, so improving prospects of social justice. Still, boundaries and exclusive membership criteria have to be there first. And in moral terms, they require no justification other than the intersubjective "recognition" of fellow-members.

Here, then, are two disturbing ambiguities in the way Miller relates constitutive and constitutional values in his defense of nationality. First, Miller clearly doesn't value nationality *only* because and insofar as it supports republican values. He also invests the constitutive functions of nationality with an "intrinsic" ethical value, which has more to do with the importance people ascribe to their particular group attachments per se than with their capacity to motivate just conduct.[40] And second, he frequently implies that the identity-conferring functions of nationhood are more important than republican principles of justice, since the latter cannot thrive without the former. But this raises the question: what if someone were to advance Miller's arguments defending nationality in a place where republican practices were weak or nonexistent? The ideal would doubtless be to urge people to embrace both parts of the package deal at once. But some of them might argue, quite consistently with Miller, that since republican values have to be framed by strong, bounded national identities, there is a good case for developing these identities first, and worrying only later about high constitutional ideals. This could then pave the way for oppression and violence in the name of national unity. Miller certainly does not want to countenance these nastier forms of "nationalism." The question is, does he provide clear and consistent grounds for opposing them?

To answer this question, let us look more closely at the moral and political implications of the way Miller distinguishes nationality's connection to republican values from its connection to "identity." When discussing these broadly "constitutional" and "constitutive" issues, Miller makes two distinct arguments about how nationality contributes to justice.[41] He presents them as mutually indispensable, but in fact they can easily come apart and point in very different moral and political directions.

One argument can be called the political justice–supporting argument. It says that nationality is good because and insofar as it supports principles of political justice, in this case those embodied in republican theory and deliberative democracy. The second can be called the prepolitical justice argument.[42] It says that the value of nationality is relatively independent of specific political considerations. Nationality in the constitutive sense—shared, bounded identity based on sentiments and belief—is the precondition for political justice, for this identity defines the communities that make political justice possible and motivates people to recognize and meet their political obligations. This argument still links nationality to justice, then, but not through the medium of particular political principles. Instead, the values of particularity and sentiments of national attachment are themselves among the basic sources of justice.[43]

Now the crucial difference between these arguments is that the first locates the value of nationality in its contribution to other goods, while the second sees it as an intrinsic value, and indeed as a core component of political justice. Yet the arguments are often run together, or assumed to have a natural affinity that they don't in fact have.[44] To see why this assumption is wrong, the claim made in the prepolitical justice argument needs to be distinguished clearly from other, similar-sounding arguments about the value of nationality in relation to other political values.

The argument that nationality has an intrinsic, prepolitical connection to justice is different from at least three other types of argument about how the national principle can contribute to justice.[45] It is different, first, from the *pragmatic* argument that national claims must sometimes be given a high priority as a matter of practical necessity, even though they have no intrinsic moral weight, and should not be confounded with the basic principles of political justice. It is also different from the *remedial-justice* argument that national claims should be met because they have been provoked by past injustice, aggression, and oppression, or simply because the members of a nation believe that they have not had a fair deal because of their national identity. Both of these arguments say that it is sometimes prudent and/or just to support national claims. But they see the connections between justice and nationality as contingent, not intrinsic or constitutive. Moreover, they do not suggest that the principle of nationality embodies built-in values that tend to support justice rather than injustice. Pragmatic and remedial arguments in defense of nationality may go along with a sober recognition of the risks involved in meeting national claims. At the same time, they uphold more basic, non-national principles of justice that both justify and limit the recognition of national claims.[46]

Both pragmatic and remedial arguments about the value of nationality can appear under the broader heading of political justice–supporting arguments. A third type of argument can also be made under this heading: the *conditional* argument, which says that even if national claims involve very important values, they should be met only if they respect conditions laid down by an independent theory of justice. Conditional arguments can take different forms, some leaning toward the justice-supporting, others toward prepolitical justice. In its justice-supporting form, the conditional argument subordinates national claims to basic principles of justice. National values might have a certain intrinsic, prepolitical importance, but they have less moral weight than the other principles that set conditions on nationality and cannot trump those principles. When conditional arguments lean in the other direction, they give more independent moral weight to nationality. Since national values are seen as constitutive of justice, the principle of nationality is itself one of the basic principles of justice, alongside liberty, equality, autonomy, equal dignity, and so forth. Therefore, it cannot be simply subordinated to more basic conditions, but instead must be balanced against other principles in often complex and delicate ways. The various, sometimes colliding principles that are basic to justice should check and limit each other, even if none have overriding status.

I take this second version of the conditional argument to be what Miller wants to defend. On the one hand, national claims cannot simply be subordinated to "higher" principles of political justice, since national identities have an intrinsic, prepolitical value. But this does not mean that national claims should be accepted unconditionally. Within a republican conception of justice, they would always be checked and balanced by other core republican values: liberty, social solidarity, democratic participation, and so forth. It is Miller's faith in this checking-and-balancing process that allows him to shrug off liberal anxieties about giving too much weight to prepolitical national values. He trusts that his framework of republican values and institutions is strong enough to keep national claims benign, channeling them toward justice and away from negative exclusivity, aggression, and undue intervention with personal freedom.

But I am not sure that Miller has done enough to convince readers "of liberal and pacific disposition" that this framework is strong enough. After all, the republican values that are supposed to keep nationality within the bounds of *political* justice have no clear moral priority over Miller's national principle. Indeed, as we have seen, Miller explicitly rejects the view that nationhood and national self-determination are valuable only so long as they remain "within the bounds laid down by justice," since the appropriate standards of justice vary according to each nation's particular way of life. In effect if not intent, this "contextualist" ethics gives the claims of national identity an independent and, indeed, a fundamental moral standing, whether or not they are linked to republican values. After all, Miller argues, national self-determination "creates the conditions under which people can live together on terms of justice"—but in deciding what "terms of justice" are, reference must be made first of all to national identity and "public culture."[47] This argument paves the way for nationalists to make very strong demands based on the prepolitical justice argument, while seriously weakening the arguments that could be used against them. If national claims have at least equal standing with other principles of justice, as Miller implies they do, then it becomes much harder to check them when they become inflated. There is then a risk that national claims can take on such high, independent value that they can override the very principles of justice that Miller claims to defend. One could perhaps ignore this risk if national claims rarely became inflated. The problem is, they do very frequently get inflated and clash with other principles of justice.

This is my main reason for thinking that Miller has dealt the principle of nationality too strong a hand and so, for all his moderate intentions, endowed it with the potential to do as much harm as good. I see at least four more specific reasons for this concern.

First, Miller presents the "principle of nationality" in an overwhelmingly positive light, while downplaying its problematic sides. Constitutionally, it is the natural partner of democracy and justice, while in the wider world it maintains a healthy constitutive arrangement of well-ordered states against the "threats" of globalization, substate nationalism, and quarrelsome identity politics. Most of his arguments defending a benign, constructive, democracy-friendly form of nationality focus on internal politics and the good things nationality can do for the ethical health of particular societies. National boundaries have constructive effects, enabling "large masses of people to work together as citizens," along with the other advantages mentioned previously.[48] The negative and exclusive effects of these boundaries are scarcely mentioned. Moreover, Miller says very little about how his principle of nationality should operate as a principle of international order and justice.

When he does touch on the conflictual features of "nationalism," this is mainly to declare that his arguments have little to say about "hard cases" of what he calls "rival national groups," such as Israelis and Palestinians, Serbs and Croats in Yugoslavia, Catholics and Protestants in Northern Ireland.[49] His points about self-determination and secession in such cases are cautious and mainly pragmatic, implying that moral principles can give little guidance in adjudicating such deep conflicts.

Most of his normative discussion is confined to the comparatively easier cases of what Miller calls "nested nationalities," that is, "when two or more territorially-based communities exist within the framework of a single *nation* [my italics], so that members of each community typically have a split identity." Miller stresses that "they do not experience this as schizophrenic, because their two identities fit together reasonably well." States containing nested nationalities include "Belgium, Britain, Canada, Spain and Switzerland."[50] He implies that because the "nested nationalities" inside these "nations" already inhabit the same state, and because the states he mentions also happen to be liberal democratic ones, normative arguments are more likely to play a role in resolving national tensions than in the "hard" cases. But a political theory of nationality that avoids confronting its potential for generating conflict and injustice looks willfully risk averse. After all, the negative features of national politics have always been present alongside the positive ones. In many times and places, they have been far more salient. Readers with any interest in history, or in the international repercussions of national claims, are unlikely to accept Miller's somewhat whitewashed version of the national principle without further questions.

This leads straight to a second concern. Miller's decision to focus on softer types of national claim produces an uneasy dualism in his argument. On the one hand, parties to less-hard cases of national conflict may be subject to very demanding moral and political constraints. The members of "nested nationalities," for example, are expected to strive for consensus with members of the dominant nation in the state they share, even over hotly disputed questions of boundaries, self-government, and cultural policy. When Miller turns to the harder conflicts of "rival nationalities," on the other hand, he suddenly demands very little reciprocal moral and political responsibility from the different sides. The ambitious republican goals of consensus are not the only ones to fall out of the picture. So does the much weaker principle that parties to a national dispute should be obliged to seek genuine compromises and agreements in the longer term, and the even weaker requirement that parties respect clear moral prohibitions on the means they may use to press their claims or face severe penalties. At times, Miller seems to suggest that moral arguments are simply impotent in the face of strong national conflicts. These, he implies, are best dealt with through a mixture of pragmatic interest-balancing and tough-minded *realpolitik*. But then his arguments about nested nationalities and ethnic minorities in democratic states go to the other extreme, insisting that citizens of the same state belong to a very thick kind of moral community even if they don't think so themselves.[51]

This dualism arises partly because Miller chooses to concentrate on cases where national values can help to sustain commitments to political and social justice that already have some institutional support. He is not very interested in working out arguments to encourage constitutional compromises where people are currently in an uncompromising or combative mood. This is doubtless a prudent approach, but some readers will find it unnecessarily cautious, if not conservative. By consigning problems of intense national conflict to the margins of normative political theory, Miller implies that we must wait for luck or power politics to resolve them. It then appears that the only appropriate audience for a normative theory of nationality consists of citizens of already constituted states, preferably ones with established liberal democratic institutions and pacific political cultures. And this looks odd from both sides of the divide. It looks depressing for people outside the few such fortunate states that now exist, since it denies that moral principles can do much to shield them from nationalist power politics or help them to resolve national conflicts. To people inside liberal states, Miller's ideal of mutually respectful, consensus-seeking minorities and subnations may look too optimistic. In both cases, Miller seems to think that existing state boundaries exert a powerful moral influence, negative toward the outside and positive inside, no matter what people say or do. This makes him sound complacent about prospects for resolving ethnic and national conflicts inside liberal societies and, at the same time, unduly fatalistic about the need to accept morally unsound means to resolve the disputes of "rival nations."[52]

My third concern about Miller's argument points to a deeper conceptual problem behind his dualistic morality of nationhood. I have said that Miller places most of his hopes for developing constructive forms of nationality on republican politics inside states. At the same time, he takes a rather deterministic view of current national boundaries and identities and doubts that there is much point in subjecting these to moral criticism. Another way of putting this is that whereas Miller is willing to engage with constitutional questions about nationality, he treats constitutive questions as less susceptible to critical discussion. States and nations are just there, as both objective historical entities and "psychological facts." Political theorists have to take their boundaries and identities more or less as they are, although they can try to persuade members to reform their political systems. These assumptions lie behind the tension between Miller's republican idealism and the empiricist realism of his views on relations between nations that lack a common state. The problem, though, is not just that Miller is uncritical toward constitutive national questions. It is, as I suggested earlier, that he frequently allows constitutive concerns to take priority over concerns about political justice.

The most striking example of this is Miller's remark that in "tragic" cases where governments cannot readily be persuaded to protect minorities, "it may be necessary to contemplate some exchange of populations so that two more or less nationally homogeneous entities can be created."[53] Miller presents this view as one based on reluctant yet hardheaded realism. In fact, it rests on the very dubious assumption that the decisive principle in such cases is a purely constitutive one, aimed at creating unitary, bounded nations. This principle is apparently so weighty that the most basic rights and security and well-being of the minority population may have to fall down before it.[54] In practice, constitutive national values simply trump other principles of republican justice. Though Miller implies that in this case the national principle's authority is mainly pragmatic, elsewhere he conflates the ethical and practical reasons for putting constitutive concerns before concerns for political justice. But if this is the price demanded by Miller's strong principle of nationality, one can see why many people of a liberal and pacific disposition might balk at it.[55] If national identities are conceived from the outset as the nonnegotiable, constitutive basis of all other political values, and moreover as the source of effective morality, then one must conclude that political theorists can't have much to say about the moral dilemmas of nationhood. They should just accept it as a fact, build on its strengths wherever this is possible, and steer well clear of the battles fought in its name. To question the constitutive premise that unitary, bounded, particularist entities are the best available basis of political and international order would, it seems, be way out of line. This cautious approach is consistent with Miller's moral empiricism and raises the question of whether an approach that takes so many psychological and political facts as "given" can help us to deal with the most pressing national issues that face us today.

My fourth doubt concerns the republican values that Miller presents as the natural allies of nationality. I have already suggested that Miller gives the constitutive claims of nationhood a strong, independent weight in his theory of justice. This makes it harder for other principles of political justice to place limits on national claims, since in practice those claims often take priority over justice. But there is a further problem with the way Miller formulates his republican ideal. Out of a rich and ancient repertoire of values that republicans have espoused over the centuries, Miller deliberately picks out those that tend to overlap with modern national values while opposing liberal individualism and universalism. The values of participation, solidarity, and particularity are more or less congruent with what I have called the core national values of strong, continuous identity and distinctiveness. Miller might also have chosen, like Mazzini, to stress "duties to humanity" as a core republican imperative, or, like many Roman authors, to stress personal liberties against state intrusion. He does not bring out these republican virtues, however, because he wants to distance his republican ideal from universalist and individualist principles.

The problem is that Miller lets constitutive national values shape his political ideal from the outset, more than the other way around. Miller's republican values are so nearly identical to national values that they have scarcely any independent bite. This makes it all the harder to see how republican principles of justice can effectively constrain excessive national claims. A further problem is that if national values are famously two-faced and susceptible to "corruption," so are republican ones. The degenerate side of republican values has come to be symbolized by tales of terror, persecution of minorities and free-thinking individuals, and crusading national arrogance during the French Revolution. Even worse excesses were committed in the twentieth century in the name of republican revolutionary and national virtues: solidarity (vice: collective unity), participation (mass mobilization), and particularity (exclusive "particularism"). In most parts of the world, experience has shown that the vices corresponding to these political virtues cannot be warded off without a firm constitutional commitment to more basic, limiting principles. That is why the states that come closest to Miller's republican ideal are liberal democracies, with laws and constitutions that clearly restrict the pursuit of solidarity and so forth by states or groups within society. Miller's republican ideal, however, is too dependent on a national constitutive ideal—and shares too many of its possible vices or excesses—to generate independent limiting principles.

III

Miller might respond to these doubts by pointing to other elements of his argument that I may not have considered closely enough. One possible response relates to my last point about the inability of republican politics to ward off inflated national claims. But, one might ask, what about the procedures Miller describes in his account of deliberative democracy? Surely the claims of national majorities or extremists can be kept in check by the procedural demands for reflective rather than emotional discussion, for ensuring that minority views get a fair hearing, and for public legitimation of collective decisions? This is certainly what Miller intends when he links his defense of nationality to the theory of deliberative democracy. But this linking does not suffice to address the concerns outlined previously. In the first place, the procedural constraints are added almost as an afterthought, while more fundamental and very strong national principles are left intact. The principles behind Miller's deliberative democratic procedures are in fact more liberal than republican: they reflect a concern to protect individual and minority rights of expression, political pluralism, and the equal dignity of citizens regardless of their background. But Miller apparently thinks that these procedural values can only come into play after prior, constitutive national values have been realized. Therefore, they cannot do much to restrict constitutive claims about boundaries and membership per se, even though these are just the kind of claims that tend to become most inflated. Democratic constraints only operate in the exceptional and fortunate settings of already constituted, liberal democratic states with coherent "national" cultures in Miller's sense.

Moreover, Miller confuses the ethical picture by undermining the very liberal principles he tacitly depends on. His sharp critiques of individualism and "ethical universalism" weaken his own case for a moderate nationality, since individualist and universalist arguments give crucial support to practices that have helped to pacify strong nationalism in many parts of the world. To take Miller's own cases of nested nationalities in Europe, we are frequently reminded today that the overarching "national" identities shared by Scots and English, Francophone Quebecois and Anglophone Canadians, Catalonians and Castilians did not just grow up organically, with occasional help from the accidents of war and peace. National coexistence has also been supported by liberal constitutions, the emergence of tolerant and pluralistic political cultures, and a willingness to see the devolution of certain powers as a normal part of democratic politics rather than as a mortal threat to national unity. In other words, the conditions that make Miller's nice nationality possible are the product of doctrines that he relentlessly criticizes. Liberal and pluralist principles form the bedrock of politics in Miller's "nesting" nation-states. If the divisions reemerging in them no longer involve popular violence, such as one sees in the conflicts between "rival" nations, this is due in no small part to political arrangements grounded in liberal principles of justice. Further support for these arrangements in Miller's best-case countries comes from international organizations like the North Atlantic Treaty Organization (NATO) and the European Union. Far from being a natural outgrowth of Western national cultures, these organizations were designed, *inter alia*, to check the competitive excesses of nationalism that had done so much to destroy European stability and prosperity in the past. And while prudential motives are extremely important for defenders of strong international institutions, "ethical universalist" principles have also inspired them, attracting support because they hold out feasible alternatives to old-fashioned, overly demanding national states.

A second possible response to my criticisms might refer back to Miller's moral epistemology. In Miller's defense, some readers might say that I have not offered a convincing alternative to his empiricist perspective. Perhaps there is no good alternative, especially in view of the "social psychological research" which suggests that sentiments of a national-collective type are needed to motivate just conduct. Whether we like these conclusions or not, we may simply have to face facts and build them into our political theories. The facts of human psychology will of course generate awkward tensions between ideals and realities, but this is unavoidable.

The problem with this argument is that it is profoundly unreflective. It simply fails to show that the facts it invokes must shape moral and political norms in the way Miller says they must. Many questions about Miller's "basic facts" would have to be answered before we could agree that they have the kind of fundamental role he gives them in political theory. For example, just what kind of fact is a basic "psychological fact"? Is it a fact about what makes people tick at a given time, in circumstances that may be changed? Or is it a more permanent, context-independent disposition, that is to say, an anthropological fact or a fact of human nature? Miller is unclear on this point, but it goes directly to the question of how far the facts of current national attachments should influence our basic moral and political principles. If national sentiments are asserted strongly in particular circumstances but weakly in others, then even a good empiricist might conclude (1) that wider circumstances can alter psychological facts, and (2) that those facts, therefore, should not be given too much moral authority in themselves. When contingent facts are given such high authority, the political theorist will find it harder to take a reflective distance from current situations, and thus to suggest ways of altering certain attitudes and the conditions that foster them. Because it clings so uncritically to current dispositional facts, Miller's theory is unable to encourage practices that tend to promote supranational duties or sentiments of humanitarian justice. Indeed, it discourages active measures toward developing these sentiments and loyalties, dismissing them from the outset as empirically unsound.

A further problem arises when current dispositional facts are treated as sources of basic political norms. Whose interpretation of such facts should be taken as authoritative: that of the people involved, or that of the political theorist? Once again, Miller's position is not always crystal clear. On the one hand, he criticizes other "philosophers" for failing to take peoples' avowed beliefs and sentiments seriously enough.[56] This leads one to believe that Miller is no friend of second-guessing and that he accepts "subjective" declarations as the main basis for reaching legitimate democratic decisions. On the other hand, Miller also implies that the most important psychological facts of national identity can be identified objectively by observers, even when the people observed deny them. This, at least, is the thrust of his argument against "full independence or secession" for Scotland.[57] Even if a great majority of Scots should express the wish for these arrangements through democratic procedures, Miller says that they would be wrong, because there is an objectively recognizable British national identity that has a deeper psychological importance for Scots and other Britons than they themselves may realize. Miller's argument suggests that an objective observer like himself can recognize this importance, and thus rightly second-guess the results of a democratic plebiscite favoring independence. For "we can say that for Scots to renounce their higher-level British identity would . . . be to fail to understand who they are, and what makes them the people they are today."[58] Miller is not the first political theorist, or the first nationalist, to change roles so subtly in the course of argument. At one moment he appears as the champion of popular sentiments against the stern moralizing of Kantian "philosophers," in the next as self-appointed authority on how people *should* properly understand their own identities.[59] One need not be a Scot to suspect that Miller has let his own sentimental attachment to the United Kingdom get the better of empiricist consistency, as well as of democratic justice.

A third response might still be open to Miller, this time harking back to his argument about the links between nationhood and democratic justice. Whatever else one might say, it is hard to deny that most stable, democratic states are based on distinct national identities. And a sense of common nationality can surely help to promote justice within particular societies. These statements are not especially controversial. But they do not amount to a strong argument for preferring nationality over other constitutive principles that can frame democratic societies. First, it is easy to poke holes in the argument that since democracies *so far* have taken a national form, there must be some *necessary* connection between nationality and democratic values.[60] Some of the oldest democratic states—Switzerland, Britain, the United States, Canada—have been federal or multinational, if one understands these terms conventionally instead of following Miller's definitions.[61] Some of the other states that Miller sees as exemplifying the deep links between nationality and democracy, notably France and Spain, have been only intermittently democratic over the past two centuries. They became reliably so only in the past few decades, and this was due more to internal liberalization and membership in European institutions than to any inherently democracy-friendly features of their nationhood.

Second, although national values can support democracy if they are appropriately restrained, they can otherwise undermine it. Democratic republics that ask citizens to display unitary, particularistic national identities have often been internally illiberal and aggressive toward nonnationals. This is why national values should be treated not as basic but as supplementary values for democracy. Criteria for national boundaries and membership, as well as the authority of national sentiments in politics, should be constrained by more basic principles of individual liberty, humanitarian justice, and political reason.

IV

David Miller's arguments for nationality are original and provocative. They invite readers in secure, liberal democratic states to reflect on the role of national identity in their own societies and highlight advantages of nationhood that may have to be surrendered in the face of globalization and European integration. But there are not so many secure, liberal democratic states in the world today. And this means that there are not many cases of reliably moderate nationalist movements, either—that is, movements that can be counted on to work within the rational limits of deliberative democracy to achieve consensus (or even compromise) with other "nationalities" in the state.

This kind of national politics is exceptional, and exceptional conditions are needed to sustain it. These conditions include, first, a basic sense of trust between citizens and government, so that neither feels vulnerable to arbitrary or violent attacks from the other; and second, a wider sense of geopolitical security, so that the national tensions inside a state are unlikely to precipitate international violence. Such conditions will probably continue to hold for Scotland and Great Britain, Quebec and Canada, Corsica and France, Flanders and Belgium, even if both state-based and substate nationalisms become more assertive. If the significance of national identity seems to be growing in these countries, its real impact on political, economic, and security issues will remain far less than it was in the past. People in Britain or Scotland, Quebec or Canada can assert their own historical and cultural claims to nationhood as much as they want. For the foreseeable future they will still cooperate closely within wider international institutions, "pooling" their sovereignty—the ultimate prize of classical nineteenth- and twentieth-century nationalism—in the key areas of economics and defense.

This is why Miller is right to say that we need not be alarmed by demands to strengthen "nationality as a form of identity" in these countries. But he takes for granted the conditions that make benign nationality possible. And because he takes them for granted, he fails to ground his defense of nationhood in clear limiting principles and undervalues the individualist and universalist norms that have helped to foster the conditions that keep popular nationalism moderate in countries like Britain and Canada. His arguments thus do little to encourage readers to create or maintain these conditions. This might not worry readers in safely liberal parts of northwestern Europe and North America. It cannot help people who want to think about the role nationality should play in promoting order and justice in the wider world, or in places where constitutional trust and international security cannot be taken for granted.

NOTES

1. Miller, *On Nationality* (Oxford: Oxford University Press), 7.
2. In fact, since its earliest appearances in the late eighteenth century, the word *nationalism* has been used mainly in a pejorative sense. It has usually meant an excessive, power-hungry form of partiality for one's own country. The label "nationalist" became acceptable in the mid- to late-nineteenth century in smaller countries fighting against "imperial" or authoritarian rule, such as Ireland and the Basque country. See Erica Benner, "Nationality without Nationalism," *Journal of Political Ideologies* 2 (1997): 189–198.
3. Miller, *On Nationality*, 8, 1.
4. John Stuart Mill's writings on nationality, for example, place utilitarian criteria of "civilisational" progress and human development alongside concerns for individual autonomy and equal human dignity. The former override the latter in some of Mill's most controversial judgments, notably his view that the claims of smaller, less-civilized "nationalities" like the Scots, Basques, and Welsh should be subordinated to the higher demands of human progress. See Mill, *On Liberty and Other Essays* (Oxford: Oxford University Press, 1991 [1861]), 431–432. Few liberals today openly embrace these utilitarian strands of Mill's argument, since they have been used to justify the oppression and cultural denigration of weaker peoples.

5. For contemporary writings that offer a similar "core" liberal position, see Yael Tamir, *Liberal Nationalism* (Princeton, N.J.: Princeton University Press, 1993); and various essays in *The Morality of Nationalism,* ed. Robert McKim and Jeff McMahan (Oxford: Oxford University Press, 1997); and Ronald Beiner, ed., *Theorizing Nationalism* (Albany: State University of New York Press, 1999).

6. See especially Yael Tamir, *Liberal Nationalism;* and Will Kymlicka, *Liberalism, Community, and Culture* (Oxford: Oxford University Press, 1989) and *Multicultural Citizenship* (Oxford: Oxford University Press, 1995).

7. Miller, *On Nationality,* 48–80; Miller, *Citizenship and National Identity* (Cambridge: Polity, 2000), 25.

8. See Miller, *On Nationality,* 73–80; Miller, *Citizenship,* 89–96, 167–179.

9. See Adam Swift in this volume.

10. Miller, *Citizenship,* 25.

11. Miller, *Citizenship,* 25.

12. Miller, *Citizenship,* 166.

13. Miller, *Citizenship,* 25.

14. Miller, *Citizenship,* 27.

15. See Miller, *Citizenship,* 38, 167–167.

16. Miller, *Citizenship,* 10, 62–80, 142–160.

17. Miller, *On Nationality,* 49–80.

18. Miller, *Citizenship,* 157–158.

19. Miller, *Citizenship,* 40.

20. Miller, *Citizenship,* 3.

21. Miller, *Citizenship,* 82–83.

22. Miller, *Citizenship,* 84.

23. Miller, *Citizenship,* 65.

24. Miller, *Citizenship,* 9, 83–84; Miller, *On Nationality,* 150–151.

25. Miller, *On Nationality,* 194–195; Miller, *Citizenship,* 31–33.

26. Miller, *Citizenship,* 81.

27. Giuseppe Mazzini, *The Duties of Man and Other Essays* (London: J. M. Dent, 1906).

28. See Avner de-Shalit in this volume.

29. Miller, *Citizenship,* 3–4.

30. Miller, *Citizenship,* 62–80, 142–160.

31. Miller, *Citizenship,* 3.

32. I have drawn this distinction in Erica Benner, "Is There a Core National Doctrine?" *Nations and Nationalism* 7 (2001): 162–170.

33. See Miller, *Citizenship,* 162–163.

34. Miller, *Citizenship,* 81.

35. Miller, *Market, State and Community* (Oxford: Clarendon Press, 1989), 245.

36. See Miller, *Market, State Community,* 245, where Miller says that nationality and citizenship "complement one another" and should ideally go hand in hand. In *On Nationality* Miller sometimes writes as though republican principles are already built into nationality, as when he claims, "the principle of nationality points us towards a republican conception of citizenship and towards deliberative democracy as the best means of making political decisions"; *On Nationality,* 150.

37. Miller, *Citizenship,* 31.

38. Miller, *Citizenship,* 38–9.

39. Miller, *Citizenship,* 122.

40. See Miller, *On Nationality,* 58–65; Miller, *Citizenship,* 32, 164–179.

41. As I try to show later, I think it is fair to say that Miller "makes" both arguments even though he does not develop them explicitly in all his writings on nationality, and at times seems to shy away from spelling out their connection to more specific positions.

42. Although Miller uses different terms to describe these two arguments, he distinguishes them in essentially the same way as I do here. In *Market, State and Community,* for example, he

distinguishes two sets of reasons for linking social justice to national community. One has to do with "the intrinsic value of overall community" given that "Nations are the only possible form in which overall community can be realised in modern societies"; the other has to do with the implications of such community for distributive justice (234, 245). Miller makes a similar distinction in *Citizenship* in discussing national self-determination, which he says has "both intrinsic and instrumental value. It is instrumentally valuable because, *inter alia*, it provides the optimum conditions for the pursuit of social justice" (Miller, *Citizenship*, 208, fn. 8). But while admitting that "instrumental justifications may turn out in the end to be stronger than the intrinsic one that I sketch here," Miller proceeds to defend the intrinsic value of national self-determination even when it "oversteps the boundaries" of general principles of justice. True, he sketches three republican-humanitarian conditions that he says should ideally be met by movements seeking national self-determination. But these conditions, like Miller's principles of global justice, are presented as perfectionist, somewhat unrealistic demands rather than as principles setting firm limits on acceptable nationalist conduct (Miller, *Citizenship*, 166–179).

43. By calling this the "prepolitical justice" argument, I do not mean that Miller has a naturalistic or entirely unhistorical understanding of nations per se. Miller often insists that he sees nationhood as essentially constructed, through both the contingencies of power politics and deliberate design. The prefix *pre-* refers to the *moral* significance of national identity before it is weighed against other political principles. It does not suggest chronological priority.

44. See note 39.

45. These arguments are discussed in more detail in Erica Benner, *Nationality and the State of War* (Oxford: Oxford University Press, forthcoming), ch. 3.

46. Although Miller often cites John Stuart Mill as an early proponent of his strong principle of nationality, I read Mill's chapter on nationality in *Representative Government* as a tentative, somewhat reluctant defense of a pragmatic and remedial national principle. He clearly worried about the risks of endorsing a general principle of nationality, not because it would lead to uncontrollable secessionist demands, but because it might encourage people to draw a "broadly marked . . . distinction between what is due to a fellow countryman and what is due merely to a human creature," a distinction "more worthy of savages than of civilised beings" (Mill, *Representative Government*, 430). Unlike Miller, Mill strongly denied that particularity should be seen as a basic political value, and that national identity should limit the scope of justice.

47. Miller, *Citizenship*, 172.

48. Miller, *Citizenship*, 88.

49. Miller defines *rival national groups* as "groups with mutually exclusive national identities each seeking to control all or part of the territory of the state"; Miller, *Citizenship*, 128.

50. Miller, *Citizenship*, 129.

51. Miller's clearcut distinctions between "rival nations," "nested nationalities," and "ethnic minorities" are dubious. In fact, cases that seem to fall into one category today often change quite quickly to fit another tomorrow. Catalonia has not been cheerfully "nested" inside Spain for very long; Miller does not say whether the Basques are a nested, rival, or ethnic nationality. Quebec and Scotland have shifted in the other direction, moving from seemingly quiet nestedness a few decades ago to asserting much stronger—and for some nationalists, rival—identities. This suggests that normative debates cannot be avoided by simply bracketing off different types of nationalism, since the types are neither pure nor static.

52. In a characteristic passage, Miller concedes that "international peace, international justice," and other such ideals "are very important objectives, and we must *hope* that republican citizens will *choose* to promote them externally" (Miller, *Citizenship*, 96 [my italics]). This seems to imply that political theorists shouldn't bother trying to persuade people to make these choices; they can only sit back and "hope."

53. Miller, *Citizenship*, 120–121.

54. Miller does not only make these arguments for "tragic" cases. His argument against Scottish independence rests on the same premise that the constitutive concern to preserve a "given" national identity may trump the democratic principle of consent. See my discussion which follows.

55. I am not implying here that when the principle of nationality conflicts with other principles of justice, such as liberty or equal human dignity, "the only sane response to national aspirations is to try to damp them down as quickly as possible" (Miller, *Citizenship*, 126). This is of course a gross caricature of liberal responses to such conflicts, which can take a variety of subtler forms. As I suggested previously, liberals can recognize national claims on pragmatic, remedial, or conditional grounds while denying that these claims have the same fundamental moral standing as principles of individual autonomy, equal human dignity, and so forth. See my earlier criticisms of Miller on these lines in "Nationality without Nationalism," 202–203.

56. Miller, *Citizenship*, 24.

57. Miller, *Citizenship*, 131–140.

58. Miller, *Citizenship*, 138.

59. A similar tension appears in *On Nationality*, 15, where Miller implies that while philosophers should take ordinary people's national sentiments seriously, they should not take people so seriously when they deny having strong national sentiments, since such denials probably involve self-delusion. It seems that Miller's arguments against second-guessing only apply to views that support his own positions.

60. See Miller's version of this argument in Miller, *Citizenship*, 88. Miller declares, "Genuinely multinational states have either been held together by force . . . or else have been empires which allowed a substantial degree of self-determination to their constituent parts." Since Miller denies that Britain, Spain, Belgium, Switzerland, or Canada can be called "genuinely multinational," the argument looks completely circular.

61. Miller asserts that states like Canada, Britain, and Switzerland are not really multinational at all, on his historicocultural definition of nationality. Miller, *Citizenship*, 131.

12

Is Republican Citizenship Appropriate for the Modern World?

Daniel A. Bell

Philosophers such as Aristotle and Rousseau argued that ordinary citizens should be active participants in the political life of their community, and that they should be motivated by the common good, not by their own particular interests. This classical ideal of republican citizenship assumes (1) that the state can control the political community's own destiny and (2) that people strongly identify with their own political community.

In the modern world, however, both of these assumptions can be questioned. Regarding (1), the problem is that, as Daniel Bell (the distinguished American sociologist, not to be confused with the present author) put it, the state is too small for the big things and too big for the small things. On the one hand, environmental disasters, regional economic upheavals, humanitarian crises, and major security threats often seem to require transnational solutions. On the other hand, welfare aid and development projects often seem to require decentralized political arrangements that give local communities and ethnic groups more political control over their own affairs. Regarding (2), competing allegiances also seem to pull away from the state in opposite directions. On the one hand, highly educated professionals, successful entrepreneurs, and Internet surfers often feel more at home among foreigners with similar interests than with their own conationals. On the other hand, modern states seem to be breaking up into competing centers of identity focused on ethnicity and race.

In short, the ideal of republican citizenship might seem obsolete. David Miller courageously argues otherwise and provides a forceful and eloquent defense of republicanism for contemporary liberal-democratic states.[1] But does it work? Not quite. The essay will present arguments from three different perspectives—liberal realism, socialism, and communitarianism[2]—against

Miller's conception of republican citizenship. Liberal realists will raise doubts about the feasibility of republican citizenship in the modern state, and socialists and communitarians will raise (different) questions concerning the desirability of this ideal. I will conclude by sketching a qualified ideal of republican citizenship that meets objections from all three perspectives.

THE LIBERAL REALIST PERSPECTIVE[3]

Liberal realists view citizenship as a set of rights enjoyed equally by every member of the society in question.[4] The government has an obligation to secure basic rights,[5] but liberal realists do not expect more than that. Ordinary citizens do not have an obligation to actively engage in politics, or to engage in politics for the "right" reason. The large majority can stick to their own private affairs, so long as they respect the rights of others. And those who participate in politics do not need to think or act with a view to secure the common good—they can bargain, cajole, pressure, and resort to dubious rhetoric on behalf of their causes—so long as people's basic rights are not violated.

The republican conception of citizenship is more demanding. As Miller puts it, "It takes the liberal conception of citizenship as a set of rights and adds to it the idea that a citizen must be someone who thinks and behaves in a certain way. A citizen identifies with the political community to which he or she belongs and is committed to promoting its common good through active participation in its political life.[6] But what if "citizens" do not conform to this ideal? Unlike earlier republicans, Miller does not argue that this ideal should be *enforced*. The liberal element of contemporary republicanism means that the state cannot, for example, punish those who refuse to participate in politics. Instead, Miller seems to assume that republican citizenship can and should be voluntarily sustained in modern societies. The government can construct institutions of public deliberation to encourage deliberation, but ultimately it is up to individuals to be involved if they so choose.

The liberal realist will question this vision of political life. Republican citizenship may be feasible in small face-to-face political communities where citizens treat each other as friends, but it is simply not realistic to expect that strangers from different classes and ethnic groups will care enough about each other's fate to allow for this kind of friendly interchange in the political realm. Moreover, there is no "common good" in advanced industrialized societies; rather, there are competing interests, and the best we can hope for is a political system that allows for those interests to be negotiated in a fair way. At the very least, democratic politics has the virtue of allowing for different coalitions at different times, so that the losers can end up winners the next time around. Nor is it realistic to expect that ordinary citizens will devote a substantial chunk of their lives to participate in the distant, day-to-day administration of a large state. In short, contemporary political communities are not informed by the sense of mutual trust and common identity that would allow for the ideal of republican citizenship to be realized.

Miller's reply is that the *nation*-state can, and does, supply these goods. Nationality, he argues, can "maintain solidarity among the populations of states that are large and anonymous."[7] Miller recognizes that citizens of large nation-states will not necessarily agree on substantive values, but what matters is that they try to resolve those conflicts "through an open and uncoerced discussion of the issue at stake with the aim of arriving at an agreed judgment."[8] If particular groups want to defend their interests, they cannot appeal simply to those interests. Citizens must appeal to "reasons that can persuade those who initially disagree with us."[9] What counts as a persuasive reason is a function of the dominant political culture, and political actors therefore need to frame their arguments in terms of that culture. Miller argues that this is a practical requirement for political success in contemporary nation-states: "In *all* cases the success of any particular demand will depend upon how far it can be expressed in terms that are close to, or distant from, the general political ethos of the community."[10]

But this is an overstatement. In American politics, for example, it has become a truism that powerful interest groups such as the National Rifle Association can get their way simply by funding compliant legislators, even though the large majority of citizens would prefer radically different policies.[11] Still, Miller can grant these "exceptions" and defend the weaker claim that particular interest groups are *more likely* to be successful if they frame their demands in terms that appeal to the political culture of the majority.[12] In the case of conflicts over material interests, for example, all "sides" can frame their arguments in terms of shared principles of social justice. This may sound like pie-in-the-sky theorizing, but Miller draws on experimental evidence to demonstrate that there is a reasonable degree of cross-class consensus in people's thinking about social distribution.[13]

The problem, however, is that agreement in the abstract about principles of social justice does not translate into agreement regarding the fairness of actual distributions of valued goods in existing societies. Not surprisingly, those on the bottom have different perceptions from those on the top—"we find widespread agreement between rich and poor, men and women, on the principle that jobs and offices should be allocated on the basis of merit, but significant disagreement about the extent to which jobs and offices are actually allocated by meritocratic criteria—the worse-off groups being more likely to think their society operates in unjust ways."[14] In terms of real politics, it is quite likely that, for example, respectful dialogue over the rate of taxation will be stymied by conflicting perceptions of actual distributions in existing societies. The fact that all parties may agree about abstract principles of social justice will not help; if anything, it will poison the atmosphere. When it is evident that people disagree about moral principles (e.g., disputes over abortion), they can recognize the depth and sincerity of the other side's commitments and perhaps agree to practical solutions that do not blatantly offend these commitments.[15] But

when people have radically diverging interpretations about the extent of in-
stantiation of shared moral principles, they are likely to accuse each other of
twisting facts to suit their own advantage. In such cases, respectful dialogue
will come to an end, and interest groups are more likely to achieve political
success precisely by means of argumentation that Miller rules out of court
(e.g., "I claim that group A—farmers, say, or policemen—should get more
money"[16]). If the group is a well-financed interest group, behind-the-scenes
lobbying should do the trick. If not, it may have to resort to "I'll scratch your
back and you scratch mine" bargaining with other economic interest groups
to get its money. This kind of politicking, arguably, more accurately describes
the likelihood of political success in existing liberal democracies.

To be fair, however, Miller seems to have ethnic groups in mind when he argues that groups are more likely to achieve political success by appealing to
the political culture of the majority:

> Everything will depend on whether the demand can be linked to principles that
> are generally accepted among the citizen body, such as principles of equal treat-
> ment. So, for example, in a context in which the state already supports Christian
> and Jewish schools, Muslims arguing for similar support for Islamic schools may
> validly claim that the status quo unfairly privileges some religious identities at the
> expense of others, and demeans Muslims.[17]

But here, too, counterexamples readily come to mind. For example, some
aboriginal groups in Canada resorted to radical action such as armed resistance (the Mohawks in Quebec) and illegal disruptions of logging activity (the
Mic Macs in British Columbia) to secure more aboriginal rights. These groups
were not appealing "to the majority's sense of justice and fairness."[18] Rather,
their aim was to pressure the government into granting their demands. Such
radical actions did not always succeed, but (arguably) they delivered more
benefits than decades of fruitless negotiations with the Canadian government.
This is not to deny that appealing to the majority culture is one way of securing political recognition for minority groups, but it is not necessarily the most
common (or the most effective).

But all this may miss the real point of Miller's discussion. His argument is
primarily normative, not empirical—"The argument here is that we should reassert the underlying values of republican citizenship as a form of politics and
nationhood as a form of political identity, while simultaneously thinking cre-
atively about how best to implement these values in the contemporary
world."[19] In fact, Miller recognizes that debates in existing national legislatures do not conform to his ideal of republican citizenship—"parliamentary
debates and adversarial courts, whatever their other virtues, are not good examples of deliberative democracy at work, and it is hard to imagine deliberative theorists saying otherwise."[20] How, then, can we even begin to close this
large gap between the ideal and the reality?

One possibility is to *transform* motivations, so that people will be willing to sacrifice their particular interests for the sake of the common good. Miller does appeal to experimental evidence to suggest that it may be possible to do so. He draws on psychological experiments that show that "discussion has the effect of turning a collection of separate individuals into a group who see one another as co-operators."[21] As Miller himself admits, however, all this evidence has been "obtained from research in small group contexts,"[22] which leaves unanswered the liberal objection that people are far less likely to sacrifice their own interests in large-scale political decision making. The liberal has conceded all along that republican citizenship may be appropriate for small face-to-face communities, but politics in large industrialized states is far more likely to be governed by "deal-making" between different interest groups.

Another possibility is to devolve decision making to the local level, where people are more likely to engage in respectful dialogue with their cocitizens. Miller does point to this kind of arrangement:

> Decisions may be parceled out to the sub-constituencies that are best placed to make them, or most affected by the outcome; or else lower-level deliberating bodies may act as feeders for higher-level ones, with arguments and verdicts being transmitted from one to the other by representatives. Thus, one might, for instance, envisage primary assemblies at town or city level making decisions on local matters, and at the same time debating issues of national concern in the presence of their parliamentary representatives: the latter would not be bound by the outcome, since they would themselves be involved in a deliberative process in which new arguments might be presented, but part of their job would be to convey the sense of the local meeting to the national body.[23]

The problem, however, is that issues of national concern often involve costs and benefits that are distributed unevenly in local communities. Most likely, local deliberative bodies will settle on policies that benefit their own communities/constituencies,[24] and this will lead to conflicting choices for national representatives. Consider the following examples.

The Department of Defense has to decide where to build new armaments and different local communities make competing bids for lucrative contracts.

Following extensive deliberation, most rich communities opt for Federal Housing Administration policies that favor the building of suburban homes for relatively wealthy families, and most poor communities settle on policies that promote home construction in relatively heterogeneous settings with a mixture of social classes.[25]

The federal government must decide where to put toxic waste dumps, and local deliberative bodies campaign vigorously to protect their own communities from this potential source of danger (all the while agreeing in the abstract on the need for toxic waste dumps).[26]

Deliberative bodies dominated by business groups, worried about potentially inflationary wage demands, prefer interest rate hikes by the Federal
Reserve Bank; those dominated by the workers and the less well off, worried about the likely increase in unemployment, oppose these hikes.[27]

How should national representatives decide when faced with conflicting
recommendations from local communities? Most likely, they will vote for
national policies that benefit their own constituencies, and the outcome will
be decided by means of nondeliberative bargaining between different interest groups. It could be argued that national representatives will be public-
spirited and that they will be motivated to sacrifice local interests for the
sake of the national good (or at least to frame their arguments in terms of
the respectful dialogue), but Miller has already conceded that parliamentary debates "are not good examples of deliberative democracy at work."[28]
So we are still waiting for an answer to the liberal realist objection that republican citizenship will not be workable at the national level. Let us now
turn to the objection that state-centered republican citizenship—even if it is
feasible—is undesirable.

THE SOCIALIST PERSPECTIVE[29]

Socialists look forward to a time when the large mass of humankind will be
freed from the need to engage in drudge labor. Technology would be highly developed, and machines would do most of the labor necessary to meet people's
physical needs. Unpleasant work would be limited to the maintenance of machinery and other tasks required to keep the system going, but this "realm of
necessity"[30] would not take up most of the working day. Generally speaking,
people would be free to do the things they want to do—go fishing, read books,
design and create works of beauty, and so on.

This world, however, remains a long way off. The capitalist mode of production, which treats workers as mere tools in the productive process and puts
technology to use for the purpose of enriching a small minority of capitalists
instead of the betterment of humankind, looks set to stay for the foreseeable
future. Capitalism, however, does have one virtue—it has the consequence of
developing the productive forces more than any previous economic system.
The reason is that capitalists compete with each other in order to make a
profit, hence they have a special incentive to develop new, ever more efficient
means to produce goods, and this has the effect of creating a large material
surplus without which socialism would not be feasible. Socialists thus seem resigned to view capitalism as a necessary, short-term (200 years?) evil. They will
support capitalist reforms that have the effect of modernizing the productive
forces, but they will also struggle on behalf of workers who pay the price for
rapid economic development.

More relevant for our purposes, socialists are internationalists. They will side with those who argue that we have extensive obligations to other people (especially the victims of capitalism) in foreign lands. Contemporary socialists recognize that "class" conflict is often played out in the global arena, with rich industrialized countries relying on their economic might to rig the global economic system to their advantage. In cases of conflict over material interests, socialists will (or at least should) side with relatively deprived workers in poor countries.

Socialists will be attracted by one aspect of Miller's ideal of republican citizenship. He emphasizes that large-scale solidarity is necessary to motivate people to help the worst-off groups in society.[31] To the extent that this is true, socialists will encourage the formation of large-scale solidarity, if only to mitigate the effects of capitalism. The problem, however, lies with Miller's argument that this solidarity must be realized at the level of the nation-state. Even if Miller's project is feasible, socialists will worry about the consequences of this project on nonnationals. More precisely, there is no reason to expect that citizens of one nation will be motivated to help, or to refrain from harming, the needy in other nations. According to Miller, members of nations "conceive of themselves as members of communities with a specific cultural character that set them apart from their neighbors,"[32] and they are less likely to identify with the plight of those living in distant lands. Moreover, citizens should engage in respectful dialogue with fellow citizens, and they have "a responsibility to promote the community's welfare actively"[33]—but they do not need to worry as much about the welfare of nonnationals. It seems that citizens of one nation could justifiably support needy fellow citizens even when this imposes substantial costs on relatively deprived people in foreign lands. A socialist, in contrast, would prefer to aid the worst off, wherever they are—for example, by increasing the share of GNP from industrialized countries that goes to support development projects in the Third World, even if this results in negative consequences for workers in rich countries.

Miller develops three different responses to this kind of objection. His first argument is to deny that there is an agreed-upon common denominator that would spell out what those obligations consist of. He does concede that some basic human rights should be recognized globally, but these rights are limited to a bare minimum—"food, shelter and clothing."[34] Beyond this core, the meanings of such goods as "money, work, honors, status and political power"[35] will vary from nation-state to nation-state, and democratic states should be "entitled to define the rights of their citizens in different ways, depending on the political culture of a particular national community."[36] Thus, citizens in rich industrialized countries do not need to worry about the distribution of such goods as work and health care in the Third World, because the two groups are likely to have different understandings of how those goods should be distributed. Those who argue otherwise may be guilty of "cultural imperialism," that is, of riding roughshod over local understandings in the name of a "universal" theory of justice.

The socialist will be skeptical, and Miller's use of examples will only rein-force that skepticism. Consider what he says about the different significance of work in different communities—"whether being without a job *in itself* constitutes a form of deprivation, aside from the loss of income that accom-panies it, will vary from one community to the next."[37] The question left "aside," however, is far more significant in many capitalist societies. For hun-dreds of millions of workers in the Third World, the whole point of work is precisely to earn an income, and they will not agonize over the meaning of work beyond that. Marx's description of work as a "means of life" rather than life's prime want still holds true for most of the world.[38] Given this wide-spread consensus about the meaning of work in capitalist societies,[39] it is dif-ficult to argue for a "hands-off" policy by appealing to the possibility of con-flicting shared understandings.[40]

In the same vein, Miller argues that "even a good such as medical care, whose meaning may appear to be fixed by its physical relationship to human health, turns out on closer inspection to have a significant (and variable) cul-tural content."[41] This example is not developed, but it is worth noting that Michael Walzer, who inspires much of this discussion about cultural variation, refers to the example of medieval Europe. In those ancient times, the "cure of souls" mattered more than the "cure of bodies," with the consequence that the community did its best to provide equal access to church services and worried less about securing the "right" to decent health care.[42] But this does not trans-late into an argument that, say, contemporary Chinese care less about health care than Westerners do! In most of the world, the major problem is lack of funding for basic health care, not irreconcilable differences over the meaning of that good. This is not meant to deny that understandings of what consti-tutes vital human interests underpinning conceptions of human rights vary from community to community, but rights to work and health care are far less controversial than Miller makes them out to be.[43]

Miller's second argument also seeks to minimize the extent of conflict be-tween caring for conationals and meeting our obligations to the worst-off in other countries. He does this by questioning the feasibility of alternatives to nationalist forms of republican citizenship. For example, he criticizes argu-ments for cosmopolitan citizenship on the grounds that they fail to take seri-ously the preconditions for citizenship. But one does not have to rely on a global conception of active, public-spirited citizens to secure international ob-ligations.[44] From a socialist perspective, it seems dogmatic to insist on either national or global citizenship as means for securing social and economic rights. If, for example, the formation of a regional monetary fund in East Asia helps to prevent another financial crisis that throws millions of people out of their jobs,[45] then that's the way to go. This fund may have the effect of con-ceding a nation's sovereign right over monetary policy to a regional central bank—and hence, may have the effect of further diluting the quality of citi-zenship in nation-states[46]—but that will be a price worth paying.

Nor will socialists readily give up on the ideal of transnational citizenship if this can help to secure our obligations to the most deprived members of the human species. To be fair, Miller does not do so either, but he argues that national solidarity is a precondition for transnational solidarity—"possibilities for transnational citizenship as may exist depend upon first strengthening citizenship and inculcating civic virtue within national boundaries, and then hoping that these qualities may carry across to wider boundaries."[47] There are some obvious counterexamples, however. Most recently, church groups from around the world organized an international movement (called Jubilee 2000) designed to pressure Western governments to "forgive"[48] crippling debts owed by the world's poorest countries. This movement was partly successful at achieving its ends (as well as increasing solidarity among fellow-minded activists from different countries), and fortunately, organizers did not wait for the ideal of nation-based republican citizenship to be realized before launching their international campaign.[49]

Miller's third response to (what I've labeled) the socialist critique is to concede that obligations to conationals may conflict with obligations to needy foreigners, and to set forth some basic principles of global justice that set limits to the pursuit of national justice. One such principle is the obligation to refrain from exploiting vulnerable communities and individuals in foreign countries. Miller suggests that exploitation may not be uncommon in the contemporary world—"Pervasive global inequality means that opportunities for international exploitation are legion, whether this takes the form of states imposing onerous conditions on the governments of poorer countries in return for (economically vital) access to investments and markets, or corporations employing workers in these countries on terms that would be wholly unacceptable in developed countries." Miller then recognizes the need for a mechanism to deal with this problem, but he says that we must first meet the challenge "to provide criteria for identifying exploitative transactions that are neutral as between different societal cultures."[50]

Once again, Miller may be exaggerating the extent of actual or potential conflict over cultural meanings. It will be much easier to agree upon abstract criteria for identifying exploitative transactions than to agree on the extent of exploitation in actual cases, when people's judgments will likely be biased by their own economic interests.[51] And even if there is agreement about how those principles are instantiated, the real challenge will be to get multinational corporations and rich industrialized countries to shape up their ways. If it is true that the rich and powerful benefit from global economic relations that exploit the poor, why should they be motivated to change the status quo?

One possible reply is that nationalist republican citizenship can produce the right motivation. If citizens deliberate more about issues of international justice, they will come to appreciate the need to refrain from exploitative relations at the global level. Miller does not produce any evidence for this claim and it is difficult to feel optimistic. For one thing, the foreign victims of exploitation will not be part of the national deliberations, and the deliberators will not be under any obligation "to find reasons that can persuade those who initially disagree with us."[52] Perhaps nationalist deliberators will want to consider the interests of exploited foreigners anyway, but why should they be motivated to care about the interests of those with whom they do not have affective relations of any sort—not to mention those with whom they have a hostile relationship.[53] And the problem is not just that citizens will refuse to recognize the fact of exploitative relations. Many Americans are fond of driving sport-utility vehicles, and they worry about the fact that such vehicles contribute to global warming. According to one survey, however, they are still unwilling to pay for environmentally responsible products or to sacrifice polluting features on their vehicles.[54]

In short, a detailed investigation into the actual workings of the international political economy and the conditions needed to overcome exploitative relations may well yield conclusions that undermine Miller's ideal of republican citizenship. But this is ultimately an empirical dispute over the extent of exploitation and the best means of dealing with it. Those concerned about global inequality might also want to challenge Miller's principle that rich countries only have a negative obligation to refrain from exploitation. Even if rich countries do not exploit the poor, does that mean they do not have any obligation to help needy foreigners?

This brings us to Miller's principle that we also have "the obligation to provide all political communities with opportunity to achieve self-determination and social justice."[55] He argues, however, that national communities do not have an obligation to act on this principle until they first meet the requirements of national justice—"it seems legitimate for nation-states to give priority to creating regimes of justice among their own citizens before undertaking whatever actions may be necessary to create such regimes elsewhere."[56] The socialist will question this argument. An economic policy might be justified if, for example, it generates immense material benefits for a poor country and imposes relatively marginal costs on a rich one. Consider the "unequal" trading relationship between several East Asian countries (Korea, Japan, and Taiwan) and the United States in the post–World War II period. These countries were allowed to sell their products at low tariffs to the United States and to maintain high tariffs at home to protect local industries,[57] an arrangement that helps to explain the rapid economic takeoff of the East Asian region.[58] No doubt the costs were often borne by American producers who had to compete with relatively cheap imports, but the overall benefits (considered globally) outweighed the costs. This would be a problem for the American nationalist republican, but not for the socialist internationalist.

Miller could once again reply that nation-based republican deliberators could be made to endorse economic policies that benefit outsiders and penalize locals, but this would be stretching the limits of the possible.[59] In the real political world, the people most directly affected by other-regarding policies are (understandably) the least inclined to accept them, and it often takes "progressive" elites to push these policies through, often by means of limiting public participation and discussion. For example, the Clinton administration had a difficult time persuading the American public of the benefits of permanently establishing normal trade relations for China, given the fact that this will almost inevitably result in the loss of American jobs (hence U.S. labor's vehement opposition to this policy). Part of the administration's strategy was to limit public debate, for fear that it would be counterproductive. Most notoriously, Clinton canceled a television address to the nation on the grounds that, as the White House spokesman put it, "We made the judgment that in order to win, we would be better off without the speech."[60] A nationalist republican would oppose this decision, on the grounds that more deliberation with those affected by particular policies is better than less. But a socialist internationalist might support moves to curb deliberation and resist popular pressure, if the benefits from the standpoint of global justice outweigh the costs. In this case, the number of Chinese workers who benefit from WTO is likely to exceed the number of American workers who lose out,[61] and the socialist might well side with the Clinton administration's decision to curb counterproductive debate.[62]

In sum, the socialist will worry about the real possibility that there are trade-offs between global justice and nationalist republican citizenship. Let us now turn to the communitarian perspective. The communitarian will also question the ideal of nationalist republican citizenship, though for different reasons.

THE COMMUNITARIAN PERSPECTIVE

Modern-day communitarianism began as a critical reaction to the recent resurgence of rights-based liberal theory. Drawing primarily on the insights of Aristotle and Hegel, communitarian theorists argued that liberalism rests on an overly individualistic conception of the self. Whereas liberals argue that we have a supreme interest in shaping, pursuing, and revising our own life plans, they neglect the fact that our selves are often defined or constituted by various communal attachments (e.g., ties to the family or to a religious tradition) so close to us that they can only be set aside at great cost, if at all.

Moving from "ontology" to politics, communitarians dispute the liberal assumption that the principal task of government is to secure the liberties and economic resources individuals need to lead freely chosen lives, as there may also be a need to sustain and promote the forms of communal life crucial to our sense of well-being and respect. The actual remedy will depend on the particular context, but the point is that our interest in freedom does not automatically "trump" our interest in community. In Western liberal democracies, basic human liberties are generally secure, and communitarians argue that the main political task is to promote policies meant to stem the erosion of communal life in an increasingly fragmented world. Thus, "political" communitarians such as Amitai Etzioni propose a moratorium on the minting of new rights and argue for such "family-friendly" policies as laws that force corporations to provide six months of paid leave and eighteen months of unpaid leave.[63]

More relevant for our purposes, contemporary communitarians argue that our loyalties stretch to more than one community—family, hometown, profession, religion, nation, and so on. Whereas earlier communitarians defended the ideal of *Gemeinschaft*—a static, orderly, rooted conception of community, where people are tied to fixed modes and hierarchies of status and power and their behavior is regulated by an instinctive, unqualified attachment to the local community—today we value many different kinds of communities.[64] Some of our communal attachments may conflict in practice, and once again there is no universal answer to the question of how to deal with competing commitments. In Japan, for example, the obligations of the workplace may be too demanding, and there may be a need to revitalize family life; in more family-based societies, the challenge may be to encourage commitment to the workplace.

From a communitarian perspective, the main problem with Miller's ideal of nation-based republican citizenship is that it threatens to overwhelm all our other communal commitments. According to Miller, commitments to the nation have "depth . . . which may not be shared by other more immediate forms of association." The nation "is a community of obligation." People are born into and they owe obligations to conationals "who practice mutual aid among themselves."[65] In practice, this means each person must be willing to sacrifice on behalf of the nation and act as an "active citizen who takes part along with others in shaping the future direction of his or her society through political debate. . . . To be a citizen one must think and behave in a certain way: one must have a sufficient measure of what the older republican tradition called public virtue."[66] It would seem, then, that the nation is the most important communal attachment that should override others in cases of conflict.

Communitarians will worry about this ideal. One obvious area of conflict is with family life. Favoring the ideal of active citizenship is likely to erode commitments to the family, as few persons have sufficient time and energy to devote themselves fully to both.[67] Surely it is no coincidence that republican societies in the past (ancient Athens, or America in Tocqueville's day) relied on active, public-spirited, male citizens largely freed from family responsibilities; conversely, societies composed primarily of persons leading rich and fulfilling family lives (such as contemporary Singapore) tend to be ruled by paternalistic despots who can rely on a compliant, politically apathetic populace. Communitarians would want to strike a balance between these extremes, but Miller seems to side entirely with the republicans.

One possible reply is that the contemporary ideal of republican citizenship is less demanding than the classical version. As Miller puts it,

[W]e need to distinguish what (some) classical republicans have said from what the republican view of citizenship actually requires. What it requires is something weaker: that it should be part of each person's good to be engaged at some level in political debate. . . . Some people may be engaged in [politics] on a full-time basis, while others may listen to the arguments being presented but only become involved from time to time, when major issues are being decided. One need not, then, regard political activity as the summum bonum in order to adopt the republican view, but can hold the more modest position that although politics is indeed a necessary part of the good life, different people can be expected to give it a different weight according to their own personal values.[68]

This diluted version of republican citizenship, however, still seems to place too much emphasis on politics. The claim that "politics is indeed a necessary part of the good life" is presented as a universal truth, but there may be feasible and desirable societies where most people devote themselves almost entirely to other obligations and leave political decision making to a tiny, public-spirited elite.[69] Even in liberal-democratic societies, it may not seem appropriate to condemn those who abstain from politics because they are committed to different communities—someone, say, completely devoted to family and religion. Is it really "necessary" to participate in politics "from time to time" to lead a good life?

More pertinently, perhaps, this "weak" version of citizenship also seems problematic from the perspective of some minority groups because it seems to favor the national community's political culture over the demands of minority groups in cases of political conflict.[70] That is, it does not place any obligation on the national community to take seriously the commitments of minority groups that cannot be accommodated under existing principles and frameworks. If a religious group finds itself in an overwhelmingly secular setting, for example, it should frame its political demands in terms accepted by the majority culture. The alternative may well undermine the group's basic values, but that's just tough luck. As Miller puts it, "if existing policy were to be based on the principle that all formal education must be secular in character, the claim that Islamic schools were essential to Muslim identity would have to be assessed on its own merits, and might well be rejected in a democratic forum."[71] Perhaps the closest real-life approximation of this example is the French government's decision to forbid the wearing of head scarves in French secular schools, even though (some) Muslims regard head scarves as essential symbolic expressions of their identity (not coincidentally, the republican tradition is still very strong in France). This might not be a problem for the republican, but the communitarian will worry about this (democratic) assertion of majority culture. In this case, the costs to the majority culture seem relatively marginal, and it seems justifiable to give priority to the strongly held commitments of the religious group.

This "weaker" form of republicanism will even seem too demanding from the perspective of citizens inclined to public-spirited political participation.

While it leaves some room for the assertion of other communal responsibilities, presumably these must still be set aside when "major issues are being decided." But why should a parent with a sick child, say, become an active participant in the debate on WTO for China? Surely, there are times when even "good citizens" can justifiably set aside their political obligations.

In sum, even this "weak" version of republican citizenship is still too "strong" for the communitarian, because it seems to justify overriding competing communal commitments in cases of conflict.

TOWARD AN APPROPRIATELY QUALIFIED IDEAL OF NATION-BASED REPUBLICAN CITIZENSHIP

Notwithstanding the preceding criticisms, my intention is not to undermine the ideal of nation-based republican citizenship. On the contrary, this ideal is appealing in many respects, and I hope that it can be reformulated so that republicans can meet some of the objections noted previously. In this concluding section, I briefly sketch one possible reformulation.

The ideal of nation-based republican citizenship contains two main elements: (1) the *psychological* disposition to be public-spirited, in the sense that one is willing to sacrifice one's interests for the sake of the national good, or at least to be willing to present one's political arguments in a way that is close to the general political ethos of the national community and aims at arriving at an agreed judgment; and (2) the tendency to *behave* as an active citizen that participates in the nation's political affairs, or at least the tendency to become involved when major issues are being decided. In my view, a feasible and desirable conception of nation-based republican citizenship will retain the psychological component and discard the behavioral one. That is, most citizens will have, in latent form, the disposition to be public-spirited, but they will be largely inactive in political affairs. In actual fact, people will spend most of their time pursuing their private interests and fulfilling their duties to nonpolitical forms of communal life, but they can be mobilized for nation-based public-spirited political action on relatively rare occasions, if need be. Let me now show why this ideal of *occasional* public-spirited citizenship—applicable in the context of contemporary Western liberal democracies—might appeal to liberal realists, socialists, and communitarians.

From the liberal realist perspective, the main problem with the ideal of republican citizenship is that it is not feasible at the level of the nation-state. There are too many conflicting interests in large industrialized states, and politics is more likely to be characterized by interest group bargaining than by public-spirited deliberation. Nor will "citizens" be inclined to participate in the political decision making of the distant state apparatus. To the extent that large numbers of citizens participate in national politics, they will often by partaking of a zero-sum game of different constituencies fighting for their own interests. This is, so to speak, an unavoidable fact of everyday "bourgeois" politics.

Nonetheless, even the most hard-nosed liberal realist will want to acknowledge the importance of sustaining a degree of public-spiritedness that can be mobilized if need be. Liberal realists care about basic rights, and they will want people to defend their rights when they are in danger of being taken away. The most serious threat occurs when liberal states are threatened militarily by authoritarian or totalitarian states. Fortunately, citizens of liberal states have manifested the willingness to sacrifice on behalf of their nation in such cases—World War II is an obvious example. Once these threats are put down, then citizens can, and do, revert to ordinary bourgeois behavior.

Liberal realists, in short, will not question the feasibility of the ideal of occasional public-spirited citizenship, since it allows for the fact that most people do not usually participate in national politics (and when they do, they often seem motivated by parochial concerns). But this psychological disposition to be public-spirited can be tapped in exceptional circumstances if need be and this is a good thing because citizens of liberal states can (on rare occasions) be mobilized to sacrifice their own interests for the state when hostile nonliberal forces threaten to take their rights away. In short, the liberal realist will be attracted by this reformulated republican ideal on grounds of both feasibility and desirability.

From the socialist perspective, the main problem with the ideal of nation-based republican citizenship is that it may have negative consequences for those lying outside the national community. Even if this ideal is feasible, nationalist republicanism is worrisome because it seems to favor meeting the obligations owed to cocitizens over those owed to needy foreigners, or at least, it does not provide any account of the motivation that would lead citizens to sacrifice the national good in order to secure global justice. In the capitalist global economy, rich industrialized states often benefit from economic rules that disadvantage the rest, and there is often a conflict between economic policies that benefit rich Western countries and those favoring the Third World. In such cases, nationalist republicans and internationalist socialists are likely to be at loggerheads.

But there will not *always* be a trade-off between national and global justice. In such (rare?) cases, the socialist will join efforts to draw on the public-spirited, nationalist solidarity that underpins the welfare state in rich industrialized countries. The rest of the time, however, the socialist may prefer to minimize political participation in rich states, for fear that "the people" will fight to maintain economically exploitative relations vis-à-vis the rest of the world or refuse to sacrifice national interests to aid the Third World. If nonparticipatory and nondeliberative modes of political activism—such as behind-the-scenes maneuverings by progressive political elites and radical activism by internationalist NGOs (street theater, economic boycotts, etc.)—stand a better chance of realizing global justice, then the socialist will welcome passivity on the part of public-spirited, nationalist citizens. So, the socialist may well come to the conclusion that occasional public-spirited citizenship is preferable to the active variety.

From the communitarian perspective, the worry is that nation-based republican citizenship threatens to overwhelm all our other valued forms of communal life. Even the diluted form of participation in major political decisions seems demanding from the point of view of someone with obligations to, say, family and religion. And the republican does not seem to allow for the possibility that nonpolitical obligations can sometimes override obligations to the nation-state in cases of conflict.

But the communitarian will be attracted by the ideal of nation-based public-spirited citizenship. Nationality is an important focus of identity and allegiance in the contemporary world (for most people), and this entails certain obligations to promote the common national good. So, the communitarian will welcome public-spirited motivation in political life. If political actors tend to behave in overtly self-interested ways, the communitarians will try to remedy the situation, for example, by means of citizenship training in public schools and national civil service programs,[72] so long as commitment to the common national good does not have the effect of radically undermining other communal commitments.

Once again, the ideal of occasional public-spirited citizenship can preserve the advantages of republicanism without the drawbacks. Citizens will be motivated by the common good when they participate in politics, but politics need not occupy a central place in their lives. People will have plenty of time to fulfill their other commitments, and it is not assumed that political obligations have automatic priority. Finally, the communitarian will endorse the contingent defense of occasional public-spirited citizenship as applicable in the context of contemporary Western democracies, thus leaving open the possibility that other political ideals may be more appropriate elsewhere.

NOTES

I would like to thank Ronald Beiner and Avner de-Shalit for helpful written comments on an earlier draft of this chapter.

1. This chapter draws primarily on Miller's book, *Citizenship and National Identity* (Cambridge: Polity Press, 2000).

2. The use of labels to describe different "perspectives" is meant to provide a useful typology of arguments, but this should not obscure the fact that (at the end of the day) my arguments against Miller should be judged on substantive grounds, regardless of the labels.

3. The first and second sections draw on my review of *Citizenship and National Identity* in the *Times Literary Supplement*, June 1, 2001, 12.

4. My use of the term *liberal realist* corresponds roughly to Miller's own usage of the term *liberal* (Miller, *Citizenship*, 43–44). The addition of the term *realist* is meant to distinguish this perspective from normative liberal theory that typically develops normative ideals and worries less

about feasibility. Liberal realists begin with very low expectations regarding human nature and potential for reform and work out normative views shaped by these constraints.

5. There is of course disagreement within the liberal realist "camp" with respect to the content of basic rights, but the need to secure civil and political rights is not controversial.

6. Miller, *Citizenship*, 53.

7. Miller, *Citizenship*, 31.

8. Miller, *Citizenship*, 9.

9. Miller, *Citizenship*, 55.

10. Miller, *Citizenship*, 57.

11. Another example is the House of Representatives' recent decision to repeal an inheritance tax that was levied almost exclusively at the very well off and yielded $30 billion per year to the public purse. As the economist Paul Krugman put it, "The truth is that the vote to repeal the inheritance tax was just an unusually blatant demonstration of a much simpler power law, the one that says that money talks" ("Pity the Pain of the Very Richest," *International Herald Tribune*, June 15, 2000).

12. I leave aside the question of hypocrisy, that is, interest groups that insincerely appeal to broader principles when in fact they are motivated by more narrow interests. In my view, it is generally easy to identify these groups in political debate. For example, no one appeared to be fooled when U.S. labor groups appealed to "human rights" in China to justify their opposition to permanently establishing normal trade relations with China. Their real motivation—to protect American jobs—was quite obvious to most commentators.

13. See David Miller, *Principles of Social Justice* (Cambridge, Mass.: Harvard University Press, 1999), ch. 4.

14. Miller, *Principles*, 162. The possibility that there may be different understandings of what constitutes "merit"—which may be particularly relevant in cross-cultural studies—will pose additional problems. For example, Kwok Leung reports a study that shows that Americans put more emphasis on performance in judging the fairness of pay levels, whereas Koreans place more emphasis on seniority and educational background (Kwok Leung, "Social Justice from a Cultural Perspective," in *The Handbook of Culture and Psychology*, ed. D. Matsumoto (New York: Oxford University Press, forthcoming). I thank Professor Leung for sending me an advance copy of this paper.

15. Miller, *Citizenship*, 151.

16. Miller, *Citizenship*, 9.

17. Miller, *Citizenship*, 57. Note that this discussion is meant to evaluate the empirical claim that minority groups are more likely to succeed if they appeal to the political culture of the majority, but one might also raise doubts about the normative claim that minorities should adopt this strategy—see the third section of this chapter.

18. Miller, *Citizenship*, 5.

19. Miller, *Citizenship*, 3.

20. Miller, *Citizenship*, 146. More surprisingly, perhaps, Miller does not provide a single example of political debate in a national legislature that conforms to his ideal. In comparison, Amy Gutmann and Dennis Thompson often illustrate their arguments for deliberative democracy with examples from American politics (see Gutmann and Thompson, *Democracy and Disagreement* [Cambridge: Harvard University Press, 1996]). The glaring gap is the Gutmann/Thompson book is the lack of attention paid to the psychological mechanisms (e.g., a sense of solidarity and mutual trust) underpinning deliberative democracy. Both Miller and Gutmann/Thompson fail to describe the institutions of deliberative democracy in any detail.

21. Miller, *Citizenship*, 17.

22. Miller, *Citizenship*, 22.

23. Miller, *Citizenship*, 23.

24. It could be that local communities opt for policies "in the national interest," but this is most likely when those policies do not impact directly on the local community (i.e., local communities are unlikely to favor national policies that harm their own community). This leads to a

problem that is left aside by Miller—"the question whether citizens will be sufficiently motivated to take part in debating assemblies if these are brought into existence" (Miller, *Citizenship*, 23). It seems to me that the likely answer is negative—particularly when national policies do not impact directly on a particular local community—and this by itself is sufficient to cast doubt on the feasibility of Miller's proposal.

25. The reality in the United States, unfortunately, is that the Federal Housing Administration plays an active role in promoting relatively homogenous Residential Community Associations for the well off. See my essay, "Civil Society versus Civic Virtue," in *The Freedom of Association*, ed. Amy Gutmann (Princeton, N.J.: Princeton University Press, 1998), esp. 246–247.

26. One possible solution is to pay relatively poor foreign countries that are willing to take toxic materials (not an imaginary scenario), but this leads to problems of global justice that are considered in the following section.

27. I leave aside the question of expertise. In this case, it is difficult for noneconomists to make informed judgments regarding the probable outcome of particular policies. In the case of foreign policy, it is even more difficult for non–area experts to make informed judgments regarding particular policies.

28. Miller, *Citizenship*, 146.

29. Some defenders of global justice refer to themselves as "liberal egalitarians" (e.g., see the contributions by Caney and Fabre in this volume). My view is that the concern for global justice emerges more "naturally" from the socialist tradition, but these labels are not philosophically relevant (though they may have political relevance) if there is agreement about the substantive arguments.

30. Karl Marx, *Capital, Volume 3*, in *The Marx-Engels Reader*, ed. Robert Tucker (New York: Norton, 1978), 441.

31. Miller, *Citizenship*, 32.

32. Miller, *Citizenship*, 87.

33. Miller, *Citizenship*, 84.

34. Miller, *Citizenship*, 168.

35. Miller, *Citizenship*, 168–169.

36. Miller, *Citizenship*, 93.

37. Miller, *Citizenship*, 173 (Miller's emphasis).

38. This is a constant theme in Marx's work, starting from the *Economic and Philosophical Manuscripts of 1844* all the way to the *Critique of the Gotha Program* (1875).

39. At least in poor countries, the quest for the "means to life" will be the main reason for work. Even in "rich" industrialized countries, however, this may be the most common motivation—how many of us would keep our jobs if we won the lottery?

40. Note that Miller is being criticized for asking the wrong (least morally and politically relevant) question. Given that most people need a job to obtain the means to life, the main task is to promote social and political arrangements that make this more feasible. This is not to deny that Miller's question has import in contexts where there are motivations for work over and above the quest for the means to life.

41. Miller, *Citizenship*, 169.

42. See Michael Walzer, *Spheres of Justice* (Oxford: Basil Blackwell, 1983), 87.

43. Conversely, "the standard range of civil and political rights" (166) is far more controversial (in the non-Western world) than Miller suggests, and this opposition to Western-style liberal democracy is not purely self-serving rhetoric by power-hungry autocrats, but it may in fact be rooted in divergent meanings about the priority and scope of those goods—see my book, *East Meets West: Human Rights and Democracy in East Asia* (Princeton, N.J.: Princeton University Press, 2000).

44. Miller himself suggests that a "thin" version of citizenship may be sufficient to invoke international law to remedy wrongs done to individuals (Miller, *Citizenship*, 92–93).

45. Japan floated the idea of an Asian Monetary Fund after Thailand and other Asian countries were hit by currency crises beginning in July 1997.

46. I say "further diluting" because I don't think the ideal of republican citizenship can be of much help even when national central banks decide on monetary policy. At the descriptive level, few citizens, as it is, participate in this kind of decision making. And there may also be good normative reasons for excluding "the many"—good-policy decisions in this context require patience, expertise, a long time horizon, and (sometimes) short-term pain, and increasing participation may work against these ends. See Alan Blinder, "Is Government Too Political?" *Foreign Affairs* 6 (1997): 115–126.

47. Miller, *Citizenship*, 95.

48. I use scare quotes because it is questionable to what extent these debts are "legitimate," as they were often incurred as a result of being in an unequal bargaining position vis-à-vis rich Western countries and "international" global institutions such as the IMF (and I use scare quotes around "international" because the IMF appears to be dominated by Western powers and often serves their economic agenda).

49. It can be argued that members of Jubilee 2000 also organized on a national scale and put pressure on national representatives as part of their international campaign (e.g., Canadian members of Jubilee met with Finance Minister Paul Martin and urged him to "forgive" the debt owed to Canada by the world's poorest countries, and they apparently received a sympathetic ear; I thank Father Ernie Schili of the Social Justice Committee of Montreal for this information). But participants were not nationalist republicans in Miller's sense—they did not think of themselves as members of a national community with a separate cultural character, nor did they agree that national citizens owe more obligations to each other than to foreigners or that each citizen should set aside personal interests for the sake of the nation. Rather, they were urging rich countries to set aside national interests for the sake of international obligations.

50. Miller, *Citizenship*, 175.

51. One is reminded of the fact that most of the world adheres to the principles spelled out in the Universal Declaration of Human Rights, yet there is profound disagreement over the application of those principles to particular cases (e.g., does the "right to life" mean that capital punishment should be abolished?).

52. Miller, *Citizenship*, 55.

53. In fact, the hostility of various groups may produce both a strong republican nationalist tradition (in the sense that many citizens are active participants in the nation's political life and deliberate about their distinctive political culture) and a willingness to exploit hostile groups. Consider the fact that Israel is perhaps the modern democratic nation that most "breathes" politics on the day-to-day level, yet it also deals with Palestinians in less than acceptable ways from the perspective of global justice.

54. Ford Motor Company, which produces these vehicles, also recognizes that sport-utility vehicles are far worse than cars in terms of contributing to global warming and emitting smog-causing pollution. However, the automaker said it would keep building them because they are so profitable (the factory in Wayne, Michigan, that builds them is the world's most profitable in any industry, generating roughly $3 billion a year in pretax profit [Keith Bradsher, "Sport-Utility Vehicles Are Really Bad, Ford Sighs, but So Profitable!" *International Herald Tribune*, May 13–14, 2000, p. 1]).

55. Miller, *Citizenship*, 177.

56. He subsequently takes back what he says with the following example—"it does not seem justifiable to claim that projects such as this [a national football stadium or a Millenium Dome] should take priority over, for example, helping to rebuild the economy of a foreign nation that has been shattered by foreign invasion or civil war" (Miller, *Citizenship*, 177–178), but Miller does not explain how he distinguishes between justifiable national projects and those that must give way to our international obligations. From a nationalist republican standpoint, it might seem that national football stadiums are particularly useful as they provide the context for nationalist football fever that often leads to a strong sense of national solidarity.

57. This is not to imply that U.S. decisionmakers were motivated by altruism. The main reason the United States tolerated this arrangement is that it wanted to maintain economically

healthy "capitalist" allies to combat Soviet influence in the region. With the end of the Cold War, the United States has been pressuring East Asian countries to open up their markets to U.S. products on more "equitable" terms.

58. Of course, there are other reasons for the East Asian "miracle," including economic policies that favored high savings rates and cultural factors such as a strong work and educational ethic.

59. One possible reply is that this might not be as much of a problem in rich states with a political culture of aiding needy foreigners—Sweden might be an example. But these nation-states are few and far between. More worrisome, Miller seems to turn this descriptive fact into a normative requirement, that is, he let's off the hook "selfish" nations if that is their political culture. He doesn't say this directly with reference to aid for the foreign needy, but one can extrapolate this implication from his argument that "solidaristic" Swedes have more extensive obligations to provide welfare for needy compatriots compared to "individualistic" Americans, who will not worry as much about aiding "fellow-Americans." This, Miller says, is "what social justice consists in" (Miller, *Citizenship*, 39), thus turning a descriptive fact into a normative requirement.

60. Quoted in Greg Torode, "Hard Bargaining for Freer Trade," *South China Morning Post*, May 21, 2000.

61. Note that this refers to the long term (ten years?), because the initial impact is likely to be negative in China as well, with millions of Chinese workers of noncompetitive state-run enterprises losing their jobs. But eventually, the increased foreign investment will likely lead to more employment opportunities (see Clay Chandler and Frank Swoboda, "Despite U.S. Labor's Claim, Some Chinese Workers Flourish," *International Herald Tribune*, May 24, 2000, p.13), and it is not entirely implausible to assume that the benefits will eventually outweigh the original costs (at least compared to the alternative of continuation of the non-WTO status quo, as many workers would have lost their jobs anyway without the hope of alternative job creation). Also, the socialist will applaud the fact that joining the WTO is likely to have the effect of forcing China to further modernize its productive forces.

62. This leads to the question of why the Clinton administration supported a policy that is likely to bring more (long-term) benefits to Chinese workers than to American ones. This was due to a variety of factors: the fact that WTO for China will bring security benefits to the United States by decreasing the likelihood that China will emerge as an implacable foe; the fact that U.S. business groups stand to benefit; and one cannot rule out the possibility there was an element of concern for the interests of the Chinese among internationalist political elites that (understandably) is lacking among relatively parochial "Joe Six-Packs" who do not know, or care about, things Chinese (not to mention U.S. workers who will have to bear the costs of WTO for China).

63. See Amitai Etzioni, *The Spirit of Community* (New York: Crown, 1993), 71–72. Etzioni emphasizes that these policies are meant to be applicable in the Western liberal democracies, more specifically, in the United States. His proposals are temporary, specific responses to a diagnosis of the American condition now: "If we were in China today, we would argue vigorously for more individual rights; in contemporary America, we emphasize individual and social responsibilities" (Communitarian Platform). In that sense, Miller is correct to argue that communitarians do not propose a universally applicable political program (Miller, *Citizenship*, 97), though Etzioni et al. would not regard this as a criticism.

64. See my book *Communitarianism and Its Critics* (Oxford: Clarendon Press, 1993), Act III.

65. Miller, *Citizenship*, 29.

66. Miller, *Citizenship*, 82.

67. This point can be illustrated with the example of the political theorist William Galston, who resigned as domestic policy adviser in the Clinton administration because he felt he did not have enough time to spend with his family.

68. Miller, *Citizenship*, 58.

69. See my book *East Meets West*, 110–116.

70. See also Michael Walzer's essay in this volume.

71. Miller, *Citizenship*, 57.

72. Note that the communitarian aspiration to public-spirited citizenship may conflict with the liberal realist's analysis of political behavior in existing liberal democracies. But the communitarian can agree with the liberal realist diagnosis and add that such policies as citizenship education in public schools can help to move the reality closer to the communitarian ideal.

The communitarian endorsement of Miller's point that nationality is an important focus of identity, and the implication that this translates into special obligations owed to conationals, also seems to conflict with the socialist emphasis on the worst off, wherever they are. The communitarian can reply that part of the point of citizenship education would be to make people more conscious of their obligations to both conationals and needy foreigners. This is similar to Miller's argument that we can fulfill obligations owed to conationals subject to the constraints of global justice, but Miller seems to go a step further by endorsing political cultures characterized by U.S.-style individualism. In contrast, the communitarian would not have the same reluctance to promote policies explicitly designed to challenge political cultures that seem to justify individual and/or national "selfishness."

In any case, my aim in this chapter is to show how Miller's ideal can be criticized from three different perspectives (and to suggest an alternative formulation that can meet the various objections), and it is not part of my argument that these perspectives need to be mutually consistent in all respects.

III

GLOBAL JUSTICE

13

Republicanism, Patriotism, and Global Justice

Stuart White

NATIONAL CITIZENS AND GLOBAL JUSTICE

One of the many interesting questions raised by David Miller's recent work concerns the possibility of globally responsible citizenship: a form of citizenship that involves an effective recognition of moral duties across national boundaries. The idea of globally responsible citizenship is often assimilated to that of cosmopolitan citizenship: a form of citizenship that is mediated through participation in supranational political institutions. In an essay, "Bounded Citizenship," Miller is explicitly skeptical about the prospects for cosmopolitan citizenship.[1] Citizenship, Miller argues, is necessarily grounded at the national level, for, under modern conditions, the call to duty is motivationally effective only when integrated with a sense of national identity and belonging. And yet, at the same time, in his essay "National Self-Determination and Global Justice," Miller advocates a demanding conception of global justice.[2] Is Miller confused? Can he consistently argue that citizenship is necessarily national in essence, but that we have demanding transnational obligations of justice? If national identity and belonging are motivational preconditions for meeting our civic duties, how can Miller expect us to act on our obligations toward strangers in foreign lands? These questions connect with a more general question that has focused the attention of political theorists in recent years: How are we to evaluate national-patriotic solidarities? Are they to be celebrated? Are they to be repudiated in favor of higher, more encompassing solidarities?[3]

One approach to these questions is suggested by another feature of Miller's recent work: his advocacy of a republican form of citizenship.[4] Some might regard this aspect of Miller's thinking only as accentuating the tension described previously.⁵ For there is undoubtedly a strong tendency in some republican thinkers to locate the claims of justice firmly within the city walls, those outside the walls having a decidedly second-class moral status. As Rousseau put it: "Every patriot hates foreigners; they are only men, and nothing to him."⁶ But there is also a strong tradition of republican thinking and practice, dating from the late eighteenth century, which locates domestic civic responsibilities in the context of wider responsibilities to humanity. Exponents of this Enlightenment republicanism, as one might loosely call it, hold that one's duties to one's nation are to the nation conceived, to put it grandly, as a servant of humanity; as a nation that affirms the universal importance of republican values and which is willing to affirm these values abroad as an extension of its respect for them at home. But the perspective of these republicans is nevertheless, like Miller's, one of a world made up of distinct peoples and nation-states, and of national identities and affections, rather than of a world state and unmediated global citizenship. Drawing on other contributions to the recent literature on republicanism, by political theorists such as Karma Nabulsi, Philip Pettit, Quentin Skinner, and Maurizio Viroli,⁷ I shall outline and defend a variant of this kind of republicanism and explain how it might resolve the tension inherent in the "national globalist" perspective that Miller's work articulates (a perspective that simultaneously locates citizenship firmly in the nation and asserts that justice is of global reach).

The argument proceeds as follows. In the first section, I briefly review Miller's theories of citizenship and global justice and why there appears to be a tension between them. In the second section, I then examine republicanism in more depth, developing an account of republican citizenship that borrows not only from Miller, but from the work of the other, aforementioned theorists. I focus in particular on the idea of patriotism and on how, in this form of republicanism, patriotic sentiments are integrated with constitutional values that are thought to have relevance for all nations. In the third section, I discuss how this specific form of republican patriotism might, in turn, support transnational solidarities of the kind necessary to achieve global justice (as defined by Miller). The republican patriotism outlined in the second and third sections bears more than a passing resemblance to the constitutional and civic patriotisms proposed by other political theorists recently, and it has been said, with some justification I think, that there is frequently something "amorphous" about these ideas.⁸ Responding to this concern, the fourth section tries to explain in more detail how universalist and particularistic, nationalist sentiments might combine in this form of republican patriotism to support action for global justice.

MILLER ON CITIZENSHIP AND GLOBAL JUSTICE

Let us begin by clarifying Miller's theory of citizenship. In his essays, "Citizenship and Pluralism" and "Bounded Citizenship," Miller maintains that citizenship ought not to be understood in merely "liberal" terms as consisting in an equality of civil, political and socio-economic rights and corresponding duties. It ought to be understood in "republican" terms as involving, in addition to this equality of rights and formal duties: (1) an active commitment to the common good and (2) a willingness to participate, responsibly, in (democratic) politics.

Miller describes the first of these two distinctive requirements of republican citizenship as follows: "[C]itizenship involves . . . being willing to take active steps to defend the rights of other members of the political community, and more generally to promote its common interests. The citizen is someone who goes to the aid of a fellow citizen who collapses in the street, or who intervenes when he is able to prevent a criminal act being committed."[9] And he describes the second of the two distinctive requirements of republican citizenship thus: "The republican citizen plays an active role in both the formal and informal arenas of politics. Political participation is not undertaken simply in order to check the excesses of government . . . but as a way of expressing your commitment to the community."[10]

To be a citizen in this republican sense, Miller argues, one must have sufficient "motivation" and "responsibility." One must have sufficient motivation "to carry out the tasks—political and sub-political—that citizenship involves," even though the tasks impose costs on one's time and "may not be experienced as pleasant."[11] It is not enough that one is merely a civic and political activist, however: citizens must "act responsibly . . . [must] not merely . . . get involved in public decision-making, but . . . promote the common good."[12] This involves "taking a long-term view of the community's interests rather than a short-term one" and "being willing to set aside personal interests and personal ideals in the interests of achieving a democratic consensus."[13] By "personal ideals" here, Miller means to refer to religious and philosophical commitments of the kind that enter into what, in contemporary political theory, is often called a "conception of the good." Responsible citizenship, in the foregoing sense, will only be stable over time, Miller argues, if each citizen has adequate assurance that other citizens will also act responsibly. Miller worries that the motivation and responsibility conditions might in practice pull against each other in that those most strongly motivated to enter politics might well also be those most strongly committed to a sectarian conception of the good.[14] The republican citizen is necessarily politically active, in contrast to the so-called "liberal" citizen for whom politics is (supposedly) just one possible lifestyle choice among others.[15] And his or her activism is focused centrally on securing the protection of a common good rather than on advancing sectional interests or sectarian ideals.

Miller's next and critical claim is that, under "modern . . . conditions," shared national identity and allegiance provide the necessary sentimental basis for republican public-spiritedness: "Rousseau's citizens were supposed to gather face to face under the shade of an oak to make laws. If modern social conditions make this impossible, something else must generate the trust and loyalty that citizenship requires. Common nationality has served this purpose in the advanced societies."[16] In Miller's view, shared nationality provides the basis for solidarity between citizens of modern polities.[17] A strong sense of national identity and belonging gives one's efforts for the polity's common good a distinctive feel; one experiences these efforts as at least partly congruent with the pursuit of one's own personal projects and welfare, for nationality is something that helps gives one's own life some of its meaning and purpose.[18] Greater willingness to contribute to the common good builds trust between citizens, which, in turn, facilitates further cooperation.

In view of the alleged importance of national identity to responsible citizenship, Miller is skeptical of the fashionable idea of cosmopolitan citizenship. Proponents of cosmopolitan citizenship look to the emergence of a new transnational political activism to help establish and sustain a range of transnational political institutions (legislative, judicial, and executive) that will, in turn, help to secure human rights, advance global distributive justice, and better manage environmental problems.[19] Miller argues that proponents of this ideal ignore the need for bases of "trust and loyalty" that citizenship demands. The trust and loyalty born of shared national allegiance must obviously weaken as we move to the transnational level at which cosmopolitan citizenship is supposed to work, and, in Miller's view, cosmopolitan idealists have yet to propose any credible alternative source for these virtues. Much contemporary transnational activism, such as radical environmentalism, is motivated by rather sectarian philosophies of the good life; and a global politics of competing sectarianisms hardly seems a promising basis on which to cultivate ongoing trust and loyalty among global citizens.[20] As sectarians, such activists lack the responsibility of the true citizen.

At the same time, however, Miller is emphatically not a skeptic about global justice. In his essay, "National Self-Determination and Global Justice," Miller argues that there are three main obligations of global justice, which obligations carry a degree of priority over purely national interests. There is, first, an obligation to "respect . . . the basic human rights of people everywhere."[21] Second, "individuals and collectivities should refrain from exploiting those who are vulnerable to their actions."[22] Third, there is "the obligation to ensure that all political communities have the opportunity to determine their own future and practise justice among their members," implying an "adequate resource base" and a "tolerable economic environment."[23] Miller claims that the first two obligations set clear limits on the domestic pursuit of social justice and other domestic goals. In the case of the third obligation, it is, so Miller argues, reasonable for each nation to prioritize the achievement of self-government and basic justice at home before looking to help with these objectives elsewhere. But this obligation will nevertheless set some limits on the pursuit of national interests.

Now one question that arises here is whether Miller is altogether consistent in rejecting cosmopolitan citizenship and advocating this conception of global justice.[24] It might be argued that implicit in the three obligations that Miller identifies, or derivable from them, there is a fourth obligation: the obligation to help establish and maintain transnational bodies that will promote respect for the three primary obligations of global justice and reduce the risk of some nations free riding on others in the effort to achieve global justice. Institutionally, therefore, Miller's conception of global justice may well point toward arrangements that correspond quite closely to some of those advocated by supporters of cosmopolitan citizenship. And, given the reasons for Miller's skepticism toward cosmopolitan citizenship, this point serves to draw out the deeper issue that I noted in the introduction: how can we expect citizens, as nationalists of a sort, to respond to the theoretical demands of global justice? If nationality is, as Miller says, the essential basis of solidarity under modern conditions, what of the transnational solidarity necessary for global justice?

ELABORATING REPUBLICAN CITIZENSHIP: THE PATRIOTISM OF LIBERTY

Perhaps one way of resolving the tension we see here is to develop further the idea that citizenship at the national level ought to take a specifically *republican* form. Miller's interest in republicanism reflects a wider resurgence of interest in republicanism among political theorists in recent years. By drawing on the work of these theorists, I think we can construct a fuller account of republican citizenship that we can then use to address the tension we have identified in Miller's thinking.

As a first step in this task of elaborating what is involved in a specifically republican form of citizenship, we need to open up the question of what constitutes the "common good" to which the republican citizen is properly committed. At the risk of great oversimplification, I would contend that the basic idea underlying modern forms of republicanism is that citizens share certain basic interests, and that, in entering political society and accepting its obligations, each acquires an equal right with other citizens to the protection of these interests. The common good consists, first and foremost, in equal protection of these *core civil interests*. These interests themselves roughly consist of life, "liberty," and "property." The interest in life generates a right to draw on the force of the community for physical protection and to secure access to subsistence. As Philip Pettit and Quentin Skinner have recently shown, the interest in liberty is typically understood in modern republican (or, as Skinner prefers, "neo-Roman") thought, through a contrast with slavery, as the state of independence enjoyed when one is not under the open-ended threat of interference by another: to be unfree is to live at the mercy of another.[25] As for the term *property*, that can be understood, at least to a first approximation, as a right of reasonable access to the wealth necessary to maintain life and enjoy effective liberty in the sense just defined.[26] A republican citizen, then, is someone who is willing to enter politics, at possible risk/cost to him- or herself, specifically with a view to securing the equal protection of these core civil interests, a goal that I shall henceforth refer to, for short, and in conformity with standard republican rhetoric, as the common liberty. Within a given republican polity, the common liberty will be embodied in a specific set of institutions, and civic obligation will thus be understood as immediately concerned with the maintenance and healthy functioning of these institutions.

Against the backdrop of this republican conception of the goals of the polity, there can now arise a specifically republican understanding of patriotism. The patriot, as a general matter, is someone who has "love of country"; but the republican patriot's love of country has a distinctive form. As Maurizio Viroli puts it, in his extended essay on the subject: "Love of country [is] understood as a benevolent love for the common liberty of our own people: we want to see them living in freedom, and to live in freedom with them, because we hold them dear."[27] Viroli cites, among many others, the English Leveller pamphleteers and Rousseau as writers who understood love of country in this way.[28] These do not seem to be exceptional cases. Indeed, Karma Nabulsi's discussion of the republican tradition of thinking about war shows how key republican activists of the eighteenth and nineteenth centuries, including Pasquale Paoli, Tadeusz Kosciuszko, Karol Bogul Stolzman, and Giuseppe Mazzini, also conceptualized love of country in these terms: as love for the home of a common liberty.[29] (Viroli also cites the case of Mazzini.) The patriot is a member of a specific people, which may be differentiated linguistically and culturally from other peoples; and this may be central to the patriot's personal identity, and even to her sense of what the institutions of the republic are intended to protect. But "love" of this people is given content by the republican ideal of the common liberty—something that is good not only for *us*, as a particular people, but good, indeed of fundamental value, *for all*. Republican love of country is love of things peculiar to one's people connected to, and potentially constrained by, a love for this thing of fundamental and allegedly universal value: the common liberty. Cultural differences may give the common liberty different shapes across different peoples, but there is a shared, universal core related to the civil interests identified previously. In the words of Mazzini: "I am an Italian, but also a man and a European. . . . I adore *our* Liberty, because I believe in abstract *Liberty*; *our* rights, because I believe in abstract *Right*."[30] As Nabulsi shows, exactly this blend of particularistic attachment to a specific people and moral universalism can be seen in the actions (as well as the writings) of republican activists like Paoli, Kosciuszko, and Stolzman; this blend was fundamental to the ideology and the practical political strategy of European republicanism as it emerged in opposition to the Vienna settlement in the years after 1815.[31]

I am not sure that all recent theorists of "republican patriotism" would find this characterization of republicanism wholly acceptable. In a recent essay, Maurizio Viroli argues that we need to distinguish republican patriotism from what he calls "civic nationalism."[32] He says: "Republican patriotism differs from civic nationalism in being a passion and not the result of rational consent; it is a matter not of allegiance to historically and culturally neutral universal political principles, but attachment to the laws, constitution and the way of life of a particular republic."[33] Quite a lot is packed into this sentence, but the central contrast seems to be between a "patriotism" focused on specific national institutions and a "civic nationalism" focused on "universal political principles." Viroli would presumably argue that the sentiment I have described previously is, in view of its universalist content, more akin to civic nationalism than republican patriotism. Now the label we give to the sentiment described before is less important to me than its substantive content. Nevertheless, I do not accept Viroli's characterization of republican patriotism, in preference to my own, for three reasons.

To begin with, were we to accept Viroli's characterization of republican patriotism, as set out in the quoted passage, I do not see how people like Mazzini, or the Levellers, whom Viroli cites as exemplifying republican patriotism, could be regarded as examples of republican patriots. For it seems clear in Mazzini's case, for example, that his republicanism was derived from a strong allegiance to "universal political principles": "I believe in abstract *Liberty*. . . . I believe in abstract *Right*." A quick glance at Mazzini's "General Instructions for the Initiators" of the Young Europe movement indicates the universalistic perspective: "'Young Europe' is an association of men [*sic*] believing in a future of liberty, equality and fraternity, for all mankind; and desirous of consecrating their thoughts and actions to the realization of that future."[34] The notions of "liberty," "equality," and "fraternity" clearly have universal content for Mazzini—they are, to a considerable extent, the same for Italians as for Germans, Poles, or any other portion of "mankind." Second, Viroli has not explained how allegiance to republican institutions, passionate or otherwise, can be divorced from a rational evaluation of those institutions by reference to background, universal principles. Imagine a polity emerges that has all the objective features of a fascist dictatorship. Could we seriously entertain the proposition that it is a form of republican polity? I think not. But a judgment of this kind makes sense only if one accepts that there are universal standards of republican government and social organization against which we can rationally assess the adequacy of any given nation's institutions.[35] Third, and unsurprisingly in view of the first two points, Viroli in fact more usually characterizes republican patriotism in ways that seem to refer to universal values and principles. "Love of country [in its republican form]," Viroli says, "presses us to feel the oppression that some of our fellows endure as an outrage. Oppression may take the form of the denial of civil and political rights or exploitation, brutality, contempt for human dignity in workplaces and social life."[36] Unless Viroli wishes to claim that the meanings of "civil and political rights," "exploitation," "brutality," "human dignity," and so on are wholly relative to specific societies with their distinctive political traditions (and there is no indication of any such radical relativism in his work) then, in passages like this, he does seem implicitly to be endorsing some universal political values and to be defining republican "love of country" partly in terms of a commitment to them.

REPUBLICAN PATRIOTISM AND GLOBAL JUSTICE

This discussion of republican patriotism brings us naturally to a pivotal idea of this chapter, the idea of *transnational republican solidarity*. A citizen may be said to exhibit the spirit of transnational republican solidarity when he or she cares about the common liberty of other peoples/nations[37] as well as that of his or her own, where "caring about" this good implies that he or she is willing to act to promote it, if need be at some cost/risk to him- or herself. Concretely, in its most intense form, this solidarity might be expressed in a decision to join the struggle of another people for the achievement of their common liberty, as did activists such as Kosciuszko and Stolzman.[38] Solidarity might alternatively be expressed in efforts to offer a safe and dignified place of refuge for the victims and critics of oppressive foreign regimes; or in support for economic sanctions, such as the support given by British workers, at great cost to themselves, to the Union's blockade of the Confederacy during the American Civil War.[39] It might be expressed in acts of criticism of, even resistance to, one's own government if it is acting in ways that clearly endanger or directly violate the common liberty in other countries.

How might a nationally based republican patriotism, of the kind sketched in the previous section, give rise, with appropriate encouragement, to this spirit of transnational republican solidarity? There are, I suggest, at least four ways in which such solidarity can emerge from a nationally based republican patriotism.

1. Prudential solidarity. First, a conscientious republican patriot may desire to show solidarity with the struggle for the common liberty of other peoples for prudential reasons. As a republican patriot I care about the common liberty of my fellow citizens. But our republic may be less secure if certain other countries do not enjoy the same freedom. If so, then if we are really motivated, in the assumed way, to secure the common liberty at home, then we ought also to be motivated to help the other relevant peoples secure their common liberty. Admittedly, by themselves, prudential considerations of this sort will produce only a contingent and limited form of transnational solidarity.

2. Humanitarian solidarity. A deep and abiding sense of the evil of subjection to arbitrary power is necessary to sustain the citizen's determination to uphold the common liberty at cost/risk to him- or herself. If, however, the republican patriot necessarily has this vivid appreciation of the evil of subjection, then he or she should immediately grasp the significance

of subjection when it is suffered by members of other peoples. And this, in turn, should motivate the republican patriot to sympathize with, and so perhaps support, the efforts of foreign peoples against oppression. Thus, the republican patriot may be drawn to support the struggle of foreign peoples for their common liberty out of humanitarian motives: from direct empathy with foreign victims of oppression. This humanitarian solidarity, growing out of nationally based republican patriotism, is, in part, what Viroli refers to when he writes: "If it is love of common liberty, patriotism can translate into solidarity beyond national boundaries. All the oppressed are the patriot's fellows."[40]

3. Honorific solidarity. The patriot, who loves his or her people, will typically desire that this people be worthy of the respect of other peoples.[41] Now many things might be thought to make a people respectworthy in this way, but, if the patriot in question is a republican patriot, as defined previously, then he or she will tend to link respectworthiness, or national honor, with a willingness to uphold the common liberty (understood as a universal good). And this desire for national honor, as a natural expression of love of country, might serve as a further motivation driving the republican patriot into solidarity with the struggle of other peoples to achieve the common liberty. As Mazzini put it, with characteristic melodrama: "[So] long as you are ready to die for Humanity [in defense of its liberty], the Life of your Country will be immortal."[42] (Note that the patriot's concern with national honor is indeed fundamentally a matter of how his or her *people*, rather than his or her government, is perceived. The patriot would like the people he or she loves to be worthy of the respect of other peoples in virtue of being a freedom-loving, freedom-defending people. Thus, the republican patriot's concern for national honor may motivate him or her to act in support of another people's struggle for the common liberty independently of the patriot's government, or, indeed, possibly even in opposition to it.)

4. Solidarity of the patriots.[43] The sentiment I have in mind here can be explained by imagining the republican patriot of one people addressing the republican patriot of another as follows: "In some respects, your struggle is not our struggle. It is not for us to lead your struggle since it is a struggle for the common liberty of your people, which you are unlikely to achieve if we assume a leadership role. Nor can we identify as closely as you can with the particular national form of life that you expect to enjoy under conditions of liberty. But in one, no less important sense, your struggle is our struggle. For you are struggling to realize for your people the same political ideal that we are struggling to achieve for ours, an ideal which we both regard as of value to all peoples. We see in the specific kind of liberty-focused love you have for your people a mirror of the kind of love that we have for ours; and that itself forms a bond between *us,* as republican patriots."

This sentiment seems to have been central to the ethos of the European republican activists of the nineteenth century, as exemplified by the Young Europe movement of the 1830s.[44] Unsurprisingly, therefore, appeals to this sentiment play an important role in the work of Mazzini. For example, in his essay, "On the Duties of Man," formally addressed to his fellow Italians, but published in England and eagerly read by a large English audience, Mazzini raises the question: "A People—Greek, Pole, Italian, or Circassian—raises the flag of country and independence, and combats, conquers, or dies to defend it. What is it that causes your hearts to beat at the news of those battles, that makes them swell with joy at their victories, and sink with sorrow at their defeats?"[45] Relatedly, he asks: "Why do you read so eagerly the prodigies of patriotism registered in Grecian history, and relate them to your children with a sense of pride, as if they belonged to the history of your ancestors?"[46] The answer, according to Mazzini, is that his audience can see a fundamental commonality between the values it holds dear and those apparently upheld in these foreign and ancient struggles: "[I]n your heart a voice cries unto you: 'Those men of two thousand years ago, those populations now fighting afar off . . . are your Brothers; *brothers* not only in community of origin and of nature, but *in community of labour and of aim.* . . . *Those* [afar off] *populations consecrate with their blood an idea of national liberty for which you too would combat.*"[47] The italicized portions of this answer describe the sentiment I am here calling solidarity of the patriots. In practice, this sentiment might well be intertwined with what I referred to previously as humanitarian solidarity. But the two sentiments are distinct because one identifies with a foreign people as the *victims* of oppression ("wheresoever a man is tortured through . . . tyranny, that man is your brother"), while the other identifies with a foreign people, or with a subset of that people, as *fighters* against oppression ("wheresoever there arises a man to combat for the right, the just, and the true, that man is your brother").[48] Humanitarian solidarity is a form of compassion; solidarity of the patriots, a form of comradeship.

I have described four plausible ways in which a republican patriot might be motivated to defend the common liberty abroad as well as at home. How might these motivations work to promote action for global justice?

Let's begin with Miller's first obligation of global justice, which mandates respect for human rights. There is a clear connection between human rights, as standardly conceived, and the basic republican commitment to uphold the common liberty. If I have a strong sentiment of transnational republican solidarity then, given my resulting commitment to the common liberty of other peoples as well as my own, I will be motivated to refrain from promoting my nation's interests at the expense of human rights. Indeed, I might well be motivated to act transnationally in support of the development and application of international human rights law. I will be motivated to help publicize cases of human rights abuses at the international level and to help get the perpetrators into an appropriate court. I may even be willing to join something like a UN Volunteer Force to help keep the peace in situations where the threat to human rights is strong, or even to intervene to resist an aggressor that is threatening human rights.[49]

Transnational republican solidarity might also work to support Miller's second and third obligations of global justice. Given the republican insight that liberty is compromised by economic dependency, a concern for the common liberty of one's own and other peoples should also make republican citizens supportive of ground rules of international economic cooperation that protect individuals and, indeed, peoples as a whole, from the material desperation that compromises independence. And, in view of the humanitarian, honorific, and other solidarities described previously, the republican patriot will naturally be sympathetic to the efforts of other peoples to construct polities that provide essential freedoms and that have sufficient economic strength to sustain these freedoms.

However, even if citizens of a republican nation might have an initial willingness, grounded in sentiments of transnational republican solidarity, to act in support of global justice, do we have any reason to think that such action could be sustained over time? In his critique of cosmopolitan citizenship, Miller makes the important point that individuals or groups are unlikely to continue to practice active and responsible citizenship if their good citizenship is not sufficiently reciprocated by other members of the polity. Is this not, perhaps, the real problem? Can the members of one republican people reasonably expect members of other peoples to reciprocate their responsible, justice-promoting activities?

I think the key point to make here is that if a number of peoples cultivate republican patriotism, so as to ensure that their citizens are willing to be active in defending the common liberty at home, then there is no reason why sentiments of transnational republican solidarity, as an extension of republican patriotism, could not be shared across these peoples. To this extent, at least, there is no reason why responsible human rights and economic justice activism at the transnational level by citizens belonging to one nation should not be reciprocated by citizens belonging to other nations. The analysis presented previously suggests that concerted activism by citizens of one republican nation will tend to bring forth a supportive response by citizens of other republican nations, motivated perhaps by a concern for national honor and/or a sentiment of comradely identification with fellow fighters for the common liberty.

REPUBLICAN PATRIOTISM: A CLOSER LOOK

Let us now recap. I have argued that republican citizenship involves a specific form of patriotism, republican patriotism; and I have argued that this particular form of patriotism, while immediately focused on the good of a specific people or nation, is capable of motivating transnational political solidarities of the kind necessary to satisfy the demands of global justice (at least as these demands are characterized by Miller). Critics might argue, however, that the notion of republican patriotism remains somewhat ambiguous. Yes, it will be said, you describe something that is a "mix" of nationalistic and universalistic sentiments. But how does this mixture work? Is it really a coherent mix? Is this notion of republican patriotism perhaps just a rhetorical dodge that fails to confront the unavoidable conflict between nationalistic sentiment and moral universalism? A number of political theorists have tried in recent years to articulate a patriotism or nationalism that embodies a mix of this kind; the literature now abounds with, not only republican patriots, but with "constitutional patriots," "civic patriots," "civic nationalists," even "cosmopolitan patriots."[50] I agree with critics like Margaret Canovan that there is a degree of amorphousness about these ideas. More work needs to be done to explain the relationship between the particularistic and universalistic sentiments that respectively constitute these imagined patriotisms and nationalisms, and why they do not simply negate, or live in conflict with, one another. This section discusses just one way in which we might elaborate the notion of republican patriotism sketched in the second section.

Step one of the elaboration is a firm endorsement of a moderate ethical universalism. All human beings have certain basic interests and have a right to the satisfaction of these interests. To a considerable extent, these correspond to the interests described in the preceding section: life; liberty, understood as a state in which one is not vulnerable to the arbitrary interference of another; and property, understood as access to the wealth necessary for life and liberty. We have an obligation to help bring about a world in which all human beings enjoy adequate protection of these interests. Call this, for convenience, the "global obligation." This global obligation corresponds quite closely to the obligations of global justice that Miller identifies: I read Miller's conception of global justice as a more detailed breakdown of what is required to satisfy this obligation.

Now, will national identity and a sense of national affiliation necessarily get in the way of our discharging the duties associated with the global obligation? This depends on the specific way in which national identity is constructed. According to David Miller's helpful analysis in his essay *On Nationality*, national identity involves a group of people (1) sharing a sense of themselves as an active community that has historical continuity (so that the actions of the community today can be slotted into a narrative that stretches some way into the past); (2) sharing a specific geographic location; and (3) sharing characteristics that add up to what Miller terms a "common public culture."[51] The common public culture, Miller points out, need not be based on common biological descent, nor need it be "monolithic and all-embracing." A republican will naturally wish to put commitment to the common liberty, in the sense outlined previously, at the heart of the common public culture. Other things might enter into this culture, and those things might affect some of the nuances of the way in which the common liberty is understood;[52] but the culture will celebrate the common liberty, understood as a universal good. This will, in turn, affect the way in which the nation develops a shared narrative concerning its history. As Miller acknowledges, the development of such narratives is an exercise in myth making.[53] By this we do not mean that such narratives are simply historically false, but that they involve a value-driven interpretation of the significance of specific events and personalities. In a republican nation, the values driving this interpretation will, of course, be the republican values at the center of the nation's common public culture. The republican patriot, then, is the individual who, as citizen, shares in this common public culture and in the corresponding national-historical "myth." The patriot will wish the nation to carry the myth forward in a way that more effectively realizes the values of the common public culture, and she will suffer a kind of shame at backsliding and regression. Her life will derive some (though by no means all) of its meaning and purpose from a sense of belonging to, and from active participation in, this national project.[54]

In some modern democratic nations, such as the United States, this form of national identity does seem to be part of the political culture (albeit in competition with other, less admirable conceptions of national identity). As Benjamin Barber puts it: "The American trick was [is?] to use the fierce attachments of patriotic sentiment to bond a people to high ideals."[55] The stories of the American Revolution, the Civil War, the Civil Rights movement of the 1960s all form part of a national-historical myth that connects national identity with republican values. Of course, in the U.S. case, the story must also incorporate, indeed emphasize, the record of slavery, genocidal wars against Native Americans, Jim Crow laws, and the judicial murder of working-class political activists. For these episodes in U.S. history represent fallings away from the national mission, understood in republican terms; and an awareness of these failures helpfully underscores the need for vigilance and for continued struggle to make the nation true to its (better) self. The link between the national-historical narrative and the values in the common public culture is helped, of course, by the centrality of the U.S. constitution in the public culture, taking the constitution in an extended sense to include documents like Lincoln's Gettysburg Address and pivotal Supreme Court decisions (and dissents) such as *Brown* v. *Board of Education of Topeka*. However, this means of forging a national identity is not necessarily unique to the United States.[56] In principle it would be possible to develop a sense of British national identity, for example, along similar lines. And, if national identity is experienced in this way, then, for the reasons elaborated in the previous section, it need not come at the expense of respecting the global obligation. The endorsement and support of the national-historical myth help to animate a sense of justice that can readily apply transnationally. How the nation acts toward injustices elsewhere becomes part of the national-historical story in terms of which citizens evaluate the meaning, purpose, and, indeed, success of their own lives.

Republican patriotism, or nationalism, is a kind of mediated universalism: it promotes respect for the global obligation by integrating the values which underpin this obligation into a public culture and a national-historical myth that, in turn, give partial meaning and purpose to individual lives. Nationality is, in this view, "an instrument for labour toward the common good, toward progress for all."[57]

CONCLUSION AND CAVEATS

I conclude, then, that there is no necessary contradiction between Miller's insistence on the nationalistic context of effective citizenship and his advocacy of a demanding conception of global justice. Reconciling the two requires that we develop further the republican dimension of Miller's political theory: specifically, that we clarify the connection between republican citizenship and the common liberty, understood as a universal value of fundamental importance; and that we then explain how this universal value might combine with nationalistic sentiments in a coherent way so as to motivate action to redress global injustice. These were my tasks in the preceding sections.

In closing, however, I do wish to enter some caveats. To begin with, one must acknowledge the essentially speculative character of this chapter's argument. I do not claim to have shown conclusively that nationalistic and universalistic sentiments can fruitfully combine in the manner suggested; to show that would require empirical research that I have not undertaken. I merely claim to have defused the objection that, as an analytical matter, nationalist, patriotic sensibilities necessarily work to undermine action for global justice. Second, nothing I have said suggests that cultivating a certain republican form of national identity is the only, or a necessary, way of promoting global justice. Participation in some religious traditions, for example, might also connect the demands of global justice to the individual's sense of what gives meaning and purpose to her personal life and so increase the individual's motivation to meet these demands. Third, my discussion has taken as a given Miller's conception of what global justice demands. There are (even) more demanding accounts of what global justice requires, however, and I do not claim to have shown that nationality and its sentiments can be reconciled with global justice when understood in these more demanding terms. If global justice requires nothing less than the elimination of brute luck inequalities in income and wealth across all human beings, for example, then the very existence of national borders becomes hard to justify, at least at the level of ideal theory.[58] Even in this case, however, the arguments set out in this chapter might have some use for purposes of second-best, nonideal theory. They perhaps shed some light on how the citizens of richer, more advantaged nations might be better motivated to help remove at least the most severe brute luck inequalities in view of the deprivation of liberty to which these inequalities give rise. Finally, we must acknowledge that many, perhaps the vast majority of, actually existing national identities and sensibilities do not have the republican form described here. It may well be that these actually existing nationalisms do obstruct action for global justice. The import of this, however, is not necessarily that we should reject nationality altogether in favor of direct, unmediated cosmopolitanism. More feasibly, perhaps, we might instead seek to construct a mediated form of global citizenship, rooted in a republican refashioning of national identities.

NOTES

I would like to thank Daniel Attas, Daniel Bell, Erica Benner, Richard Caplan, G. A. Cohen, Cécile Fabre, Diana Gardner, Cécile Laborde, Andrew Mason, David Miller, Karma Nabulsi, and Marc Stears for comments on an earlier version of this chapter and/or for helpful discussion of the subject; particular thanks are owed to Karma Nabulsi, whose work on republicanism helped to stimulate my initial interest in this subject, and, as will become apparent, has strongly influenced the shape of this chapter's argument.

1. David Miller, "Bounded Citizenship," in Miller, *Citizenship and National Identity* (Oxford: Polity, 2000), 81–96.
2. Miller, "National Self-Determination and Global Justice," in Miller, *Citizenship*, 161–179.
3. For discussion of these questions, see the essays in Martha Nussbaum et al., *For Love of Country: Debating the Limits of Patriotism* (Boston, Mass.: Beacon, 1996).
4. See, in addition to "Bounded Citizenship," "Citizenship and Pluralism," in Miller, *Citizenship*, 61.
5. See the chapter by Daniel Bell in this volume.
6. Jean-Jacques Rousseau, *Emile,* trans. Barbara Foxley (London: Everyman, Dent, 1993 [1762]), 7.
7. See Karma Nabulsi, "Hope and Heroic Action: Rousseau, Paoli, Kosciuszko, and the Republican Tradition of War," in Nabulsi, *Traditions of War* (Oxford: Oxford University Press, 1999), 177–240; Philip Pettit, *Republicanism: A Theory of Freedom and Government* (Oxford: Oxford University Press, 1997); Quentin Skinner, *Liberty Before Liberalism* (Cambridge: Cambridge University Press, 1998); and Maurizio Viroli, *For Love of Country: An Essay on Nationalism and Patriotism* (Oxford: Oxford University Press, 1995).
8. See Margaret Canovan, "Patriotism Is Not Enough," in *The Demands of Citizenship,* ed. Catriona MacKinnon and Iain Hampsher-Monk (London: Continuum, 2000), 276–297, specifically 279.
9. Miller, "Bounded Citizenship," 83.
10. Miller, "Bounded Citizenship," 83–84.
11. Miller, "Bounded Citizenship," 84–85.
12. Miller, "Bounded Citizenship," 85.
13. Miller, "Bounded Citizenship," 85.
14. I am not sure that the distinction Miller intends when he speaks of the "motivation" and "responsibility" aspects of republican citizenship is best expressed in precisely these terms. For if someone is "sufficiently motivated to carry out the tasks . . . that citizenship involves," and one such task is responsible participation in politics, then a "sufficiently motivated" citizen is also necessarily a "responsible" one. It may be more accurate to speak, as I do in the closing sentence of this paragraph, of *activism* and *responsibility* as two aspects of what it means to be a "sufficiently motivated" citizen.

15. I think this contrast between "liberal" and "republican" conceptions of citizenship is overstated. Many thinkers who are indisputably in the liberal tradition, such as J. S. Mill, T. H. Green, and Leonard Hobhouse, are also republicans in Miller's sense: they see citizenship as demanding active political engagement for the common good.

16. Miller, "Bounded Citizenship," 87.

17. See Miller, "In Defence of Nationality," in Miller, *Citizenship*, specifically 31–32.

18. See David Miller, *On Nationality* (Oxford: Oxford University Press, 1995), 56–58, 65–73.

19. See "Bounded Citizenship," 91–92.

20. Miller, "Bounded Citizenship," 95–96.

21. Miller, "National Self-Determination," 175.

22. Miller, "National Self-Determination," 175.

23. Miller, "National Self-Determination," 175–176.

24. Another criticism, that I bracket here, is that Miller's conception of global justice is flawed because it would permit considerable inequality in resources and capabilities across individuals on the basis of morally arbitrary differences in nationality. For discussion of this criticism, see the chapters by Simon Caney and Cécile Fabre in this volume.

25. See Skinner, *Liberty Before Liberalism*. The point is that freedom is not reduced only by actual interference in one's actions, but by living in a state of dependency on another such that one is vulnerable to interference. Pettit makes a similar point in *Republicanism*, though he also makes the further, distinct claim, which I do not mean to endorse here, that freedom is not reduced by actual interference if the interference is nonarbitrary, that is, promotes the common good.

26. The idea is captured in Rousseau's statement that in the well-ordered republic, no citizen should be rich enough to buy another, and none so poor that he has to sell himself. See Jean-Jacques Rousseau, *The Social Contract* (Oxford: Oxford University Press, 1994 [1762]), book 2, ch. 11, 87.

27. Viroli, *Love of Country*, 95.

28. Viroli, *Love of Country*, 51, 82.

29. See Nabulsi, *Traditions of War*, 206–213 (Paoli), 213–224 (Kosciuszko), and 228–236 (Stolzman and Mazzini).

30. Giuseppe (Joseph) Mazzini, "Letter to Messrs. Rodbertus, Deberg, and L. Bucher," March 30, 1861, in *Mazzini's Letters*, trans. Alice de Rosen Jervis (London: Dent, 1930), 173–180, specifically 175. Also quoted in Viroli, *Love of Country*, 152. This letter was also published as "Reply to the German Nationalists," in Ignazio Silone, *The Living Thoughts of Mazzini* (London: Cassell, 1939), 96–105. The crucial sentence is there translated (at p. 99) as follows: "I believe in freedom for Italians because I believe in the concept of freedom. I want rights for Italians, because I believe in rights for all."

31. Paoli's universalism is evident in his comparison of William Penn, who "founded a republic of free and happy men," with Alexander the Great, who merely "ravaged half of the entire world by his conquests." Kosciuszko's universalism is exemplified in his participation in the American Revolutionary War and by his opposition to slavery. He originated the slogan: "For our freedom, and yours." Stolzman, along with Mazzini, was a participant in the "Young Europe" movement that in the 1830s brought together republicans of different nationalities in a common struggle against the political order established at the end of the Napoleonic Wars. Alongside this universalism, however, all of these actors retained a deep and special commitment to their own people. See Nabulsi, *Traditions of War*, 209, 213–217, 227–230 (and also 236 on Carlo Bianco).

32. See Maurizio Viroli, "Republican Patriotism," in *The Demands of Citizenship*, ed. Catriona MacKinnon and Iain Hampsher-Monk (London: Continuum, 2000), 267–275.

33. Viroli, "Republican Patriotism," 273.

34. Giuseppe Mazzini, "Young Europe: General Instructions for the Initiators," in *The Living Thoughts of Mazzini*, ed. Ignazio Silone (London: Cassell, 1939), 91–95, specifically 91.

35. One can, of course, assert a belief in universal political principles without holding that these principles are, as Viroli puts it, "historically and culturally neutral." Quite why universalism of this kind should be accompanied by such a doctrine of neutrality is obscure. I certainly do not regard the conception of republicanism outlined here as being historically and culturally neu-

tral; it stands in opposition to all cultures that celebrate, or merely tolerate, relationships in which some have power of arbitrary interference in the lives of others.

36. Viroli, *Love of Country*, 143.

37. Although it is sometimes important to distinguish these two ideas, I treat "people" and "nation" almost as interchangeable terms in this chapter (and as both having a sufficiently clear and shared intuitive meaning to readers).

38. For an in-depth discussion of the activities of the first two in support of the republican ideal at home and abroad, see Nabulsi, *Traditions of War*, 213–217, 227–238.

39. For a realistic, balanced account of British working-class solidarity with the Union and the antislavery cause, see Royden Harrison, *Before the Socialists: Studies in Labour and Politics, 1861–1881* (London: Routledge and Kegan Paul, 1965), 40–77.

40. Viroli, *Love of Country*, 143–144 (italics added). I stress that humanitarian solidarity, based on empathetic identification with the foreign *victim* of oppression, is only one aspect of what Viroli is articulating in this passage. I think Viroli is also implicitly referring here to what I describe later as the "solidarity of the patriots," a sentiment of transnational solidarity based on empathetic identification with the foreign *fighter* of oppression.

41. Presumably, the patriot will also desire that his or her people *are actually respected* in virtue of their respect-worthiness; note, however, that this desire is importantly different from the desire to be respected at any price, for example, at the price of doing what the patriot him- or herself regards as unworthy of respect.

42. Mazzini, "On the Duties of Man," in Mazzini, *Life and Writings of Joseph Mazzini: Volume IV* (London: Smith, Elder, 1891), 209–378, specifically 281.

43. I am particularly indebted to Karma Nabulsi for this idea.

44. On the origins, activities, and legacies of this movement, see Nabulsi, *Traditions of War*, especially 227–238.

45. Mazzini, "Duties of Man," 262.

46. Mazzini, "Duties of Man," 263.

47. Mazzini, "Duties of Man," 263 (italics added).

48. Mazzini, "Duties of Man," 272. Victims of oppression (by which I mean, of course, denial of the common liberty) need not necessarily be fellow fighters against oppression; and fellow fighters against oppression need not necessarily be victims of the oppression, or even members of the same people that is subject to oppression.

49. Note that intervention need not necessarily take a military form. Solidarity might alternatively express itself, quite consistently with what I argue here, in the form of nonviolent direct action. The relative ethical and practical merit of military and nonviolent forms of assistance is an issue I bracket here.

50. See, for example, Jurgen Habermas, "Citizenship and National Identity," in *Between Facts and Norms* (Cambridge, Mass.: MIT Press, 1996), app. II on "constitutional patriotism"; Benjamin Barber, "A Constitutional Faith," in Nussbaum et al., *Love of Country*, 30–37, on "civic patriotism"; and Kwame Anthony Appiah, "Cosmopolitan Patriots," in Nussbaum et al., *Love of Country*, 21–29, on "cosmopolitan patriotism." Canovan, "Patriotism Is Not Enough," provides a thoughtful review and critique of these ideas.

51. Miller, *On Nationality*, 23–25.

52. I assume that there are some trade-offs between different elements of the common liberty and that different peoples will reasonably resolve these trade-offs in different ways that express their distinctive values. Republican peoples might reasonably differ, for example, over the proper scope of antiracist "hate speech" laws, the content of the social wage that protects citizens against economic dependency, appropriate electoral systems for national assemblies, patterns of political devolution, and so on.

53. Miller, *On Nationality*, 33–42.

54. For suggestive discussion of this ethical integration between individual and collective life, see Ronald Dworkin, "Liberal Community," in Dworkin, *Sovereign Virtue* (Cambridge, Mass.: Harvard University Press, 2000), 211–236, especially 231–234 on "liberal civic republicans."

55. Barber, "Constitutional Faith," 32.

56. I do not mean to imply that the public culture of the United States is fully republican. Rogers Smith argues that historically it has contained a mix of value systems, including ascriptivist values that contradict republicanism. See Rogers Smith, *Civic Ideals: Conflicting Visions of Citizenship in U.S. History* (New Haven, Conn.: Yale University Press, 1997).

57. Mazzini, "Reply to the German Nationalists," 99. It is absolutely clear in the context of this passage that by *all* Mazzini is referring to all of humanity and not (just) to all of one's conationals.

58. For related criticism, see Canovan, "Patriotism Is Not Enough," 286–288, 290–291.

14

Miller on Distributive Justice

Daniel M. Weinstock

Some philosophers[1] believe that the world now comprises a full-blown economic system that distributes benefits and burdens to the world's population. As such, they argue, it ought to be subject to norms of distributive justice. In his recent writings, David Miller has cast doubt on the idea that the scope of theories of distributive justice should extend beyond the bounds of the nation-state. In this chapter, I want to assess the arguments that Miller develops to support his skepticism about the possibility of international distributive justice. I argue that Miller has failed to make his case against global justice, and I suggest that aspects of Miller's arguments themselves tell against a restriction of distributive justice to the bounds of the nation-state. I run through what I take to be the most important arguments developed by Miller to justify the scope restriction, and in a concluding section I highlight some of the principles for which Miller has argued, and which in my view can be made to argue powerfully for the *extension* of principles of global justice to the world's population.

I

The most basic nationalist argument simply invokes alleged facts about human sentiment and emotional attachment. Whatever might be the case from the point of view of disembodied reason, the argument runs, it is just a hard fact that people feel greater loyalty toward their *concitoyens* and that any theory that is based on a contrary assumption will simply fail to take motivational hold. As Miller puts it in an early article on the principle of nationality, "There can be no question of trying to give rationally compelling reasons for people to have national attachments. What we can do is to start from the premise that people generally do exhibit such attachments and allegiances, and then try to build a political philosophy which incorporates them."[2] The point is made in slightly less sentimentalist language in *On Nationality*. There, Miller emphasizes the fact that people tend to have national identities to which they accord importance and claims that part of what possessing a national identity involves is the recognition of greater obligations toward the national community. "Because I identify with my family, my college, or my local community, I properly acknowledge obligations to members of these groups that are distinct from obligations I owe to people generally."[3]

In Miller's view, these facts about the way people are render universalist ethics in general, and international theories of distributive justice, in particular, suspect. They claim that, from the vantage point of the "view from nowhere," all humans matter equally, and that we therefore have no reason to give greater weight to the interests and needs of some at the expense of others. But, Miller claims, we do not occupy such a disembodied perspective. Rather, our national allegiances matter to us. Miller espouses a Humean moral epistemology that, "rather than dismissing ordinary beliefs and sentiments out of hand unless they can be shown to have a rational foundation, leaves them in place until strong arguments are produced for rejecting them."[4] On his view, we therefore have reason to take these allegiances as moral data. And universalist theories that enjoin us to treat all humans alike offend against these data.

I don't want to devote too much attention to this argumentative path toward the denial of the possibility of international distributive justice, as I have already devoted an article to it.[5] In a nutshell, my argument was, and is, that our intuitions and spontaneous judgments about justice are at least in part artifacts of the institutional orders in which we live. We must therefore be wary of giving such intuitions anything like the moral weight that Miller ascribes to them until we have been able to satisfy ourselves that these institutions are morally defensible and that they socialize us in morally defensible ways. It may very well be the case that we tend to give greater weight in our reckoning of our obligations to the needs and interests of our compatriots than we do to those of people from other lands. But this might have something to do with the fact that we live in nation-states and that the persistence of the nation-state depends in large measure upon the continued support of its citizens. This being the case, modern nation-states have gone to great lengths to ensure (through their control of public education, through other state institutions mandated to promote national identity) national partiality and the patriotic allegiance of their citizens. That people tend to feel special obligations toward their compatriots might simply be a sign that nation-states have been successful in their nation-building campaigns. Thus, the sense that we have special obligations toward those with whom we share political institutions does not constitute the moral bedrock Miller takes it to represent.

There is moreover evidence from Miller's most recent writing that he now concedes the larger, methodological points I have just made, though he has as yet not seen how damaging they are to his attempt at defending national partiality. First, Miller recognizes that proximity can give rise to the distortion of our moral judgments. We tend to accord disproportionate importance to the interests of the near and dear simply *because* they are near and dear. Now, Miller makes this point because he is concerned that our intimate relationships distract us from our obligations *as citizens of the same nation-state*. He writes that:

> We are most directly aware of our family and other community relationships; next of our immersion in economic and other instrumental relations; and finally of citizenship, which is, for most people, a remote and poorly understood mode of association. Because of these conceptual shortcomings, we are prone to give too much weight to the demands of justice stemming from our immediate communities, and too little to the demands stemming from citizenship.[6]

Now if it is the case that our sense of obligation toward those to whom we are intimately related makes it more difficult for us to fully appreciate the obligations we have toward fellow citizens, surely, by parity of reasoning, we should conclude that the (perhaps weaker) sense of obligation that binds us to our fellow citizens makes it more difficult for us to appreciate our *broader* obligations, those that bind us to humanity at large. On the face of it, the point seems to be a general one: we must be wary of assigning too much objective moral weight to our prima facie weightings of moral import, because these might be colored in a morally dubious manner by our contingent attachments to the communities that lie close at hand. Unless independent argument can be given to substantiate the claim that our obligations toward our fellow citizens are real, and that it is thus to be deplored that our more intimate relationships sometimes blind us to them, whereas our international obligations are somehow less real, so that we have no reason to regret the fact that our national allegiances prevent us from taking on a broader perspective, the argument should tell against our tendency to favor the claims of kin as against those of fellow citizens *and* against the tendency to privilege fellow citizens as against other human beings.

Second, Miller argues in *Principles of Social Justice* that we ought to be wary not only of those intuitions that reflect too great a proximity, but also of those that reflect sectional interests. Criticizing Rawls's method for determining "considered judgements" as too solipsistic, he makes the point that we ought to consider the broader socioeconomic context in which such judgments are made, in order, for example, to winnow out the insidious effect upon our judgment of self-interest.

> Suppose . . . that on some issue better-off people tend to believe p and worse-off people tend to believe not-p; I am better off and I believe p. Suppose also that adherence to belief in p serves the sectional interest of the better off—for instance it helps to justify economic institutions from which they benefit disproportionately.

Taken together, these constitute good grounds for placing rather little confidence in the truth of p. Should I not then be similarly skeptical about my own belief in p?[7]

For p, read "that we have greater obligations toward our fellow citizens," a belief that Miller claims is widespread in affluent countries and one that most assuredly serves as a justification for the persistence of the international economic system from which they benefit enormously, and you have, or so it would seem, an *indictment* of the thesis according to which we have greater obligations toward our fellow nationals.

Miller thus seems in *Principles of Social Justice* to have moved away quite substantially from the Humean metaethics of his earlier work on nationalism. Whereas he argued there that we ought to give credence to people's spontaneous moral judgments and intuitions, he now thinks that we ought to be suspicious of such judgments because they might reflect sectional interest and/or an undue privilege to those who are nearest and dearest. The context in which these points are made in *Principles of Social Justice* makes clear that Miller takes them to tell *for* a kind of impartiality *among* citizens of the same state and *against* partiality for substate units such as the family, the ethnic community, and so forth. But he owes us an account of why the "hermeneutic of suspicion" he now enjoins us to practice vis-à-vis our spontaneous moral judgments should not apply to the belief many of us hold that we owe more to our fellow citizens than we do to the rest of humanity.

I want briefly to bring up a third methodological theme from *Principles of Social Justice* that would seem to have implications subversive of the substantive points that Miller wants to make about the scope of distributive justice. One of the central themes of that work is that there is a strong link between the three apparently mutually exclusive distributive principles that need, desert, and equality represent and different "modes of relationship." But Miller warns against a simplistic reading of his thesis that would have the causal arrows going in one direction only, from mode of relationship to distributive principle. He claims, plausibly, that the choice of a distributive principle can sometimes modify a mode of relationship. "The distributive principle chosen not only *reflects* the character of group relations but also helps to constitute those relations in the future."[8] The point is that modes of relationship are dependent variables. It is not etched in stone that relations between individuals of different types will always necessarily be of one specific *kind* or other. Much will depend upon human *decisions* as to the principles that will underpin these relationships.

Now, this point about the "plasiticity" of human communities seems sensible and sane. But, as we shall soon see, much of the rest of Miller's argument against the possibility of transnational distributive justice rests upon the claim that international community is not the right *kind* of community to sustain institutions and practices of distributive justice. We should in what follows keep Miller's methodological point about the plasticity of communities firmly in mind, for it is possible that Miller's case against international distributive justice rests upon a violation of his own methodological principle.

My point is that the larger methodological pronouncements made by Miller in *Principles of Social Justice* stand in some tension with his denial that principles of distributive justice can apply transnationally. We need an independent account, one which does not simply rely on people's spontaneous judgments and intuitions about the "specialness" of their relationship with their fellow nationals, to explain why it is that nation-states, but not communities spanning more broadly, can be appropriate sites of distributive justice. Let me now consider Miller's attempts at demonstrating this specialness.

II

I want to deal quite briefly with a first argument that Miller has recently put forward to attempt to provide such an independent account. The argument, briefly stated, is that material inequality does not *mean* the same thing when it occurs within the bounds of the nation-state and when it occurs between members of different states. When it occurs "at home," inequality requires a justification. There is a strong prima facie case for the state guaranteeing equally those rights that it has been created to uphold. Lack of equal treatment with respect to those rights betokens lack of equal status. "To treat people unequally would amount to a failure of recognition and respect; it would be to declare that those who receive a smaller quota of advantages are not members in full standing but mere adjuncts."[9] In contrast, when inequality occurs between members of different states, questions of respect and status do not arise, because there is no *presumption* that citizens of different countries ought to be afforded exactly the same bundles of rights, or that the material inequality that obtains between rich and poor raises at least a prima facie ethical concern.

To begin with, I would question whether the psychological facts line up in the manner suggested by Miller's claim. Do members of the poorer countries of Europe or the Americas simply accept that their lesser level of well-being is a function of their different political culture, and that it in no way betokens a difference in status relative to members of more affluent countries? Is it implausible to think that (for example) Mexican workers might form the belief that their impoverished condition relative to workers in other parts of North America is due to the fact that they are part of a continental economic system which treats them as a cheap labor pool, and thus, that they are members in less than full standing of that system? Would they spontaneously put the differences down to morally innocent differences in political culture? I doubt it. Though I cannot marshal the empirical evidence that would substantiate my suspicion that transnational economic inequalities are in fact in a great many cases *experienced* as inequalities of status, I would point out that Miller has not done anything to warrant his view that questions of status are not experienced as arising transnationally.

Now it would of course be open to Miller to claim that the argument from status is in no way grounded in people's subjective *experience* of status differentials. People who believe that the fact that they have lesser life chances relative to others simply by virtue of where they happen to have been born betokens that they are accorded lesser status in the global political and economic system might simply be *wrong*. There may be some *objective* difference that makes it appropriate for people within the same nation-state to experience differences in life chances as marks of lack of status, but inappropriate for transnational differences to be experienced the same way.

What might account for this difference? According to Miller, nation-states are, whereas transnational communities are not, the right *kinds* of communities for interpersonal comparisons of status to be made. That is because they are in Miller's view possessed of three properties, which transnational communities lack. First, their members share an identity *as* citizens of this or that nation-state; second, they are bound together by a shared ethos made up of common understandings and common purposes; and third, an institutional structure exists that allocates rights and resources to members.[10]

Let us assume that we have enough of a handle on the concept of "identity" to agree that members of a nation-state share one.[11] The first point to keep in mind is that national identities are, to a significant degree, artifacts of the institutions of the nation-state. Whether in Europe or in the postcolonial world of Africa and the Americas, modern nation-states at their inception only rarely encompassed fully formed, homogenous national identities. Rather, they had rather deliberately to fashion some degree of cohesion out of a motley of regional identities and a variety of languages and cultures. The point is not that present-day national identities are thereby debased or worthless. As Miller and others rightly have claimed, identities can come to matter a great deal to people despite their somewhat "artificial" origins.[12] Rather, it is that the acknowledgment that national identities were at least in part the result, rather than the cause, of the emergence of those national political and economic institutions which came to be seen as instrumentally necessary[13] involves the recognition that people's political identities are at least in some measure malleable. Political institutions and leaders can therefore seize on this malleability to fashion identities that are congenial to them. Were transnational political institutions to become instrumentally required for reasons analogous to those that gave rise to the nation-state, there is no reason in principle why people's identities might not be refashioned so as to cohere with these new institutions.[14]

More problematically from a moral point of view (and in keeping with the methodological theses which I have culled from Miller's *Principles of Social Justice*), the belief that members of the same nation-state share a morally important identity should be questioned, both because it might prevent us from reaching a proper awareness of our broader responsibilities, and because it serves the self-interested purposes of those who can thereby justify to them-selves their lack of concern for nonmembers. Let me illustrate the latter point with a deliberatively provocative example. One of the most insidious aspects of the apartheid system in South Africa was its homelands policy. Despite the obvious economic and social interpenetration of all segments of South African society, the South African government created a legal fiction whereby black la-borers could be viewed as "foreigners" without legal or political standing in the South African State. White South Africans were thus able to "have their cake and eat it." They benefited from a vast pool of cheap labor of black workers, but were able through the legal fiction of the homelands to deny blacks basic civil rights and material welfare. What's more, they could con-gratulate themselves with the idea that, far from constituting rank exploita-tion, the homelands policy was in fact in line with the principle of national self-determination.[15]

This was clearly a case in which the belief in separate national identities served the purpose of the most well-off members of South African society. What's more, it is likely that most people came to form the belief in separate, morally significant national identities *because* it served their interests to do so. Can we be sure that we in the well-off Western world are not re-creating the apartheid system on a global scale, justifying the banishment of foreigners from the scope of our institutions of distributive justice with the belief that we do not share an identity with them?

The simple fact that the world's population is divided along the lines of na-tional identity is therefore not in and of itself sufficient to justify the refusal to extend principles and institutions of distributive justice transnationally. What about the two other properties mentioned previously that, in Miller's view, dis-tinguish national from transnational communities?

I will postpone my discussion of the "argument from shared meanings" un-til the following section. The third property invoked by Miller as justifying the limitation of distributive justice to national populations consists in their pos-session of appropriate institutional vehicles for the dispensation of distributive justice. Briefly stated, there must, in order for international distributive justice to be conceivable, be institutions allocating resources, and thus affecting the life chances of individuals, and there must be some agency capable of reform-ing these institutions in the manner required by appropriate principles of dis-tributive justice. And though international institutions are clearly evolving both in the scope of issues which fall under their purview and in the extent to which they can enforce international norms, this condition is still clearly sat-isfied to a much greater degree by modern nation-states than it is by interna-tional and transnational institutions.

What moral weight should we give to this fact? Very little, I would claim. We must be very wary indeed of reading substantial ethical conclusions from insti-tutional facts, as these facts can embody significant injustices that we would thereby be legitimizing. To revert again to the example of apartheid South

Africa, we would not have taken very seriously the claim that white South Africans had no responsibilities of distributive justice toward blacks because no institutions existed to administer such justice. Surely, the absence of such institutions was a very serious *symptom* of injustice, rather than a fact on the basis of which standards of justice might be derived. The proper relation of norms to institutions in normative political philosophy should be that norms set constraints for institutions. We must, preinstitutionally, determine where the bounds of justice lie and argue for institutions that produce outcomes within those bounds.

There is evidence, moreover, that Miller accepts this broader methodological point, though he curiously does not see its relevance for discussions of transnational distributive justice. In the discussion of desert contained in *Principles of Social Justice*, Miller insists that we should not conceive of desert as an institutionally defined concept. People do not simply "deserve" whatever falls out of a given institutional order's operations. Rather, Miller claims, the concept of desert must be spelled out preinstitutionally, and it must constrain institutional design and allow for the external criticism of existing institutional orders. "Desert is predominantly a preinstitutional notion. When we invoke it, we are very often assessing the way our institutions work in the light of prior ideas about what constitutes a fitting response to individual performances."[16] Generalize this very plausible point, and a methodological prescription emerges that tells quite decisively against any attempt at deriving too much normative freight out of mere institutional facts.

III

Miller wants us to see that there is something about national communities that makes them particularly fitting contexts for the administration of distributive justice. We have just seen that the first and third properties identified by Miller, which point to the existence of robust national identities and to the presence in nation-states of appropriate institutional structures, do not do any work to justify this claim. What about the second? The claim here is that there is little prospect for transnational distributive justice because there is no transnational consensus on the meaning and worth of the various goods that institutions allocate. How can we come up with transnational norms of distributive justice when people in different societies do not agree on the absolute and relative worth of different goods and resources? To illustrate with one of Miller's examples, rich arable land particularly suited to the cultivation of vines means something completely different for a wine-drinking culture and for a culture in which the consumption of alcohol is proscribed for religious reasons.[17] How could a transnational system of distributive justice determine if a potentially wine-growing country was resource-rich or resource-poor? And to invoke an example of Michael Walzer's, whose theory of complex equality is clearly the principal inspiration for Miller's views on these issues, different cultures rank the care of bodies and the care of souls differently. How could they come to an agreement as to the proportion of resources that ought to be allocated to (physical) health care?[18] The point is that different societies will value different goods differently, and what's more, they will bring differing distributive criteria to bear on the question of how these goods ought to be distributed. They will moreover, according to Miller, have different understandings of distributive criteria such as desert.[19] In such a context, how could the project of transnational distributive justice ever get off the ground?

Two responses seem warranted here. The first is that Miller (and Walzer) clearly overestimate the extent to which modern nation-states are characterized by the kind of "shared understandings" upon which the foregoing argument depends. Let me focus on the claim that there is some degree of consensus over the meaning and import of the *goods* that national systems of distribution must allocate. It seems plainly belied, to invoke just one kind of example, by the experience of countries with regionally based industries. In Canada, for example, entire "forms of life" have emerged out of industries concerned with the extraction of various natural resources. For inhabitants of fishing villages of Newfoundland, of the farmlands of the Prairies, or of the logging villages of British Columbia, the resources that they harvest represent more than just fungible goods, the full value of which might be fully expressed in monetary terms or traded off against other goods. Rather, they are laden with meaning and symbolic value, as befits resources around which a community has organized its life. The situation with respect to these resources is completely different, say, for urban dwellers within the same country. It is much more likely that they will have a more pragmatic dollars and cents approach to these resources. This fact becomes apparent when the industries in question are placed under pressure, either (to refer again to the Canadian context) because of environmental concerns, because of the resolution of land disputes with aboriginal communities, because of sudden drops in demand for certain resources (e.g., asbestos, coal, slate), because of the terms of economic treaties (such as NAFTA) which might make the support Canada provides to seasonal industries illegal, or because of other factors. Whereas "locals" tend to bemoan the disappearance of a way of life and accept only with great difficulty that their communities be geared toward new economic activities, citizens of other parts of the country, or of cities, will evaluate the costs and benefits of maintaining the industry in question, radically discounting the symbolic import of these resources and their centrality to the way of life of local communities. Recent Canadian history has been replete with example of such disparities of evaluation, and my guess is that the same can be said about regional industries elsewhere, such as coal mining in Great Britain and farming in the United States. Examples such as these reveal that national communities are often bitterly divided over the correct meaning to ascribe to different kinds of resources and of the relative weight they ought to be granted in the cost-benefit analyses and assessment of trade-offs, which necessarily go into the making of the national budget of even a moderately complex national society.[20]

Miller might respond to this that his point was not to claim that debates about distributive justice can only *get off the ground* when people antecedently agree about the right way to evaluate a set of goods, but rather that such debates must ultimately *give rise* to such shared understandings. In other words, Miller might be claiming that democratic deliberation must have as one of its *telos* that members of a national community together arrive at a way of understanding the goods that they must allocate.[21] His thesis would therefore not depend upon the implausible claim, examined previously, that national communities might be marked by preexisting normative agreements. The argument from shared meanings would therefore not be that distributive justice requires *preexisting* shared meanings, and that only national communities have them, but rather that distributive justice requires debate and deliberation *giving rise* to shared meanings, and that such debate and deliberation can only, or should only, occur within national communities.

I will set aside possible interpretations of this (reconfigured) argument from shared meanings that point to the technical difficulties associated with the establishment of democratic institutions in mass societies. Prudent institutional design has already been employed in the history of democratic nation-states in order to overcome difficulties related to size, and there is no reason to think that it could not help to offset difficulties which transnational democratic institutions would have to face. And in any case, as Robert Dahl has quite effectively shown, the ideal of a truly deliberative democracy, in which citizens participate as equals in deliberation, is a mirage. He calculates, for example, that a meeting would have to go on for 208 eight-hour days in order for every citizen of a small town of 10,000 to have a say of ten minutes on a single issue![22] So, if the practical objection to large-scale, transnational democratic deliberation is that it would extend the bounds of democracy too broadly to allow for meaningful participation, then most modern nation-state democracies are *already* too vast for "real" democracy.

I will concentrate instead on the normative construal of the reconfigured argument from shared meanings. It claims that democratic deliberation *ought not* to extend beyond the bounds of the nation-state, because if it did, it would offend against the value of *national self-determination*.

Miller suggests two considerations to sustain his claim that the value of national self-determination has independent force relative to the claims of global justice. The first analogizes national self-determination to individual autonomy. "Just as individual people want to be able to shape their circumstances to suit their aims and ambitions, so groups want to be able to decide how to organize their internal affairs and to dispose of their resources."[23] And the second points to the range of phenomena that falls under the effective control of an individual agent when she combines her forces with that of her fellow citizens. "The group as a whole can achieve much more than I as an individual can achieve, so by belonging I have a smaller say over a bigger range of issues than I have as a private person."[24]

Neither one of these considerations can go very far in establishing the value of national self-determination. Putting aside the question of its hypostatization of the nation as a kind of individual agent writ large, the first consideration gives us no reason to privilege the nation as against all other groups, be they sub- or supranational, that might want to exercise control over their internal affairs. (Miller does mention the fact that people tend to *identify* with their nation, but as we have already seen, it would be wrong to view such attachments as some kind of law given to which moral theory should simply adapt.) What's more, even if we were to accept for the sake of argument that nations are particularly important collective agents, the argument limiting democratic deliberation to nation-states, whatever the material impact on citizens of other societies, does not flow as easily as Miller seems to assume. Indeed, moral theories do not tend to accord value to exercises of individual autonomy that, say, violate the harm principle, and so there is no reason to think that *national* autonomy should impose constraints upon global distributive justice, rather than the other way around.

Moreover, in the context of an increasingly globalized economy, the second consideration mooted by Miller actually seems to me to argue *against* limiting democratic deliberation about distributive justice to the nation-state. It has become a truism that the interdependency of national economies and the transnational nature of international capital have combined to reduce the range of economic and fiscal issues over which nation-states can effectively exercise control. If economic and financial processes are to be effectively "steered" by democratic political forces, it will have to be by the creation of political institutions operating at the same transnational or international level that modern-day financiers and industrialists operate today. So, if one of the points of national self-determination is to give individual citizens a share in making decisions over a greater range of issues affecting their well-being, then surely the conclusion must be that we must democratize transnational institutions, or make them answerable to democratic pressures. In the present context, limiting democratic debate about distributive justice to the arena of the nation-state *violates* the requirement set by Miller, to the effect that our political institutions must, to as great a degree as possible, extend the political "reach" of ordinary citizens.[25]

It is hard to see how either of the considerations raised by Miller might be mobilized to mount a successful defense of national economic self-determination against the claims of global justice. Are there better arguments for national self-determination than those suggested by Miller? I don't think that the value of national self-determination can be assessed independently of the specific contexts in which claims of national self-determination are made. Clearly, it performed a considerable role in decolonization struggles and is still today invoked by national minorities seeking to acquire powers of self-government within the context of larger, multination states. But it can also be invoked in order to close borders to immigrants and refugees, to shirk international obligations, and to enact repressive legislation. This "in-built ambivalence" of the concept of national self-determination has been noted by Antonio Cassese: "In the hands of would-be States, self-determination is the key to opening the door and entering into that coveted club of statehood. For existing States, self-determination is the key for locking the door against the undesirable from within and outside the realm."[26] The point is that national self-determination cannot simply be invoked as a value constraining the pursuit of global justice. On the contrary, its value has to be determined on a case-by-case basis in the particular contexts in which it is invoked. And its value is questionable when it is used by rich countries to justify immunizing their own economic systems from broader claims of justice.[27]

IV

We have seen thus far that the limitation of the scope of the principles and institutions of distributive justice to the citizens of nation-states cannot be justified by appeal to intuition and sentiment, by reference to the specialness of national communities, or by the invocation of the independent value of national self-determination.

One final move that is open to Miller is, as it were, to meet the defender of transnational distributive justice on her own ground and to claim that the setting up of institutions of distributive justice on a transnational scale that would be empowered, among other things, to redistribute resources between richer and poorer individuals, wherever they happen to live, would itself violate norms of distributive justice. The claim would be that it is actually *unfair* to transfer resources in a manner that might be suggested by abstract principles of global justice.

Miller develops this argument in "Justice and Global Inequality" with the parable of two hypothetical societies, "Ecologia" and "Affluenza." The first adopts policies of conservation and sustainable development, and its citizens thereby over time come to enjoy a higher per capita share of global resources than those of Affluenza, who, having pursued wasteful short-term consumerist policies, end up relatively resource poor, having squandered their resources in an imprudent manner. Miller's argument is that transferring resources from Ecologians to Affluenzians would give rise to a structure of perverse incentives, as there would in such a system of transfer be nothing to gain from adopting prudent national economic policies. What's more, it would be *unfair*. Ecologians should be allowed to derive long-term benefit from their short-term sacrifices. "It is wrong to frustrate this achievement by transferring resources to people who have made no such sacrifices."[28]

Miller is clearly applying the classic "expensive tastes" argument to the international sphere.[29] The argument in a nutshell is that agents, be they individual or collective, should not in a just society expect to be compensated when they knowingly enact policies through which they use up significant proportions of their allotment of resources for questionable return. If Affluenzians consistently voted for political parties that enacted wasteful, imprudent policies, then they should accept the consequences of so doing and not expect to be baled out by frugal, self-denying Ecologians.

What is the moral of this story as far as international justice is concerned? It is clearly that, to the extent that some of the poverty in the world today results from the imprudent decisions taken by political leaders in some societies, it is not unjust. In order for the fable to have relevance for the world we find ourselves in, we would need to be able to see the wasteful, imprudent, inefficient, and thus poverty-creating political cultures of the world as so many "expensive tastes."

But this is highly problematic. People can simply not be held responsible for their political cultures in the same way that individuals can be held responsible for their tastes and preferences. Among other things, the political cultures which characterize different societies reflect their history of interaction with other societies. In the world today, poverty is concentrated in the previously colonized world. The political cultures of the states in the poorest regions of the globe are creations of interaction with colonizers most obviously in that these states are in large measure *creations* of colonization. The model of the European state was in large measure imposed upon the colonized world, and borders were drawn that reflected the interests of Europeans rather than indigenous logic. Much civil strife has resulted from such impositions, and it has clearly prevented such societies from turning their attention to the creation of wealth.

What's more, the political choices made within such societies by political leaders clearly reflect the impact of the colonial period. It may very well be the case that, from a cool, dispassionate point of view, it would have made more sense for, say, African states to have mimicked the liberal-democratic political systems and market economic models of the West. But in the period immediately following colonization, decisions were understandably not being made from such a cool, detached perspective. To revert to the example of African political cultures discussed by Miller, it seems wildly implausible to claim that the ill-advised policies and corrupt political cultures that emerged from decolonization reflected some set of decisions adopted "in a cool hour" by African citizens. Numerous studies make plain that they are causally related to the colonial period itself.[30] For example, why would African leaders trust markets, when markets had been used against them so savagely during the colonial period? Miller's argument is clearly premised upon a wildly voluntaristic and idealistic conception of the formation of political cultures. Such cultures form not as a result of calm, rational reflection, but as a reaction to specific political and economic contexts. Many of the poorest countries of the world are former colonies, and their political cultures still bear the imprint of colonialism. It would be the height of injustice for the nations that benefited from colonialism to point to the inefficient and corrupt political cultures that colonialism wrought as proof that the peoples of those countries have only themselves to blame for their suffering!

The claim that political cultures are the main determinant of a country's economic situation cannot therefore be used in an argument for the broader claim that global inequality is a result of the choices made by individuals, because, as we have seen, political cultures are in large measure part of the circumstances of individuals rather than a reflection of their choices. There are, moreover, independent reasons to deny this claim. In an interdependent economic world, national economies are often hostages to decisions made elsewhere, decisions which in their intent and impact fall well short of outright exploitation.[31] It is said that when Alan Greenspan sneezes, the whole world catches a cold. The kernel of truth in this witticism is of course that the fiscal decisions of the world's most powerful economies can have catastrophic ripple effects through smaller national economies. We could multiply ad infinitum the various ways, large and small, in which decisions (including, for example, seemingly trivial consumer decisions) taken at one corner of the globe can have repercussions in other parts. Given the interdependence of the world's economies, it seems simplistic to draw too much of a connection between a society's political culture and its overall level of economic well-being.

Thus, even if we accept that Ecologians owe nothing as a matter of justice to Affluenzians, this should not lead us to conclude that rich countries in the real world owe nothing to poorer countries. A disproportionate number of the latter have the political cultures they have because of the exploitative and oppressive relations Europeans had with societies in the colonized world over the entire course of the only recently ended colonial period.

V

I have canvassed what I take to be David Miller's central arguments against the desirability of transnational norms and institutions of distributive justice, and found them wanting. Let me conclude briefly by highlighting a certain number of themes from the earlier sections of this chapter, in order to mount a defense of such norms and institutions grounded in what I take to be impeccably Millerian ideas.

Arguing for transnational justice might seem utopian in the pejorative sense of the term.[32] Indeed, the kinds of institutions that would have to be in place in order for a full system of transnational justice to be realized do not presently exist.[33] There would be significant motivational problems to getting people to accept that their hard-earned wages might be taxed for the benefit of strangers living at the ends of the earth. Clearly, we do not conceive of ourselves as inhabiting the same community as those people who are separated from us by great geographical, cultural, religious, and linguistic distances.

What I want to claim is that Miller provides us with ways in which to counter this pessimism about the possibility of international distributive justice. As I have already noted, and as I want to make salient here, he argues in *Principles of Social Justice* for a set of methodological prescriptions which, taken together, defuse the threat suggested by the foregoing paragraph. Now Miller puts forward these prescriptions as arguing for impartiality among citizens within already-existing nation-states, but it is hard to see how he can block the natural transnational drift of these prescriptions.

The methodological principles that I have culled from Miller's work are the following:

The distorting impact of intimacy. Miller warns us that our feelings and sentiments are most naturally and immediately engaged by those who are closest to us, both geographically and in terms of personal intimacy. But these feelings do not of themselves settle the question of our moral obligations. We must be wary of judgments formed on the basis of such feelings, moreover, because they risk blinding us to our broader, but less intensely felt, obligations.[34]

The distorting impact of self-interest. We have a tendency toward self-deception in the formation of our moral judgments. That is, we tend sometimes to believe that certain principles are true, not on the basis of a dispassionate assessment of the evidence and arguments, but rather because they serve our self-interest. We ought to be wary of those judgments that are held principally by those who benefit from them and deny principally by those upon whom these principles bear hard.[35]

The principle of the principle-dependence of community. Our conception of the kind of relationship in which we stand to other individuals does not merely reflect "brute facts" about these relationships. Rather, they are at least in part artifacts of the distributive principles we decide to enact in relation to these people.[36]

The principle of the institutional independence of distributive principles. Moral argument, rather than institutional fact, should determine the principles our institutions of distributive justice instantiate. We need to view principles of distributive justice as independent constraints upon the design of such institutions. They cannot simply be read off the operation of those institutions as we happen to find them.[37]

Taken together these principles represent a powerful set of tools against conservatism and complacency in the area of distributive justice. The first principle warns us that our obligations might very well span more broadly than our feelings might indicate. Though we may feel more of an obligation toward our families and loved ones, we should not allow this to blind us to our obligations toward our *concitoyens*. And by parity of reasoning, though we may feel a greater sense of obligation toward our *concitoyens*, we should not allow this to blind us from the obligations we might have toward humanity as a whole. The second principle puts even greater pressure on the belief we might have that we have only derivative or residual obligations toward humanity as a whole. Indeed, such a belief serves the interests of those who inhabit the richest countries in the world. Recognition of broader obligations would involve significant curtailments of present-day privileges. There is therefore a powerful incentive to be self-deceptive with respect to the scope of our obligations.

The third principle suggests that our lack of a sense of community with inhabitants of other countries is at least as much an artifact as it is a cause of our having chosen not to enact principles of distributive justice to regulate our relations with them. We cannot infer from the fact that no norms and institutions of distributive justice presently exist that they *ought* not to exist. As the principle of the institutional independence of distributive principles tells us, we must on independent ethical ground determine what principles ought to be enacted to regulate our relations, rather than simply assuming that the present (lack of) institutional order gives us access to the right principles. And I take it that the principle of the distorting impact of intimacy establishes at least a prima facie case that, whatever these principles should be, they ought to extend globally.

I think that this argument-sketch has a lot going for it. I want to stress in any case that it has been built on the basis of impeccably Millerian principles. Is David Miller a globalist *malgré lui*?

NOTES

I wish to thank David Miller, Daniel Bell, and Avner de-Shalit for their kind invitation to take part in the colloquium devoted to David's work and to the volume that grew out of it. Thanks are moreover due to Daniel Bell for his extensive written comments.

1. The philosopher who has articulated this position with the greatest care is Thomas Pogge. See, most recently, his "Priorities of Global Justice," *Metaphilosophy* 32 (2001).

2. David Miller, "In Defence of Nationality," in Miller, *Citizenship and National Identity* (Oxford: Blackwell, 2000), 25.

3. David Miller, *On Nationality* (Oxford: Oxford University Press, 1995), 65.

4. Miller, *Citizenship*, 25.

5. See my "National Partiality: Confronting the Intuitions," *The Monist* 82 (1999).

6. David Miller, *Principles of Social Justice* (Cambridge, Mass.: Harvard University Press, 1999), 40.

7. Miller, *Principles*, 55.

8. Miller, *Principles*, 65.

9. David Miller, "Justice and Global Inequality," in *Inequality, Globalization, and World Politics*, ed. A. Hurrell and N. Woods (Oxford: Oxford University Press, 1999), 189.

10. Miller, "Justice and Global Inequality," 190.

11. I question this assumption in a pair of forthcoming articles: "Les identités sont-elles dangereuses pour la démocratie?" in *Repères en mutation: Identité et citoyenneté dans le Québec contemporain*, ed. J. Maclure and A. Gagnon (Montreal: Éditions Québec-Amérique, 2001) 227–50; and "Groups, Identities and Democracy," *Annual Review of Political Science*, forthcoming.

12. See David Miller, *Citizenship*, 165: "Whatever their ultimate origins, national identities once created are remarkably tenacious, and often remarkably resistant to being reshaped to fit existing political boundaries." See also John Rawls, *The Law of Peoples* (Cambridge, Mass.: Harvard University Press, 1999).

13. I remain agnostic as to which of the various "stories" about the emergence of the nation-state ought to be accepted. For two leading accounts, see Ernest Gellner, *Nations and Nationalism* (Cambridge: Cambridge University Press, 1983); and Liah Greenfield, *Nationalism: Five Roads to Modernity* (Cambridge, Mass.: Harvard University Press, 1992). What matters to my account is that instrumental, "modernist" accounts as a class be more plausible than "primordialist" ones. For a remarkably exhaustive account of the literature, and of the debate between modernists and primordialists on the issue of the emergence of nations, see Michel Seymour, "Questioning the Ethnic/Civic Dichotomy," in *Rethinking Nationalism; Canadian Journal of Philosophy Supplementary* 22 ed., J. Couture, K. Nielsen, and M. Seymour.

14. I develop this point in more detail in "Prospects for Transnational Citizenship," in *Ethics and International Affairs* 15 (2001).

15. On the Bantustan policy see *inter alia* Richard Abel, *Politics by Other Means: Law in the Struggle against Apartheid, 1980–1994* (London: Routledge, 1995); Steve Biko, "Let's Talk about Bantustans," in Biko, *I Write What I Like* (London: 1978), 80–86.

16. Miller, *Principles*, 142.

17. David Miller, "Justice and Global Inequality," 192.

18. The example is from Michael Walzer, *Thick and Thin: Moral Argument at Home and Abroad* (South Bend: University of Notre Dame Press, 1994). For the *locus classicus* for the view that distributive justice ought to take its cue from the shared understandings latent in a given society's political culture, see his *Spheres of Justice* (New York: Basic Books, 1983). For Miller's qualified endorsement of Walzer's theory, see David Miller, "Complex Equality," in *Pluralism, Justice, and Equality*, ed. David Miller and Michael Walzer (Oxford: Oxford University Press, 1995).

19. See Miller, *Citizenship*, 168–169.

20. For an account of differing perceptions of the fishing industry, see David Griffith, *The Estuary's Gift: An Atlantic Coast Cultural Biography* (Pennsylvania State University Press, 1999). One of the most compelling accounts of national divisions in the understanding of how specific resources are central to the lives of local communities is George Orwell's *The Road to Wigan Pier* (New York: Harvest Books, 1973).

21. This interpretation is reinforced by passages from *On Nationality* where Miller speaks of the indeterminacy of national public cultures and of the obligations that such cultures encompass. He speaks of obligations of material aid between citizens as flowing "from a shared public culture which results from rational deliberation over time about what it means to belong to the nation in question." See Miller, *On Nationality*, 70.

22. Robert Dahl, *On Democracy* (New Haven, Conn.: Yale University Press, 1998).

23. Miller, *Citizenship*, 164.

24. Miller, *Citizenship*, 164.

25. At the end of *Principles*, Miller does discuss the impact of globalization upon the nation-state's ability to continue to administer social justice. He concludes that even in the context of a globalized economy, there might be instrumental reasons for firms to continue to support nationally based institutions of distributive justice (though he fears that need-based claims, as opposed to merit-based or citizenship-based ones, might fall by the wayside). He does not consider the possibility that transnational institutions might in the context of a globalized economy more effectively dispense justice. See Miller, *Principles*, 254–260.

26. Antonio Cassese, *Self-Determination of Peoples: A Legal Reappraisal* (Cambridge: Cambridge University Press, 1995), 6.

27. In the same way, President George W. Bush's invocation of American national self-determination—"The American way of life is not negotiable"—rings hollow when it is used to justify the United States' refusal to ratify the Kyoto protocols on climate change.

28. David Miller, "Justice and Global Inequality," 194.

29. The *locus classicus* of this argument is Ronald Dworkin's "What Is Equality?" pt. 1 and 2, most recently reprinted in his *Sovereign Virtue: The Theory and Practice of Equality* (Cambridge, Mass.: Harvard University Press, 2000).

30. See, for example, M. Mamdani, *Citizen and Subject, Decentralized Despotism, and the Legacy of Late Colonialism* (Princeton, N.J: Princeton University Press, 1996).

31. Miller believes that well-off nations have an obligation not to *exploit* poorer ones. See "Justice and Global Inequality," 204–209, and *Citizenship,* 175–176. My point here, however, is that massive inequalities can result in the world economy from patterns of interaction that involve neither exploitation on the part of the rich nor bad economic decisions on the part of the poor.

32. For an attempt to distinguish legitimate and illegitimate utopian arguments, see Thomas Nagel, *Equality and Partiality* (Oxford: Oxford University Press, 1991), ch. 2.

33. For an argument to the effect that international distributive justice would not require significant institutional change, see Thomas Pogge, "An Egalitarian Law of Peoples," *Philosophy and Public Affairs* 23 (1994).

34. Miller, *Principles,* 40.

35. Miller, *Principles,* 55.

36. Miller, *Principles,* 65.

37. Miller, *Principles,* 142.

15

Entitlements, Obligations, and Distributive Justice
The Global Level

Simon Caney

This chapter examines David Miller's analysis of global justice. Much has been written about whether there are global principles of distributive justice and, if there are, what they specify. For some writers, including realists like Hans Morgenthau, the idea that states are under obligations of distributive justice to aid foreigners is utopian and unrealistic.[1] For others, global ideals of distributive justice are unattractive because they do not show adequate respect to the sovereignty of the state. A good example of this position is Terry Nardin's *Law, Morality and the Relations of States*.[2] Others, however, including Charles Beitz, Brian Barry, Onora O'Neill, and Thomas Pogge, adopt a cosmopolitan position, contending that we should adopt global principles of distributive justice.[3]

My aim in this chapter is to examine Miller's contribution to this debate.[4] He provides a characteristically rich and sophisticated treatment of the distributive principles that should govern global politics. He outlines both a critique of alternative conceptions of distributive justice and a defense of his own distinctive view. This chapter concentrates on three aspects of Miller's account of global justice. Section I focuses primarily on Miller's critique of alternative conceptions of global justice and in particular his claim that there can be no global comparative principles of distributive justice. Section II outlines and evaluates Miller's own positive account of global justice and in particular his defense of three principles of global justice. I then turn from Miller's account of people's entitlements (as specified by global principles of distributive justice) to his account of people's duties. Section III thus analyzes Miller's claim that the duty to secure people's global entitlements should be attributed to fellow nationals or citizens.

I

Let me begin by considering Miller's critique of certain approaches to global justice. Following Joel Feinberg, Miller distinguishes between noncomparative and comparative principles of distributive justice.[5] The former stipulate some fixed amount to which persons are entitled, and whether justice is served for a person does not depend on how well he or she does in comparison with other people. People's entitlements can be defined without reference to other people's entitlements. Comparative principles of distributive justice, by contrast, make reference to other peoples' conditions. To give one obvious example, egalitarian principles are comparative principles of distributive justice.

A

Employing this distinction Miller then makes three distinct claims. These can be stated as follows:

1. Nationalist-specific principle. Nations are, as a general rule, the largest form of association within which comparative principles of distributive justice apply.
2. Anti-cosmopolitan-specific principle. Comparative principles of distributive justice do not apply at the global level.
3. General principle. Comparative principles of distributive justice only apply within associations.

Before proceeding further, let me make good these exegetical claims, examining each in turn.

B

(1) is deliberately worded cautiously. Miller does not, for example, claim that there are no transnational situations within which comparative principles of distributive justice apply: the words "as a general rule" are therefore essential.[6] His view, as I understand it, is that the largest context within which comparative principles normally apply is the nation.[7] Second, Miller does not deny that comparative principles apply within subnational institutions, like families or businesses or university departments.[8]

Let us turn now to (2).[9] The relations between (1) and (2) are not straightforward. Note, for example, that one may deny (1) but affirm (2): someone might, for example, think that comparative principles apply at a transnational level (like the European community) while denying that comparative principles apply at the global level. One might also affirm (1) but deny (2). This arises because (1) allows that there might, in exceptional circumstances, be transnational comparative principles and hence is open to the possibility that there might, in exceptional circumstances, be a global comparative principle of distributive justice (a possibility denied by [2]). (Consider, for example, a global scheme like the World Cup. A proponent of [1] can allow that it makes sense to talk of the best football team in the world.) Setting aside such relatively insubstantial matters, however, it is of course true that (1) broadly supports (2). Miller's view, as I interpret it, is that (1) only allows there to be global comparative principles for relatively trivial phenomena—like prizes—and does not mean it to allow there to be comparative principles of distributive justice dictating the distribution of income, wealth, and opportunities to ordinary men and women in their everyday lives. I shall, for this reason, hereafter set aside the exceptional global comparative principles that (1) allows and write as if (1) entails (2).

(2), if true, is an important finding because several important theories of justice affirm global comparative principles. Hillel Steiner (and before him Brian Barry) has defended global equality of natural resources.[10] In this volume, Cecile Fabre also defends global egalitarianism, defending the idea of global equal access to advantage.[11]

Underpinning (1) and (2) is the general principle articulated by (3). Miller affirms (3) in a number of places. For example, in "The Limits of Cosmopolitan Justice," he writes:

> In order for comparative judgements of justice to have force, they must apply to persons who are connected together in some way, for instance by belonging to the same community or association. Once a common membership is established, it makes sense to ask whether individual members are enjoying their fair share of advantages (or carrying their fair share of burdens) in comparison to other members. In the absence of such a common membership, on the other hand, only noncomparative questions of justice arise. In an encounter with a stranger from another community, there are certain things I may not do—I may not injure him or steal his property—and certain things that I must do—if he is ill or in pain I must do what I can to help him—but it makes no sense for either of us to try to apply comparative principles—for instance to insist on equality in some respect.[12]

This, note, says not just that comparative principles apply within "associations": it makes the strong claim that comparative principles only apply within associations. The same strong claim is also affirmed in *Principles of Social Justice*. Miller writes that in applying principles of distributive justice,

> we have to assume *a bounded society* with a determinate membership, forming a universe of distribution whose present fairness or unfairness different theories of justice try to demonstrate. *This assumption is most obviously needed when the principles of justice we apply are comparative in form*—that is, they concern the relative shares of advantages or disadvantages accruing to different groups of people. Is it fair that skilled workers should earn higher wages than unskilled workers? Is it fair that women should perform more domestic labor than men? In asking questions such as these we presuppose that the groups in question belong to a single universe of distribution. (emphasis added)[13]

The background of a "bounded society" is thus "needed" (that is, necessary) for "principles of justice [which] are comparative in form."

We should note one complication to Miller's affirmation of (3). In his discussion of equality in chapter 11 of *Principles of Social Justice*, Miller contrasts three ways in which one might argue that justice mandates an equal distribution. Justice demands equality, says Miller, when (a) there is an object to which no one has a special entitlement (on grounds of need or desert).[14] It also demands equality when (b) there is uncertainty about likely outcomes; here, it is appropriate to grant everyone equal entitlements.[15] Third, justice demands equality when (c) people belong to particular social groups: "[T]here are certain social groups whose members are entitled to equal treatment by virtue of membership."[16] This might lead someone to argue as follows: [I]f Miller is to maintain the distinction between the first two cases and the third, he must claim that justice can mandate equality between people even if they are not members of the same association. Otherwise, the first two cases are not distinct from the third. Miller must, then, reject (3) and must allow that there can be comparative principles of distributive justice outside of an association.

This reasoning is not, however, necessarily compelling. Miller can make two different responses. The key to the first is to distinguish between different types of association. Miller *might* be arguing that all comparative principles apply within some association (where the latter is defined in a broad sense) and hence all three cases where justice demands equality presuppose an association (broadly defined). He might, however, also be arguing that equality follows directly from certain specific associations, that is, not just any old association but an association with some extra specific features (an association narrowly defined). In this way Miller can *both* affirm that comparative principles apply only within associations (the broad conception) *and* maintain his distinction between those egalitarian principles that are entailed by a specific association (the narrow conception) and those that are not. That is the first response.

The second is simply to revise (3) to state that comparative principles only apply within associations but to add two exceptions (namely positions [a] and [b]). We would thus have (3*) revised general principle: comparative principles only apply within associations except when either (a) or (b) apply, in which case equality, a comparative principle, applies.

I will not arbitrate between either response and nothing that follows rests on which of the two we adopt. For simplicity's sake I will use (3).

C

Having outlined Miller's position, I wish to consider its plausibility and want, in what follows, to challenge each of the preceding three claims. Comparative principles apply at the transnational (but subglobal) level (and hence [1] is false). They also apply at the global level (and hence [1] and [2] are false). Claim (3)—that is, the claim that comparative principles of distributive justice only apply within associations—is also false, I want to argue, if we work with Miller's account of the sort of associations to which comparative principles apply. I also want (more tentatively) to suggest that (3) is also false no matter what account of an association one adopts, since we have some reason to think that comparative principles can apply to persons who are not members of an association (on any plausible definition of an association).

D

Prior to arguing for these claims, I want to note an important unclarity in Miller's treatment of comparative justice. The unclarity concerns the nature of the association to which comparative principles apply. Miller's wording is vague and it is difficult to discern the properties and morally relevant features of the associations to which comparative principles apply. Consider the following descriptions that Miller employs when affirming the context within which comparative principles operate. The latter apply to

"persons who are connected together in some way, for instance by belonging to the same community or association"[17]
"a common membership"[18]
"a bounded society with a determinate membership, forming a universe of distribution"[19]
"a connected body of people who form the universe of distribution"[20]
"a social universe within which distributions can be judged fair or unfair"[21]
"bounded communities"[22]

It is far from clear what properties these "associations" or "groups" have such that it is appropriate to say that comparative principles can be applied.[23]

Given the general tenor of Miller's work and his emphasis on *social* justice and *nationality* I think that his work rests upon what one might call a communitarian, or social, conception of an association. As I shall use this term, a communitarian, or social, conception comprises (a) an "identity" component (the members identify with one another), (b) a "cultural" component (they share some common values), and (c) a "motivational" component (they are more willing to bear burdens for their fellow members than they are for non-members).[24] This model, I believe, coheres best with the terms Miller uses—invocations of community are frequent and Miller objects to global comparative principles of distributive justice in one place on the grounds that there is no "world community."[25] Comparative principles of distributive justice, he says, obtain where there is a "common identity and sense of belonging to a group."[26] One might add, moreover, that the communitarian conception is needed if Miller is to sustain the nationalist claim affirmed by (1). For example, defining an association in purely economic terms will not yield (1) given suprastate and global economic interdependence.[27] The communitarian conception thus coheres best with Miller's overall political theory. In what follows, I shall then tentatively assume that when Miller claims that comparative principles only apply in associations, he means that they apply only in communities.

E

Let us now begin the evaluation of Miller's claims, starting with (1). This, recall, maintains that nations are, as a general rule, the largest form of association within which comparative principles of distributive justice apply. (1) is, I believe, contradicted by a number of persuasive counterexamples. Consider, for example, the following examples.

Example 1: The common agricultural policy. This policy dictates how various burdens (taxes) and benefits (quotas, compensation, and subsidies) are distributed among the member countries of the European community. It represents a paradigmatic case of comparative justice since it is concerned with questions such as "how much should each member state (and their members) pay when compared to other members?" "how much may the farmers of one country be subsidized?" and "how much is it fair to ask people of another country to bear the cost?"

Example 2: The common fisheries policy. Again this is a straightforward case of comparative justice since the policy determines comparative questions concerning the proportion of the resources to which members are entitled. It raises questions about how the proportions are to be identified and justified. In other words comparative decisions are made about what size of the pie members are entitled to and what distributive criteria should be applied.

Example 3: International institutions and humanitarian intervention. Comparative questions arise when we consider international institutions like the United Nations or World Bank or IMF. These require funding and thus comparative questions arise about how much each member should pay. The same sort of questions arise when we consider legitimate humanitarian interventions (assuming that there are some). Who should supply food, resources, and military aid and on what basis? One common strand of American realist work maintains, for example, that the United States is being asked to do more than its fair share and that it should not be required to be the world's police officer.

Example 4: Environmental policy. What I have in mind here are environmental bads that affect more than one country. (For simplicity's sake, let us consider those bads that are natural disasters and are not brought about by a specific state or group of people.) Comparative questions arise here about who should bear the cost and on what basis. Should it be equal amount per person? Equal amount per state? Should payment reflect ability to pay? Should payment reflect the degree of harm it inflicts (and what if different people have different attitudes to the physical effects)? It is hard to think of an adequate treatment that does not address these questions and which therefore does not have a comparative character to it.[28]

Example 5: Refugees. Consider the aftermath of natural disasters or repression or interventions: frequently these result in mass emigration and questions then arise as to how refugees should, as it were, be distributed. In Britain, for example, comparison was made of the meager proportion of refugees from Kosovo that Britain admitted as compared, say, with Germany. The suggestion, in other words, is that countries should take their *fair share* of refugees.

The examples could go on. The preceding, however, suffice to bring out several important points that I now wish to identify. First they establish that (1) is incorrect. The phenomena referred to previously are sufficiently common and also sufficiently important not to be dismissed as exceptional phenomena and constitute counterexamples to the claim that comparative principles do not apply to transnational contexts.

They also cast doubt on Miller's general principle as articulated by (3). We can perhaps retain the claim that comparative principles apply in associations but only if we abandon Miller's conception of an association. It is true that most (perhaps all) of the preceding examples ascribe comparative principles in contexts in which there is an association but none of them correspond to the communitarian conception of an association that I suggested Miller invokes. Recall, the three features normally associated with a community—identification, cultural commonality, and motivation. Consider now the examples: examples 1 and 2 refer to comparative principles that arise within the association that is the European community. It is far from clear, though, whether this meets Miller's ideal of the sort of context in which comparative principles arise. It does not score well on the identification index (its members do not think of themselves as Europeans); cultural commonality is very thin if nonexistent; and so is the motivational commitment.[29] In short it is difficult to think of the European community as a *community*. The same point is borne out by example 3: comparative principles do apply within institutions like the UN. Given, however, the heterogeneous nature of the UN—to which, we should note, countries as diverse as the United States, China, Russia, Iraq, Saudi Arabia, and Germany belong—there is no conceivable way in which one could say that the members are socially integrated. Nor is it plausible to say that the UN possesses the identity and motivational features of a community. Or take example 4: we have no reason to think that those afflicted with a common environmental problem have anything in common bar their vulnerability to this problem. In short, while it *may* be plausible to say that all of the examples listed rely, in some sense, on there being an association of some kind, they do not rely on (and are incompatible with) the social conception of an association.[30] In short each shows that comparative principles can and do apply when community is absent. Comparative principles, thus, apply outside of a "community" or a "bounded society" or "bounded communities."[31] (3) is thus suspect (as, indeed, is [2], which rests on it).

F

Let us now consider Miller's general principle (3) in more depth. Why does Miller think we should accept it? Miller's reasoning, I take it, is that correct political principles should follow people's intuitions closely *and* that people's intuitions are that comparative principles apply to the members of groups.[32] On Miller's view, then, our intuitions are that "comparative judgements of justice" should not be invoked except in communal contexts.[33] Our intuitions do not support supracommunal comparative principles.

How might one respond to these claims? Let me make three points.

a. First, as I have argued previously, I think that the examples in I.E cast doubt on the model of an association that Miller's argument employs. Additional examples (that do not invoke transnational phenomena), I believe, cast even more doubt on (3). Consider, for example, the following:
A country contains a slave population that lives with and is owned by a slave-owning class. The former labor for the latter and as such greatly affect their quality of life and vice versa. The slave-owners and slaves are, in no plausible sense, members of the same community. The identity component is absent. They do not share any cultural traits or common cultural practices. Furthermore, they do not care greatly for each other. The slaves are aggrieved, rightly thinking that they do not receive their fair share, and the slave owners dislike the slaves.[34]
If we employ the communitarian conception of an association, (3) entails that we should not apply comparative principles to the members of this country. Such a conclusion is, though, hard to accept and it is, surely, plausible to apply comparative principles to such a country. The presence of communal relations is, thus, not necessary for the application of comparative principles.

b. A second point: We might strengthen this conclusion further by moving from counterexamples and analyzing the very concept of distributive justice. When we do so, we find that it is hard to see why social unity or identification or cultural similarity have any relevance for people's distributive shares. These, I think, fit ill with our considered views about distributive justice (and indeed with our considered views about penal justice and civil and political justice). This surely also links in with a deeper point about the nature of justice, namely, that justice should be blind to factors like people's communal membership or their regional identity or race. What matters is not *what* socioeconomic or cultural group they belong to (e.g., their class identity or cultural identity) but *what* they have done (e.g., have they contributed to an economic project?) and *what* their general entitlements are (e.g., any general rights). Claiming that comparative principles are only appropriate within communities clashes with our normal understanding of justice.

c. A third point: Miller gives an example designed to bring out the intuitive appeal of his claim that comparative principles apply solely within social groups. In a passage already quoted previously, Miller writes:

> In an encounter with a stranger from another *community*, there are certain things I may not do—I may not injure him or steal his property—and certain things that I must do—if he is ill or in pain I must do what I can to help him—but it makes no sense for either of us to try to apply comparative principles—for instance to insist on equality in some respect [emphasis added].[35]

Does this not support Miller's claim that there are no comparative principles outside of a community? I think not, and a proponent of supracommunal comparative principles can reply that this is not asking the right question. Here it is helpful to use a distinction invoked by Thomas Pogge between "interactional" and "institutional" approaches to global justice. The former specify those principles that apply directly to individuals, whereas the latter refer to those principles that should regulate the basic structure.[36] Pogge's position is that global principles of justice should apply to the context in which individuals behave. And if we adopt this conception, Miller's example has little force, for his example focuses solely on the duties that *individuals* owe and not on the nature of the basic structure. There is nothing at all counterintuitive in stating that there should be global comparative principles that specify the conditions under which people of different communities can and do interact. Miller's example, and his focus on what duties apply to an *individual*, thus does not establish that comparative principles apply only to members of the same *community*.

G

Having criticized the communitarian conception, let me suggest an alternative conception of the type of associations to which comparative principles apply. Consider the following: The "causal interdependence" conception of an association stipulates that comparative principles apply to people who causally affect and are affected by others or who are subject to the same economic forces.

This conception is drawn from the work of Pogge, Beitz, and Onora O'Neill and is, to use the terms introduced in the last section, an "institutional" approach.[37] On this view, principles of justice apply to what Pogge terms "institutional schemes," where these refer to "the ground rules and practices that regulate human interactions."[38] (None of the preceding distinguish between comparative and noncomparative principles in this context.) The relevant criteria for identifying who is incorporated within the scope of comparative principles is, then, *not* communal membership but who affects and is affected by whom. Where two people are affected by the same socioeconomic forces, they form part of the same institutional scheme. This conception of an association has two virtues. First, it is not vulnerable to the argument against the communitarian conception (I.F). It would, for example, find that comparative principles apply to all in the slave society: slaves should not be excluded from the distribution of benefits. Second, it supports and explains the examples presented in I.E—each of the examples referred to an institutional setup in which persons are causally affected by a common set of practices. (We might also note that in two of the passages from Miller quoted previously, Miller refers to "connectedness.")[39] The causal-interdependence conception of an association is thus to be preferred to the communitarian one I have suggested Miller employs.

H

This, however, has (as Beitz, O'Neill, and Pogge, of course, claim) radical implications for the scope of comparative principles of distributive justice. For once we conjoin this account of when comparative principles apply with factual claims about global interdependence we arrive at the conclusion that there are global comparative principles of distributive justice.[40] The empirical support for this factual claim is, moreover, very strong. As Held, McGrew, Goldblatt, and Perraton persuasively chronicle, we exist in an interdependent world in which production, finance, management, and trade are internationalized and in which there is considerable transnational migration of people.[41]

Two further points should be made about this empirical claim. First, we should record that it does not rely on extreme claims to the effect that globalization is such that states have no autonomy and that there are no borders. It claims simply that the world is interdependent and this is a much weaker claim.[42] Second, some have resisted the line of reasoning given previously because they have misunderstood the conception of an institutional scheme on which it rests. Brian Barry, for example, construes Charles Beitz as adopting Rawls's ideas of "fair play" and then claiming that there is a global scheme of mutual cooperation.[43] As Beitz pointed out in the original edition of *Political Theory and International Relations*, however,[44] and, as he has pointed out again in the afterword to the latest edition of *Political Theory and International Relations*, this is not how he construed economic schemes.[45] The causal-interdependence model thus does not claim that such interaction is mutually beneficial and, as such, avoids Barry's critique of the (Beitzian) claim that there is a global economic system.

Given, then, the causal-interdependence model and given the extent to which there is global interaction, we arrive at the conclusion that there are global comparative principles of distributive justice. (2) is false.

I

The preceding arguments are sufficient to undermine (1), (2), and (3). I want, however, to go further and to suggest tentatively that comparative principles can apply to persons even when they are not members of any common association (on any normal understanding of an association). Let me present two considerations.

The first is directed to those who adhere to any consequentialist theory of justice that issues in comparative principles of distributive justice (what one might term *comparative consequentialist* theories). If one affirms a comparative consequentialist approach (and I am not arguing that we should), then one is committed to applying comparative principles to people regardless of whether they interact with each other. From such a consequentialist perspective, what matters are states of affairs and people are duty bound to bring about good states of affairs independently of any connection or lack of connection. Consider in this light a world that contains a community (the As) that lives in isolation in a far-flung part of the world and is facing starvation. This world also contains the members of another affluent community (B) who are aware of the As but have no contact with them. From a consequentialist point of view, members of community B have a duty to assist the members of A independently of whether there exists interaction or common bonds. Comparative consequentialists should then think that principles of distributive justice apply in the absence of common membership.

The second point is this: there is a powerful rights-based line of reasoning (given by both Brian Barry and Hillel Steiner) that establishes that comparative principles apply to people independently of whether they have interacted. The argument is this: we should begin by noting H. L. A. Hart's distinction between general rights and special rights. The former refer to those rights held by all persons, qua person, whereas the latter refer to those rights held by particular individuals who possess them because of some special feature about themselves.[46] With this distinction in mind, the next step in the argument points out that the claim that comparative principles apply within associations ascribes special rights to the members of associations. (3) states that those who belong to an association have a special right to a fair share of the produce of that association—a right not possessed by other persons who do not belong to that association. But then, as Barry and Steiner both point out, if this is so, we need an account of people's preparticipation rights. With what are they entitled to trade? The special rights of participants assume that people have a set of general rights specifying their initial entitlements. And then, they reason, we have no reason to call for anything other than a set of equal rights. Thus, we have derived a set of comparative principles that apply outside of any association.[47]

It may, at this point, be appropriate to take stock. I have argued

Conclusion 1: There are transnational comparative principles of distributive justice (and hence [1] is incorrect).

Conclusion 2: The model of an association that Miller affirms is untenable (and hence his version of [3] is incorrect).

Conclusion 3: We have a better model of the type of association that yields comparative principles of distributive justice.

Conclusion 4: This model of an association yields global comparative principles of distributive justice (and so [2] is incorrect).

Conclusion 5: We have some reason to think that comparative principles apply even outside of any associations (and so [3] is incorrect whatever conception of an association one employs and further doubt is cast on [2]).[48]

II

Having analyzed Miller's treatment of comparative justice and his rejection of comparative principles of global distributive justice, I now want to consider his defense of his own preferred principles of global distributive justice. Miller outlines and defends three noncomparative principles of distributive justice. These are as follows.

First, Miller defends a set of basic rights.[49] Each person has a right to certain bare essentials on the grounds that these are prerequisites for any reasonable life. These include rights to freedom of speech and conscience and to enough material resources so as not to starve or suffer malnutrition.[50] Everyone (and that includes governments, social movements, corporations, and individuals) is required not to violate these rights.[51] Miller then makes this interesting claim:

> This requirement entails more than just an obligation not to violate human rights oneself, whether negatively by injuring people, say, or positively by failing to provide vital resources. It is also an obligation to try to present [*sic*] the violation of human rights by third parties—say foreign governments that attempt to starve dissident minorities into submission.[52]

Second, Miller affirms a principle of nonexploitation. Individuals and corporations and states should not exploit others.[53] Miller adds:

> Global justice in the form of non-exploitation is primarily a negative requirement for the political community as a whole—the obligation is to refrain from engaging in exploitative transactions—though at the same time it imposes positive obligations on governments to ensure that multinationals and other institutions under their jurisdiction also respect that requirement.[54]

Third, and finally, Miller argues that nation-states should have enough resources to be self-governing.[55]

From these three principles we can see that, on Miller's account, international distributive justice is owed to individuals (notably in his first principle) but also to nation-states (notably in his third principle).[56]

A

I want to argue, in what follows, that these are too minimal and that they also conflict with other claims Miller seeks to advance. Let me begin with the worry that Miller's three noncomparative principles are too minimal. A world that met Miller's noncomparative principles would, I believe, be unfair because it allows people to be disadvantaged for no reason other than their nationality and/or their citizenship. As such his theory needs to be supplemented by two additional principles, both comparative principles of distributive justice.

The first is a principle of global fair equality of opportunity: this states that people of the same ability and same drive should have equal opportunity to positions of the same standard of living.[57]

Why should we accept this? I have sought to defend this elsewhere and so shall be brief here.[58] The essential line of reasoning is that our commitment to equality of opportunity is underpinned by the thought that it is unfair if persons have worse opportunities because of their cultural identity. It is, for example, unfair if persons have worse opportunities because of their class or ethnicity or regional identity. But—given the same principle—it is also unfair if persons have worse opportunities because of their national or civic identity.[59] A world order that satisfied Miller's standards is, on this view, insufficient because it is compatible with a humane system of "global apartheid" in which people's basic rights are met but opportunities are skewed to those belonging to a privileged nation.[60]

B

A second global comparative principle of distributive justice which, I believe, is required and which Miller does not adopt is what might be termed the *equal remuneration principle*: this states that people should receive equal remuneration for equal work.

This principle is a variation on the equal pay principle affirmed by the United Nations Declaration of Human Rights (Article 23 section 2). The latter maintains, "Everyone, without any discrimination, has the right to equal pay for equal work."

The intuitive appeal of this principle is strong: if people do the same work (producing something of equal quality), then should they not be rewarded to the same extent? Would it not be a violation of natural justice to say, "Well, you've done the same amount of work as John Smith and produced something of equal worth but because you're Iranian you should get less"? Of course, the notion of "remuneration" employed here needs to be developed.[61] If pay is construed as "financial reward," this principle is open to the objection that it is counterintuitive to pay someone in Sweden and someone in Ethiopia the same amount of money when the latter can buy more in Ethiopia than she can in Sweden. Drawing on this, someone might argue that equal work entitles people to an "equal standard of living as specified by the norms of their own community" or an "equal standard of living as specified by some transcultural index."[62] Quite how remuneration is fleshed out, then, remains to be seen, but the underlying intuition is hard to resist.

In short, then, my suggestion is that Miller's noncomparative principles are insufficient. They sanction a world system of "global apartheid" in which people are disadvantaged because of their cultural identity. To prevent injustice, comparative principles of distributive justice should be imported.

C

Before closing my discussion let me make two further points about Miller's noncomparative principles. First, Miller has in the past argued that principles of justice, if they are to be effective, must apply within communities. He has, as a corollary, been highly critical of supracommunal principles of distributive justice.[63] Distributive principles require "communitarian relationships . . . to underpin" them.[64] This claim is, however, hard to square with his commitment to the three principles of global justice previously presented. And adherence to his views on the communal presuppositions of principles of distributive justice would undercut his commitment to any global principles of distributive justice.[65]

The second point is this: in practice the distinction between comparative and noncomparative principles becomes rather blurred. This occurs because we cannot ever eliminate rights abuses and hence we have to make judgments about which rights abuses should be addressed. Comparative judgments thus have to be made to decide which causes deserve greater priority. This does not, and is not intended to, dissolve the distinction between comparative and noncomparative principles since they are defined with respect to the ideal to which they aspire. We may, thus, say that the ideal aimed at by noncomparative principles does not require any comparative judgments, whereas the ideal aspired to by comparative principles, by contrast, necessarily does. My point is simply that in the nonideal world, even noncomparative principles require comparative judgments. Consider, in this light, Miller's statement:

> If I say that each person has a right to a fair trial, or not to be tortured, I mean that he or she is owed this whether or not other people are currently enjoying these rights: the fact that others in the society in question are being tortured or denied fair trials does not weaken or alter the force of my claim.[66]

There is a sense in which this is true (the desired ideal is one in which all have their rights and no comparative claims are required) and a sense in which it is false (in our fallen world we have to make choices about which rights violations are most deserving of our attention).

III

Having discussed Miller's critique of comparative principles of global justice and his preferred three principles of global justice, I now want to complete my analysis by considering Miller's treatment of *who* is duty-bound to ensure that people receive their just entitlements as specified by a global theory of justice.

Miller argues that the main responsibility for ensuring that people receive their global entitlements accrues to fellow nationals. Miller adduces a number of considerations in support of this claim,[67] but he develops and explicates one at greater length and I shall, accordingly, focus on that. Miller's most sustained argument makes the following claim: if a political regime has autonomy, it must take responsibility for its own decisions. Accordingly, if it makes poor decisions, it must live by them. Given that it is self-determining, the duty to ensure that its members receive their entitlements is a duty borne by the political community. Let us call this the "dynamic argument."[68]

I want to suggest that the dynamic argument is unpersuasive for a number of reasons. I argue *first*, (a) that its core idea should be rejected; *second*, (b) that it is incompatible with Miller's commitment to culture-neutral principles of global justice; and *third*, (c) that it is the wrong type of argument and when revised undermines Miller's own position.

A

Let me begin with the first problem.[69] To substantiate this claim, let me begin by addressing the assumptions underlying the argument. The argument, I want to suggest, is plausible only if we make two assumptions, namely:

(i) that persons should be responsible for their ends, and
(ii) that our conclusions about the responsibility of individuals can be applied to states.[70]

Many liberal thinkers like Dworkin and Rawls affirm (i).[71] Furthermore, it is, I believe, a reasonable claim (although it needs to be supplemented by other considerations). (ii), by contrast, is questionable. It is of paramount importance for the dynamic argument that our conclusions about the responsibility of individuals can be applied to the responsibility of states. (ii) is, however, vulnerable in two ways. The first and most important point is that the very plural and diverse nature of most states makes it difficult to conceive of states as agents making decisions.[72] Rather, they comprise diverse elements, divided by religion, class, interests, pursuits, region, and (often) nationality. The policies adopted by states are thus never the choices of all the members of that state. Second, and as a corollary of this first point, (i) actually undermines the dynamic argument. Implementing the dynamic argument will mean that some will pay the price for the policies that others (their leaders) have adopted.[73] (i) thus simply does not support the dynamic argument. It actually entails that the latter should be rejected. People are made to pay the price of choices they did not make.

Miller is, of course, sensitive to these sorts of concerns. He replies that it is appropriate to treat states as responsible agents if their decisions are democratic and if everyone's basic rights are respected.[74] Such liberal democratic states may thus be treated as autonomous and responsible agents. Two replies can, however, be made to this argument. First, many states with impoverished people are not liberal democracies. Accordingly, we cannot appeal to the dynamic argument to show that the populations of such states are not entitled to aid. Second, it is worth recording that the revised version of the dynamic argument does not address the second point. If we stick to the claim that people are responsible for their decisions, this implies that we should reject the modified version which, whilst an improvement, would still result in some suffering because of policies they did not choose and which they might heartily reject. (ii) is thus implausible because it fails to show adequate respect for the decisions of individuals and flies in the face of the intuition that persons should take responsibility for their own decisions. Treating states as responsible agents is, thus, deeply unfair to individuals who are disadvantaged because of the state's decisions. This is especially so in nondemocratic states but still applies in democratic states.[75]

B

Miller's dynamic argument faces a second (internal) problem. To appreciate the problem it is important to bear in mind that Miller criticizes other global principles on the grounds that they cannot be stated in a way that members of all cultures can accept. He makes this point, for example, about proposals to distribute resources to all persons throughout the world, arguing that people of different societies will disagree on how to value resources. Miller thus criticizes other global principles on the grounds that it is not possible to construct a culture-neutral conception of them.[76] The same charge can, however, be leveled against Miller's dynamic argument. For someone can quite plausibly argue that the value at its core embodies a set of nonneutral values. One of Miller's examples brings this point out nicely, namely, that which includes two communities, one of which restricts its population and one which does not.[77] Miller insists that the former should not have to subsidize the latter. This assumes that birth control is morally legitimate but many, of course (notably, Roman Catholics), deny this on religious grounds: this impugns the dynamic argument's claim to be culture neutral. The importance of this example is borne out by the long-standing disagreement about population control.[78] If, then, Miller is troubled by the fact that people of different cultures cannot agree on how to value resources, he should be even more troubled by the fact that they will disagree on the appropriateness of the principle at the heart of the dynamic argument.

C

Let me now present a third challenge to Miller's argument. This argument begins with the claim that, as it stands, Miller's argument appears to commit what Gilbert Ryle terms a "category mistake."[79] To see this, it is important to distinguish between statements about people's entitlements, on the one hand, (hereafter *entitlement claims*) and statements about people's duties, on the other hand (hereafter *duty claims*). Miller presents his argument as a critique of "global equality of resources."[80] The objection I am presenting suggests, however, that this misconstrues the moral claim that the dynamic argument seeks to articulate. For the latter is most plausibly construed as a claim about people's duties rather than a claim about people's entitlements. What it shows (if it is valid) is that it is unfair to require nonmembers to bale out the members of a political regime when the latter make poor policies. In other words, the dynamic argument articulates the thought "it is unfair that those who pursued sensible policies have to subsidize others for the latter's poor decisions."[81] This point can be made in another way: one can present the dynamic argument without specifying what people's entitlements in fact are. If this conjecture is correct, this is hardly surprising: its point is not directed toward people's entitlements and is directed at the question of who is duty-bound to ensure that people receive their just entitlements. (Let us call this the Category Mistake Objection.) One might then add that the dynamic argument is therefore not a direct challenge to global equality per se, and one can substitute "basic rights" or "a global difference principle" as its target. If correct, this challenge would have disturbing implications for Miller's argument since it would undermine his rejection of global equality and his affirmation of basic rights. One of the points he deploys to reject the former should—*if it has any force*—also have force against his own favored global ideals. (Let us call this the Undiscriminating Force Objection—since it claims that the dynamic argument applies in an undiscriminating way to any global distributive principle.)

In response to the Category Mistake Objection, one might rightly question the claim that the dynamic argument speaks solely to the question of duties and has no bearing on people's entitlements. To think the latter, one would have to argue that statements about people's entitlements can be utterly divorced from statements about people's duties. Such a position is implausible. If people are entitled to some amount of a good, it does seem plausible to suggest that, in some circumstances at least, others have some duty to ensure that they receive it. In other words, claims about people's entitlements inevitably have implications for people's duties. And so the dynamic argument does bear on the question not simply of what duties people have but also what entitlements people have.

This response, however, does not rescue Miller's position. It helps to exonerate the dynamic argument from the Category Mistake Objection. But it does not help Miller to meet the Undiscriminating Force Objection. The point here is that if the dynamic argument has force against global equality, it has force against *any* theory that ascribes rights to all persons and hence (following the argument of the last paragraph) ascribes duties on other persons. Miller's own view (endorsing basic rights) and the global equality view are thus both vulnerable to the dynamic argument for both ascribe duties to those who do not belong to a community to come to its aid (be it in the name of global equality or basic rights or some other principle).

Thus, if the dynamic argument tells against global equality, it also tells against Miller's basic rights.

D

This conclusion is further reinforced if we turn our attention to an important typology that Miller deploys to categorize why people lack their global entitlements (i.e., why, in Miller's case, they lack their basic rights). Miller envisages four types of scenario that are as follows:

Case 1: No government exists in a country.
Case 2: A society's political elite is corrupt or committed to a disastrous ideology.
Case 3: A society faces an adverse international economic situation.
Case 4: A society is resource poor.[82]

He then argues—and this is crucial—that the duties for outsiders vary in each case. This is part of the point of the preceding fourfold typology. In case 1 scenarios, Miller says, nonmembers have a duty to supply aid.[83] In case 2 situations, however, Miller requires more restricted action. He argues, for example, that any economic trade "should be made conditional on internal policy reforms," adding that financial institutions and governments have a negative duty "not to collude."[84] But if neither have any dealings with a country, then they have *no duty* to do anything. "Primary responsibility for putting right the injustice lies with the people themselves."[85] If we turn now to case 3, Miller maintains that, although outsiders have some duty here, the duty to secure people's rights should be attributed in the most part to their state.[86] In case 4 scenarios, outside bodies have a duty to assist.[87]

I believe that Miller is importantly right to distinguish between different causes of rights violations and to argue that these bear on the question of who is duty-bound to secure people's rights. I also think that Miller is right in arguing that case 4 is "relatively rare."[88] I would, however, like to make three critical comments.

E

The first follows on from the preceding analysis of the Undiscriminating Force Objection. As I argued previously, there is a sense (to be qualified shortly) in which entitlement claims like global equality (which Miller rejects) and basic rights (which Miller affirms) are both vulnerable to the dynamic argument. The same type of point (namely, that global equality and basic rights are in the same boat) can be applied to Miller's typology concerning who is duty-bound to secure people's entitlements. Why, one might ask, can one not affirm global equality of some sort *and* affirm his fourfold typology of when duties fall on nonmembers? Put otherwise: the dynamic argument and the preceding typology do not impel us to reject global equality. Can someone wishing to defend global equality not adopt Miller's account of when people are duty-bound to assist members of another community? We have no reason to think that one cannot combine Miller's account of when (and how much) outsiders have a duty to assist members of a community to receive their entitlements, on the one hand, *with* an egalitarian's account of what those entitlements are, on the other.

The qualification is this: global equality and basic rights are not wholly on a par because the former will ask more of outsiders than does the latter. Since it is a tougher standard to meet it is likely to involve more external aid than would a basic rights view. But then if this is the argument, the dynamic argument should be revised in such a way that makes it clear that its central claim concerns the *amount* that outsiders can be required to do. Moreover, it is open to the adherents to global equality to respond in one of two ways. First, they can hold onto equality but stipulate an upper limit on the demands that one can make on foreigners to bring about global equality (an upper limit on a par with that specified by the basic rights view). Second, they can ask why a cosmopolitan ideal can be faulted for being more demanding than a basic rights view. Of course, these rejoinders do not (and are not supposed to) settle these issues here, and further analysis would be required to settle how much it is fair to ask outsiders to do. My point is that *as they stand* the dynamic argument and Miller's typology are insufficient to persuade us to reject global equality. The latter is analogous to the view Miller himself endorses, and if the basic rights view can adopt Miller's typology of when outsiders are duty-bound to assist, then an adherent to global equality can equally easily adopt the same typology.

To recap so far, then, I have argued that the dynamic argument is flawed for three reasons: it (a) rests on an implausible account of the nature of a state, (b) conflicts with Miller's desire to construct culture neutral principles, and (c) undermines the basic rights view as well as global equality.

F

I now want to add two further critical points about Miller's typology. The first (minor) point concerns Miller's claim that only in case 4 scenarios do outsiders have a duty of justice to assist the members of a society.[89] It is not clear to me why this should be so. The thought underlying this claim cannot be, for example, that duties of justice fall on a person if she is causally responsible for an event because outsiders are not (normally) responsible for one country lacking resources. In addition, outsiders might be causally responsible for civil war (type 1) or a corrupt political elite (type 2)[90] or an adverse economic environment (type 3). Quite why resource deficiencies generate duties of justice whereas the others do not is unclear. What property is it that type 4 possesses that types 1, 2, and 3 lack?

G

Miller's typology is open to a second, more damaging objection. The problems concern Miller's treatment of case 2 scenarios. Of such scenarios Miller writes:

> Rights violations stem from the failures of a political regime which nonetheless continues to hold power and may indeed have considerable popular support. These failures might arise either from corruption in the office-holders, who are syphoning off a considerable part of the society's wealth to their own advantage, or from misguided ideological doctrines. . . . Here it is assumed that the technological and other capacities are such that if it were well governed it could protect its citizens' basic rights adequately if not easily.[91]

In such circumstances, recall, his position is that the central duty to ensure that people receive their entitlements should be attributed to their political regime and its members.[92]

But Miller's description of two-style situations loads the dice in two ways. First Miller states that the elite "*may* . . . have considerable support" (emphasis added).[93] This allows that it may not, and that may make a difference, for if an elite does enjoy support, that *might* perhaps lead us to think that the people should therefore accept the outcome resulting from the policy. But type 2 cases are compatible with the elite *not* enjoying public support: in which case, it is unfair to make people pay the price for policies that others have adopted. We should, then, distinguish between case (2a): a society's political elite is corrupt or committed to a disastrous ideology and that elite enjoys popular support; and case (2b): a society's political elite is corrupt or committed to a disastrous ideology and that elite does not enjoy popular support.

Second, Miller assumes that the society has sufficient "technological" resources. If he does so, though, the typology should be amended to include a fifth category whereby people's rights are not fulfilled because case 5: the society lacks technological ability (and more generally knowledge and expertise). As such, it is distinct from case 4 scenarios which, in Miller's construal, refer simply to material resources.

Let us suppose that Miller's typology is revised in these two ways. His analysis of type (2) scenarios is nonetheless unpersuasive for the reason set out previously in III.A. While (2a) is superior in this regard to (2b), both are unfair because they make people pay the price for the policies that others have adopted.

IV

It is time to conclude. This chapter has addressed three central claims that Miller makes about global justice. Against the first—Miller's claim that comparative principles of distributive justice normally operate within the nation and cannot be applied at the global level—I have argued that: there are transnational comparative principles of distributive justice; Miller's claim that comparative principles apply only within associations rests on an unduly narrow conception of associations; a more plausible conception of an association generates global comparative principles; comparative principles apply even outside of any kind of association.

Turning now to Miller's three principles of global justice, I have argued that these need to be supplemented by two comparative principles, and I tentatively suggested (a) global equality of opportunity and (b) the equal remuneration principle. I have also argued that Miller's affirmation of any global principles of justice conflicts with his claim that principles of distributive justice should be implemented only in communal contexts.

And finally, Miller's dynamic argument treats individuals unfairly and conflicts with his commitment to cultural neutrality. It undermines his ability *both* to affirm the basic rights view *and* to reject global equality.[94] To the extent that the dynamic argument has force, it undermines the basic rights view as well. And to the extent that his typology of duties has force, it is available to defenders of global equality as well as to defenders of the basic rights view.

Having chronicled these disagreements, it is important to add that, the preceding disagreements notwithstanding, there are many points on which I agree with Miller. I am sympathetic to his three noncomparative principles. In addition to this, he provides a subtle and nuanced exploration of why people do not receive their global entitlements and how this affects the allocation of obligations. A world order that honored Miller's principles would be an immeasurable improvement on the status quo. But it would not, if I am right, be a just world order.[95]

NOTES

1. See, for example, Hans J. Morgenthau, *In Defence of the National Interest: A Critical Examination of American Foreign Policy* (New York: Knopf, 1951); and Hans J. Morgenthau, *Politics Among Nations: The Struggle for Power and Peace,* 6th ed. (New York: Knopf, 1985).

2. Terry Nardin, *Law, Morality, and the Relations of States* (Princeton, N.J.: Princeton University Press, 1983).

3. See, for example, Brian Barry, "Statism and Nationalism: A Cosmopolitan Critique," in *NOMOS Volume XLI: Global Justice*, ed. Ian Shapiro and Lea Brilmayer (New York: New York University Press, 1999), 12–66; Charles Beitz, *Political Theory and International Relations* (with a new afterword by the author) (Princeton, N.J.: Princeton University Press, 1999); Onora O'Neill, *Bounds of Justice* (Cambridge: Cambridge University Press, 2000); Thomas W. Pogge, *Realizing Rawls* (London: Cornell University Press, 1989); and Pogge, "A Global Resources Dividend," in *Ethics of Consumption: The Good Life, Justice, and Global Stewardship*, ed. David A. Crocker and Toby Linden (Lanham, Md.: Rowman & Littlefield, 1998).

4. For a discussion of recent work on international distributive justice, see Simon Caney, "Review Article: International Distributive Justice," *Political Studies* 49, no. 5 (2001).

5. See Joel Feinberg, "Noncomparative Justice," *Philosophical Review* 83 (1974): 297–338. Miller cites this paper in "The Limits of Cosmopolitan Justice," *International Society: Diverse Ethical Perspectives*, ed. David R. Mapel and Terry Nardin (Princeton, N.J.: Princeton University Press, 1998), 180 fn. 10; and *Principles of Social Justice* (Cambridge, Mass.: Harvard University Press, 1999), 152, 305 fn. 39.

6. For brevity's sake I shall sometimes use the term *comparative principles* to refer to "comparative principles of distributive justice." In doing so, I am not assuming that one cannot have comparative principles that are not principles of distributive justice.

7. Miller, *Principles*, 18, 273 fn. 32.

8. Miller makes both of these points in the following passage:

I do not mean that such principles [principles of comparative justice] operate only at the national level; they also apply within smaller groups and associations inside national communities. Nor do I wish to exclude the possibility of there being certain transnational contexts in which comparative principles may apply. The international community of scientists is sufficiently well-formed for us to say that it is unfair that Professor Smith, an American, received a Nobel prize for Chemistry while Professor Malenkov, a Russian, was passed over. I do, however, want to deny that there presently exists an overall "world community" within which comparative principles of justice apply.

On nations as the privileged locus for implementing comparative principles of justice, see Miller, *On Nationality* (Oxford: Clarendon Press, 1995), ch. 2–4; Miller, "The Limits of Cosmopolitan Justice," 180 fn. 14.

9. Miller's commitment to (2) is evident in his statement that "our thinking about global inequalities should be guided not by comparative principles, such as principles of equality, but by the noncomparative ideas of *protecting basic rights* and *preventing exploitation*" (see Miller, *Principles*, 19). There is a footnote after the word *exploitation*, in which Miller refers to "Justice and Global Inequality" and "The Limits of Cosmopolitan Justice"; see *Principles*, 273–274 fn. 33. The essay "Justice and Global Inequality" is published in *Inequality, Globalization, and World Politics*, ed. Andrew Hurrell and Ngaire Woods (Oxford: Oxford University Press, 1999), 187–210.

10. Hillel Steiner, *An Essay on Rights* (Oxford: Blackwell, 1994), 235–236, 262–265, 270. See also Brian Barry, "Humanity and Justice in Global Perspective," in *Liberty and Justice: Essays in Political Theory 2* (Oxford: Clarendon, 1991), 196–203; and Barry, "Justice as Reciprocity," in *Liberty and Justice*, 226, 237–239. See also Brian Barry's affirmation of global comparative principles of distributive justice in "International Society from a Cosmopolitan Perspective," in *International Society*, 147–149. Miller's arguments in "The Limits of Cosmopolitan Justice" are explicitly directed toward Barry's arguments in this paper.

11. "Global Egalitarianism: A Defensible Theory of Justice?" sec. 2. For the concept of equality of access to advantage cf. G. A. Cohen, "On the Currency of Egalitarian Justice," *Ethics* 99, no. 4 (1989).

12. Miller, "Limits of Cosmopolitan Justice," 171. Miller includes a footnote reference (footnote 15) at the end of the passage quoted after the word *respect*. Footnote 15 cites two works,

namely: Charles Taylor, "The Nature and Scope of Distributive Justice," in his *Philosophy and the Human Sciences: Philosophical Papers, Second Volume* (Cambridge: Cambridge University Press, 1985); and Michael Walzer, *Spheres of Justice* (New York: Basic Books, 1983), ch.2; Miller, "Limits of Cosmopolitan Justice,"180 fn. 15.

13. Miller, *Principles*, 4–5.

14. Miller, *Principles*, 233–234.

15. Miller, *Principles*, 234–236.

16. Miller, *Principles*, 236. See, more generally, Miller, *Principles*, 236–239. One example of the sort of group to which this egalitarian logic applies is a "political community" like a state; Miller, *Principles*, 237. For the distinction between communal and noncommunal vindications of equality, see also Miller, "Justice and Global Inequality," 189–197, esp. 189–191.

17. Miller, "Limits of Cosmopolitan Justice," 171.

18. Miller, "Limits of Cosmopolitan Justice," 171.

19. Miller, *Principles*, 4. Miller also refers to "bounded societies" in Miller, *Principles*, 6.

20. Miller, *Principles*, 5.

21. Miller, *Principles*, 18. The passage is followed by a footnote reference (footnote 31) that refers to *On Nationality* (Oxford: Clarendon Press, 1995), ch. 3, 4; see Miller, *Principles*, 273 fn. 31.

22. Miller, *Principles*, 18.

23. As we have seen earlier (note 12), Miller cites Charles Taylor and Michael Walzer (Miller, "Limits of Cosmopolitan Justice," 180 fn. 15). Neither of these, however, provides much helpful guidance on the nature of the entities to which comparative principles of distributive justice apply. Taylor, for example, writes of "distributive justice" that it "presupposes that men are in a society together, or in some kind of collaborative arrangement"; "The Nature and Scope of Distributive Justice," 289. Walzer maintains that justice applies within "a bounded world"; *Spheres of Justice*, 31.

24. This is necessarily brief. For a good discussion of the properties of a community, see Andrew Mason, "Liberalism and the Value of Community," *Canadian Journal of Philosophy* 23, no. 2 (1993): esp. 216–228.

25. Miller, "Limits of Cosmopolitan Justice," 180 fn. 14.

26. Miller, *Principles*, 273 fn. 32.

27. See, in this light, Miller's distinction between three "modes of human relationship" to which principles of justice apply (Miller, *Principles*, 25). These three modes are "solidaristic community" (the relations between friends and family members), "instrumental association" (the relations in the marketplace), and "citizenship" (the relations between fellow citizens) (Miller, *Principles*, 26; cf. 26–41). The second relationship, I believe, causes problems for Miller's commitment to (1) and (2). The problem stems from three points: first, Miller states that "the relevant principle of justice [for those participating in an instrumental relationship] is distribution according to desert" (Miller, *Principles*, 27; cf. 27–30). Second, he states that desert claims often employ a comparative principle of distributive justice (Miller, *Principles*, 151–154). Third, market relations (the paradigmatic case of an instrumental association) frequently transcend the borders of states and nations and are sometimes global. The conjunction of these three points, however, implies that comparative principles apply in the market and that since markets are transnational, and sometimes global, there are (on Miller's own criteria) transnational, and sometimes global, comparative principles of distributive justice.

28. Miller does say that a complete account of global justice would provide an account of "how the costs of environmental protection should be shared between states, and so forth"; "National Self-Determination and Global Justice," in Miller, *Citizenship and National Identity* (Cambridge: Polity, 2000), 209 fn. 22. My point is that it is difficult to see how one could share such costs fairly without comparative principles.

29. Miller, *On Nationality*, 160–162.

30. Suppose someone denies that the examples employed also contain an "association." Suppose, for example, that they claim that in example 5 the duty to accommodate refugees should be

attributed to all societies and not just those affected in some way. This suits my argument fine since it supports there being global comparative principles of distributive justice and since I entertain the possibility that such principles apply outside of associations later in the chapter: section I, subsection I.

31. For these three phrases see, respectively, Miller, "The Limits of Cosmopolitan Justice," 171; Miller, *Principles*, 4; and Miller, *Principles*, 18.

32. Miller, *Principles*, 18, 273 fn. 32.

33. For this phrase, see Miller, "Limits of Cosmopolitan Justice," 171. As an example of Miller's position, see his discussion of equality in "Justice and Global Inequality":

> I protest when I discover that the standard of medical treatment offered to me is markedly inferior to that enjoyed by my compatriots in the next city, but I make no such complaint when told that French citizens enjoy certain rights that British citizens do not. (I might think that the French system is a better one and that we ought to introduce it in Britain, but this is a different argument: it is not a complaint that the inequality between the two countries is unfair to the citizens of one of them.)

See Miller, "Justice and Global Inequality," 190.

34. The example is an adaptation of one used by Charles Beitz to establish a slightly different point: *Political Theory and International Relations*, 131.

35. Miller, "Limits of Cosmopolitan Justice," 171. Miller includes a footnote reference (footnote 15) at the end of the passage quoted after the word *respect*. Footnote 15 cites two works, namely: Charles Taylor, "The Nature and Scope of Distributive Justice"; and Walzer, *Spheres of Justice*, ch. 2. See Miller, "Limits of Cosmopolitan Justice," 180.

36. Thomas Pogge, "Cosmopolitanism and Sovereignty," in *Political Restructuring in Europe: Ethical Perspectives,* ed. Chris Brown (London: Routledge, 1994), 90–91. The concept of a "basic structure," of course, comes from Rawls, *A Theory of Justice,* rev. ed. (Oxford: Oxford University Press, 1999), 6–10.

37. See, for example, Pogge, "Cosmopolitanism," 90–98; Beitz, *Political Theory*, 129–132; and Onora O'Neill, *Towards Justice and Virtue: A Constructive Account of Practical Reasoning* (Cambridge: Cambridge University Press, 1996), 101, 105–106, 112–113. See also Henry Shue, "The Geography of Justice: Beitz's Critique of Skepticism and Statism," *Ethics* 92, no.4 (1982): 719; and Thomas Scanlon, "Rawls' Theory of Justice," in *Reading Rawls: Critical Studies of a Theory of Justice,* ed. Norman Daniels (Oxford: Blackwell, 1985), 202.

38. See Thomas Pogge, "Cosmopolitanism," 90, 91, respectively.

39. The two passages come from Miller, "Limits of Cosmopolitan Justice," 171; and Miller, *Principles*, 5.

40. See Beitz, *Political Theory*, 143–152; O'Neill, *Towards Justice and Virtue*, 113–121, but esp. 114, 115, 121; Pogge, *Realizing Rawls*, esp. 8–9, 11–12, 35–36, 226–227, 234–241, 262–265, 273–280; Pogge, "Global Resources Dividend," 504–507; and Pogge, "Cosmopolitanism," 90–98.

41. See David Held and Anthony McGrew, David Goldblatt, and Jonathan Perraton, *Global Transformations: Politics, Economics and Culture* (Cambridge: Polity, 1999).

42. David Held is at pains to stress this point: see, for example, Held, "The Transformation of Political Community: Rethinking Democracy in the Context of Globalization," in *Democracy's Edges,* ed. Ian Shapiro and Casiano Hacker-Cordón (Cambridge: Cambridge University Press, 1999), 97–98, 103–104.

43. Brian Barry, "Humanity and Justice," 194–195. For Rawls's ideas of fair play, see *Theory of Justice*, 96–98, 301–308.

44. See Beitz, *Political Theory*, 131. Beitz writes, "It would be better to say that the requirements of justice apply to institutions and practices (whether or not they are genuinely cooperative) in which social activity produces relative or absolute benefits or burdens that would not exist if the social activity did not take place"; *Political Theory and International Relations*, 131. See more generally *Political Theory and International Relations*, 129–132.

45. See Beitz, *Political Theory and International Relations*, afterword, 200–205 (esp. 200–203).

46. H. L. A. Hart, "Are There Any Natural Rights?" in *Theories of Rights*, ed. Jeremy Waldron (Oxford: Oxford University Press, 1984), 84–88.

47. For the argument of this paragraph, see Barry, "Justice as Reciprocity," 235, 237; Barry, "Humanity and Justice in Global Perspective," 195–203; and Steiner, "Just Taxation and International Redistribution" in *NOMOS Volume XLI Global Justice*, ed. Ian Shapiro and Lea Brilmayer (New York: New York University Press, 1999), 172ff. See also Charles Beitz's critique of the claim that the only rights persons have are special rights arising from cooperation: *Political Theory and International Relations*, 140–141. Thus, although he is often seen as defending a purely "institutionalist" approach, this is inaccurate; see his discussion of natural resources, *Political Theory and International Relations*, 136–143. Beitz defends a hybrid view according to which some principles of justice arise from cooperation and some apply independently of cooperation.

48. Cécile Fabre also defends this view in her chapter in this volume; see chapter 16, Fabre's "Global Egalitarianism: An Indefensible Theory of Justice?" section 2.3.

49. See Miller, *On Nationality*, 74; Miller, "Justice and Global Inequality," 198–204; Miller, "National Self-Determination," 174–175.

50. For a full statement of exactly what rights are entailed and why, see Miller, "Justice and Global Inequality," 198; Miller, "National Self-Determination," 174.

51. Miller, "National Self-Determination," 175.

52. Miller, "National Self-Determination," 209 fn. 20.

53. Miller, *On Nationality*, 104; Miller, "Justice and Global Inequality," 204–209; Miller, "National Self-Determination," 175.

54. Miller, "National Self-Determination," 175.

55. Miller, *On Nationality*, 105–106; Miller, "National Self-Determination," 175–177.

56. See further Miller's outline and defense (in Miller, *On Nationality*, 104–105) of five principles of international justice that are owed by states to other states.

57. This is a globalized version of Rawls's principle of "fair equality of opportunity." See *Theory of Justice*, 63, 72–73. An early proponent of global equality of opportunity is H. G. Wells, *The Rights of Man or What Are We Fighting For?* (Middlesex: Penguin, 1940), 101; and *The New World Order: Whether It Is Attainable, How It Can Be Attained, and What Sort of World a World at Peace Will Have to Be* (London: Secker and Warburg, 1940), 139–140.

58. See Simon Caney, "Global Equality of Opportunity and the Sovereignty of States," in *International Justice*, ed. Anthony Coates (Aldershot: Ashgate, 2000), 131–132; Caney, "Cosmopolitan Justice and Equalizing Opportunities," *Metaphilosophy* 32, nos. 1/2 (2001): 113–134; and Pogge, "An Egalitarian Law of Peoples," *Philosophy and Public Affairs* 23, no. 3 (1994): 196, 198. For another, different conception of global equality of opportunity, see Allen Buchanan, "Rawls's Law of Peoples: Rules for a Vanished Westphalian World," *Ethics* 110, no. 4 (2000): esp. 711–712. Buchanan's principle differs from that defended in the text in a number of ways. First, he distinguishes between positions that are part of the global basic structure (what one might term GBS-jobs) and those that are part of a society's domestic basic structure (what one might term DBS-jobs). On his principle, people should have equality of opportunity to positions that are part of the global order (GBS-jobs) but not to those positions that are not part of it (DBS-jobs) (711–712, esp. 712 fn. 14). As he puts it, there should be equality of opportunity to "desirable positions and roles in the most important international economic institutions and in global corporations" (711). It thus requires equality of opportunity to some positions, not all. A second, related, difference is that his principle is, as Buchanan notes, compatible with there being a "lack of equality of opportunity within states" (711). It allows cases where two people within a state have unequal opportunities to DBS-jobs. This is, however, prohibited by the principle defended in the text above. Buchanan's principle is, furthermore, compatible with some people in one state having worse opportunities than people in another state.

59. My line of reasoning here draws on, and is indebted to, the rationales for cosmopolitanism developed by, among others, Brian Barry, Charles Beitz, Thomas Pogge, and Peter Singer. See,

respectively, inter alia, Barry, "Statism and Nationalism," esp. 34–40, 53; Beitz, "Cosmopolitan Ideals and National Sentiment," *Journal of Philosophy* 80, no. 10 (1983): 593, 595; Pogge, *Realizing Rawls*, 247; Pogge, "Egalitarian Law of Peoples," 198; Peter Singer, *Practical Ethics* (Cambridge: Cambridge University Press, 1979), 14–23, 171–172. See also Samuel Black's lucid discussion "Individualism at an Impasse," *Canadian Journal of Philosophy* 21, no. 3 (1991): esp. 355–357. See also Simon Caney, "Nationality, Distributive Justice and the Use of Force," *Journal of Applied Philosophy* 16, no. 2 (1999): esp. 128–133. I have argued elsewhere that almost all defenses of cosmopolitanism rest on this line of argument: "Review Article: International Distributive Justice," sec. I. See, too, the additional references cited therein of those who appeal to this cosmopolitan line of reasoning.

60. Richard Falk employs the concept of "global apartheid" to characterize the current world order: *On Humane Governance: Toward a New Global Politics* (Cambridge: Polity, 1995), 49–55.

61. For illuminating discussion, see Henry Shue, "Transnational Transgressions," *Just Business: New Introductory Essays in Business Ethics*, ed. Tom Regan (Philadelphia: Temple University Press, 1983), 274–283, esp. 277–278. See also Hugh Lehman, "Equal Pay for Equal Work in the Third World," in *Ethics and International Relations*, ed. Anthony Ellis (Manchester: Manchester University Press, 1986), 155–162.

62. This, of course, raises the questions addressed by Cohen, Dworkin, Sen, and others on "equality of what?" See, for example, G. A. Cohen, "On the Currency of Egalitarian Justice"; Ronald Dworkin, "What Is Equality? Part 1: Equality of Welfare," *Philosophy and Public Affairs* 10, no. 3 (1981); Dworkin, "What Is Equality? Part 2: Equality of Resources," *Philosophy and Public Affairs* 10, no. 4 (1981); and Amartya Sen, "Equality of What?" in *Choice, Welfare and Measurement* (Oxford: Blackwell, 1982).

63. See, for example, David Miller, "In What Sense Must Socialism Be Communitarian?" *Social Philosophy and Policy* 6 (1989): 58–60.

64. Miller, "In What Sense?" 59.

65. Erica Benner has argued more generally that Miller tends to criticize universalist principles and then to assume them; see, for example, her "Nationality without Nationalism," *Journal of Political Ideologies* 2, no. 2 (1997): 202–203. If I am right, this is an instance of this phenomenon.

66. Miller, "Limits of Cosmopolitan Justice," 170.

67. For these other considerations, which are not examined here, see Miller, *On Nationality*, 75, 77–78.

68. For this argument, see Miller, "Justice and Global Inequality," 193–197. I call it the dynamic argument because its central point is that principles of justice should not be treated in a static fashion but should reflect a dynamic view; "Justice and Global Inequality," 193.

69. This section is taken from an earlier paper: Simon Caney, "Global Equality of Opportunity and the Sovereignty of States," in *International Justice*, ed. Tony Coates (Aldershot, U.K.: Ashgate, 2000) 142–143. © Ashgate Publishing Company. Used with permission.

70. See, for example, Peter Jones, "Universal Principles and Particular Claims: From Welfare Rights to Welfare States," in *Needs and Welfare*, ed. Alan Ware and Robert Goodin (London: Sage, 1990), 48; and Jones, *Rights* (Basingstoke: Macmillan, 1994), 166.

71. See, for example, John Rawls, "Fairness to Goodness," *Philosophical Review* LXXXIV (1975): sec. VII; and Ronald Dworkin, "What Is Equality? Part 1," esp. sec. VIII.

72. McMahan, "The Ethics of International Intervention," in *Ethics and International Relations*, ed. Anthony Ellis (Manchester: Manchester University Press, 1986), 28–29.

73. See Michael Green, "Review Article: National Identity and Liberal Political Philosophy," *Ethics and International Affairs* 10 (1996): 200; Jones, "Universal Principles and Particular Claims," 49.

74. Miller, "Justice and Global Inequality," 194–196.

75. Moreover, as Cécile Fabre rightly points out, Miller's view is especially troubling in cases where later generations are disadvantaged because of the decisions of earlier generations: "Global Egalitarianism," sec. 4.1.

76. See Miller, "Justice and Global Inequality," 192–193; Miller, *On Nationality*, 106. For an evaluation of this argument, see Simon Caney, "Cosmopolitan Justice and Cultural Diversity," *Global Society* 14, no. 4 (2000): 549–550.

77. Miller, "Justice and Global Inequality," 194.

78. For another example, consider Buddhism. Given that Buddhists deny the existence of permanent selves and given that the dynamic argument holds people to account for their past decisions, it is reasonable to expect Buddhists to be skeptical of the force of the dynamic argument. For a relevant discussion, see Derek Parfit, *Reasons and Persons* (Oxford: Oxford University Press, 1986), 323–326. For the similarity between his view and that of Buddhists, see *Reasons and Persons*, 273, 280, 502–503.

79. Gilbert Ryle, *The Concept of Mind* (London: Hutchinson, 1949), 16–18.

80. Miller, "Justice and Global Inequality," 193.

81. See, for example, Miller, "Justice and Global Inequality," 194.

82. For all four, see Miller, "Justice and Global Inequality," 201–203.

83. Miller, "Justice and Global Inequality," 201.

84. Miller, "Justice and Global Inequality," 202.

85. Miller, "Justice and Global Inequality," 202.

86. Miller, "Justice and Global Inequality," 202.

87. Miller, "Justice and Global Inequality," 203.

88. Miller, "Justice and Global Inequality," 202. See Michael L. Ross, "The Political Economy of the Resource Curse," *World Politics* 51, no. 2 (1999): 297–322.

89. Miller, "Justice and Global Inequality," 203.

90. On which see Thomas Pogge, "Priorities of Global Justice," *Metaphilosophy* 32, nos.1/2, 18–22.

91. Miller, "Justice and Global Inequality," 201.

92. Miller, "Justice and Global Inequality," 202.

93. Miller, "Justice and Global Inequality," 201.

94. There may, of course, be arguments that explain the disanalogous treatment of basic rights and global equality. (Perhaps the former but not the latter are inalienable or necessary for a regime to be self-determining.) My claim is that we haven't been given such an argument.

95. An earlier version of this chapter was presented at Nuffield College at the symposium on David Miller's political thought. I am grateful to the participants, and to Andrew Williams, for their comments. I am particularly indebted to David Miller for many discussions on the issues discussed in the chapter and to Avner de-Shalit for his detailed written comments.

16

Global Egalitarianism
An Indefensible Theory of Justice?

Cécile Fabre

1. INTRODUCTION

Over the last twenty years or so, many political theorists have argued that principles of distributive justice apply not only within nations but also between them. Whereas thinkers such as Brian Barry, Charles Beitz, and Thomas Pogge have advocated extensive global distributive policies, others, such as Charles Jones, John Rawls, and Henry Shue have argued that national communities only have duties to help other countries meet the basic needs of their members and be viable economically.[1] David Miller belongs to the latter camp and explicitly rejects the view that *egalitarian* principles of justice should apply globally. His criticism of global egalitarianism as set forth in his most recent works is one of the most sophisticated of those on offer, and my aim, in this chapter, is to rebut it.[2]

Miller does not simply think that principles of global equality are hard to formulate and impossible to implement: he thinks that it does not make sense to talk of such principles as principles *of justice*. For justice, or so he argues, "assumes the form of a principle of equality only in certain contexts. . . . In the absence of a politically-organized global community, this context cannot be stretched in such a way as to make global inequalities unjust merely by virtue of their being inequalities."[3] This is not to say that rich nations have no obligation whatsoever to help poor nations. According to Miller, however, those obligations are much more limited in content than global egalitarianism. Having said that, my concern, here, is not with the principles of global justice he endorses. In his chapter "Entitlements, Obligations and Distributive Justice: The Global Level," Simon Caney shows not only that Miller's own principles are not demanding enough, but also that they conflict with Miller's contention that principles of justice *must* apply only within communities.[4] I agree with Caney's analysis of Miller's account and need not dwell on it further. Rather, my concern is with the principles of justice Miller rejects. Thus, my target is more narrow than Caney's, who addresses not so much Miller's criticism of global egalitarianism as his contention that comparative principles of justice, which need not be egalitarian, cannot apply at global level. Here again, I side, unsurprisingly, with Caney. Indeed, Caney is right to claim that comparative principles of justice, whereby one assesses individuals' entitlements by comparing their situation with that of others, can operate outside national communities. Consequently, *pace* Miller, the fact that egalitarian principles are comparative does not disqualify them as principles of global justice. This having been said, Miller makes a number of points against egalitarian principles per se, which are worth examining.

In section 2, I assess Miller's rejection of global egalitarianism. I conclude that even if global egalitarianism is flawed, Miller's arguments against it are unsatisfactory. However, as I hope to show in section 3, some of his criticisms highlight a number of the issues that a theory of global egalitarianism must address.

2. MILLER'S REJECTION OF GLOBAL EGALITARIANISM

For the purpose of this chapter, global egalitarianism can be described, roughly, as follows: "the worse off, wherever they happen to reside, have a claim for compensation against the better off, wherever they happen to reside, but *only* if (a) they live in a country which is poorly endowed with natural resources and/or which is bad at producing wealth, and (b) they are not responsible for the fact that their country is bad at creating and distributing wealth."

An entirely plausible interpretation of Miller's argument against that view can be formalized as follows:

1. What justice requires largely depends on the cultural and social milieu within which these goods will be distributed.[5]
2. The values that shape that milieu, and thus what justice requires, can best be articulated through deliberative procedures.[6]
3. National communities are the best locus for large-scale deliberative democracy.[7]

Therefore,

4. To speak of global egalitarian principles of justice is deeply problematic.

In this section, I argue that premises (1) to (3) are false, which leaves claim (4) unsupported.

2.1

Claim (1) is a claim about the way in which we should conceive of justice. According to Miller, people disagree about three things when they try to formulate a conception of justice: they disagree about the *goods* which fall under the purview of justice, the *principles* which should regulate the distribution of those goods, and the *social context*—family, firm, political community—within which the distribution is to occur. Conceptions of justice will vary from one community to another depending on their understanding of each of those three elements, and in particular on their understanding of the first.

Now, to echo briefly concerns raised in this volume by Avner de-Shalit, Andrew Mason, and Adam Swift, it is rather unclear to me why the views of the members of a given community determine what counts as a principle of justice. To be sure, trivially, they determine what count as a principle of justice *for them*; but why should we take that at face value? We do not, in fact Miller himself does not, believe that it is never possible to deem certain practices as unjust, even though those who endorse those practices regard them as just. So why does he argue that meeting foreigners' basic needs is a duty of justice, no matter what, but that trying to do more than that, let alone trying to equalize access to advantage (or resources, or opportunities, or welfare) cannot count as such?

In an article that does not appear in *Citizenship and National Identity*, Miller, in effect, answers that question.[8] Global egalitarianism, he argues there, must give an account of what it would mean for a distribution of resources among various individuals to count as an equal distribution. Insofar as natural resources are heterogeneous, and are valued differently by different societies, it is hard to see what equality would mean. Miller describes, and rules out, a Dworkinian solution to that problem. Dworkin imagines an auction, where individuals are given an equal number of clamshells, with which they bid for available resources. Equality obtains, or so Dworkin argues, when each individual thinks that, given the number of clamshells she had and the resources available for auction, she has made the best possible set of bids.[9]

According to Miller, one cannot transfer Dworkin's auction to the global level. For before one bids for a given resource, one must know how one will be able to use that resource. Suppose now that a country has land that, if turned into a vineyard, would yield very rich harvests; suppose further that the inhabitants of that country have prohibited the production and sale of wine for religious reasons. To them, that land is not a source of wealth, whereas to someone else, it would be. To assume that it *is* a source of wealth and to allow people to bid for it already presupposes that it is legitimate to produce and sell wine. But that is precisely what the population of that country disputes.

If Miller is correct, one cannot give a coherent account of global equality of resources. But I do not think that he is correct. True, in considering the land auctionable, one is assuming that producing and selling wine are legitimate. Yet, there is nothing in the auction that would prevent the population of that country to bid for the land as well, thereby ensuring that the land will *not* be used to produce wine. Of course, someone might be tempted to reply (and I am not saying that Miller himself would do so) that one cannot in a Dworkin-ian auction ask communities to bid for resources that already happen to be on their territory. For if the community is outbidded by a wine-producer enthusi-ast, it must accept the presence on its territory of someone who engages in ac-tivities that it finds illegitimate. This, in turn, would unacceptably violate its interest in national self-determination.

I am not suggesting that this would be Miller's objection to the point that the population of that country can be made to bid for the land: I simply do not know what Miller would say here. The important point, though, is this: as-suming that we ought to conclude that the land should not be part of auc-tionable resources on the grounds that it would unacceptably jeopardize the community's interest in national self-determination, we will not have thereby rebutted global egalitarianism. Rather, we will have shown that, in situations of conflicts between implementing equality at global level and promoting the value national self-determination, we should give precedence to the latter over the former.

2.2

I shall return to that point in section 3. For now, let me address claim (2), which states that one can arrive at a conception of justice through deliberative democracy.

Now, when I formalized Miller's claims against global egalitarianism at the outset of section 2, I claimed that it was "an entirely plausible inter-pretation of Miller's argument," as opposed to "Miller's argument." In-deed, this chain of argument is not to be found in Miller's recent works in the form in which I state it here. In particular, Miller might take exception to the ways in which I recruit his claims on deliberative democracy to the cause of his antiegalitarianism. And yet, his account of deliberative democ-racy, while flawed in some ways, nevertheless rescues claim (1) from the charge of relativism leveled in section 2.1, thereby making his antiegalitar-ianism more interesting than it would be otherwise.

Thus, the second step in the four-step rejection of global egalitarianism con-tains a Millerian answer to the question I asked at the close of section 2.1. To quote that step in full:

> How are we to go about finding [the] best interpretation of social justice? . . . It is not the *purpose* of deliberative democracy to generate a widely-shared concep-tion of social justice; its purpose is to take practical decisions on issues facing the community. But it may be a *side-effect* of a well-functioning deliberative democ-

racy that it does just this, by inducing participants to revise their original judgements about what's fair when confronted by fellow-citizens who hold different views.[10]

Now, a regime is a deliberative democracy if the process for reaching decisions is one "whereby initial preferences are transformed to take account of the views of others."[11] In defending one's view as to how society should be shaped, one must only advance reasons that others can accept. Miller thus appeals to a weak form of impartiality, whereby one formulates one's claims (in content and basis) in such a way that they appeal to the wider political community.[12] Insofar as citizens are motivated so to formulate their claims and, generally, to act in good faith, they can develop an understanding of which goods should be distributed, how and to whom; by virtue of being worked out through deliberative procedures, such understanding is the best conception of justice citizens may hope for.

Miller's argument is convincing only if it is plausible that a conception of justice articulated by a given community will always be acceptable to all. But consider the situation of someone who values a good to which he does not have access, which is not considered as highly valuable by the society in which he lives, and which nevertheless does not cost more than goods which are considered as so valuable. Thus, consider a nomadic religious ascetic, who claims that he needs resources to print out religious tracts instead of housing, and who happens to live in a very secular society which regards housing as much more important than printing religious tracts. Miller argues that the ascetic does not have a claim to those resources, even though they would not exceed the amount needed to provide him with housing, on the grounds that "someone's preferences, no matter how strong, cannot ground claims of need."[13] If society has decided, through deliberative procedures in which the ascetic had a voice, that housing is a good that falls under the purview of justice whereas printing religious tracts does not, the ascetic has no claim. But why should that particular outcome—housing is a need, tracts are not—be acceptable to him? The good he requires, his preference, as Miller puts it, is not more expensive than housing. Furthermore, he has good reasons to protest that the majority's *preference* for housing is arbitrarily elevated to the status of a need, simply in virtue of being held by the majority.

A Millerian answer to the latter point would be, I think, that the preference of the majority for housing is elevated to the status of a need through deliberation. Can it be so, though? The difference between preferences and needs is a conceptual one, and as such it does not depend on the views of the democratic majority. As David Wiggins puts it, whether I prefer x to y depends on my state of mind, whereas whether I need x as opposed to y depends on the state of the world.[14] Thus, it is not up to me that I need food in order to survive, indeed, that I need to print tracts, or to have housing, in order to live a fulfilling life. And what counts, for me, as a fulfilling life is not always up to me either. To be sure, whether or not my conception of the good life is such that it requires that I print tracts or live in decent accommodation is, to some extent, a matter of choice. But insofar as what my conception of the good life requires is not a matter of choice, whatever that conception is, Miller cannot claim that housing is a need whereas printing tracts is not in virtue of the fact that the democratic majority reached that conclusion. What he cannot avoid saying, in order for his treatment of the case of ascetic to survive, is that if the democratic majority decides to privilege conceptions of the good which require housing as opposed to conceptions of the good which require tract printing, then the ascetic must accept that as his community's understanding of justice.[15]

Quite why he would want to say that remains unclear. We need here an account of the reason why deliberative procedures coupled with weak impartiality deliver *justice*. But no such account is forthcoming.[16] In fact, Miller's own commitment to deliberative democracy coupled with weak impartiality seems to entail that (some) requirements of justice are arrived at independently of democratic procedures. Endorsing deliberative democracy and weak impartiality amounts to requiring that citizens actually act accordingly, that is, only make claims that fellow citizens can reasonably accept. This requirement, in turn, rests on the view (or something like the view) that human beings all have a claim to be treated with equal concern and respect. There is, then, a moral prescription as to how one should act toward others, which is not yielded by deliberative procedures but rather underpins citizens' commitment to them. But if that prescription is correct, why not allow that it entails other, more detailed requirements to act toward others in certain ways? Thus, it does seem to entail the requirement that we should not murder, torture, or rape other human beings. But if that is true, why not allow, further, that it entails certain requirements to distribute resources in certain ways— requirements that could be deemed requirements of justice? Miller actually does think that rich countries are under duties of justice to help poorer countries meet the basic needs of their people. Those duties of justice are not the outcome of deliberation conducted among the citizens of rich countries, and although Miller does not tell us where they stem from, one can plausibly surmise that they stem from the view that not helping people meet those needs, and thereby allowing them to suffer severe deprivation, violates one's commitment to basic equality. But if it is true that those duties do not stem from deliberative procedures, then one cannot rule out without further ado the possibility that more stringent duties of justice, such as duties to redress inequalities, can be arrived at outside those procedures.

2.3

I may have given the impression of needlessly digressing away from global justice into the territory of metatheories of justice. Yet, it is crucial for Miller's case against global egalitarianism that deliberative procedures do indeed deliver justice. For if they do not, and if it is possible to construct a theory of justice without appealing to procedural criteria for justice, Miller's case is much weaker than appears at first sight. To see why, let us examine the third and fourth steps in Miller's rejection of global egalitarianism. They go as follows: (3) National communities are the best locus for large-scale deliberative democracy, from which, together with steps (1)—what justice requires depends on the community within which the distribution takes place—and (2)—what justice requires is articulated through deliberative democratic procedures—it follows that (4) global egalitarianism is incoherent. Thus, if (2) is false, it is not so clear why stringent principles of global justice above and beyond the meeting of basic needs can only apply within national communities, why, in short, global egalitarianism is incoherent.

Let us assume for the sake of argument that claim (2) is true. Claim (4) remains unsupported, for claim (3), or so I shall now argue, is false. Miller holds it to be true for the following reason. You recall that he is committed to weak impartiality and to the institutions through which it can operate, to wit, deliberative democracy. To be impartial means to be willing to give people who disagree with us reasons that they can accept. This presupposes that there is enough common ground between us and them that we can find such reasons; in particular, we need to be able to understand each other's own standpoint, so as to arrive at a shared understanding of what counts as valuable resources to be distributed. Now, insofar as we make comparative judgments of *fairness*—is it fair that I have x amounts of goods whereas they have $x + 10$?— primarily with fellow nationals and not with non–fellow nationals, such shared understanding must be located within a national community.[17] Thus, even if we developed the institutions we would need in order to have deliberative democracy at a global level, we would not be able to come up with an acceptable understanding of which goods should be distributed, and how.

Let us assume that Miller is correct to claim that individuals primarily make judgments of fairness in comparison with their fellow nationals. It still does not imply that they have no strong claim of fairness against foreigners. Imagine a group of women who, for cognitive reasons, do not know that their husbands are doing much better than they are financially, or that they do know it, but see nothing wrong in this, as they have always been told that this is the way things are, that men, solely by virtue of being men, should have more. Those women may compare how they fare relative to one another and think that it is unfair that some of them get more from their husbands than others. But they may not deem it unfair that their situation is worse than their husbands'.[18] Should we, in all those cases, deny that women have a claim to more resources than they currently get? Miller would not reach that conclusion: he would agree, I think, that the mere fact that some people do not think that what they get is unfair does not constitute a reason to forbear to give them resources. So, his claim, once reconstructed, seems to be that against a fair background of correct information and appropriate perception of their moral status as human beings, people tend to make judgments of fairness primarily in comparison to fellow nationals.

Well, even if that is true, it does not follow that they should persist in doing so. Moreover, it is not clear at all that it is true. Within supranational entities, such as the European Union, people do develop a sense of justice across borders. Thus, within Europe, redistribution to poor countries from rich countries, but also to poor _regions_ (within countries) from rich countries, is underpinned by an increasing awareness that it is possible to make such comparative judgments of fairness between national communities who, while maintaining many of their national characteristics, belong to the same supranational entity. As Caney argues persuasively,[19] the common agricultural policy, the common fisheries policies, indeed, at global level, humanitarian intervention, and refugee policies are all instances where comparative judgments are being made across borders on what people get, give, ought to get, and ought to give. Granted, those are not instances where strong egalitarian principles operate. Nonetheless, it remains the case that Miller cannot convincingly object to such principles on the grounds that people do not make comparisons across borders.

There is another problem with Miller's argument in favor of restricting stringent claims of justice to members of the same national community. He thinks that deliberative democracy, which helps formulate a conception of justice, best works within national communities, for it is within such communities that shared understandings of what counts as needs and advantages is developed. But such understandings also develop within subnational groups. Thus, one can very well imagine that an orthodox Jewish community, or a fundamentalist Christian group, would deny that girls should get the same education as boys, that sex education should be part of the curriculum, and so on. Why not, then, consider each of those groups as a "community of justice," whose members together decide how to allocate goods among themselves, provided that they each deploy in support of their proposals reasons that other members of that group who disagree with the proposals can find persuasive? Such reasons could, for example, revolve around scriptural interpretation. Just as it is unclear why the ascetic has no claim of justice to the resources he needs to print out tracts, it is unclear, in the context of Miller's views on shared values, that the understanding of the good of education developed by the majority should have precedence over the understanding developed by the minority. It is beyond the scope of this chapter fully to address that issue. Suffice it to say that _if_ it is true that weak impartiality can only operate among people who have the same understanding of what counts as valuable resources (a conditional which, I, for one, do not endorse), then it does not seem always to recommend _national_ principles of justice over _global_ principles of justice. It may well recommend _local_ principles over any other.

Miller would deny that we should accede to the conception of justice developed by subgroups, first, on the grounds that a national community can accommodate the demands of its cultural and ethnic minorities, and second, on the grounds that the proper way for members of a national community to regard one another is as equals. If a national community allowed different groups to distribute certain fundamental goods in their own ways, and especially in ways that contradict the fundamental principle that individuals should not be discriminated against on grounds of race and gender, it would fail to confer equal status on all its members. In a Western liberal democracy, that would be clearly unjust. Now, even if the first prong of his response is true, which I doubt,[20] the second is vulnerable to the charge that after all, the proper way for members of the human race to regard each other is *also* as equals, which may very well require that efforts be made to develop a global, egalitarian conception of justice.

Miller would resist the foregoing points by pointing out that global principles of distribution above and beyond the meeting of basic needs, and by implication egalitarian principles, cannot be principles of social justice. For "the principles we advance must apply to an identifiable set of institutions whose impact on the life chances of different individuals can also be traced." Moreover, there must be "some agency capable of changing the institutional structure in more or less the way our favored theory demands."[21] Such institutions must therefore be global in scope. However, they are neither in place nor desirable.[22] Therefore, there can be no such thing as global principles of justice above and beyond the meeting of very basic needs, the prohibition on exploitation, and the requirement that each country be economically viable.

At first sight, Miller's argument seems convincing: in order for the ideal of weak impartiality to work, institutions are necessary where citizens can advance to another reasons they can all accept. However, if it is correct, Miller's own principles of global justice are vulnerable to the same criticisms as egalitarian principles, since, presumably, global institutions are also necessary in order to implement them: after all, just as the religious community described in section 2.1 has a certain understanding of what counts as valuable resource, a community whose members are very needy, or which is not economically viable, has a certain understanding of what counts as a basic need there and as to what counts as economic viability. Accordingly, global institutions would be necessary where it can advance its claims, on behalf of its citizens. As it happens, global institutions as they currently exist clearly do not seem to do the job. So, given that the international institutions that would be needed to achieve what Miller wants to see done at global level do not currently exist, it is doubtful, on Miller's own premise (i.e., "global institutions are necessary to generate global principles of justice") that there can be any kind of principle of justice at that level.

In any case, I am not convinced that such a global community is *necessary* to devise global principles of justice. A given citizen body does not simply make decisions as to how its members should behave toward one another; it also makes decisions as to how it should behave toward other citizen bodies. Suppose that members of community C1 must decide how much to distribute to members of community C2, which happens to be poorer than they are. It is entirely plausible to think that the ideals of weak impartiality and deliberative democracy require that whatever decision members of C1 make must be informed by reasons that members of C2 know they could and would accept if, counterfactually, they were part of the decision-making process.[23] For example, were members of C1 to decide that they cannot give extra resources to poorer members of C2 on the grounds that the natural resources under C1's territory belong to C1, they would be producing a bad, self-serving argument, which no potential C2 claimant could be expected to accept, whether or not she actually takes part in C1's deliberative process.

However, although global institutions are not necessary to *devise* principles of justice, they are necessary to *implement* them. And it is true that institutions strong enough to do so are lacking at global level. Or rather, it is true that those who currently control our global institutions do not believe that justice requires more than meeting the basic needs of foreigners; if they do believe that it does, they certainly do not have the political will to act accordingly. Yet, I do not think that this undermines our characterization of more stringent principles than the basic needs principle as global principles of *justice*. The lack of global institutions only tells us that global principles of justice cannot yet be implemented and that we have to settle, as a matter of policy, for a less global distribution. It does not tell us that we should look for other global principles of justice, or that global egalitarian principles cannot be deemed principles of justice.

3. NATIONAL (DEMOCRATIC) SELF-DETERMINATION AND GLOBAL EGALITARIANISM

3.1

Egalitarians are concerned with delineating what equality requires; but not all of them have spent much time solving conflicts between equality and other values. More specifically, when they have articulated theories of egalitarian global justice, they have not solved conflicts between global equality and democratic national self-determination. Miller claims that there is no conflict between stringent principles of global justice (which encompass egalitarian principles) and democratic national self-determination, since stringent principles of justice can only exist as such at national level. I have argued that his denial that there can be such principles at global level is not adequately supported. In what follows, I show that such conflicts can arise, by examining Miller's claim that global egalitarianism fails to account for the importance of collective responsibility, and thereby of national self-determination.

But first, it is important to distinguish ideal from nonideal theories of justice. Ideal theories set out what justice requires of each individual, on the assumption that no one will default on their duties. Nonideal theories set out what justice requires of individuals when others default on their duties. In both ideal and nonideal theories of global justice, there are conflicts between equality and national self-determination. Miller's aforementioned claim is deployed as part of a nonideal theory of global justice, and I shall deal with it right away, postponing my account of ideal theory until section 3.2.

In section 1, I claimed that under global egalitarianism, the worse off, wherever they reside, have a claim for compensation at the bar of justice, which may impose duties on foreign countries to provide them with the required resources. I qualified that statement by pointing out that individuals have that claim to the extent that they are not responsible for being worse off. Miller would strongly disagree with that argument: states, in his view, should not be "compensated for errors of economic management, or for making expenditure choices that detract from the pursuit of justice (for instance, to stockpile large quantities of armaments)."[24] Thus, suppose the citizens of a given country, call it Affluenza, whose predecessors implemented consumerist policies, have a smaller per capita share of natural resources than the citizens of another country, call it Ecologia, whose predecessors engaged in sustainable, environment-friendly development. Similarly, imagine two countries, Procreatia, which allows for a 5 percent per annum population growth, and Condominium, which implements strict family-planning policies and thereby achieves a stable population. Inhabitants of Procreatia, who are more numerous, have fewer resources than inhabitants of Condominium.[25] According to Miller, Affluenzian and Procreatians do not have a claim of justice for extra payment against, respectively, Ecologians and Condominians. Communities, in his view, should be held collectively responsible for their fate, and individual members of badly off communities therefore do not have a claim of justice against better-off members of better-off communities to compensation for their unequal situation.

In so arguing, Miller overlooks the fact that as the effects of such mistakes may sometimes only be felt a generation or two later, they are felt by individuals who were not adult, or even born, when those mistakes were made. By virtue of the principle that people should not be adversely affected by factors they are not responsible for, those individuals, presumably, do have a claim for compensation against richer states. Consider, analogously, the case of two families, in a same country, of equal size and wealth at time *t*: family A saves and is industrious, while family B adopts a leisurely lifestyle, with the effect that forty years later, family A is richer than family B. Miller nowhere says in *Principles of Social Justice*, which addresses relationships of justice between fellow nationals who are members of different families, that families whose wealth derives from decades of wise investments should not be taxed in order to compensate poor families whose poverty comes from decades of money squandering. And, indeed, he could not say it, as a fundamental principle of his is that, from the point of view of the government, people's standing and their claims of justice do not stem from the family in which they are born, but from their status as equal individual moral agents. By the same token, Miller should accept that an individual member of Affluenza whose poverty at time t_{40} is due to management mistakes made at time t, before he was born or of adult age, has a claim against citizens of Ecologia (many of whom, incidentally, at time t_{40}, benefit from, without having contributed to, wise policies conducted by their forebears).

Moreover, in the case of Procreatia versus Condominium, Miller's argument implies that the children of Procreatians who failed to check population growth can be denied compensation for being worse off, on the grounds that their parents could have decided not to have them. Insofar as it penalizes them for something they have not chosen themselves, to wit, for being born, Miller's principle is unjust.

In the two scenarios I have just described, that individuals may not be responsible for being worse off does not seem too hard to ascertain. More difficult to decide is the validity of claims of justice made by people who are made worse off than members of other countries as a result of policies conducted by their contemporary fellow citizens. Imagine two countries, Frugalia and Profligata. The government of Frugalia is conducting policies such that its members not only are in an equal situation compared with one another, but they also enjoy a very high standard of living. By contrast, the government of Profligata is conducting policies such that its members enjoy a much lower standard of living than they would if they were members of Frugalia (for example, they have spent billions of dollars on spatial programs, the usefulness of which is rather dubious). Now, it is my contention that *at the bar of equality*, a badly off Profligatean who opposed the policies conducted by his government has a claim for extra payment against Frugalia, just as he would have such a claim if he were living under a dictatorship and had absolutely no say in the way economic policy is shaped, or if he were denied the right to participate in Profligata's decision-making process on the grounds that he is not a national of Profligata.[26]

Miller rejects that argument, on the grounds that the position of the dissenting Profligatean "is then essentially no different from that of anyone who holds a minority view amongst his contemporaries . . . if he holds his newfound ideals sincerely, his position is in some respects an unfortunate one, but he does not have a just claim to resources transfers from [Frugalia]."[27] Similarly, you recall, the ascetic does not have a claim against better-off fellow citizens to the resources he needs to print religious tracts. Well, it is equally unjust, I contend, to impose disadvantages on the ascetic and on dissenting Profligateans simply because they happen to be in the minority. What people can claim as a matter of justice does not depend on what the democratic community decides that they should get.

There is another consideration that Miller deploys in support of his claim that a badly off individual does not have a claim against foreign governments that he be made as well off as his fellow citizens or as those governments' members. Miller claims that, up to a point, ordinary citizens of democratic regimes must bear unjust policies conducted by their government, because "in some sense they share in the responsibility for [such policies]."[28] There are two claims here. The first one states that if I participate in democratic procedures, I share responsibility for the outcome yielded by those procedures; the second one states that as I share such responsibility, I do not have a claim against other countries for compensation for unjust outcomes. The former claim is wildly implausible, as it would imply, for example, that German Jews who voted in the last, democratic, election of the Weimar Republic in some sense share responsibility for the victory of the Nazi party and for the monstrous treatments the Nazi regime meted out to them. The second claim captures an important insight, namely, that the fact that we are not responsible for unjust policies does not entail that we have a claim for compensation against foreign countries. For as Miller rightly points out, "we cannot value self-determination, and at the same time seek to nullify its effects whenever it leads to outcomes that appear to us mistaken."[29] And so it could very well be that national self-determination overrides egalitarian justice.

3.2

A similar point can be made with respect to ideal theories of global justice. Let us assume, then, that egalitarian principles of justice are in place at global level, and that no one defaults on their duty to contribute. What would such a world look like? Each government would have to pay a tax to a global fund, in proportion to the wealth it creates and to the wealth of its inhabitants. Each government would have to redistribute to its citizens what global egalitarianism would dictate that they get. Individuals and communities would thus be required to give away what can be traced to good brute luck. There would be rather little scope, in such a world, for countries to accumulate vast amounts of wealth and to engage in the kinds of collective ventures that rich countries typically engage in: monument building, high-tech research, highly developed health care and education system (e.g.: Western countries have the means to provide their AIDS patients with sophisticated and reasonably effective treatments, but they simply do not have enough resources to help AIDS patients in developing countries to the same extent), and so forth. Now, some will balk at such picture on the grounds that it is an inefficient way of allocating resources (some inequalities may actually benefit the worst off, wherever they are). But one may also reject global equality on the grounds that it does not leave much space for national self-determination.

In short, egalitarian justice is but one of the many values that we should seek to promote. The values of national self-determination and of democratic decision making are important values, too, and they may indeed require that we abide by the will of the national, democratic majority. It is beyond the scope of this chapter to adjudicate between those competing values. Rather, it is only through careful argument that one can decide which value is the most important—global justice, where justice demands equality, or democratic, national self-determination. Miller does not believe that there is a conflict between those values, since, in his view, global equality does not make sense as a conception of justice. Although his argument to that effect is flawed (or so I have argued), his skepticism about global equality is a healthy reminder that globally minded egalitarians should spend more time than they have working out a solution to that conflict.

4. CONCLUSION

To conclude, I have made the following points:

Miller is wrong to reject global egalitarianism on the ground that democratic deliberation delivers the best conception of justice and that national communities are the best locus for such deliberation.

More generally, Miller is mistaken in thinking that what counts as a principle and a claim of justice depends on what the individuals among which goods are distributed think about justice.

However, he is right that if we do away with collective responsibility, and if we seek to implement egalitarian policies at global level, we will jeopardize the value of democratic national self-determination.

I have not solved the conflicts between egalitarian justice and democratic national self-determination. I believe, though, that just as it is important that individuals be allowed to flourish in their private lives, be it, within limits, at the expense of other individuals, it is important that, as members of national communities they be allowed to embark on various collective ventures, be it, within limits, at the expense of members of other national communities. Where to draw the line is one of the hardest tasks at hand: I would actually go further than to say that the basic needs of everybody should be met and that nations should be given an opportunity to be economically viable and claim (not unproblematically) that countries have a duty to ensure that everybody in the world has the resources to lead what counts as a flourishing life in his or her community. Even if Miller were to agree that providing people with the means for a flourishing life, rather than meeting their basic needs, is a requirement of global justice, he would argue that such a world, where vast inequalities would be allowed, would be just. Unlike him, I contend that it would be unjust, albeit desirable. This divergence of views may sound like quibbling over the meaning of words: but as I hope to have shown, it does, in fact, denote a profound disagreement not simply over the meaning of justice, but over the ways in which we should conceive of it.

NOTES

An earlier draft of this chapter was written for a symposium on David Miller's recent works, which was held at Nuffield College, Oxford, July 11–13, 2000, and was subsequently presented at McGill University's Political Philosophy Workshop in September 2000. I am grateful to the participants at the symposium and the workshop for very helpful suggestions, and to G. A. Cohen and A. de-Shalit for written comments.

1. Brian Barry, "Humanity and Justice in Global Perspective," in *Ethics, Economics and the Law: Nomos XXIV*, ed. J. R. Pennock and J. W. Chapman (New York: New York University Press, 1982); C. Beitz, *Political Theory and International Relations* (Princeton, N.J.: Princeton University Press, 1979); Thomas Pogge, *Realizing Rawls* (Ithaca, N.Y.: Cornell University Press, 1989) and "An Egalitarian Law of Peoples," *Philosophy and Public Affairs* 23 (1994): 195–223; C. Jones, *Global Justice* (Oxford: Oxford University Press, 1998); John Rawls, *The Law of Peoples* (Cambridge, Mass.: Harvard University Press, 1999); Henry Shue, *Basic Rights: Subsistence, Affluence and U.S. Foreign Policy* (Princeton, N.J.: Princeton University Press, 1980).

2. See David Miller, *Principles of Social Justice* (Cambridge, Mass.: Harvard University Press, 1999), and *Citizenship and National Identity* (London: Polity Press, 2000).

3. Miller, *Citizenship*, 174.

4. Simon Caney, "Entitlements, Obligations and Distributive Justice: The Global Level," in this volume.

5. Miller, *Citizenship*, 168–171.

6. Miller, *Citizenship*, 171.

7. Miller, *Principles*, 18–19. See also Miller, *Citizenship*, ch. 4 and 5, as well as his *On Nationality* (Oxford: Oxford University Press, 1995), ch. 4.

8. See his "Justice and Global Inequality," in *Inequality, Globalization, and World Politics*, ed. A. Hurrell and N. Woods (Oxford: Oxford University Press, 1999).

9. Ronald Dworkin, "What Is Equality? Part Two: Equality of Resources," *Philosophy and Public Affairs* 10 (1981): 283–345.

10. David Miller, *Citizenship*, 171.

11. Miller, *Citizenship*, 9.

12. Miller, *Citizenship*, 56. One displays strong impartiality, by contrast, when one gives other people's desires, attachments, and projects equal weight as to ours. See, for example, Brian Barry, *Justice as Impartiality* (Oxford: Oxford University Press, 1995); and Thomas Nagel, *Equality and Partiality* (Oxford: Oxford University Press, 1991).

13. Miller, *Principles*, 211.

14. D. Wiggins, *Needs, Values, Truth* (Oxford: Basil Blackwell, 1987), 6.

15. Notice that Miller's argument against the claims of the ascetic does not bode well for any claim to certain resources that a minority group might want to make.

16. Moreover, as de-Shalit shows in his "Deliberative Democracy: Guarantee for Justice or Preventing Injustice?" in this volume, Miller's endorsement of deliberative democracy rests on dubious empirical assumptions. In particular, it is not at all clear that deliberation actually changes people's preferences. Accordingly, or so de-Shalit argues, the outcomes of the deliberative procedures merely tend to reflect existing, unreconstructed views and prejudices—not the best material with which to construct principles of justice.

17. Miller, *Principles*, 18–19.

18. For a recent account of such cases in contemporary India, see Martha Nussbaum, *Women and Human Development* (Cambridge: Cambridge University Press, 2000).

19. Caney, "Entitlements, Obligations, and Distributive Justice," this volume.

20. See note 15.

21. Miller, *Principles,* 5–6. For that reason, he would remain unmoved by my claim that Europeans do make judgments of fairness in comparison with one another and that this is evidence that common understandings of justice can develop transnationally: he would point out that the reason why Europeans make such judgments is precisely because there are (supranational) institutions that allocate resources among states and regions.

22. Miller, *Citizenship,* ch. 5.

23. A brief reminder: I am not arguing here that this is how we should devise principles of global justice. Instead, I am assuming that Miller's claim that deliberative procedures deliver justice (claim [2] in his four-step argument against global egalitarianism set out previously) is correct. My point is to show that if one accepts that claim, one can endorse the view that these procedures can deliver an egalitarian principle of global justice even if they only exist at national level.

24. Miller, *Citizenship,* 177.

25. See Miller, "Justice and Global Inequality," 193–195. For a similar argument, see J. Rawls, *Law of Peoples,* 116–117.

26. I am here implying that from the point of view of what equality requires, the democraticness or lack of it of a regime is irrelevant. However, when balancing equality against other values, it might very well be that we would want equality to override the political autonomy of dictatorship, while we may not want it to override the political autonomy of a democratic regime.

27. Miller, "Justice and Global Inequality," 195.

28. Miller, *Citizenship,* 176.

29. Miller, *Citizenship,* 176.

17

Nonbasic Environmental Goods and Social Justice

Mathew Humphrey

If we do not share Friedrich Hayek's view that social justice is a "mirage," then the question of what goods are goods of social justice is a live one. That is, if we believe that there are certain things in the world to which human beings have a right, grounded in justice, then the question of *which* things in the world has to be addressed. One class of goods that might be included in a list of goods appropriate to distribution under the rubric of justice is environmental goods. Now, what counts as an "environmental good" will itself be a subject of debate, but suitable candidates for inclusion would include such items as the quality of the air, water, and soil that people have available to them; the distribution of, and quantities of, certain species of plants and animals; and the accessibility of, and quality of, other features such as forests, lakes, and seas.

This question of whether environmental goods are goods of social justice, if so which environmental goods these might be, and among whom these goods should be distributed, has received increasing attention in recent years.[1] To get a clearer perspective on this problem, it is useful to distinguish environmental goods that seem basic to human welfare from those that do not (or at least that are far less obviously so). Breathable air, potable water, and adequate supplies of nutrition might all be considered goods that are basic to a human life; without them our functioning is impaired, and radical deprivation will lead to death. Such goods are, in the terms of this chapter, basic environmental goods. They can be assumed to be rationally desired by everyone, whatever comprehensive conception of the good people happen to possess. Other environmental goods do not seem to be basic in this sense. My preference for the existence of a bird called the Dartford Warbler may be strongly felt, but the argument that I could not function as a human being without the existence of this bird in the world would be controversial. An argument that other people would be equally deprived even if they had never heard of the Dartford Warbler would be even more so. Such environmental goods, which are not obviously essential to human functioning, will be considered "nonbasic" in this chapter.

I would suggest that the case for considering basic environmental goods to be goods of social justice is relatively straightforward. If human beings should be considered as entitled to basic goods, then environmental basic goods would surely be included given their necessity for any adequate human life. The case for including *nonbasic* environmental goods as goods of justice is far less obvious, and it is with this latter question that this chapter concerns itself. We will use, as an entry point to this question, David Miller's recent attempt to disbar nonbasic environmental goods from the list of goods demanded by social justice.

In his 1999 book *Principles of Social Justice*, Miller visits, briefly, the question of the relationship between nonbasic environmental goods and justice. Despite the brevity of his remarks, which are discussed later, the question he raises regarding the relationship between the preservation of nonbasic environmental goods and distributive justice is of great importance for those of us working in the field of environmental ethics. Furthermore, we have more than the passing remarks contained in *Principles of Social Justice* to go on, as Miller treats the same questions more expansively in his chapter in Andrew Dobson's recent collection *Fairness and Futurity*.[2] Miller's suggested resolution to the problem of how to consider nonbasic environmental goods runs counter to the arguments put forward by a significant number (probably a majority) of environmental ethicists. This may be no bad thing, as Miller's views present a challenge to what has become "conventional wisdom," for some, in a problematic area of environmental philosophy. Such conventional wisdom being that the elimination of contingency in environmental argument is possible through the establishment of an argument for the intrinsic value of nature.[3] I suggest that Miller's treatment of the problem of nonbasic environmental goods raises genuine problems for those who want to argue for the preservation of these goods on the grounds of their intrinsic value, and that these problems are due to the ineliminability of contingency in the class of arguments that intrinsic value addresses. However, I go on to argue that if we compare the loss of certain nonbasic, nonenvironmental goods with the destruction of nonbasic environmental goods, we will see that there are two different types of change involved. Opportunity costs are nearly always present in environmental decision making, which often trades off different types of irreversible change. However, within the field of irreversible change there is a distinction to be made between irrecoverable costs and irreplaceable loss, the importance of which is argued for. If the import of this distinction is recognized, then the distribution of (some) nonbasic environmental goods should, *pace* Miller's objections, be treated as a matter of distributive justice, regardless of questions of intrinsic value.

The chapter proceeds in three sections. First, I challenge David Miller's line of reasoning in his rejection of the accounts of the value of nature to human lives put forward by John O'Neill and Robert Goodin. This raises a broader question about Miller's method for establishing the adequacy of principles of justice. I claim that Miller's stance on this also seems to contradict the claims he makes elsewhere about objective values and human life. Second, I go on to argue that even if we accept Miller's objections, we still have reasons to believe that nonbasic environmental goods can be goods of justice. Finally, I consider a possible objection to my argument grounded in the doctrine of welfare compensation and briefly sketch some of the implications of the argument in this chapter for the problem of intra- versus intergenerational justice.

To begin, then, with Miller's brief treatment of this topic in *Principles of Social Justice*, where it appears in a more general discussion of the relationship between public goods and distributive justice (itself nested in a section of the book dealing with meritocracy, desert, and justice). Miller asks whether the value of public goods can be measured by the amount of utility they generate. There is, he says, a possible challenge to this approach, which is that some public goods can be seen as "merit goods," which are valuable independently of any welfare-generating properties, and this is where the discussion of environmental goods begins.

First, there is the case in which a particular good is taken to have its own intrinsic value, independent of existing human preferences. Features of the natural environment are sometimes regarded in this way, as having value independent of the satisfaction human beings derive from experiencing them (it's good that there are tigers living freely in the wild even if nobody gets pleasure from watching them).

> It does not seem justifiable for the social value of public goods to be affected directly by judgements of their intrinsic value. Rather, such judgements should be seen as considerations that can be advanced politically, which if successfully done would then alter the content of people's preferences. Thus if you believe that wild tigers have intrinsic value, then you may try to persuade others that this is so; to the extent that you succeed, people will want to have tiger habitats preserved, and this becomes a genuine public good. If by contrast people are not persuaded, then the judgement cannot be grounded in claims of justice: I cannot demand a reward for my activities in securing tiger habitats on the ground that this is a public good, any more than in market contexts I can claim rewards for making things that I judge are valuable for people to have but that they are not willing to buy.[4]

One thing of note about this passage is that, if correct, it effectively undermines one aspect of the common distinction between ecocentric (nature-centered, broadly speaking) and anthropocentric (human-centered) ethics in environmental philosophy—not at the level of ethical argument itself, but in terms of the foreseen practical effects of making the distinction. Part of the reason why ecocentrists make preservationist arguments in terms of intrinsic values in nature is to remove the question of nature preservation from the contingencies of whether or not such preservation is believed beneficial to human welfare.[5] If wild tigers are intrinsically valuable at a sufficient level to generate a moral demand for their preservation, then such preservation is demanded irrespective of human welfare benefits. Miller's approach suggests that contingency reenters the equation at another juncture. One has to convince a majority of people via the political process that one's judgment about intrinsic value is correct—that is, generate enough tiger-preserving preferences, and then, and only then, does tiger preservation become a "genuine" public good.[6] Thus one form of human-based contingency (human welfare in anthropocentric arguments) is replaced by another (the number of people with sufficiently strong tiger-preserving preferences). The mistake that intrinsic value theorists make, I believe (although this is not an argument I can defend here), is in believing that contingencies such as these can be avoided by going down the intrinsic value route. This will be true in terms of support for environmental public policies whether one is wedded to an objectivist or (more obviously) a subjectivist position on value. I should add that this is not to argue that an environmental ethicist ought to disavow intrinsic value theory if he or she believes it is true. The point is rather that the apparent prospect of eliminating contingency through the use of intrinsic value arguments does not (pace Eckersley) provide a reason for supporting an intrinsic value argument. This is both because the hope of eliminating contingency is in itself a poor reason and also because the apparent prospect is a false one.

More pertinently to this argument, consider the posited relationship here between public goods and goods of justice. Miller suggests that on the generation of a sufficient number of tiger-preserving preferences, tiger preservation becomes a "genuine" public good. He is certainly correct insofar as if we agree that knowledge of wild tigers is a good, it is a public one—both nonrival and nonexcludable. I cannot deny you the pleasure of living in a world with tigers so long as I also enjoy that benefit, and my "consumption" of this good does not affect yours.[7] The quality of being a public good, however, does not necessarily entail the existence of that good as a good of justice. We may agree that knowledge of the existence of wild tigers is a public good. This view does not, logically, bind us to a view that people deprived of this knowledge are being treated unjustly. Conversely, material wealth is both rival and excludable, and yet normally features in a metric of the goods of social justice. It is thus worth bearing in mind that we are enquiring here into the status of nonbasic environmental goods as *goods of justice* rather than as public goods.

This brings us to a problematic element of Miller's argument—the idea that this question of justice pivots upon a demand for an agent-based reward for "activities in securing tiger habitats" that is directly analogous to a (mistaken) claim for rewards for producing goods one believes others ought to demand in the marketplace. The problem here is that demands for preservation based on claims about intrinsic values in nature are presented as the demands of disinterested ethics, not as demands based upon the activities of the agent making the claim (although personal utility gains may of course be generated as a by-product). To take one intrinsic value argument as an example: the argument that organisms displaying the property of autopoiesis (the ability to self-regenerate and maintain their own boundaries) are of intrinsic value because they "matter to themselves" in an appropriate way,[8] rests upon the "argumentative competence" (such as plausible premises, consistency, and coherence) of the argument itself. It does not depend upon claims of merit on the part of the author (for producing, say, a clever philosophical argument). The instrumental nature of producing goods for the market stands in direct contrast to this, and I would suggest the analogy between one and the other in Miller's argument does not survive critical scrutiny, even at the illustrative level. If I produce goods *for* the market, I could never reasonably complain that a set of values, which should exist *independently* of the actual valuations of people in the marketplace, ought to be realized in the market with respect to these goods. This would be to make a fundamental mistake about the nature of production for the market. A more appropriate analogy would be with an artist who believes she is producing art that is itself of intrinsic value. This person could complain that her art is not valued as it should be, that its *true* value was not reflected in market valuations. If I produce goods that I believe to be of *intrinsic* value, it is not clear why I would want rewards from others for bringing such value into existence, even if I feel that others *should* value what I have produced in an appropriate way. If I believe this value to be intrinsic, I should also believe that such value exists independently of the subjective evaluations of others. Is it not thus sufficient for me that nobody *destroys* the value I have brought into the world? (Thus, this line of reasoning seems to imply a preservationist stance.) This suggests, among other things, that the positioning of the discussion of environmental goods in the part of Miller's book dealing with merit and claims of *desert* may itself be inappropriate.

We need, at this stage, to delve a little more deeply into the case for rejecting the demand for the preservation of natural objects and categories such as species as being a demand of justice. In his "Social Justice and Environmental Goods," Miller considers whether the demands of social justice can be reasonably said to include demands for the preservation of nonbasic environmental goods. Alternatively, such demands can be considered (as in *Principles of Social Justice*) as *political* demands, but not demands of *justice*. Such political demands have to take their chance in the democratic arena along with other policy preferences—your preference for tiger preservation along with my preference for urban development. That nonbasic environmental demands are political rather than justice based is, broadly, the position endorsed by both Rawls and Dworkin on Miller's account.[9]

One way of treating demands for preservation as political demands is to attempt to measure them through a process of contingent valuation,[10] whereby people are asked to value natural objects through the common denominator of a monetary scale. This approach has little to offer for a basic good demanded by justice on the grounds that it satisfies a fundamental human need (nobody is likely to ask me how much I value your being free from arbitrary arrest and torture, and nor should they). Contingent valuation is much more promising for certain types of political policy decision (would you rather the council provided a swimming pool or a football field?). Miller rejects one challenge to this approach—that "environmental goods are incommensurable with goods like money—it is simply impossible to say how much money would compensate you for the loss of an environmental feature."[11] As long as you accept the possibility of rationally choosing between two different environmental goods, you are committed to a principle of comparability and welfare compensatibility. It is, Miller suggests, probably not rational to deny yourself a "consistent way of choosing between different packages of goods."[12] Even within a value subjectivist (utility-based) framework, however, it is not clear that a refusal to trade two different categories of good against each other is nonrational. Assuming both an environmental good W (say, the existence of a species) and a marketed good X (say, money, as the most fungible form) generate utility, limits to comparability between the two exist when preferences are lexicographic.[13] In this case "no increase in X can compensate the individual for a reduction in W, but increasing X with non-declining W does increase utility."[14] Thus, we may well be willing to trade tokens of species W for economic gain, but when species viability is threatened, and the remaining tokens have come to instantiate the species, then we would cease being willing to trade any increase in X for a reduction of W. I see no reason to suppose that the holding of lexicographic preferences is irrational per se.[15] We may of course at times have still to make "tragic" choices between losing one environmental good or another, but this reflects real-world constraints on choice sets. It does not impugn the rationality of lexicographic preference orderings between different categories of good.

Miller is also rather too quick when he dismisses another argument against the use of contingent valuation as the appropriate way of making decisions about nonbasic environmental goods. This argument is that we should value environmental goods "not by some more-or-less sophisticated form of cost-benefit analysis, but according to an objective account of the value they have for human lives."[16] John O'Neill's Aristotelian account of human virtue and Robert Goodin's account of the human need for a nonanthropogenic framework to life are the chosen examples of this kind of argument. What I want to suggest is that the weaknesses in these accounts of the conditions for human flourishing that Miller claims to find are not sufficient to entail their outright rejection, as he suggests. Furthermore, if there are at least components of a good human life that can be delineated independently of people's subjective conceptions of the good, then we can make a morally relevant distinction between compensatability and (strict) substitutability of goods. This in turn offers support to the contention that the preservation of (some) nonbasic environmental goods is a matter of justice.

We should first briefly examine the arguments from human flourishing of O'Neill and Goodin, before going on to assess the plausibility of Miller's critique. John O'Neill[17] bases his argument on an objectivist account of the human virtues that is explicitly Aristotelian in character. On such an account of the human virtues, a life lived absent a capacity to understand and appreciate natural objects is a life lived as a less than fully flourishing human being. O'Neill states, "The best human life is one that includes an awareness of and practical concern with the goods of entities in the non-human world."[18] More generally, his book "develops an Aristotelian conception of well-being according to which well-being should be characterized not in terms of having the right subjective states . . . but rather in terms of a set of objective goods a person might possess."[19]

Goodin's account is not objectivist in the way that O'Neill's is. Goodin claims that people need to live their lives in a wider context that is relatively stable and unchanging if they are to have "sense and pattern" to their lives. Furthermore, "the products of natural processes, untouched as they are by human hands, provide precisely that desired context."[20] As this framework of "sense and pattern" is taken by Goodin to be essential to our psychic health, the existence of untouched natural features in the world is by deduction also essential. He, however, "traces the value of setting our lives in a larger context beyond ourselves to the satisfaction of our subjective desires in that regard, rather than to anything objectively valuable in that."[21] So, Goodin is claiming a sufficient intersubjective commonality with respect to the desire people have for a nonanthropogenic context in which to live their lives in order to further claim that an object's nonanthropogenic history is capable of imparting value. A similar argument about the value of a natural, nonanthropogenic context to human life is provided by Bill McKibben in *The End of Nature* (a work cited by Goodin in support of his own view), although McKibben's case does rely upon the validity of the "realist" argument.

Miller takes both of these views to be overstated. These are no more than "conceptions" of a meaningful life and very far from "universal truth." Moreover, as they are only conceptions of meaningful life for *some* people, "we are right back to the central problem . . . how to set your interest in preserving certain natural features against my interest in having land available to build a bigger and better football stadium for my team to play in, and so on, with the interests of everybody else."[22] Crucially: "It is not reasonable to establish a regime of distributive justice which by privileging environmental goods assumes that people already value nature in that way when empirically we know that they don't."[23]

This, however, is a question-begging response, in two different ways. John O'Neill is certainly not suggesting that people do, now, value nature in the way that he believes they should. Nor, for that matter, does he claim that they do not, for such subjective beliefs on the part of the public are not relevant to the validity of his argument (although he would clearly prefer a world in which people did value nature in an appropriate way). O'Neill is merely suggesting that there are particular, objectively ascertainable components to a fully human life, and that an appropriate valuation of nature is one of them. Thus, if your failure to value nature renders you deficient as a human being, the appropriate response is not to feed your preferences into a democratic decision-making machine on the same basis as a nature appreciator's preferences. It is rather to try and enable you to lead your life as a fully flourishing human being through bringing you to an appreciation of natural objects in an appropriate way. Preserving natural objects would constitute an important prerequisite for this process. One might add here that in his defense of a republican conception of citizenship, Miller appears to endorse a view that there are certain objective goods to a human life, in this case engagement with politics.

One need not regard political activity as the *summum bonum* in order to adopt the republican view, but can hold the more modest position that although *politics is indeed a necessary part of the good life*, different people can be expected to give it different weight according to their own personal values.[24]

Similarly, O'Neill is not suggesting that nature appreciation is the supreme good of a human life, but he is claiming it as a necessary part of such a life—although people will give it a different weight according to their own personal values. This would still seem sufficient to ground a demand for nature preservation on the basis of preserving the possibility of a good human life.[25]

The relationship of Miller's dismissal to Goodin's argument is more complex, because Goodin clearly does claim that people *want* to see a sense of order and pattern in their lives[26] and that *given* this brute empirical fact nature is paradigmatically capable of satisfying this subjectively felt need. But again, Goodin's claim is only that people feel a need for this sense and pattern, *not* that they currently value nature in a particular way. His message is that given a felt need for sense and pattern, people *should* value natural processes because these processes have all the qualities necessary to satisfy the felt need. The normative call for nature preservation is derived, rather than foundational. That said, one can certainly accept Miller's contention that Goodin's argument overstates the supposedly singular importance that an unaltered nonhuman nature has in providing an appropriate context to endow human beings with such sense and pattern (religion would be a good possible alternative that does not necessarily imply nature preservation).

It is also worth pondering, at this point, on the demands that Miller's riposte seems to imply for the standards that a theory of distributive justice is expected to meet. If we agree with Miller, we are denying nonbasic environmental goods a status as goods of distributive justice because there *is* not, empirically (rather than "could not be, categorically") agreement in society that these goods are of an appropriate value to be the subject matter of justice. This seems to conform to Miller's general methodological approach to establishing the validity of ethical principles, whereby the intuitions of the members of a society are seen as a crucial aspect of validation. Miller states that "an adequate theory of justice must pay attention to empirical evidence about how the public understands justice, and in particular to the way in which different norms of justice are applied in different social contexts."[27] In this case "how the public understands justice" clearly includes the question of which goods count as goods of justice.

Miller considers a number of possible objections to his approach, such that there may be systematic differences between people's intuitions about justice according to different characteristics or background, or that such intuitions are adaptive to the existing distribution of social advantages. He does not consider either of these objections to be strongly supported by the empirical evidence available.[28] A more fundamental objection, however, is surely that such empirical evidence of social beliefs is merely irrelevant to the correctness (and therefore the validity) of a theory of justice. If I believe my preferred theory is correct, why should I care about common intuitions about justice in society? Perhaps, however, on Miller's account validity and adequacy are treated as separate conditions that a theory of justice has to satisfy. The notion of adequacy may have as an integral component the condition that it implies for a theory of justice conformity with common intuitions about what justice demands abroad in society at the time. But this would only push the problem back one stage, as we then have to ask why this should be accepted as a reasonable condition for the adequacy of a theory. If a society believes in the justice of slavery, both on the part of the free citizens dependent upon the slave economy, but also on the part of the miserable slaves, should this entail that a theory denying the justice of slavery (based on a belief, say, in the moral equality of all humanity) is inadequate because it fails to engage appropriately with the intuitions of the members of that society? It is not clear why such a condition should constitute a test of adequacy. The equality based antislavery conception would be explicitly transformative and would seek to present this society with a new way of thinking about itself. If it is based upon a belief in the objective equality of human beings, it would not be susceptible to a set of social beliefs about human inequalities, nor is it clear that it ought to be.

Environmental theories of justice also fall under the category of potentially transformative beliefs that seek to present society with a new way of understanding the relationship between itself and nonhuman nature. Arguments such as O'Neill's (or arguments such as Holmes Rolston's on the intrinsic value of nature)[29] appeal to a set of supposedly objective ethical criteria (with regard to the valuable form of human life, on the one hand, and the direct value of nature, on the other) in support of the normative views they put forward. To the extent that both arguments are taken by their authors to be philosophically correct, why should they entertain the possibility that they are *inadequate* because they fail to engage with "empirical evidence about how the public understands justice"? If it was somehow possible to know, in advance, that one's chosen principles could never, under any circumstances, win public support, this might be a reason to consider one's preferred theory inadequate (even if philosophically valid). This, however, is an entirely distinct question from that of whether one's preferred theory accords with common intuitions about justice held in a society at this moment. One could point to a changing public understanding of environmental questions to suggest that public beliefs can follow transformative ideas, but the point is that, absent such knowledge of future judgments, if I hold what I believe to be philosophically valid principles of justice, this should be sufficient to also believe them adequate.

All that said, I want to argue that even if we concede Miller's point that objectivist accounts of human flourishing have well-documented and insuperable problems, a sound argument for considering certain goods of nature to be goods of justice can still be made. Furthermore, we can assume that nature preservation forms part of a comprehensive conception of the good and will only form a part of the comprehensive conception of the good for some people in contemporary societies. Given this, would it then be "unreasonable" to make demands for the preservation of natural objects on the grounds of distributive justice (in the sense that, having conceded this much, nature appreciators would no longer have any good reasons for making such a demand)? An affirmative argument to this question, of the sort that Miller delivers, is crucially dependent upon there not being any qualities of nonbasic environmental goods that would themselves be sufficient to ground these as an object of distributive justice, regardless of the nonuniversal character of nature appreciation. I want to suggest that there is at least one such, relating to the qualitative difference in costs between the loss of (certain categories of) environmental, nonbasic goods and the loss of nonenvironmental, nonbasic goods.

I label these two types of loss *irrecoverable* and *irreplaceable* (both falling within the more general category of irreversible change).[30] The language is arbitrary to an extent, although I hope the meaning of the distinction will still be clear. *Loss* here involves the disappearance of a resource or potential resource,[31] and opportunity costs are inevitably involved in the decision situations appropriate here—typically a choice between undertaking a development or preserving a natural object. If we as a society decide to build a shopping mall on the final habitat of a small plant known as the divided sedge, we incur species loss.[32] If we forego the shopping mall and preserve the sedge, we incur the loss of the economic benefits the mall would bring. All of this is obvious enough,[33] but the distinction I want to add to this is the following. Irrecoverable costs are costs that can never be regained. Energy only flows one way; the energy we expend in development cannot be used elsewhere or be regained (or at least not all of it; there is always waste in the process of energy–mass conversion)—entropy cannot be gainsaid. Some losses, however, are not merely irrecoverable but also irreplaceable. An irreplaceable loss is a loss that cannot be recovered; it cannot be reconverted *even with the acceptance of additional irrecoverable costs*. We could build a shopping mall, and then knock it down to develop a park. We could then decide this was a mistake and rebuild the mall. We could go through this cycle ad infinitum. This might make us a rather odd society, apparently acting on an intransitive preference ordering, but as long as we are prepared to incur a new set of costs at each juncture, we can, *ceteris paribus*, redeem ourselves from the less-preferred situation we have placed ourselves in.

However, if we destroy our divided sedge, we are committing ourselves to a situation from which, prepared as we may be at some future time to incur fresh costs in order that we might again live in a world with the divided sedge, we (barring miraculous *Jurassic Park*–style developments in genetic engineering) cannot. This is the intuitive distinction between an irrecoverable and an irreplaceable loss, which I want to suggest can work in favor of the inclusion of some nonbasic environmental goods among the demands of distributive justice, even within an anthropocentric and subjectivist ontology of value.

There is a categorical distinction to be made between the costs to humans involved in allowing the destruction of certain types of environmental goods (commonly and importantly, species loss, but also, for example, the status of an area as never having been developed) and the costs involved in foregoing development or other types of nonbasic nonenvironmental goods. This distinction entails a substantive difference between present-orientated distributive justice and distributive justice between generations, of a sort that Miller denies.[34] Species loss is irreplaceable; the loss of undeveloped natural features is also irreplaceable if it violates the authenticity of nature in the way suggested by, for example, Elliot.[35] The costs of foregone development are irrecoverable, but it is far from certain that foregoing development presents us with losses that are irreplaceable should society, at some future point, have a change of heart. To use a parochial real-world example, the decision taken by British Railways in the Beeching era to close thousands of miles of branch line imposed a set of costs on a set of people (and benefited others). That there is now active discussion about restoring several of the lines to service shows that, socially, Beeching did not impose an irreplaceable loss, although another set of costs will have to be born if the lines are to be reconstructed. All of these costs are of course irrecoverable. In the cloud forests of Costa Rica, the golden toad had almost certainly become extinct over the past fifteen years, the most likely explanation for which is the drying out of the Costa Rican cloud forest as a result of global warming. Should a future society decide that it wants nothing more than to be part of a world in which the golden toad exists, it will be unable (whatever the costs it would be prepared to bear) to redeem the situation in which it finds itself.

This raises the question, is it unjust to impose irreplaceable losses onto future generations (and/or certain sections of the present generation) even if it is not unjust to impose irrecoverable costs onto future generations (and/or sections of the present generation)? The substantive difference between irrecoverable and irreplaceable losses is that the latter *close down options* in a way that the former do not. To impose irreplaceable losses onto a future generation is to close down a possibly valued option permanently regardless of any changes in valuations and preferences occurring in the future. A world without nonanthropogenic tigers is destined to remain such. To impose irrecoverable costs on a future generation is not to close down an option at the same general level, although it will of course close down specific options within the general option (history cannot be rewritten, but the social situation can be redeemed). This distinction between irrecoverable costs and irreplaceable losses is not intended to imply that in all cases preservationist concerns must prevail over developmental ones. What I am suggesting is that in many cases the imposition of irreplaceable losses should weigh heavily in our calculations merely by virtue of their very irreplaceability. This may well be sufficient to render the preservation of natural objects a matter of concern for distributive justice whatever, empirically, people think about natural values in the here and now. The irreplaceable removal of an object from the world also removes the possibility a valuing agent would otherwise have had to value that object. It reduces the scope of a valuing agent's domain and is thus at least arguably damaging to the agent. At the very least, proponents of the subjective judgment arguments of the type David Miller puts forward need to explain to the rest of us why it is acceptable, as a question of justice, to impose avoidable irreplaceable losses onto future generations.

This brings us back, briefly and by way of closing this chapter, to two points made previously: the appropriateness of the doctrine of substitutability and the possibility of a relevant structural difference between present-generation and intergenerational justice with respect to nonbasic environmental goods. The distinction I am seeking to draw between irrecoverable costs and irreplaceable losses might appear to rest upon a denial of the doctrine of welfare compensatability. Does this distinction suggest that people could never be compensated adequately (at least hypothetically) for being forced to live in a world without wild tigers or the golden toad? I have claimed that the world that loses the golden toad has suffered an irreplaceable loss because, however much we might value this creature in the future, we can never live in a world with it again. By the doctrine of substitutability we could accept that this is true but trivial. We can compensate those in the world today who value the golden toad highly through other means. If they are not irrational, they will accept that there is *some* level of compensation that will be sufficient to equalize their level of welfare with respect to living in a world in which the golden toad still exists. Similarly, if future generations are materially better endowed due to our economic activities, this will compensate them for living in a world with fewer species or a more anthropogenic environment.

There are two points to make about this that are relevant to the foregoing discussion. First, it may be (as discussed previously) that if we countenance lexicographic preferences, *irreplaceability* implies the impossibility of compensation. Furthermore, if there are some objective goods of human flourishing, then there may be an ethically relevant distinction between *compensatability* and *substitutability*. Second, the possibility referred to previously of a relevant structural difference between present-generation and intergenerational justice might also do some work here.

With respect to the conmpensatability/substitutability distinction, imagine the (real) possibility of certain inhabited Pacific and Indian Ocean islands disappearing underwater if sea levels rise sufficiently as a result of global climate change. One might not see this as an insuperable ethical problem, because of the doctrine of substitutability. The people who live on (say) the Maldives can be relocated and compensated—places to live are substitutable. Of course, there is a normative element present in the sense that fairness dictates that these people should be compensated—their fate is thus a matter for distributive justice. But the disappearance of their homeland per se is of no ethical consequence. Is this the only rational view? It seems to me that we could draw a distinction between a strict substitutability and compensatability here, which will have some purchase if there are at least objective *elements* to a satisfactory account of human flourishing.[36] A homeland, that is, the existence of a place with both individual and social memories of development and ties between environment and people is not strictly substitutable even if it is compensatable. If we believe that having a homeland (an imprecise concept, I accept) is of objective importance to human well-being, it might also follow that this outweighs the raw fact of compensatable levels of welfare. Those who have lost their homeland suffer an irreplaceable loss, whatever compensation they are given, if this is about objective human goods as well.

It is worth noting that this argument is not quite the same as the standard bread and water argument against the belief in complete welfare substitutability (see earlier, note 14). We can assume that compensation is monetary and that, as the most fungible good, money can restore welfare to prior levels. It is suggesting that a homeland is a merit good of the sort Miller refers to previously, and so welfare levels are not the only relevant metric here. On this view species loss is also strictly nonsubstitutable, even when it is compensatable. The "sense and pattern" I get from living in a nonanthropogenic world where species such as tigers exist is eroded as anthropegeneity increases. I lose an objective good, which cannot be substituted for even if my welfare levels are restored through (say) monetary compensation for what would otherwise be my increasing misery.

Second, even if species loss is a compensatable cost to those in the present generation, is this mode of reasoning an appropriate framework for thinking about the interests of future generations with respect to this matter? The values of future generations cannot be, by the very fact that they do not yet exist, fed into any calculations of costs and compensation. And yet, when we exterminate a species we close down the options for future generations in a "hard" way by imposing an irreplaceable loss. Given the strict nonsubstitutability of species, is this, when avoidable, a justifiable thing to do to future generations? While this is more suggestive than definitive, it implies that there is an answer to the question "how can these future persons have claims of justice to environmental goods unless at least some of our contemporaries have such claims, too?"[37] The answer would lie in the injustice of imposing such losses onto these future people whose value judgments can play no part in coming to the decision to impose such costs.

Miller's work on the status of nonbasic environmental goods raises important questions for environmental ethicists. These are not idle speculations; estimates of the rate of human-induced species loss vary from 1,000 to 10,000 times background rates over the world as a whole.[38] It matters whether these losses are seen as of no consequence, as clearly we must prefer to live in a world where species are sacrificed to development if our subjective judgments are being satisfied, or of the utmost consequence as visiting a grave injustice upon future generations. My argument, contra Miller, is that the imposition of irreplaceable losses on future generations, via the destruction of nonbasic environmental goods such as species, is an act of the utmost consequence and should weigh heavily, although not always decisively, with the present generation as a question of justice. Furthermore, as Miller does not succeed in rebutting the notion that there are objective goods to a human life, and even seems to endorse that view on some occasions, his argument against the notion that nonbasic environmental goods should be seen as objective elements in a fully human life requires more work if it is to be convincing.

NOTES

1. See for some book-length examples Andrew Dobson, *Justice and the Environment* (Oxford: Oxford University Press, 1998); Andrew Dobson, ed., *Fairness and Futurity* (Oxford: Oxford University Press, 1999); Avner de-Shalit, *Why Posterity Matters* (London: Routledge, 1995); Hampson and Reppy, *Earthly Goods* (Ithaca, N.Y.: Cornell University Press, 1996); Peter Wenz, *Environmental Justice* (New York: SUNY Press, 1988). Note that this discussion has taken place along two dimensions. First, whether environmental goods are goods of interhuman justice, and second, whether justice is owed to nonhuman entities (e.g., Paul Taylor, *Respect for Nature* [Princeton, N.J.: Princeton University Press, 1986]). We will herein be concerned only with the first of these questions, and so with environmental goods as goods for human beings.

2. David Miller, "Social Justice and Environmental Goods," in *Fairness and Futurity*, ed. Andrew Dobson (Oxford: Oxford University Press, 1999), 151–172.

3. *Intrinsic value* here taken to mean, broadly, value that is of the object taken to be valuable, or at least some properties of that object, and is completely nonderivative. This is contrasted to instrumental or "extrinsic" value, that is, value toward a good situated outside of the object in question. I might consider you as intrinsically valuable as a member of the kingdom of ends, or instrumentally valuable if I am employing you to proofread an essay of mine (as Kant noted, these two types of value are not, of course, mutually exclusive). The literature on the nature of intrinsic value is more complex than this brief characterization can suggest, and O'Neill (see John O'Neill, *Ecology, Policy, and Politics* [London: Routledge, 1993], ch. 2) gives a useful typology. Examples of intrinsic value arguments are widespread in the literature on environmental ethics, often offered in conjunction with other arguments, such as self-realization. See, for example, Arne Naess, *Ecology, Community, and Lifestyle* (Cambridge: Cambridge University Press, 1989); Robyn Eckersley, *Environmentalism and Political Theory* (London: UCL Press, 1992); Holmes Rolston III, *Environmental Ethics* (Philadelphia: Temple University Press, 1988). For a recent ro-

bust defense of the idea of the objective existence of intrinsic value, see Robin Attfield, "Postmodernism, Value and Objectivity," *Environmental Values* 10 (2001): 145–162.

4. David Miller, *Principles of Social Justice* (Cambridge, Mass.: Harvard University Press, 1999), 196–197.

5. "An anthropocentric framework is . . . likely to wind up reinforcing attitudes that are detrimental to the achievements of comprehensive environmental reform in the long run, since human interests will always systematically prevail over the interests of the non-human world"; Eckersley, *Environmentalism and Political Theory*, 38.

6. It should be noted here that the intrinsic value of tigers is not the only reason why one might have tiger-preserving preferences. The point is rather that, according to Miller, if you generate enough of this type of preference, then tiger preservation "becomes a *genuine public good.*"

7. I am assuming no informational constraints that would allow me to deceive you about the existence of tigers in the wild.

8. See Eckersley, *Environmentalism and Political Theory*, 60–61; and Warwick Fox, *Toward a Transpersonal Ecology* (Totnes: Green Books, 1995), 165–176.

9. See David Miller, "Social Justice," 155–160.

10. See, for example, David Pearce et al., *Blueprint for a Green Economy* (London: Earthscan, 1989).

11. David Miller, "Social Justice," 162.

12. David Miller, "Social Justice," 163.

13. See, for example, David Stern, "Limits to Substitution and Irreversibility in Production and Consumption: A Neoclassical Interpretation of Ecological Economics," *Ecological Economics* 21 (1997): 197–215.

14. David Stern, "Limits to Substitution and Irreversibility," 204.

15. The standard example of such nonsubstitutability involves bread and water. A well-fed person dying of thirst would have lexicographic preferences between a single glass of water and a potentially infinite supply of bread (assuming, as with species existence, that the glass of water cannot be subdivided into smaller units).

16. David Stern, "Limits to Substitution and Irreversibility," 204.

17. See John O'Neill, *Ecology.*

18. O'Neill, *Ecology*, 24.

19. O'Neill, *Ecology*, 3.

20. Robert Goodin, *Green Political Theory* (Cambridge: Polity Press, 1992), 37.

21. Goodin, *Green Political Theory*, 30, fn. 25. He notes here that a stronger realist argument "might also be true," but his own argument is not reliant upon such truth. Similarly, he later states, "A contingent preference along these lines would suffice for my purposes, just as long as that contingency was sufficiently common and the resulting preferences socially standard ones" (Goodin, *Green Political Theory*, 38). He is clearly happy to assume such a standard preference ordering, sufficiently to claim that natural processes "help to 'locate the self,' in a deep psychological sense that matters enormously to people" (Goodin, *Green Political Theory*, 39).

22. Miller, "Social Justice," 164.

23. Miller, "Social Justice," 165.

24. David Miller, *Citizenship and National Identity* (Cambridge: Polity Press, 2000), 58 (emphasis added).

25. I believe this relates to a more general problem in David Miller's self-positioning with respect to particular types of argument. When arguing against environmentalists, he tends to adopt a liberal, neutralist form of argument, stressing the invalidity of imposing a particular conception of the good upon the rest of society. However, when discussing the demands of citizenship and deliberative forms of democracy, he tends to adopt a republican form of argument that celebrates political activity as a necessary part of the good human life. Compare Miller, "Social Justice," with Miller, *Citizenship*, ch. 3.

26. Goodin's claim is thus clearly empirical, and one may well have sympathy here with Miller's call for such claims to be supported by valid evidence.

27. Miller, *Principles*, 42. Thus, Miller takes Rawls to task for not "placing much greater emphasis on empirical evidence about how people do in fact understand justice" (Miller, *Principles*, 58).

28. See Miller, *Principles*, ch.4.

29. See Rolston, *Environmental Ethics*.

30. See Mathew Humphrey, "Three Conceptions of Irreversibility and Environmental Ethics: Some Problems," *Environmental Politics* 10 (2001): 138–154.

31. Describing nature as "resource" would of course be offensive to ecocentric sensibilities, but is appropriate here.

32. A choice being considered by Essex County Council some years back.

33. Which is not to say that how we should measure these losses against each other is obvious.

34. Miller, "Social Justice," 153.

35. Robert Elliot (*Faking Nature* [London: Routledge, 1997]) argues that a restored natural landscape, even if identical in every respect to an untouched natural landscape that existed prior to development, possesses less value than its predecessor because of a loss of the quality of authenticity.

36. The argument as presented here falls back on the notion of objective goods, and so the denial that David Miller has successfully refuted such views becomes relevant again.

37. Miller, "Social Justice," 153.

38. Data from the World Wide Fund for Nature website: < www.panda.org/resources/factsheets/general/temp/26biodi.htm.> Accessed March 2000.

IV

FORMS OF JUSTICE

18

A Response

David Miller

The title of this book, *Forms of Justice*, was chosen by its two editors, but it captures perfectly in a single phrase ideas I have been trying to express over a number of years about justice and its place in human societies. Every society that we know about, or indeed can imagine, understands and practices justice in a recognizable form. Every society, that is to say, must develop rules and principles that allow it to answer questions such as these: How far should any individual member of the society be free to act as he or she chooses? and how far must constraints be imposed in the interests of others? How should resources—land, tools, human labor—be allocated among the members? Who is to exercise political authority in the society, and on what terms? What can people who are sick or starving claim from their fellows, and who is responsible for meeting these needs? How should members treat strangers from other societies? What should be done in the case of those who violate the rules—legal or moral—established to answer the previous questions? And so on. Justice, then, is a pervasive feature of human societies. But the shape that it takes—the set of answers it provides to questions such as those listed—changes not only as we move between societies but also as we move between different spheres of human life within them.

So, there are forms of justice, but there is no Form of Justice in the Platonic sense. According to Plato, knowing what justice is means identifying a transcendent standard, a supreme measuring rod, that can be applied to all the social and political institutions that human beings have developed. Societies are more or less just, on this Platonic view, the more or less closely their rules and institutions match up to this single standard. The popularity of this view remains undiminished, notwithstanding the fact that the standard Plato himself proposed, after much dialectical to-ing and fro-ing—"justice is keeping to what belongs to one and doing one's own job"[1]—has found few supporters. Neo-Platonists must think that it is only a matter of finding the right principle, or principles, to encapsulate justice. Once we have achieved that, we will be able to measure societies on a single scale. We can say, simply, what justice requires, and how close any part of humankind, or indeed humankind as a whole, has come to achieving it.

This is a heady prospect, and its attractiveness may appear to increase still further when we consider the alternative. If we say that there are forms of justice, not just a single Form, then we seem to be committed to two further propositions. The first is that, since every society arranges its affairs differently—has its own family structure, legal system, political institutions, economic arrangements, and so on—there will be as many justices as there are societies—indeed as many justices as there are subspheres within those societies, if we accept the idea that in different areas of human life, different standards of justice apply. Studying justice will be more like stamp collecting than doing philosophy. The second is that the idea of justice loses its critical purchase. We will be reduced to saying, with Pascal, that justice is simply what established practice requires in any place.[2] We will no longer be able to look at the rules and institutions that presently exist and say that they treat people unfairly and need to be reformed, or even revolutionized.

I believe that neither implication need follow if we think about justice in the way that I advocate, a way that I call "contextualist."[3] Contextualists argue that we can best understand justice by seeing it as embracing a number of distinct principles, each of which applies in a particular social context. There are different possible ways of identifying the relevant contexts, but my own preferred account defines contexts by reference to the kind of social relationship that exists among the parties between whom justice is to be done. People may be related to one another in a variety of different ways—for instance, in family or kinship groups, in communities of various kinds, as comembers of productive enterprises, in bureaucratic hierarchies, as fellow citizens, and so forth—and the principle of justice that determines how they are to treat one another, in particular how resources are to be allocated between them, will depend on which kind of relationship obtains. Moreover, these social contexts tend to be reiterated across societies: I don't mean that each of them is to be found in every society, but that many of them reappear, though with differences of detail. Because of this reiteration, we can develop a contextualist *theory* of justice, worthy of the name. We can discover systematic connections between contexts and principles of justice, so that whenever we find a society that includes human relationships of type C, we can say that those relationships ought to be governed by principle P.

So, contextualists can avoid the stamp-collecting charge, and by the same token they can avoid the charge that justice in their hands becomes merely a legitimation of established practice. For it may turn out that people in the society that includes context C fail to apply P in that context; they may not only fail to govern those relationships in the way that P demands, they may not even recognize that P is the appropriate principle to apply. In that case, contextualists should have no hesitation in saying that they have got it wrong, that the society is to that extent radically unjust. Of course, wholesale misunderstanding of that kind will be unusual. What is much more common is the distortion that occurs when contexts are not properly distinguished, so that the principle that applies in C1 is carried across to C2 where it has no place. So, the idea of justice retains its critical character even though there is no single Form, no transcendent measuring rod, that can be applied to all societies no matter how they are constituted.

So much by way of introduction. The contextualist approach sketched in the last two paragraphs opens up a daunting research program—an attempt to map the forms of justice that have recurred in human societies across cultures and across history—that it would take a lifetime to complete. The research that has provoked the present book is narrower, in the sense that it focuses on justice in the contemporary world, in particular on the demands of social justice in liberal democracies and on what justice requires rich countries to do for poorer countries. The essays collected here raise so many interesting questions and criticisms that I cannot hope to deal with each one individually. Instead, I have organized my remarks under four headings: first, questions of method, and in particular my appeal to empirical evidence about popular conceptions of justice as a way of grounding my theory; second, my analysis of the principles of social justice that apply within democratic societies, especially the principle of desert; third, my defense of the nation-state as a privileged site of justice, and of republican citizenship as a privileged means of delivering it; fourth, my analysis of what justice requires at global level, and how it differs from justice within nations.

QUESTIONS OF METHOD

In order to understand justice, we must first grasp how people generally—people who are not philosophers or academic specialists of other kinds—understand it, or so I claim. Our theories of justice must be tested against common opinion. But why do I require this? Adam Swift points out that there might be two quite different reasons. The first is epistemological: There is no standard of truth in this area that is independent of popular opinion. In other words, the question what justice is cannot be radically separated from the question what people in general take justice to be. The second is political: If we want our theory of justice to have some practical effect—we want it to influence the way that people in our society or across the globe actually behave—then we need to develop a theory that is not too far removed from what they are already inclined to take justice to be. Swift is sympathetic to the second reason—like me he thinks political philosophy should have some practical relevance—but not to the first. He thinks that we need to hold on to a distinction between what justice is and what is "a realistic amount of justice to pursue now." His worry is that the political reason may induce us to lower our sights too far, to present as an account of justice itself what is really a second-best compromise with present-day political realities, reflected in the opinions of the general public.

I agree that there is a danger here, and I agree that I may sometimes have fallen into it, dismissing proposed accounts of justice merely on account of their political infeasibility. But I am still inclined to think that there is a closer connection between the two reasons for paying attention to common opinion than Swift allows. We can bring this out by asking what exactly is the point of (normative) theorizing about justice. Why should we be interested in discovering the correct theory? Our interest, presumably, is practical: we find it valuable that people should live in a just society, where this means not only that they are living according to the right principles, but that they are living according to principles that they themselves recognize to be right.[4] So, it is a condition for a theory's being valid that it should be possible for people to come to accept it and live according to its principles. Clearly, this is not the same as saying that they must accept it *now*. But unless one thinks that as far as ethics go people are blank slates on to which more or less anything can be inscribed, it does constrain the content of the theory. Putting the point more positively, what people now believe about justice tells us a good deal about what they could freely come to believe, especially if we assume that the society they will be living in has many features in common with our own (I shall talk in a moment about the ways in which popular beliefs might be improved by appeal to common accepted standards of rationality).

My claim, then, is that the political and epistemological reasons for attending to popular opinion about justice ultimately converge. A theory of justice isn't worth propounding unless people could be rationally persuaded to accept it; but beyond that, it can't be the correct theory, for these people, unless that condition holds. And rational persuasion must involve starting with people's firmly held beliefs—what Rawls calls their considered judgments of justice—and working them up into a consistent whole.

How far from the starting point—raw public opinion, as it were—can this take us? Let's quickly review some reasons why raw opinion might be found defective. People's beliefs about justice might simply be inconsistent—they might hold two opposed principles which they deployed on different occasions without realizing that this generated contradictory judgments. Their beliefs might rest on erroneous factual assumptions—they might apply a principle to a situation thinking that it had features A, B, C, whereas in fact is has features D, E, and F (if they knew that, they would apply a different principle). Beliefs might be warped by self-interest—people might use a principle in a way that advantages them individually or as a group, whereas if they had to make a judgment on the same issue but without knowing how they personally would be affected, they would reach a different conclusion. Beliefs might also be adaptive, by which I mean that people's ideas about what is just may be over-influenced by prevailing practice—instead of considering what justice requires and then applying this to existing rules and institutions, they start with the rules and institutions and generalize from them. So there is plenty of scope for theories of justice that aim to be coherent, empirically sound and impartial in ways that popular opinion often is not, and yet can be justified to people by appeal to basic beliefs that they already hold.

To illustrate, consider one case of inconsistency that Andrew Mason high-lights in his discussion of common intuitions about desert: people appear to think that people should be rewarded for their *achievements*, but they also ap-pear to think that they should be rewarded for their *efforts*, and these two cri-teria clearly conflict whenever achievement depends on factors other than ef-fort. So, should we simply set popular notions of desert aside as self-contradictory? This needn't follow. First, it may be that both effort and achievement deserve reward, but on different occasions and in different tangi-ble ways. Provided we can demarcate the circumstances in which each princi-ple applies clearly, the apparent inconsistency vanishes. Second, there may re-main some cases in which people are genuinely unsure which principle to use, even when the circumstances have been spelled out fully. Desert of reward for productive work appears to be one of these—people when asked about what people deserve to be paid for their work are liable to vacillate between the view that more productive workers deserve more and the view that everyone who tries equally hard deserves the same no matter what they achieve.[5] Here one can try to work out a view that goes some way to accommodate each of the conflicting intuitions. So, starting from the effort side, one can point out (as Mason does) that not just any effort should count: it must at least be ef-fort intelligently directed at worthwhile aims. Starting from the productivity side, one can point out that it is not achievement as such that should count, but achievement for which the producer can properly take credit—in other words, one needs to factor out various kinds of luck, such as the luck that can turn a mediocre performance into an exceptional one. Once these refinements are made, the gap between the two positions narrows to the following ques-tion: if two people make equally good use of their talents, in the sense that they work (and have trained) equally hard and use their capacities in equally intel-ligent ways, given what others are doing, but one manages to produce more than the other simply by dint of having greater natural talents, does that one deserve greater reward? Political philosophers disagree in the answers they give to this question (I defend an affirmative answer in *Principles of Social Jus-tice*, ch. 7). But notice that in very many cases, either answer will lead us to draw roughly the same practical conclusion about how people deserve to be rewarded for their productive work—what matters, in many cases, is not nat-ural talent itself, but how people decide to deploy their talents, and how far the results of their effort depend on various kinds of luck for which they can-not be held responsible. So, what initially looked like an unbridgeable rift in common opinion over the basis of desert can be transformed, by theoretical work, into a minor divergence.[6]

A theory of justice should correct for various biases and distortions of perspective that are liable to infect popular opinion. Daniel Weinstock, taking note of the ways in which I follow this injunction in *Principles of Social Justice*, thinks that it takes me away from the Humean moral epistemology to which I have pledged allegiance in my writing on nationality, and in particular that it should lead me to abandon my arguments against global distributive justice. But we need to be clear that Hume's ethical theory, while recognizing that moral judgments are based in feelings or "sentiments," does not take these sentiments to be incorrigible. On the contrary: one of the philosopher's aims is precisely to correct for the effects of personal interest or personal location (in space or time) on the judgments that people ordinarily make. But Hume never thought that the correction should go all the way, as it were, because this would introduce too sharp a divorce between judgment and feeling and render morality impotent. Even if our unreflective sentiments attach too much weight to the claims of our close associates, say, we should not aspire to complete neutrality as between them and strangers. So, although I argue that people generally attach too little weight in their understanding of justice to their relations as citizens, by virtue of the remoteness of that relationship from everyday experience, I don't argue that this relationship should dominate all others—indeed, I criticize certain liberal egalitarian theories, such as those of Rawls and Dworkin, for understanding justice within societies entirely from the perspective of citizenship. When we come to international justice, I agree with Weinstock that people generally give too much weight to the claims of their compatriots and too little to the claims of foreigners. But the answer once again is not to erase the distinction, but to work out some principles that give a proper account of what we owe to people outside of our political community. I shall return to the substance of these principles later, but I have no doubt that they require us to do more, materially speaking, for needy strangers and poverty-stricken communities than we do now. So, the bias and self-interest of popular opinion needs correcting, in this area and in others, but not by obliterating the real difference between what justice requires of people related as members of the same political community and what it requires of people related as members of different communities, or simply as human beings.

This last remark does, however, raise a further methodological issue, touched upon both by Weinstock and by Marc Stears. If one adopts the contextualist view that different principles of justice govern different types of human relationship, so that to know what justice requires in any concrete case one has first to examine how the parties among whom justice is to be done are related to one another, one seems to subordinate justice to existing practice. What if the prevailing relationships are themselves unjust, or inadequate in other ways? The kind of theory that I recommend seems unable to generate the radical critique of existing institutions that justice may demand. Stears gives the example of the American "new nationalists," whose diagnosis of the condition of the America of their day embraced the claim that a state capable of delivering social justice did not yet exist and contrasts this with my view that the very idea of social justice presupposes the existence of an agency capable of reforming a society's basic structure in the way that justice requires. Stears finds this second view, and the general methodological position from which it derives, too conservative, and Weinstock likewise (though using a different example) cautions against "reading substantial ethical conclusions from institutional facts, as these facts can embody significant injustices that we would thereby be legitimizing."

My view, however, is not that we should begin our thinking about justice with "institutional facts," or indeed with people's beliefs insofar as these merely reflect institutional facts (see my previous remark about correcting for adaptive beliefs). We need to draw a distinction between a mode of human relationship and the institutional form that such a relationship takes at any given time and place. We can distinguish the family, as a form of relationship characterized by intimacy and mutual support, from its current institutional structure—the moral and legal rules that distribute rights and obligations among family members, the domestic division of labor, and so forth. Having decided what justice among family members requires—and if my argument is correct, the demands of justice will be specific to this relationship[7]—we can then assess the family's existing institutional shape and argue for its reform.

In a similar way, we can ask what justice requires among the citizens of a political community, and then look to see whether its present institutional structure is well designed to meet those requirements. This will include the question whether the existing state apparatus is capable of bringing about the necessary changes. But we should avoid any sort of ahistorical utopianism here. One of the questions that has interested me, and that I hope to explore at greater length in the future, is why the idea of *social* justice began to be used sporadically in the closing decades of the nineteenth century and then became central to the political discourse of the twentieth, whereas before then it was unknown. It seems clear that a conceptual shift of this kind must correspond to a real change both in the social and political world and in the way that that world was understood. My hunch is that two concurrent changes explain the shift: first, the development of political economy and the social sciences made it increasingly possible to trace the distributive effects of economic and social institutions and so to see individuals' life chances as being determined by those institutions; second, the state was increasingly involved in moderating those effects, as it began to reassign property rights, regulate the market economy, create rudimentary welfare institutions, and so forth. In that kind of world, it makes sense to think about *social* justice, whereas in medieval Europe, say, justice was understood in terms of the duties of persons occupying particular social roles, and the state's function was to maintain a system of law that stabilized these duties.[8] But it does not follow that someone thinking about social justice in America in 1915 must find the existing American state adequate to the task of delivering it. All that is required is that such a person should be able to conceive of feasible reforms to existing institutions that would turn them into effective vehicles for social justice, drawing inspiration, perhaps, from institutions found in other places. If that condition is met, then a theory of social justice becomes a serious political theory—as it surely was for the American progressives Stears describes—rather than a piece of utopian wishful thinking.

Returning now to the question of popular beliefs and the place they should hold in a theory of justice, Avner de-Shalit suggests that we might want to give special weight to the views of those who are politically active, engaged in reasoning about real cases that involve ethical dilemmas (he calls this the search for a "public reflective equilibrium" as contrasted with the versions of reflective equilibrium favored by Rawls and Walzer). He does not say very explicitly why this weighting would be justified, so it is worth considering some possible reasons. One would be that activists, by virtue of being engaged with real cases, have to sharpen their principles to deal with practical conflicts. In other words, whereas the public at large can register its agreement or disagreement with general propositions such as "it is the responsibility of government to see that everyone has a standard of living above the poverty line" or "the income people receive should depend on how hard they work," those who are politically engaged may be faced with situations in which people choose not to work at jobs that would provide them with an adequate income; they must then decide which proposition carries greater weight. Another reason might be that the experience of political engagement simply improves people's ethical thinking, or as J. S. Mill put it, "it is from political discussion, and collective political action, that one whose daily occupations concentrate his interests in a small circle round himself, learns to feel for and with his fellow-citizens, and becomes consciously a member of a great community."[9] Both reasons are sound, and they show why deliberative democracy, in particular, might prove to be a good mechanism for refining popular conceptions of justice (more on this later). But one needs to be cautious. Political activism can take different forms. Some activists are driven by personal interests or personal philosophies that can blind them to the requirements of justice. Faced with real cases, their concern to get the "right" outcome can override any attempt to balance the conflicting interests at stake. And if political discussion occurs within groups of activists, all of whom begin with the same raw beliefs, the effect may simply be to consolidate those beliefs, making group members impervious to evidence or argument from outside. The rationalizing effect of deliberative democracy depends crucially on the presence within the deliberating body of a wide range of perspectives—ideally all of the perspectives that are significant in the wider community. Beliefs are improved by having to confront, and trying to persuade, those who disagree with you (or as de-Shalit concludes, "deliberation is important when it is heterogeneous, broad and includes mixed subjects"). So, if a theory of justice aimed to be consonant not with raw public opinion but with public opinion "improved" through political discussion, a good deal of thought would have to go into constructing the deliberative mechanisms whose outputs would be used to test the theory.

SOCIAL JUSTICE AND DESERT

I argue in *Principles* that social justice involves the application, in their appropriate contexts, of three sets of principles: principles of need, principles of desert, and principles of equality. The most controversial aspect of this argument is probably my claim that desert plays a key role in contemporary understandings of distributive justice, and in particular that in the economic sphere justice requires that people should be rewarded in proportion to their productive contributions. The chapters by Daniel Attas, Mathew Humphrey, Andrew Mason, and Serena Olsaretti all address this claim, so in this section of the chapter I shall mainly be responding to their challenging critiques.

My claim about economic desert really has two parts to it: one is that productive contribution (rather than, say, effort) should be taken as the basis of desert in this sphere; the other is that in suitable circumstances market prices—what others are prepared to pay to have the goods or services that someone produces—can serve as a measure of contribution. I should emphasize right away that none of this should be seen as an attempt to justify the market economy as we see it in operation around us; in my view, existing markets are seriously unjust. I do, however, want to make two claims: One is that the *project* of reconstituting a market economy so that its outcomes match the requirements of social justice more closely is not absurd. The other is that anyone who wants to hold on to the idea of desert as at least an important element of social justice cannot avoid using market prices as a measure of contribution in a wide range of cases: there is no plausible way of estimating how much different people are contributing that makes no reference to what others are willing to pay to receive those contributions.

To defend the second claim in particular, I need to stand back a bit and introduce a basic assumption that guides my thinking about social justice. I assume that if the idea is to make sense at all, in a society in which there is much diversity, both cultural and individual, in the things that people ultimately value, we must be able to reach agreement on the currency of justice. That is to say, we must be able to agree both about what it is that people can claim as their just entitlement, and about the basis on which they can claim it. This applies to principles of need and equality as well as to principles of desert. Agreement will be possible only if the currency in question is suitably neutral as between ultimate values. Of course, it may be impossible to discover such a neutral currency, in which case the very idea of social justice may collapse before our eyes. Chandran Kukathas and Daniel Weinstock both suggest in their contributions that existing cultural diversity within nation-states makes any such assumption of agreement on the currency of justice problematic. Responding to this challenge must involve a careful exploration of the way that cultural differences impact (or fail to impact) on people's conceptions of social justice, and this is a project I hope to undertake in future work. But for now I only want to assert the following: that we cannot substitute our own (contestable) standard of value for the common currency and argue that what justice requires is determined by that standard.

This means, then, that if we decide that justice requires that people should be rewarded according to what they have contributed to society (I shall come back to examine the contribution principle itself shortly), we cannot measure contributions by asking what is the "real value" of what people have done, where *real value* invokes such a contestable standard. Daniel Attas suggests, for example, that "the value of culture is independent from its market-determined price." But is this simply Attas's assessment or is it supposed to be a shared assessment across society? If the latter, there is a puzzle here: if it is generally agreed that cultural experiences—looking at art, listening to music, reading books—are worth more than people are currently paying for them, then why are they unwilling to pay more? How can it make sense to say "we all agree that, objectively speaking, a night at the opera is worth the equivalent of $150 in regular consumer goods, but in practice very few of us are willing to spend more than $40 to attend"? Now there are certainly contingent reasons why people may pay more, or less, for goods and services than they are really worth to them, and Attas lists a number of these—manipulative advertising, lack of information, addiction, for instance. This shows why market receipts don't always track value, where value means simply the amount of utility people get from the goods or services they have purchased. But this observation doesn't justify a wholesale substitution of "real value" for market-determined value in our thinking about justice. The key point about the market here is that it takes what someone produces and sets it against the whole range of individual valuations of the item in question. You may value a Bible very highly as a repository of spiritual truth; I may place a very low value on it as simply one among a number of stout volumes that I might use as bookends. Both of our valuations feed in, along with millions of others, to determine the price at which Bibles sell and what publishers can make by selling them.

Market valuations don't work, of course, when what is produced is to a significant degree a public good—its benefits are not confined to any particular purchaser—because here there will be a systematic difference between what individuals are willing to pay and the social value of the product. We need here to find an analogue to the market: a way of assessing the value of public goods that takes into account the different values individuals place on them.[10] Here, too, I want to resist appeals to "objective value." Mathew Humphrey takes up this issue in relation to environmental goods, where I argue that, except in the case of certain "basic" goods, these have to be treated as on a par with other public goods that people might value.[11] They have no special standing in the theory of justice. Humphrey suggests, in contrast, that valuing nature in a certain way might form an intrinsic part of a good human life, whether or not people currently recognize it to be. This, he implies, would mean giving environmental goods like the preservation of endangered species more weight in our thinking about justice than they would have if we regarded them simply as the preferences of some individuals.

I fully agree with Humphrey that establishing the right kind of relationship with the natural world is an integral part of a good human life, and if we engaged in a seminar on the question "how ought one to live?" I would be pressing this view as strongly as anyone. But I would still be reluctant to build the answer into a theory of social justice, for two reasons. First, there are many kinds of good life, and even if one thinks that a relationship to nature forms some part of each, still the *weight* that attaches to that element may vary considerably vis-à-vis the rest. I am not a subjectivist about conceptions of the good life, but I am a pluralist. So, the question how to value environmental goods is not resolved by arguing that they are necessary to fully human lives. Second, if we are to live together with others on the basis of justice, we must try to reach agreement on principles that are widely acceptable to people whose personal conceptions of value may diverge. In searching for agreement, we must take these conceptions of value as given, and deliberate on that basis, rather than proceeding on the assumption that everyone must accept our own favored conception. (In a similar way, atheists seeking to reach agreement with believers about freedom of religious expression and other such matters must take religious beliefs at face value *in this context*, even though on other occasions they are of course perfectly entitled to try to convince their opponents of the falsity of their beliefs.) Since the value of environmental goods is still a contentious matter, we cannot give them a privileged place in our deliberations about justice, any more than we can cultural goods or other kinds of goods favored by particular sections of our society.[12]

So, to return to the issue of desert and contribution, my argument is that if we are to reward people fairly for what they have produced, then we need to find a way of measuring contribution that is not tied to particular conceptions of the good life. Market valuation can serve this purpose in standard cases; where public goods are involved, we need to find a way of aggregating preferences that as far as possible embodies the same kind of neutrality. But now I must tackle the question whether contribution, however measured, is the right principle in the first place. For what people contribute is determined in part by what they are able to contribute, and that depends in turn on their luck in the genetic lottery and other such arbitrary factors. Many political philosophers have concluded that desert cannot be so determined by luck; its basis must be narrowed to features of individuals (such as the efforts they make) for which they can be held fully responsible.

In *Principles* I laid out a two-pronged response to this argument. First, I distinguished between different kinds of luck and claimed that not all forms of luck undermined desert to the same degree. Second, I argued that if one wanted to eliminate the effects of luck completely, one would have to abandon the idea of rewarding desert altogether, since all forms of desert will bear the imprint of luck. Serena Olsaretti suggests that this response overlooks the distinction between desert as such and *differential* desert—one person's deserving more than another. Luck, she suggests, only nullifies desert of the second kind. But we need differential desert judgments to support the claim that market-derived distributions can be socially just.

We can think of cases that support this suggestion. Imagine two girls taking an entrance exam to a top university, only one of whom has been educated at an excellent school. Apart from that they are equally talented and equally well motivated. The exam goes true to form and the first girl but not the second is offered a place. We are likely to say that she deserves her place—her performance is such that we can reasonably judge that she will make good use of the opportunity—but that she does not deserve to go to a better university than the second girl. It was only the latter's bad luck in having gone to a second-rate school that prevented her from turning in an excellent performance.

But other cases are more problematic. Consider the person who gets a lucky job break: he falls into conversation with an employer while sitting on a train, gets offered a job, and turns out to do it well, so he fully deserves the (fair) wage he then takes home. There are other people to whom none of this happened and who as a result are earning less, though they are also earning a fair wage for what they are doing. Should we say that the absolute amounts are deserved but the differential is not? But this seems incoherent: what one deserves by way of wages is always implicitly what one deserves relative to others. Each person is being rewarded in proportion to the value for his performance. Luck here simply enabled one person to put in a performance that others might also have put in had they been given a similar break.

Olsaretti says, "for differential deserts to be justified, it has to be the case that individuals have a fair opportunity to acquire differential deserts." This certainly seems to explain our judgments in the case of the two girls; it is because the second girl was not given a fair opportunity to acquire academic merit that we refuse to say that the first girl deserves a better university education. But what ought we to say about the second case? Was there a fair opportunity to become differentially deserving here? Should we say that the employer acted unfairly by offering a job on the strength of a train conversation (but suppose he had advertised it, and only this person happened to notice the ad)? Or should we say that the employee showed enterprise by flagging his credentials in the course of the conversation? It was reflection along these lines that led me to conclude[13] that "circumstantial luck always lies in the background of human performances, and only when it intrudes in a fairly clear and direct way on what different people achieve relative to one another do we allow it to modify our judgements of desert."

Andrew Mason examines my account of one particular form of desert, desert of jobs or opportunities of other kinds. There is something puzzling about desert of this kind, namely, that in standard cases one deserves benefits (or harms for that matter) as a result of an intentional performance already carried out, whereas in the case of deserving a job, the relevant performance has yet to come. My solution is to say that desert of this kind is secondary: the person who deserves the job is the person who, in the light of her present qualities, is most likely to perform it in such a way that she *will* deserve the income and other benefits it carries with it. But Mason points out that there may be circumstances in which we can say that A is most likely to deserve some benefit if given an opportunity, and yet we don't judge that he deserves that opportunity: he gives the examples of Athenian councillors being chosen by lot and soldiers being selected for a dangerous mission by the same method.

My reaction to these cases is that the connection between the opportunity and the performance that might deserve reward is far more tenuous here than in the case of a job or an educational place. One can bring this out by asking why selection by lot might be a reasonable procedure to use in these circumstances. In the Athenian case, selection by lot was intended to express citizen equality and to try to prevent wealthy and influential men from dominating the council. The assumption was that any citizen could adequately carry out the tasks associated with being a councillor. That some citizens might turn out to deserve honors for exceptional service would appear in this context as an unexpected bonus. To the extent that citizens were differentially capable of undertaking the job itself (as some Athenians, including Aristotle, believed), selection by lot from the whole body would be irrational. Similarly, for the military mission. If soldiers are chosen at random, this is because the mission only requires qualities that any soldier may be expected to possess (if specialists are needed, one would surely choose *them*). In the course of the mission, any member of the party may find himself in circumstances where a courageous act is required. There is no predictable link between being selected and being likely to deserve a medal.

I agree with Andrew Mason when he says that giving jobs to the best-qualified candidates is a way of showing respect for persons. But I am also inclined to think that we show respect for persons, in general, by treating them in whatever way morality requires. So, we have to establish that justice requires us to give the job to the most deserving (rather than, say, the neediest) candidate *before* we can say that this is what respecting persons demands. There is more to say here, but I remain unconvinced that we can explain why the best-qualified candidate deserves the job without referring to the further fact that a person who performs well in a job deserves the income and other advantages that the job brings with it. And this in turn requires us to accept the idea that people can deserve benefits for their performances, provided those performances are intended and under their control, despite the fact that the performances in question require talents that others may not possess—the central plank in my theory of desert.

In conclusion, let me underline two aspects of my theory of social justice that may help to place this discussion of desert in its proper context. The first is that I see desert principles operating alongside (and sometimes in potential conflict with) principles of equality and principles of need—a just society is one whose basic institutions are arranged so that each of these principles is given its proper scope. Desert properly governs the distribution of benefits in economic enterprises and other forms of instrumental association, and it should not be allowed to influence distributions in other contexts. The second is that, even within its proper sphere, desert is a radical principle: it gives us a weapon to attack the existing distribution of resources in capitalist societies, since that distribution results to a considerable degree from exploitation and from unmediated forms of luck that have nothing to do with desert. Even "raw" popular opinion recognizes that many current economic and social inequalities are undeserved, and a theory that aimed to correct and systematize these judgments in the way outlined in the previous section would go further still in this direction. Holding on to desert doesn't mean capitulating in face of the status quo.

NATIONALITY AND JUSTICE

I turn now to the idea that nations, when properly constituted, are privileged sites of justice, and in this section I shall try to defend the claim that nation-states are capable of delivering justice internally, leaving until the next section the issue of global justice.

My understanding of nationality includes the idea that nations are a special form of community, and this in turn gives the practice of justice among fellow nationals a certain kind of primacy. Of course, we practice justice at many levels, from families at the smallest level up to humankind at the highest, but national communities, so I claim, make special claims on us. Many critics have found this argument hard to swallow: some point out that, as individuals we identify with communities and associations of many different kinds—local communities, churches, ethnic groups, transnational political communities, and so on—and it seems arbitrary to single out nations in the way that I do; others go further still and argue that the very idea that nations can be regarded as communities imposing demands of justice upon us is suspect.

In the present volume, both Daniel A. Bell and Michael Walzer, while not rejecting the idea of nations as communities, express concern that my privileging of nationality as a form of identity and citizenship as a political status may lead to intolerance toward minority groups, particularly groups that make "totalizing" demands on their members, such as certain fundamentalist religious groups. I have argued that democratic states can demand that such groups should accommodate themselves to the requirements of democracy, most notably in allowing their children to be educated in a way that prepares them for citizenship. I concede that the effect of this may be to change the character of the groups themselves, in effect ruling out full-blown versions of the way of life that their members embrace in favor of "liberalized" or "democratized" versions. But I do not see this as a serious objection. Although cultural pluralism is in general valuable, one need not be committed to the preservation of all cultural forms no matter what; speaking personally, I would not regret the disappearance of fundamentalist forms of religion, although I would be happy to tolerate their existence so long as those who practiced them were at the same time engaged in, and committed to, the institutions of democratic citizenship.

What can be said to a member of a totalizing group who does not want his culture changed in this way—who says that citizenship and nationality mean nothing to him, but what matters greatly is that the traditions of his community should be preserved? Two things, I believe. First, in a modern democratic state, he and his children must live alongside and interact with others not of his faith, and to do that they must be educated in such a way that they acquire the linguistic and other cultural skills needed for success in this wider environment. Second, engagement in politics may very well be necessary to protect and win respect for his culture, and effective engagement requires mastering the political language of the national community. In other words, isolation—trying to live within a cultural community as though the larger society did not exist—is normally impossible and always risky.[14] And no subcommunity can hope to engage with the national community entirely on its own terms; it needs to demonstrate its commitment to shared principles and its willingness to deal with other groups on the basis of reciprocity. So, even if learning to be a democratic citizen imposes costs on the children of would-be totalizing groups, these are costs that are well worth paying.

In a chapter directly informed by the experience of teaching citizenship to cultural minorities, Meira Levinson points out that students belonging to these minorities must travel much further than others in order to learn the "language of power" that they need to use in order to be effective citizens and that this may have a determining effect on their future identities. There is no denying this, though one should keep in mind that the political community's language—its vocabulary, principles, rhetorical devices, historical reference points, and so forth—is one that every child must learn; it comes "naturally" to no one. Levinson is also right to point out that the substance of citizenship, particularly in its historical dimension, will look very different depending on the primary experience of the group the student belongs to. It is important to underline, therefore, that in democratic states national identities are always open to contest and revision, and this ought to be reflected in the way that citizenship is taught in schools. But these difficulties do not in my view justify Levinson's conclusion that minority groups may be better served by an adversarial rather than a deliberative form of democracy, on the ground that adversarial democracy allows groups to wield power directly rather than having to convince others through reasonable argument. For minorities will typically have fewer of the resources that are needed for the exercise of power; nor do I think that, except in a few specific cases, they will be able to form effective coalitions with other minorities. What they have mainly is "the power of speech," and this of course is a form of power only if others are willing to listen and to be persuaded of the justice of the minority's cause. That is why I argue that justice in multicultural societies is best served by creating forums in which, whether directly or by means of representatives, different groups are able to confront one another's arguments and reach agreements or compromises as the case may be.[15] What should concern us is creating the conditions of trust under which such reciprocal listening and persuading can take place.

This defense of democratic deliberation has at least two objections to confront. One, well expressed in Bell's chapter, is that democracy so conceived is simply infeasible in modern large-scale societies. I agree that we need to think more about how to create institutions that would allow democratic deliberation to proceed effectively, but it is important not to regard this as an all-or-nothing issue. While preserving existing parliaments and other representative institutions, we can devise ways of encouraging deliberation within them, while at the same time setting up extraparliamentary forums to draw in a wider public. Some of these might be locally based and have local issues as their primary focus. Others might involve selecting participants so as to gather in a wide range of interests and perspectives and setting them to debate an issue of national concern. Numerous experiments along these lines, in the form of citizens' juries and deliberative opinion polls, have already been conducted, and it is not utopian to envisage these becoming a regular part of democratic decision making. Their role would not be to reach concrete decisions, but to establish principled guidelines within which such decisions could be taken by more specialized bodies. Especially where decisions have to be taken on controversial issues, their legitimacy would be enhanced by showing that a randomly selected group of citizens, invited to deliberate on the issue, had reached such-and-such a conclusion.

This brings us, however, to the second objection. Why suppose that deliberation actually works in the way that its advocates claim, changing initial beliefs and preferences so as to produce an ethically superior final judgment? Avner de-Shalit produces evidence that shows, he says, "it is not the case that people become more flexible and open when they are engaged in such deliberations; instead many of them become more stubborn." I am not sure, however, that this is the right conclusion to draw. De-Shalit's own experiments involve *simulated* deliberation—respondents are asked for their views on certain contentious issues, then they are presented with arguments against and counterarguments for the views they have expressed, following which they are asked to express a further opinion, and so on. These experiments certainly tell us something about how people think politically, but in one important respect they lack the dynamic element present in real deliberation; they cannot model the effects of seeing others modify their views in the search for agreement. De-Shalit's results also show that people quickly become confused when over-loaded with information from different sources, and there is certainly a lesson to be drawn here about the kind of informational input that successful delib-eration requires. His pessimism is not however borne out by the research that has been done on citizens' juries and deliberative polling, which reveals citi-zens coping well with complex issues, being open to have their original opin-ions modified by force of argument, and generally displaying a high degree of social responsibility.[16]

I do not claim that deliberative democracy is an appropriate political mech-anism in all circumstances. On the contrary, I believe that it can succeed only where there already exists a fairly high level of mutual trust in the deliberat-ing body, which is why I argue that a shared national identity is close to being a necessary prerequisite. But this of course raises a problem in political com-munities where no such shared identity can be presupposed—multinational states, for example. What does my defense of the principle of nationality have to say about such cases?

Recognizing that the world's populations do not divide themselves into neat homogeneous groups, each occupying a single territory—a state of affairs that I assume would render the application of the nationality principle relatively un-problematic. I argued in *Citizenship and National Identity*, chapter 8, that the best form of government for culturally divided societies must depend on the na-ture of the division. I distinguished three basic types—ethnically divided societies, rival nationalities, and nested nationalities—while conceding that we would find mixed or intermediate cases in practice. Both Erica Benner and Tamar Meisels think that I make too much of the distinction between rival and nested nations. Benner claims that when I discuss rival nationalities—intermingled groups with incompatible claims to territorial self-determination and no overarching national identity in common—I abandon both republican and liberal principles in favor of "pragmatic interest-balancing and tough-minded *realpolitik*."

In one way I plead guilty as charged, because I certainly do not think that one can solve these very difficult cases simply by demanding that liberal-democratic institutions of the familiar kind be put in place. I believe that until there exists a political community whose members trust one another sufficiently that liberal freedoms can be enjoyed and democratic procedures enabled to operate, more basic considerations must dominate the discussion. The most basic consideration of all is that people should be spared the horrors of civil war, ethnic cleansing, and the like and that a state of some kind be created that will protect their fun-damental rights. This may in some cases involve redrawing political boundaries, in other cases encouraging people to move across them in an orderly and super-vised way, in yet others using external authority to put in place a compromise arrangement whereby power is shared between the contending communities. These, it should be said, are medium-term solutions. They are not meant to de-tract from the longer-term aim of democratic nation building, whereby the rival groups, if they choose to remain together, come to develop their own shared identity linked to the territory they inhabit. But this *is* a long-term project. When one looks back at the historical formation of those nations in which democracy now flourishes, one can't help but be struck both by the time it took to reach that goal and at the often illiberal methods that were used to bring minority groups into the national community. The problem for contemporary liberals is that they recoil from the means while still willing the end.

Meisels focuses on the issue of territory. Whereas in the case of nested nationalities, I argue against secession for the smaller nations partly on the ground that the encompassing nation has a claim to maintain its territorial integrity; I appear not to recognize an equivalent claim when rival nations settle their differences by dividing territory between them. What if the territory taken by nation A contains sites of great historic or cultural value to nation B? My view is that this interest is certainly significant, but that it is trumped by the interest both nations have in creating viable political communities that can move to democratic self-government. Serbs have a historic claim to the site of the battle of Kosovo Polje in 1389, but given that this now stands in territory predominantly occupied by Kosovo Albanians, and given that Serbs and Albanians cannot live together in a national community, that claim cannot be met.[17] The Kosovo Albanians need territorial autonomy, and for the Serbs, too, it may in the end prove better to have a democratic Serbia within narrower borders than an autocratic Serbia ruling hostile minority nations. Even in the case of nested nations, I did not intend historic claims to territory to serve as trump cards, but rather as factors affecting the justifiability of secessionist demands. If the Scots, or the Catalans, or the Quebecois finally judge that their legitimate claim for self-determination requires full independence, the territorial rights of the larger nations in which they are presently nested must yield to this judgment.

I want finally here to return to the link between nationality and justice. Just how strong is it? Benner points out that national identities, in the real world, are often such as to entail injustice toward groups not regarded as belonging to the nation. I agree that sharing a national identity is no guarantee of just behavior. My claim is weaker: that in the absence of such identities it is very difficult, to say the least, to motivate people to sacrifice liberty and resources to help people they do not know, and also, as argued earlier, to deliberate together on the means of implementing justice. Chandran Kukathas points out that nation-states have not proved, in practice, to be very effective at practicing social justice among their members; he thinks they are often too internally diverse and also that the holders of effective power are likely to be the rich, who have no reason to want to redistribute their resources. Again, I agree with these cautionary remarks. It may be that states like the United States, China, and India, even leaving their national minorities aside, are simply too large and culturally diverse to be effective vehicles of social justice. On the other side of the coin, the states that have come closest to implementing social justice as

I understand it are the relatively small and (until recently) relatively homogeneous Scandinavian democracies. But it is important to be clear about the benchmark that we are using when we judge nation-states in this way. What alternative mechanisms for allocating rights, freedoms, and resources are we envisaging? If the answer to this is "the free market" or "the free market plus voluntary charitable transfers" then we need to look at the likely outcome of *that* mechanism before writing off the nation-state as a preserve of the rich.

GLOBAL JUSTICE

Even if nation-states are the best means we have for delivering justice to their own populations, they may still be obstacles to achieving justice for humanity as a whole. Liberal political philosophers often argue that principles of distributive justice should apply at global level and that the practice of justice is therefore distorted if we assume that people have special obligations to their compatriots. In the present volume, Simon Caney, Cécile Fabre, and Daniel Weinstock all present arguments of this kind. They do not of course deny that de facto people see themselves as belonging to particular political communities, but they regard this as irrelevant from the point of view of justice. Caney, for example, commits himself to a principle of equality of opportunity that holds that it is "unfair if persons have worse opportunities because of their national or civic identity."

Given my contextualist approach to forms of justice outlined earlier in this chapter, I make no such assumption about the scope of principles such as equality of opportunity. In trying to understand what global justice requires, I begin by asking how people are related to one another at the global level, and in the light of that suggest what justice requires them to do for one another. My answer, in brief, is that we are subject to three such requirements: the obligation to respect basic human rights worldwide; the obligation to refrain from exploiting vulnerable communities and individuals; and the obligation to provide all political communities with the opportunity to achieve self-determination and social justice. Specifying these obligations does not by itself tell us how the accompanying responsibilities should be distributed—where rights are being violated, for instance, it does not tell us who should step in to prevent the violations. I have attempted to deal with this issue elsewhere.[18] It is meant to indicate simply what individuals and communities can demand of one another, as a matter of justice, at international level.

My argument that global justice must be understood in terms of these principles, rather than *comparative* principles such as principles of equality, rests on certain assumptions about the character of international society. These assumptions could be disputed. For instance, one may argue that the international economy and the international political system have now become sufficiently integrated that there is no relevant difference between domestic contexts of justice and international contexts. That argument does not itself challenge my view that principles of justice are context-specific. So, when Weinstock, for instance, claims that Mexican workers may begin to consider themselves as relatively deprived compared to other North American workers, because they come to think of the North American economy as an integrated system, I tend to agree. The bounds of communities and of cooperative practices are always shifting, and in the present period often expanding, and so one can't say a priori how wide the reach of comparative principles of justice will be. My claim about global justice is only that we have not yet reached the point where we can speak meaningfully of a world community, or see people's life chances as the effect of a common "basic structure" of rules and institutions, to borrow Rawls's term. It would be foolish to deny that we might get there sometime in the future.

Caney points out that I have not always been consistent in my specification of the units within which comparative principles of justice apply, and he is right to draw attention to this. Recall that my contextualist approach to *social* justice distinguishes three forms of human association—I call them solidaristic community, instrumental association, and citizenship—within which different principles of justice—need, desert, and equality, respectively—apply. When discussing international society, it is the relative absence of *any* of these forms of association that grounds my claims about the nature of global justice, but he says correctly that I sometimes speak in a looser sense about the absence of "communities" or "bounded societies" or "associations" when making the point. He is also of course perfectly correct to say that there are forms of international cooperation within which issues of comparative justice arise. But these are characteristically of the kind: how should the burdens of cooperation be shared among the peoples who are engaged in it—in humanitarian interventions, in environmental cleanups, and so forth? The issue is not directly about the comparative treatment of individuals. Equally, where genuine international organizations exist—multinational corporations and the like—comparative questions about the pay and other benefits received by individual members in different places naturally arise. But this falls far short of Caney's much stronger principle of equal remuneration, which requires that people should be paid the same for doing the same work whether or not there are any associational or communal ties linking them.

My position here relies on a distinction between people being associated with one another, whether by participating in a common practice, being subject to the same set of institutions, belonging to the same community, or in some other way, and people merely having a casual impact on one another's situation. Since, as we have often been told, a butterfly's wingbeat in China can cause a hurricane in Florida, it is undeniable that anything any of us does will have a (probably minuscule) impact on the economic or political fortunes of distant strangers. Connectedness *at this level* is sufficient to bring into play the three basic obligations of global justice outlined previously, but not, I claim, comparative principles of the kind favored by Caney and other liberal egalitarians.

I reject these principles partly because I do not think that international society currently provides the contexts that can support them, but also partly because of my views about national self-determination. In a world of culturally diverse political communities, each enjoying some measure of autonomy, we should not expect equality of opportunity for individuals to persist over time, even if we could define an initial starting point where it had been achieved. Just as we hold individuals responsible for the use they make of their opportunities, so, I argue, we can be justified in holding nations collectively responsible for the way they organize themselves internally and use their human and natural resources. The extent of this responsibility depends on the extent to which we can reasonably interpret collective decisions as reflecting the beliefs and values of their members. Both Fabre and Weinstock raise doubts about this argument. Fabre highlights the position of minorities who dissent from the decisions and policies favored by the majority. Why should they suffer when these turn out to have disastrous consequences? I agree that we do not want to extend responsibility for the Nazi regime to German Jews simply because they participated in the election that (indirectly) brought Hitler to power. But in many other cases, we do think that groups who lose in a democratic debate can properly be asked to bear their share of the costs that result from the decision reached. This is a matter of fairness: when groups are on the winning side they benefit from the compliance of the minority who opposed the decision, and so they can be asked to comply in turn when they lose. So, we need to draw a line somewhere that limits, without annihilating, the responsibility of dissident groups for national decisions. Further work is needed on this: I have made a start in other papers.[19]

Weinstock mounts a different challenge: citing the case of postcolonial nations, he argues that such peoples cannot be held responsible for their political decisions since "political cultures are in large measure part of the circumstances of individuals rather than a reflection of their choices"—in this case a kind of conditioned reflex to the experience of colonialism. However, as Weinstock surely knows, providing a causal explanation for someone's beliefs or attitudes does not, in general, relieve that person of responsibility for holding them. I am certain that Weinstock would not cease holding the colonizers themselves responsible for what they did on production of some plausible explanation of the origins of the colonialist mentality. If we are to treat people everywhere as responsible agents, capable of reflecting on their inherited beliefs and desires and changing them in the light of circumstances, then this must entail collective responsibility, too, provided of course that the people in question have the chance to exercise those capacities. There are regimes that prevent this: autocracies and theocracies that brainwash their subjects so effectively that only the most resilient are able to resist, and here responsibility for the results should indeed lie with the powerholders and not the people. But most states, not only democracies, rely on there being a broad consensus of values between rulers and ruled, and here I want to insist that political autonomy entails taking responsibility for the results, good or bad, of the policies that are chosen.

The third element in my account of global justice is the obligation to provide peoples everywhere with the opportunity to be self-determining and pursue social justice. In *Citizenship*, chapter 10, I argued that this obligation seemed to be a straightforward corollary of the claim to national self-determination. If we value self-determination for our own political community and seek to maintain the conditions under which it can be exercised, then we must surely try to ensure that other communities have the same opportunity (not all self-determination claims can be met in full, for reasons given in my discussion of rival nationalities, but every national group can and should enjoy at least partial autonomy). Stuart White draws attention to the republican roots of this idea: the republican, moved first of all by a concern for the common liberty of his own people, comes to identify with the liberation struggles of oppressed people everywhere. This can generate what he calls "transnational republican solidarity" whereby citizens show themselves willing to promote republican values abroad even at some cost to themselves. I find this both appealing and plausible. Although there are few good republicans among us, democratic citizens are already open to the argument that it is worth sacrificing something in order to help build or shore up democratic regimes abroad. As White notes, this is partly a matter of prudence. I write this in the aftermath of the September 11 attacks on New York and Washington, at a time when there seems to a growing recognition that democracies cannot be kept safe from similar attacks in the future without addressing the root causes of terrorism; and that this may require a major restructuring of the world economy to help poor countries on to the path of democratization. Republicans would also see it as a matter of principle. This may underline the point, made by White but not I think sufficiently acknowledged by the other three contributors discussed in this section, that my conception of global justice is a demanding one, requiring very significant changes in the way that rich states now behave.

A just world, according to this conception, would be one in which many forms of justice flourished, but always within certain parameters. Societies would not be equally wealthy. Some would give a high priority to increasing consumption, others to reducing work and expanding leisure, yet others to the promotion of spiritual or environmental values. All, however, would grant their members full rights of citizenship, and none would discriminate on grounds of sex or race.[20] People everywhere would be guaranteed a decent standard of living, understood as having the capacity to perform a set of core human activities—working, playing, building dwellings, raising families, and so forth—given the conditions prevailing in their own society. Normally, this guarantee would be made effective by the political community to which each person belongs, but if for any reason local provision broke down, other communities would step into the breach. Intercommunity relations would be governed by norms of fair exchange and the equitable sharing of the costs of joint action. This is not the utopia of which egalitarians dream, but it is very different indeed from the world we presently inhabit.

NOTES

I am very grateful to Daniel A. Bell and Avner de-Shalit for their many helpful suggestions on an earlier draft of this chapter.

1. Plato, *The Republic*, trans. H. D. P. Lee (Harmondsworth: Penguin, 1955), 182.

2. B. Pascal, *Pensées*, trans. A. J. Krailsheimer (Harmondsworth: Penguin, 1966), 239.

3. For a fuller account of this approach, see my article "Two Ways to Think About Justice," *Politics, Philosophy and Economics* 1 (2002): 5–28, which I have drawn upon in the following two paragraphs.

4. Swift suggests that this conflates justice with legitimacy—that the requirement that people should accept the principles by which their society is governed is a requirement of legitimacy rather than of justice itself. I disagree. In a particular case we can of course distinguish between the justice of a law, say, and its legitimacy—its having been enacted through a certain procedure. But if we ask more generally what conditions must hold for a society to be just, I do not think that it is sufficient for freedoms, powers, resources, and so forth to be distributed in the way that justice requires. It must also be the case that the principles governing the distribution are reasonably acceptable to the members—meaning that if they do not accept them already, it must at least be possible to give them reasons for acceptance given the beliefs they already hold. Here, then, I agree with Rawls that justice requires the public justifiability of its principles.

5. John Stuart Mill used precisely this example to illustrate the conflicts that arise among common precepts of justice in *Utilitarianism*, ch. 5 (see J. S. Mill, *Utilitarianism, On Liberty, and Considerations on Representative Government*, ed. H. B. Acton [London: Dent, 1972], 54). For evidence that popular opinion is indeed divided on this question, see, for instance, J. Hochschild, *What's Fair: American Beliefs about Distributive Justice* (Cambridge, Mass.: Harvard University Press, 1981), ch. 5.

6. I hope, obviously, that the refined version of the productivity view that I propose in David Miller, *Principles of Social Justice* (Cambridge, Mass.: Harvard University Press, 1999) will eventually win over those who start with the effort view, but I recognize that this may not happen. The point is that the best version of the productivity view and the best version of the effort view will deliver the same practical verdict on many occasions.

7. I don't mean to imply that we can work out a theory of justice in the family that is completely independent of our theory of justice in other contexts, because the way that the family is structured will have causal effects elsewhere—on the economy and on citizenship, for example, as Susan Okin shows effectively in *Justice, Gender and the Family* (New York: Basic Books, 1989). But taking this into account, we can still develop an account of justice that applies to the family specifically, and not to other contexts of distribution.

8. Daniel A. Bell has pointed out to me that concerns about the distributive effects of economic and social institutions have been present in Confucian political theory for over 2000 years: he instances the responsibility ascribed to the state by Mencius for ensuring that land was properly distributed. There are parallel concerns to be found in pre-modern Western political thought, and no doubt in other political traditions as well. So, we should perhaps say that the idea of social justice existed in embryonic form in earlier periods. I still believe, however, that the state's having an inclusive responsibility to regulate the basic institutional structure so as to ensure fairness in the distribution of resources to individuals is a distinctively modern idea.

9. J. S. Mill, *Considerations on Representative Government*, in Mill, *Utilitarianism*, 278–279.

10. I made a preliminary foray into this area in *Principles*, ch. 9, but the issue needs much further work.

11. By basic environmental goods I mean goods such as clean air and flood defenses that are either essential to human life in any form, or that directly affect the value of other primary goods like liberty and property, as for instance when I cannot safely walk on polluted land. We agree that goods of this kind enter the theory of justice at ground level, so to speak. The issue that divides us is what justice has to say about nonbasic goods such as species preservation or the conservation of natural landscapes.

12. Humphrey also points out, correctly, that some environmental goods are irreplaceable: once destroyed, they cannot be recreated. The existence of particular species is the prime example. He is right to say that, because our conceptions of value might change in such a way that we come later to attach a higher value to these goods, their loss should weigh heavily in our deliberations. He also suggests that we owe it to future generations to keep such options open. But I cannot myself see how we can decide our obligations to the future except on the basis that their values and priorities will be like ours (for a developed theory that supports this assumption, see A. de-Shalit, *Why Posterity Matters: Environmental Policies and Future Generations* [London: Routledge, 1995]). They will value the preservation of natural species, but like us they will care more about the preservation of tigers, say, than mosquitoes. So, provided we give irreplaceable environmental goods the appropriate weight in our own deliberations, this will also take care of our obligations to the future.

13. *Principles*, 146.

14. In practice, liberal democracies are able to tolerate the existence of small groups who try to isolate themselves as far as possible from the surrounding society, and such toleration may be justifiable if the costs of integration would be high, so long as the groups in question respect the basic rights of their members and pose no threat to democratic values. But one should be clear that this is a second-best solution.

15. Evidence about the effects of including members of disadvantaged minority groups in legislative bodies is reviewed in M. Williams, *Voice, Trust, and Memory: Marginalized Groups and the Failings of Liberal Representation* (Princeton, N.J.: Princeton University Press, 1998), ch. 4. Williams concludes that inclusion can have a significant impact on the way that issues relevant to minorities are discussed and resolved.

16. See J. Fishkin, *The Voice of the People* (New Haven, Conn.: Yale University Press, 1995), esp. ch. 5; G. Smith and C. Wales, "Citizens' Juries and Deliberative Democracy," *Political Studies* 48 (2000): 51–65; J. Fishkin and R. Luskin, "The Quest for Deliberative Democracy" and G. Smith, "Toward Deliberative Institutions," both in *Democratic Innovation: Deliberation, Representation and Association*, ed. M. Saward (London: Routledge, 2000).

17. It may be possible, in this case and others like it, to secure rights of access to members of the nation that is denied territorial control of the site in question. This would depend on the territorial settlement being accepted by both sides and would not of course meet the full self-determination claim of nation B, but it represents a possible compromise. Joint sovereignty is also a possible solution, but this is unlikely where the two nations in question remain rivals.

18. D. Miller, "Distributing Responsibilities," *Journal of Political Philosophy* 9 (2001): 453–471.

19. See D. Miller, "Holding Nations Responsible" (unpublished); D. Miller, "National Responsibility and International Justice," in *The Ethics of Assistance: Morality and the Distant Needy*, ed. D. Chatterjee (Cambridge: Cambridge University Press, forthcoming).

20. I believe that this requirement of equal citizenship is appropriate if we are setting down the conditions for a just world order, though it is arguable than in present circumstances differentiated citizenship may sometimes be acceptable as the lesser of two evils. Daniel Bell makes a case to this effect in "Equal Rights for Foreign Resident Workers? The Case of Filipina Domestic Workers in Hong Kong and Singapore," *Dissent* 48 (4) (fall 2001): 26–34.

Index

About the Contributors

Daniel Attas is head of the Philosophy, Economics and Political Science Program, Hebrew University of Jerusalem.

Daniel A. Bell is associate professor, Department of Public and Social Administration, City University of Hong Kong. He is the author, most recently, of *East Meets West: Human Rights and Democracy in East Asia* (Princeton, N.J.: Princeton University Press, 2000).

Erica Benner is associate professor in nationalism studies at the Central European University and Humboldt Special Research Fellow at the Free University, Berlin. Her most recent book is *Nationalism and Political Judgement* (Oxford: Oxford University Press, forthcoming).

Simon Caney teaches political philosophy at the University of Newcastle. He is currently completing a book entitled *Global Political Theory* for Oxford University Press.

Avner de-Shalit is associate professor of political theory at the Hebrew University and an associate fellow of the Oxford Centre for the Environment, Ethics, and Society. His most recent book is *The Environment: From Theory to Practice* (Oxford: Oxford University Press, 2000).

Cécile Fabre is a lecturer in political theory at the London School of Economics. She is the author of *Social Rights under the Constitution: Government and the Decent Life* (Oxford: Oxford University Press, 2000).

Mathew Humphrey is a lecturer in political theory at the University of Nottingham. He has a forthcoming book on the philosophy and politics of nature preservation, to be published by Oxford University Press.

Chandran Kukathas is associate professor of politics at University College, University of New South Wales, at the Australian Defence Force Academy. His book, *The Liberal Archipelago,* will be published by Oxford University Press in 2002.

Meira Levinson is the author of *The Demands of Liberal Education* (Oxford: Oxford University Press, 1999).

Andrew Mason is professor of political theory at the University of South ampton. His most recent book is *Community, Solidarity and Belonging* (Cambridge: Cambridge University Press, 2000).

Tamar Meisels teaches in the Department of Political Science, Tel-Aviv University.

David Miller is Official Fellow in Social and Political Theory, Nuffield College, Oxford.

Serena Olsaretti is a university assistant lecturer, Faculty of Philosophy, and fellow, St. John's College, Cambridge. She is the author of a forthcoming book on the justice of market inequalities.

Marc Stears is fellow in politics at Emmanuel College, Cambridge, and teaches in the Faculty of Social and Political Sciences. He recently published *Progressives, Pluralists and the Problems of the State* with Oxford University Press.

Adam Swift is fellow and tutor in politics and sociology at Balliol College, Oxford. His most recent book is *Political Philosophy: A Beginners' Guide for Students and Politicians* (Cambridge: Polity Press, 2001).

Michael Walzer is Professor of social science at the Institute for Advanced Study, Princeton University. His books include *Spheres of Justice* (New York and London: Basic and Basil Blackwell, 1983).

Daniel Weinstock is Canada Research Chair in Ethics and Political Philosophy at the Université de Montréal. He is the author of a forthcoming book on the normative foundations of the design of political institutions in multination states.

Stuart White is tutorial fellow in politics at Jesus College, Oxford. He is the author of a forthcoming book entitled *Civic Egalitarianism: A Theory of Economic Citizenship*.